Fromm

Prague and the Best of the Czech Republic

Here's what the critics say about Frommer's:

"Amazingly easy to use. Very portable, very complete."
—Booklist

♦

"The only mainstream guide to list specific prices. The Walter Cronkite of guidebooks—with all that implies."
—Travel & Leisure

♦

"Complete, concise, and filled with useful information."
—New York Daily News

♦

"Hotel information is close to encyclopedic."
—Des Moines Sunday Register

♦

"Detailed, accurate and easy-to-read information for all price ranges."
—Glamour Magazine

Other Great Guides for Your Trip:

Frommer's Europe

Frommer's Europe from $60 a Day

Frommer's®

3rd Edition

Prague and the Best of the Czech Republic

by John Mastrini, Hana Mastrini, &
Alan Crosby

IDG Books Worldwide, Inc.
An International Data Group Company
Foster City, CA • Chicago, IL • Indianapolis, IN • New York, NY

ABOUT THE AUTHORS

John Mastrini, once a TV news anchor from the United States, ventured to Prague soon after the 1989 revolution and decided to stay after falling in love with his future coauthor and the city. He still works in Prague as a journalist after serving as press secretary for an international diplomatic institution.

   Hana Příhodová Mastrini, a native of Karlovy Vary, moved to Prague in 1987 to attend university and joined the student demonstrations that led to the 1989 Velvet Revolution. She and her husband John are coauthors of *Frommer's Europe from $60 a Day* and *Frommer's Europe.*

   Alan Crosby is a journalist who has lived and worked in Eastern Europe for the last decade.

IDG BOOKS WORLDWIDE, INC.

An International Data Group Company
919 E. Hillsdale Blvd.
Suite 400
Foster City, CA 94404

Find us online at **www.frommers.com**

ISBN 0-02-863626-0
ISSN 1086-220X

Editor: Justin Lapatine
Production Editor: Suzanne Snyder
Photo Editor: Richard Fox
Design by Michele Laseau
Staff Cartographers: John Decamillis, Roberta Stockwell
Page Creation by Melissa Auciello-Brogan, David Faust

SPECIAL SALES

For general information on IDG Books Worldwide's books in the U.S., please call our
Consumer Customer Service department at 1-800-762-2974. For reseller information,
including discounts, bulk sales, customized editions, and premium sales, please call our
Reseller Customer Service department at 1-800-434-3422.

Manufactured in the United States of America

5   4   3   2   1

Contents

Appendix B: Useful Terms & Phrases   259

Index   264

List of Maps

AN INVITATION TO THE READER

In researching this book, we discovered many wonderful places—hotels, restaurants, shops, and more. We're sure you'll find others. Please tell us about them, so we can share the information with your fellow travelers in upcoming editions. If you were disappointed with a recommendation, we'd love to know that, too. Please write to:

Frommer's Prague and the Best of the Czech Republic, 3rd Edition
IDG Travel
1633 Broadway
New York, NY 10019

AN ADDITIONAL NOTE

Please be advised that travel information is subject to change at any time—and this is especially true of prices. We therefore suggest that you write or call ahead for confirmation when making your travel plans. The authors, editors, and publisher cannot be held responsible for the experiences of readers while traveling. Your safety is important to us, however, so we encourage you to stay alert and be aware of your surroundings. Keep a close eye on cameras, purses, and wallets, all favorite targets of thieves and pickpockets.

WHAT THE SYMBOLS MEAN

✪ Frommer's Favorites

Our favorite places and experiences—outstanding for quality, value, or both.

The following abbreviations are used for credit cards:

AE	American Express	EURO	Eurocard
CB	Carte Blanche	JCB	Japan Credit Bank
DC	Diners Club	MC	MasterCard
DISC	Discover	V	Visa
ER	EnRoute		

FIND FROMMER'S ONLINE

Arthur Frommer's Budget Travel Online (www.frommers.com) offers more than 6,000 pages of up-to-the-minute travel information—including the latest bargains and candid, personal articles updated daily by Arthur Frommer himself. No other Web site offers such comprehensive and timely coverage of the world of travel.

The Czech & Slovak Republics

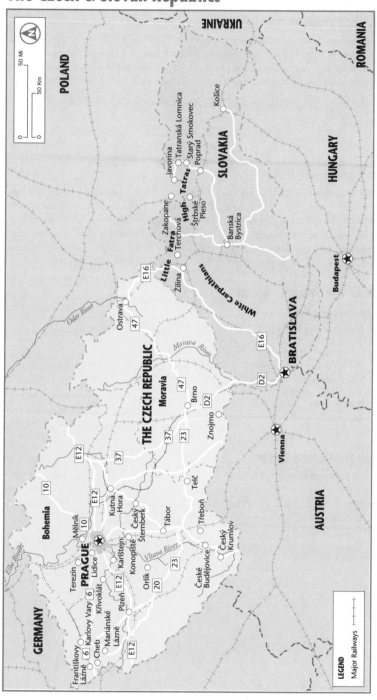

Introducing the City of a Chaotic Millennium

by John Mastrini & Hana Mastrini

For the romantic or cynic, aesthete or critic, historian or news junkie, beautiful and quirky Prague is the quintessential millennium destination.

Here, the last 1,000 years of triumphs in art and architecture have collided, often violently, with power politics and religious conflicts. While Bohemia has been the fulcrum of wars over the centuries, it has settled into a post–Cold War peace, spiked with a rough transition to a capitalist economy.

While Prague's rich collection of Gothic, baroque, and Renaissance buildings have stood stoically through all the strife, the streets and squares fronting the grand halls have often been the stage for tragedy. The well-worn cobblestones have felt the hooves of king's horses, the jackboots of Hitler's armies, the heaving wheels of Soviet tanks, and the shuffling feet of students in passive revolt. Today they're jammed with armies of visitors jostling for space to experience the aura of "Golden Prague" only to be bombarded with peddlers trying to make a quick buck or mark (or crown when the home currency is stable).

The spaghetti strands of alleys winding through Old Town have become so inundated with visitors during high season that they now resemble an intricate network of trails for scurrying ants. This town wasn't built for tourists.

The lifting of the Iron Curtain after 1989's bloodless "Velvet Revolution," one of a flurry of citizens' revolts ending Communist rule in Eastern Europe, has attracted many Westerners to finally come search for the secrets of the other side. But the city sees itself as the westernmost of former East Bloc capitals, on the map and in the mind. Praguers wince at using the term "Eastern Europe" to describe their home.

Still, conflicts past and present give the city an eclectic energy. The atmosphere continually reminds us that monarchs and dictators have tried to possess this city for much of the past millennium.

THE CITY OF A THOUSAND SPIRES

As you view Prague from high atop Vyšehrad, the 10-centuries-old citadel at the city's south end, the ancient city hugs the hills rising from the river Vltava (Moldau as it is commonly known from the German). Rows of steeples stacked on onion domes pierce the sky, earning Prague the moniker "The City of a Hundred Spires"—a flawed title. We've counted many more.

The World Comes to Prague in 2000

Prague has been chosen by the European Union as a *European City of Culture* in 2000, making for a yearlong series of artful events and celebrations. Although Czech officials have taken heat from local organizers who say the Prague fete has been heavily underfunded compared to the other eight cities chosen for the jubilee year, the lineup of performances and parties looks pretty rich. (See chapter 2 for a selection of events.)

Meanwhile, the government has poured a fortune into reconstructing the Communist-era Palace of Culture to host the **International Monetary Fund/ World Bank Annual Meeting** in September 2000, where the planet's power elite—including presidents, prime ministers, potentates, and top CEOs—will chew the fat for a few days.

Sadly, in the four decades of vacuous Communist rule, the city's classical heart was infected by faceless architecture and neglect. Now, while rediscovered owners clean up the grime on decaying masterpieces and rebuild facades on many forgettable follies, the city is recapturing its more avant-garde tastes. Regrettably, a new army of self-commissioned "artists" has laid siege with another weapon: graffiti. The "sprejer" (sprayer) problem is the latest chapter in Prague's cyclical battle of moderating freedom against repression—a conundrum Czech expatriate author Milan Kundera called *The Unbearable Lightness of Being* (see "Recommended Films & Books" in appendix A).

The Czech Republic was branded an economic miracle in the early years of the transformation to a free-market economy, but an experiment in rapid privatization of Communist-era companies led to a massive wave of corruption, turning the dream into a nightmare for many.

Thanks in part to tourism, Prague has been spared the worst impact of a deep recession in the late 1990s, although you should be forewarned that the Czech currency, the crown, remains very volatile and can significantly affect the price of your stay (see "The Czech Koruna" in chapter 2).

But while Prague's rebirth has come with labor pains of inflation, traffic jams (with new Western cars), and the ever-present pounding of construction crews, the stately spires of this living baroque and medieval museum rise above it all. Despite the furious development and reconstruction popping up all over, the classical monuments remain the city's bedrock. Prague Castle's reflection in the Vltava or the mellow nighttime glow of the lanterns around the 18th-century Stavovské divadlo (Estates' Theater) give the city a Mozart-really-was-here feel.

1 Frommer's Favorite Experiences in Prague & the Czech Republic

- **Having a Cup and a Debate at the Kavárna Slavia:** The reincarnation of Prague's favorite dissident cafe—reopened in late 1997 after being closed since 1993 in a real estate dispute—maintains its former art deco glory. The cloak-and-dagger game of secret police eavesdropping on political conversations may be gone, but there's still an energy that flows with the talk and java at the Slavia—and it comes with a great view. See chapter 5.

- **Making Your Own Procession Down the Royal Route:** The downhill jaunt from Prague Castle, through Malá Strana (Lesser Town), and across Charles Bridge to Old Town Square is a day in itself. The trip recalls the route taken by the carriages of the Bohemian kings; today it's lined with quirky galleries, shops, and cafes. See chapter 6.

- **Getting Lost in Old Town:** Every week a new cafe or gallery seems to pop up along the narrow winding streets of Staré Město (Old Town). Prague is best discovered by those who easily get lost on foot, and Old Town's impossible-to-navigate streets are made for it. See chapter 6.

- **Spending an Afternoon in the Letná Beer Garden:** Nice weather sends Czechs in search of open air and affordable beer. The tree-covered Letenský zámeček (Letná Chateau) garden on the Letná plain is a hidden treasure that serves up both a local favorite brew from Velké Popovice—called Kozel (Goat)—and a great city view. See chapter 6.

- **Taking a Slow Boat Down the Vltava:** You can see many of the most striking architectural landmarks from the low-angle and low-stress vantage point of a rowboat you pilot yourself. At night, you can rent a dinghy with lanterns for a very romantic ride. See chapter 6.

- **Riding a Faster Boat Down the Vltava:** For those not willing to test navigational skills or rowing strength, large tour boats offer similar floating views, many with meals. Be sure to check the direction of your voyage so it flows past the castles and palaces. See chapter 6.

- **Visiting a Large Communist-Era Housing Estate:** Anyone wondering how most latter-day Praguers live should see the mammoth housing blocks called *paneláky.* The size astounds and piques the debate over form versus function and living versus surviving. See chapter 6.

- **Picnicking on Vyšehrad:** Of all the parks where you could picnic, the citadel above the Vltava standing guard over the south end of the Old Town is the most calm and interesting spot close to the center. Its more remote location means less tourist traffic, and the gardens, city panoramas, and national cemetery provide pleasant walks and poignant history. See chapter 6.

- **Sharing a Moment with the Children of Terezín:** On display at the Ceremonial Hall of the Old Jewish Cemetery are sketches drawn by children held at the Terezín concentration camp, northwest of Prague. These drawings are a moving lesson in the Nazi occupation of Bohemia and Moravia. See chapter 6.

- **Strolling Across Charles Bridge at Dawn or Dusk:** The silhouettes of the statues lining the 6-centuries-old crown jewel of Czech heritage hover like ghosts in the still of the sunrise skyline. Early in the morning you can stroll across the bridge without encountering the crowds that'll be there by midday. At dusk, the statues are the same, but the odd light play makes the bridge and city panorama completely different than in the morning. See walking tour in chapter 7.

- **Romping Late at Night on Charles Bridge:** "Peace, Love, Spare Change" describes the scene, as musicians, street performers, and flower people come out late at night to become one with the bridge. Why not join them? See chapter 9 for more nightlife options.

- **Stepping into History at Karlštejn Castle:** A 30-minute train ride south of Prague puts you in the most visited Czech landmark in the environs, built by Charles IV (Karel IV in Czech—the namesake of Charles Bridge) in the 14th century to protect the Holy Roman Empire's crown jewels. This Romanesque hilltop bastion fills the image of the castles of medieval lore. See chapter 10.

Your struggle to preserve what you have inherited, and to reintegrate it into the values and character of the society you are rebuilding, is a struggle you must win, or there will not be much hope for any of us.

—Prince Charles to Prague's leaders (May 1991)

- **Jumping into "4-D" at Orlík:** After exploring Orlík Castle, south of Prague, and taking a relaxing stroll through the gardens, you can jump into the fourth dimension, in a variation of bungee jumping. It's quite a quick pick-me-up. See chapter 10.
- **Checking Out a Festive Beer Hall in České Budějovice:** Forget touristy remakes. In Bohemia's České Budějovice, the spirit of Masné krámy conjures up the feel of an 18th-century Czech pub, and the brew is as fresh as the bread. See chapter 11.
- **Enjoying New Year's Eve in Český Krumlov:** At midnight in Bohemia's Český Krumlov, the Na plášti bridge at the castle overlooking the town turns into a mini–United Nations, as revelers from all over gather to watch and light fireworks, see who can uncork the champagne the fastest, and just plain celebrate. See chapter 11.
- **Relaxing in Třeboň:** If you're looking for a small Czech town not overrun with tourists, travel to Třeboň in Bohemia. This serene place, surrounded by forests and ponds, is a diamond in the rough, a walled city that time, war, and disaster have failed to destroy. See chapter 11.
- **Walking Through the Šatov Wine Cellar:** Some of the finest Moravian wine is produced at the Šatov vineyard, and at this wine cellar you'll find more than the local product. The cellar's walls are carved and painted in intricate detail with scenes from Prague Castle and *Snow White*. See chapter 12.

2 Best Hotel Bets

- **Best Panoramic Views:** The pride of the former Communist tourism industry was the **Hotel Forum,** which has since been privatized, sold again, and renamed the **Corinthia Towers Hotel** (☎ 02/6119 1111). Each north-facing room at this high-rise south of the city center provides a wide-angle view stretching to Prague Castle and beyond. (See warning for American tourists in this hotel listing in chapter 4.)
- **Best Malá Strana Views:** Upper floors of the **Hotel U tří pštrosů** (☎ 02/5732 0565) offer some of the best old-world views over Malá Strana's red rooftops. The corner rooms are best, giving glimpses of Charles Bridge and Prague Castle.
- **Best Bohemian Country Setting:** The **Romantik Hotel U raka** (☎ 02/2051 1100), in a secret ravine minutes from the castle in Hradčany, has cozy rustic rooms and a tastefully folksy atmosphere.
- **Best Hotel Closest to Prague Castle:** The **Hotel U krále Karla** (☎ 02/5753 3594), on the main castle-bound thoroughfare Nerudova, tries hard to provide a stay to match its Renaissance motif. It's a few steps above the main turn to the castle, avoiding much of the noise, which has become a nuisance to rivals down the street.
- **Best for Business Travelers:** Just off náměstí Republiky near the imposing Czech National Bank, the new **Prague Marriott Hotel** (☎ 02/2288 8888)

comfortably fits the bill for those who need to get in, use their laptops, cut a deal, and then get out to see the city (especially if your firm is paying the bill).

- **Best Luxury Hotel:** The **Hotel Savoy** (☎ 02/2430 2430) is an opulent but tasteful small selection that suggests London more than Prague, complete with afternoon tea and a library for reading by a crackling fire when it's cold outside. The Savoy also houses the **Best Hotel Restaurant,** the **Hradčany,** with exceptionally delicate and innovative continental cuisine.

- **Best Luxury Old Town Hotel:** If price isn't a concern, choose a corner room at the **Grandhotel Bohemia** (☎ 02/2480 4111) on a quiet corner 1 block from náměstí Republiky and close to Old Town Square.

- **Best Moderately Priced Hotel:** The freshly restored **Cloister Inn** (☎ 02/ 232 7700), in a former convent, offers a comfortable room at a fair price in Old Town near Jan Hus's 15th-century Bethlehem Chapel. Its sister B&B, the Pension Unitas, is even more affordable.

- **Best Romantic Pension:** Although the **Pension Větrník** (☎ 02/2051 3390) is well outside the city center, this family-run B&B is one of the friendliest and most romantic places, easily accessible by tram or taxi. It's built into an antique windmill amid lush gardens, and you can't beat it for charm and price.

- **Best Throwback to Prague's First Republic:** The restored art nouveau **Hotel Paříž** (☎ 02/2219 5195) recalls 1920s Prague, when it was one of the wealthiest cities on earth. The hotel's beauty oozes with period elegance, and it's across from another newly remodeled gem, the Municipal House (Obecní dům).

- **Best-Value District:** Staying in **Vinohrady,** a gentrified quarter above Wenceslas Square, will put you a bit off the Royal Route, but you can find no better price and selection in central Prague, especially if you arrive without reservations. This neighborhood teems with cafes and has easy metro access to the older quarters.

- **Best for Families:** Consider a **private apartment** from an agency (see chapter 4). Larger and cheaper than hotel rooms, these apartments come with kitchens so you can fix your own meals. (For more options, see the box "Family-Friendly Accommodations" in chapter 4.)

- **Best Health Clubs:** The **Hotel Intercontinental Prague** (☎ 02/2488 1111) is fully equipped with modern machines and free weights and is home to Prague's most narcissistic aerobic classes—an after-work gawking paradise for some stockbrokers. The new **Prague Marriott** (☎ 02/2288 8888) actually has a better-equipped fitness center, but is not yet as clubby as the Intercon.

- **Best Tom Cruise/Leonid Brezhnev Haunt:** The **Hotel Praha** (☎ 02/2434 1111) was once a heavily guarded bastion for visiting Communist bigwigs. The lingering chintz of the Praha has unexpectedly emerged as refuge for luminaries who want to lay low, including the star of *Mission: Impossible.* A wacky choice.

- **Best B&B Watchdog:** The **Pension Větrník** (☎ 02/2051 3390) comes equipped with Arnošt, a huge but lovable St. Bernard who moonlights as spokesdog for a Swiss insurance company. Arnošt adds a homey touch and a bit of extra security.

3 Best Dining Bets

- **Best Spot for an Important Lunch or Dinner:** The **Bellevue** (☎ 02/ 2222 1438) still has the same artful continental fare and impeccable business-friendly service as its old Parnas location, but now with a cozier atmosphere near Charles Bridge.

- **Best Czech Cuisine:** In an intricate flower-embellished setting, **U modré kachničky** (☎ 02/5732 0308) brings delicacy to Czech fare, including savvy spins on heavy sauces and wild game.
- **Best Italian Cuisine:** Despite the Slavic name, the trendy island-bound **Ostroff** (☎ 02/2491 9235) delivers excellent northern Italian fare with a delicate touch, making it one of the top choices in the city.
- **Best Romantic Dinner:** Though for years it took raps for its high prices, the now more affordable menu of the gourmand's haute haunt, **U Malířů** (☎ 02/5732 0317), brings its romance a little closer to reality.
- **Best Bird's-eye View:** The food may not be anything to write home about, but you can't beat the panorama of Prague offered at **Nebozízek** (☎ 02/537 905) on Petřín Hill.
- **Best Riverside View:** A tie. You can dine in the shadow of Prague's most famous bridge during the high season at **Kampa Park** (☎ 02/5731 3493), or bask in the glow of the National Theater with a window seat in the bar before or after dinner at **Ostroff** (see above).
- **Best Pub Guláš:** Old Town's boisterous **Pivnice Radegast** (☎ 02/232 8237) dishes out a fine spicy goulash along with its Moravian namesake brew.
- **Best Spot for a Celebration:** The **Restaurant U Čížků** (☎ 02/2223 2257) feels like a hunting lodge, with huge portions of hearty Czech food, perfect with a Pilsner lager for a festive Bohemian evening.
- **Best American Bistro:** With the death of Planet Hollywood and the California-esque Avalon, **Red Hot & Blues** (☎ 02/231 4639) remains the last best hope for Yankee food in Prague, although thankfully the menu is mostly Tex-Mex and Cajun, with a good burger thrown in.
- **Best Seafood:** Old Town's **Rybí trh** (☎ 02/2489 5447) ships in fresh monkfish, salmon, shellfish, and about anything else that swims in saltwater and serves it in an airy space in the courtyard behind Týn Church.
- **Best Fast Food:** Even with McDonald's multiplying like mushrooms here, a Big Mac can't match the Philly cheesesteak or Cajun chicken sandwiches at **Cornucopia** (☎ 02/2494 7742).
- **Best Bagels: Bohemia Bagel** (☎ 02/531 002) at Újezd in Malá Strana has filled a curious vacuum.
- **Best Kosher:** Astonishingly, it took several years after the revolution to bring a real kosher restaurant back to Prague's Jewish Quarter. The **King Solomon Strictly Kosher Restaurant** (☎ 02/2481 8752), across from the Pinkas Synagogue, finally gets it right.
- **Best Value:** A friendly family-run restaurant on a narrow Malá Strana street, **Vinárna U Maltézských rytířů** (☎ 02/536 357) feels like an old Czech home with food that tastes like babička made it.
- **Best for Kids/Best Pizza:** You can please the kids and your own cravings at **Pizzeria Rugantino** (☎ 02/231 8172), a friendly and energetic Old Town room run by an Italian family who loves kids and dogs.
- **Best Late-Night Dining:** The **Radost FX Café** (☎ 02/2251 2035) dishes out veggie burgers, burritos, and salads to the trendy postclub crowd until 5am.
- **Best Outdoor Dining:** The terrace looking up at Charles Bridge makes **Kampa Park** (☎ 02/5731 3493) a summer favorite serving grill-fired steaks and seafood.
- **Best Art Nouveau Cafe:** The reinvigorated cafe at the **Municipal House (Kavárna Obecní dům)** (☎ 02/2200 2763) has re-created the grandeur of Jazz Age afternoons.

- **Best Landmark Dissident Cafe:** Prague's prerevolution dissident mecca, the **Kavárna (Café) Slavia** (☎ **02/2422 0957**), across from the National Theater, reopened to presidential fanfare in 1997, revealing a sparsely elegant art deco space, and beckoning those seeking a post-theater literary buzz.
- **Best Student Cafes:** Although the **Globe Bookstore** (☎ **02/6671 2610**) pulls in expats with English banter, book selection, and brownies, true intellectual angst, old furniture, and huge inexpensive cappuccinos await the crowd at **Kavárna Medúza** (☎ **02/258 534**) in Vinohrady.
- **Best Picnic Fare:** The green grocers at **Fruits de France** (☎ **02/2422 0304**), across from the main post office at Jindřišská 9, stock choice produce, cheeses, and wines for your feast in Prague's gardens.

2

Planning a Trip to Prague & the Czech Republic

by John Mastrini & Hana Mastrini

Prague has been shaping up for two big international events in 2000—the year when the capital is an official **European City of Culture** and host of the **International Monetary Fund/World Bank annual meeting** in September.

While we would normally suggest visiting in September when the crowds are thinner and the weather is at its most comfortable, this year is an exception. Preparations and the massive IMF event itself at the end of the month are expected to tie up Prague's hotels, roads, and restaurants. Anyway, as you will see below, many cultural events are packed tightly into the warmer summer months.

Once in Prague, the spectacular art nouveau Municipal House (Obecní dům) at náměstí Republiky has been fully refurbished to become the focal point for civic life and a primary source for information, with a modern visitors' center near the main entrance where tickets and advice are pleasantly dispensed.

To get the most out of your stay, first find out which events are taking place (see the "Czech Republic Calendar of Events" and the special "European City of Culture" schedule). The rest of this chapter should help you plan your trip and get the most out of your stay.

1 Visitor Information & Entry Requirements

VISITOR INFORMATION

INFORMATION OFFICES The private Prague-based firm **Tom's Travel** has developed a fantastic set of Web sites, including **www.travel.cz** for general Czech tourist information and accommodation, and **www.apartments.cz** for booking private apartments online. We would suggest any trip planning start here.

The former Communist-era state travel agency **Čedok** is now privatized, so it promptly closed its only U.S. office in New York in 1997, but you can contact English-speaking staff through its London or Prague office or via the Internet. In the United Kingdom, the address is 49 Southwark St., London SE1 1RU (☎ **020/7378-6009**). You can call the Prague main office for advanced bookings at Na Příkopě 18, Praha 1 (☎ **02/2419 7643**). The Čedok English-language link on its Web site is **www.cedok.cz/en/index.html**.

A Warning About Walking

Unless you're in great shape or are a devoted walker, you should gradually prepare for your trip with a walking program to build up your legs and feet for the inevitable pounding they'll take. And make sure to do this while wearing the comfortable shoes you plan to bring. I can't stress this enough to first-time visitors, especially those with relatively sedentary lifestyles. Prague is a city of hills, steep staircases, and cobblestone streets that require strong legs and shock-absorbing shoes. Take your time and go at your own pace.

Once in the country, you'll find an **information desk** at Prague's newly remodeled Ruzyně Airport. It offers basic help but isn't yet at a standard to match most Western convention and visitors' bureaus. In the reopened **Municipal House (Obecní dům),** at náměstí Republiky, there's now an information desk giving advice and booking event tickets. Accommodation information can be found through the private firm **AVE Ltd.,** now at the airport and at two primary rail stations, or on the Internet at **www.avetravel.cz.**

For a comprehensive list of information sources once you get to Prague, see "Visitor Information" in chapter 3.

INTERNET WEB SITES   Those hooked up to the Web can find updated information in English on the official Czech Foreign Ministry site at **www.czech.cz** or on the Central Europe Online site at **www.centraleurope.com/ceo/czech**. See above for the **Čedok, AVE,** and **Tom's Travel** Web sites. For eclectic local chat and culture, try **www.terminal.cz**. For general tips, check out the Prague Information Service at **www.eunet.cz/pis/praha**. And for the latest city lights and sights, try the weekly *Prague Post*'s site at **www.praguepost.cz**.

ENTRY REQUIREMENTS

DOCUMENTS   American, British, Irish, Australian, New Zealand, and now Canadian citizens need only passports (no visas) for stays under 30 days. Note that all children, even infants, are required to have a passport.

The easiest way to legally extend your stay in the country is to take a short trip (even of a few hours) to a neighboring country like Slovakia and get your passport restamped on your return journey into the Czech Republic (usually done only on request). Health certificates aren't required for travel to the Czech Republic.

In the **United States,** direct special needs or questions about entry requirements to the Czech Embassy, 3900 Spring of Freedom St. NW, Washington, DC 20008 (☎ **202/274-9100;** fax 202/966-8540; e-mail: washington@embassy.mzv.cz). In **Canada,** contact the Consulate General of the Czech Republic, 1305 Pine Ave., West Montréal, Québec H3G IB2 (☎ **514/849-4495**). In the **United Kingdom,** contact the Czech Embassy, 26 Kensington Palace Gardens, London W8 4QY (☎ **020/7727-4918**). In **Australia,** contact the Embassy of the Czech Republic, 38 Culgoa Circuit, O'Malley, Canberra, ACT 2606 Australia (☎ **006-16/290-1386**). In **Ireland,** contact the Czech Embassy, 57 Northumberland Rd., Ballsbridge, Dublin 4 (☎ **0035-31/668-1135**).

There is no Czech representation in New Zealand.

CUSTOMS   Czech customs laws are usually lax, but official allowances for importing duty-free goods are 200 cigarettes (or 250 grams of tobacco), 1 liter of alcohol (or 2 liters of wine), and 50 grams of perfume (or ¼ liter of toilet water). Most items brought for personal use during a visit aren't liable to import duty. Gifts are taxable if the quantity and value aren't in keeping with the "reasonable needs" of the recipient.

There are no longer any currency restrictions at borders, but transactions over 500,000Kč ($14,705) must be declared by financial institutions. Live farm animals, plants, produce, coffee, and tea may not be imported, but household pets can enter with an international health certificate.

IMPORT RESTRICTIONS   Returning U.S. citizens who have been away for 48 hours or more are allowed to bring back, once every 30 days, $400 worth of merchandise duty-free. You'll be charged a flat rate of 10% duty on the next $1,000 worth of purchases. Be sure to have your receipts handy. On gifts, the duty-free limit is $100. You cannot bring fresh foodstuffs into the United States; tinned foods, however, are allowed. For more information, contact the U.S. Customs Service, 1301 Constitution Ave. (P.O. Box 7407), Washington, DC 20044 (☎ **202/927-6724**), and request the free pamphlet *Know Before You Go.* It's also available on the Web at www.customs. ustreas.gov/travel/kbygo.htm.

U.K. citizens returning from a non-EC country have a customs allowance of: 200 cigarettes; 50 cigars; 250g of smoking tobacco; 2 liters of still table wine; 1 liter of spirits or strong liqueurs (over 22% volume); 2 liters of fortified wine, sparkling wine, or other liqueurs; 60cc (ml) of perfume; 250cc (ml) of toilet water; and £145 worth of all other goods, including gifts and souvenirs. People under 17 cannot have the tobacco or alcohol allowance. For more information, contact HM Customs & Excise, Passenger Enquiry Point, 2nd Floor Wayfarer House, Great South West Road, Feltham, Middlesex TW14 8NP (☎ **0181/910-3744;** from outside the U.K. ☎ 44/ 181-910-3744), or consult their Web site at www.open.gov.uk.

For a clear summary of **Canadian** rules, write for the booklet *I Declare,* issued by **Revenue Canada,** 2265 St. Laurent Blvd., Ottawa, K1G 4KE (☎ **613/993-0534**). Canada allows its citizens a $500 exemption, and you're allowed to bring back duty-free 200 cigarettes, 2.2 pounds of tobacco, 40 imperial ounces of liquor, and 50 cigars. In addition, you're allowed to mail gifts to Canada from abroad at the rate of Can$60 a day, provided they're unsolicited and don't contain alcohol or tobacco (write on the package "Unsolicited gift, under $60 value"). All valuables should be declared on the Y-38 form before departure from Canada, including serial numbers of valuables you already own, such as expensive foreign cameras. *Note:* The $500 exemption can only be used once a year and only after an absence of 7 days.

The duty-free allowance in **Australia** is A$400 or, for those under 18, A$200. Personal property mailed back from England should be marked "Australian goods returned" to avoid payment of duty. Upon returning to Australia, citizens can bring in 250 cigarettes or 250 grams of loose tobacco, and 1,125ml of alcohol. If you're returning with valuable goods you already own, such as foreign-made cameras, you should file Form B263. A helpful brochure, available from Australian consulates or Customs offices, is *Know Before You Go.* For more information, contact **Australian Customs Services,** GPO Box 8, Sydney, NSW 2001 (☎ **02/9213-2000**).

The duty-free allowance for **New Zealand** is NZ$700. Citizens over 17 can bring in 200 cigarettes, or 50 cigars, or 250 grams of tobacco (or a mixture of all three if their combined weight doesn't exceed 250 grams); plus 4.5 liters of wine and beer, or 1.125 liters of liquor. New Zealand currency does not carry import or export restrictions. Fill out a certificate of export, listing the valuables you are taking out of the country; that way, you can bring them back without paying duty. Most questions are answered in a free pamphlet available at New Zealand consulates and Customs offices: *New Zealand Customs Guide for Travellers, Notice no. 4.* For more information, contact New Zealand Customs, 50 Anzac Ave., P.O. Box 29, Auckland (☎ **09/359-6655**).

The Czech Koruna

At this writing, U.S.$1 equaled approximately 34Kč (or 1Kč = 3¢). This was the rate of exchange used to calculate the dollar values given in this book. At the same time, U.K.£1 equaled about 55Kč.

Note: The rates given here fluctuate and may not be the same when you travel to the Czech Republic.

Kč	U.S.$	U.K.£	Kč	U.S.$	U.K.£
1	0.03	0.02	150	4.41	2.73
5	0.15	0.09	200	5.88	3.64
10	0.29	0.18	250	7.35	4.55
15	0.44	0.27	500	14.71	9.09
20	0.59	0.36	750	22.06	13.64
30	0.88	0.55	1,000	29.41	18.18
40	1.18	0.72	1,500	44.12	27.27
50	1.47	0.91	2,000	58.82	36.36
75	2.21	1.36	2,500	73.53	45.45
100	2.94	1.81	3,000	88.23	54.55

The Czech Republic issued new currency in August 1993, and all notes and coins bearing earlier dates became invalid. There are now eight banknotes and nine coins. Notes, each of which bears a forgery-resistant silver strip and a prominent watermark, are issued in 20, 50, 100, 200, 500, 1,000, 2,000, and 5,000 korun denominations. Coins are valued at 10, 20, and 50 haléřů and 1, 2, 5, 10, 20, and 50 korun.

2 Money

CURRENCY

The basic unit of currency is the **koruna** (plural, **koruny**) or crown, abbreviated **Kč.** Each koruna is divided into 100 **haléřů** or **hellers.** At this writing, the koruna remains volatile after speculation in the currency forced the central bank to let it float in May 1997. In this guide, we quote the koruna at about $0.03 in U.S. dollars: U.S.$1 buys 34Kč and U.K.£1 buys 55Kč. These rates may vary substantially when you arrive, as the koruna often gyrates wildly in the open economy.

CHANGING MONEY

The koruna is now fully convertible, though many Western banks haven't stocked up on koruna notes and coins. You probably will have to wait to get inside the country before obtaining koruny.

Hundreds of new storefront shops provide exchange services, but, if possible, stick to larger banks to make your trades. Better yet, use credit cards or bank cards at ATMs (don't forget your PIN). In both cases, rates are better and the commissions are lower. If you must exchange at a storefront shop, beware of fees, which could go as high as 10% of the transaction.

Chequepoint has outlets in heavily touristed areas and keeps long hours, sometimes all night, but their business practices are sometimes questionable. Central Prague locations are 28.října 13 and Staroměstské nám. 21 (both open 24 hours);

What Things Cost in Prague	U.S $
Taxi from Ruzynê Airport to center city	15.00
Metro, tram, or public bus to anywhere in Prague	0.35
Local telephone call	0.12
Double room at Hotel Paríz (expensive)	270.00
Double room at Hotel Betlem Club (moderate)	100.00
Double room at Hotel Orion (inexpensive)	68.00
Lunch for one at La Provance (moderate)	10.00
Lunch for one at most pubs (inexpensive)	4.00
Dinner for one without wine at Bellevue (expensive)	35.00
Dinner for one without wine at Ambiente (moderate)	10.00
Dinner for one without wine at Osmicka (inexpensive)	5.00
Half liter of beer in a pub	0.75
Coca-Cola in a restaurant	0.90
Cup of coffee	1.00
Roll of ASA 100 film, 36 exposures	4.50
Admission to National Museum	2.05
Movie ticket	3.00
Ticket to National Theater Opera	1.17–22.05

Staroměstské nám. 27 (open daily from 8am to 11:30pm); and Václavské nám. 32 (open daily from 8am to 11pm).

If you can't use your credit card at an ATM, banks are the next-best places to convert cash; there's usually a 1% to 3% commission. **Komerční banka** is the largest Czech commercial bank, with branches throughout the city and in most towns, and its ATMs are connected to the PLUS and Cirrus systems accepting Visa and MasterCard. Its main office is at Na Příkopě 33, Praha 1 (☎ **02/2442 1111**). The branches are usually open Monday to Friday from 8am to 5pm, but the ATMs are accessible 24 hours. **Živnostenská banka,** Na Příkopě 20, Praha 1 (☎ **02/ 2412 1111**), boasts Prague's most beautiful bank lobby and is open Monday to Friday from 9am to 5pm; the change bureau, on the street level, is open Monday to Friday from 10am to 9pm and Saturday from 3 to 7pm. **Komerční banka** has three Praha 1 locations with ATMs: Na Příkopě 33, Na Příkopě 3–5, and Václavské nám. 42. The exchange offices are open Monday to Friday from 8am to 5pm.

AUTOMATED-TELLER MACHINES

ATMs are popping up all over Prague. More than 100 cash machines connected to the worldwide Cirrus and PLUS networks are now online, dispensing koruny and communicating in English. Most larger banks will give you a good exchange rate and charge just a 2% transaction fee. Rarely are there lines at ATMs, and most now accept Visa, American Express, and MasterCard (if you have a PIN). Centrally located machines are in Old Town, at the bank **Česká spořitelna,** at the corner of Rytířská and Havelský trh (between Wenceslas Square and Old Town Square), or at **Komerční banka,** at Na Příkopě 33 (as you exit the Můstek metro station) next to the Powder Tower. In Malá Strana, ATMs are on **Mostecká,** the small street linking Charles Bridge with Malostranské náměstí.

A Warning About Currency Trading

Black-marketers who thrived during Communism by trading the once-fixed soft currency on the street have all but vanished. Still, during violent rate fluctuations and shortages of major currencies, the urchins known as *veksláci* may pop up. Don't trade with them. You may get ripped off on rates, or passed bogus banknotes.

CREDIT CARDS

American Express, MasterCard, and Visa are widely accepted in central Prague, but shopkeepers outside the city center still seem mystified by plastic. The credit-card companies bill at a favorable rate of exchange and save you money by eliminating commissions. You can get cash advances on your MasterCard, Visa, or American Express card from **Komerční banka,** at its main branch, Na Příkopě 33, Praha 1 (☎ **02/2442 1111**), or at most any of its branches, which now have 24-hour ATMs.

TRAVELER'S CHECKS

Those with traveler's checks will do best at **American Express** and **Thomas Cook Travel Services** offices, where rates are competitive and checks are changed commission-free. You can also change traveler's checks at banks and at some private money-change shops. Note that traveler's checks are often not accepted at shops, restaurants, hotels, theaters, and attractions.

3 When to Go

Spring, which can occasionally bring glorious days, is best known for gray, windy stints with rain. The city and the countryside explode with green around May 1, so if you're depressed by stark contrasts and cold-weather pollution, plan your trip between May and October. May is also the month of the renowned Prague Spring Classical Music Festival, drawing stars and fans of serious music from around the world. The high summer season brings a constant flow of tour buses and people watching (from practically every culture) is at its best, especially in 2000 when the European City of Culture celebrations are in full swing (see below). Most Praguers head for their weekend cottages in high season, so if you're looking for local flavor, try another time.

Late September into October is one of our favorite periods, as cool autumn breezes turn trees on the surrounding hills into a multicolored frame for the castle. The crowds are thinner and the prices are better, but in September 2000, the city is expected to be brought to a standstill preparing for the IMF/World Bank annual meeting at the end of the month. This month, just say no.

A true lover of Prague's mysticism should aim to come in the dead cold of February. It sounds bizarre, but this is when you can best enjoy the monochrome silhouettes, shadows, and solitude that make Prague unique. You'll never forget a gray, snowy February afternoon on Charles Bridge. The only drawback of a winter visit to Prague, if you can stand the cold and occasional snow, is that castles and other attractions in the provinces are closed (not Prague Castle). During this time, Praguers dress up in their finery to attend dozens of winter balls (some are open to the public; others can be tactfully gate crashed).

WEATHER

Prague's finicky weather has even rattled a few Brits who live here. The average summer temperature is about 63°F, but some days can be quite chilly and others uncomfortably sultry. In winter, the temperature remains stuck around freezing. During an average January, it's sunny and clear for only 50 hours the entire month; in February, the average is 72 hours. Pollution, heaviest in the winter, tends to limit the snowfall in Prague; however, outlying areas get blanketed. July is rainiest and February is driest.

HOLIDAYS

Official holidays are observed on January 1 (New Year's Day); Easter Monday; May 1 (Labor Day); May 8 (Liberation Day, from Fascism); July 5 (Introduction of Christianity); July 6 (Death of Jan Hus); October 28 (Foundation of the Republic); December 24 and 25 (Christmas); and December 26 (St. Stephen's Day).

On these holidays, most business and shops (including food shops) are closed and buses and trams run on Sunday schedules.

Czech Republic Calendar of Events

January

- **Anniversary of Jan Palach's Death.** On January 19, 1969, 21-year-old philosophy student Jan Palach set fire to himself on Wenceslas Square as a protest against the Soviet invasion of Czechoslovakia. He died a few days later and became a symbol for dissidents. His death is commemorated annually at a Memorial to the Victims of Communism on Wenceslas Square and at Olšany Cemetery where he's buried. January 19.

March

- **Prague City of Music Festival.** Contemporary and classical concerts are performed at this festival. For details, contact Čedok, Na Příkopě 18, Praha 1 (☎ 02/2419 7559), or most any information/travel agency in Prague (see "Visitor Information" in chapter 3). Throughout the month.

April

- **Witches' Night.** This annual bucolic ritual is meant to bring luck to the planting season. Bonfires are lit and an effigy of an old hag is thrown on the flames. Prague largely ignores this event, but blazes dot the countryside beginning at twilight. April 30.

May

- ✪ **Karlovy Vary Blessing of the Waters.** One of Europe's oldest and most famous spas (the original Carlsbad) kicks off its high season with a traditional blessing of its 12 hot springs, complete with a coronation and a reenactment of the town's founding by Charles IV. The spa zone is filled with medieval sights and sounds. For details, call the newspaper *Karlovarské noviny* at ☎ 017/322 9572 or contact Čedok at Na Příkopě 18, Praha 1 (☎ 02/2419 7559). First weekend in May.

- ✪ **Prague Spring Music Festival.** This world-famous 3-week series of classical music and dance performances begins with the anniversary of Bedřich Smetana's death on May 12. Opening night, the most difficult seat of the festival, is traditionally a performance of Smetana's symphonic poem *Má Vlast (My Country)*, attended by the president. Throughout the fest, symphony, opera, and chamber performances bring some of the world's best talent to Prague. Concert tickets are usually 250Kč to 2,000Kč ($7.35 to $58.80) and are available in advance (beginning in January) from Hellichova 18, Praha 1 (☎ 02/5732 0468). Beginning May 12.

- **Prague International Book Fair.** This trade show attracts top Czech writers and stars from the literary world, with many special readings and book signings scheduled. For tickets and details, contact the Prague Information Service's Info-Centrum at ☎ **187** in Prague; 02/54 44 44 outside Prague. Mid-May.

June

• **Slavnost Pětilisté růže (Festival of the Five-Petaled Rose).** Held annually to mark the summer solstice, the festival gives residents of Český Krumlov the excuse to dress up in Renaissance costume and parade through the streets. Afterward, the streets become a stage with plays, chess games with people dressed as pieces, music, and more. For details, contact the town's information center at ☎ **0337/711 183.** Third weekend in June.

July

❂ **Karlovy Vary International Film Festival.** This annual 10-day event predates Communism and has regained its "A" rating from the international body governing film festivals. That puts it in the same league with Cannes and Venice, though much further down the standings since it doesn't yet have the star-drawing power of the more glittery stops. A blanket ticket policy putting 1-day advance-sell seats at a buck each means that screenings are mostly filled with students willing to stand in line the day before. Early July.

August

• **Chopin Festival.** Karlovy Vary's younger and smaller sister spa town of Mariánské Lázně (Marienbad) honors one of its past guests, Chopin, with an annual 8- to 10-day festival. Concerts and recitals, mostly for piano, are held throughout the town. For details or tickets, contact Městské InfoCentrum at ☎ **0165/625 892.** Late August.

September

• **Prague Autumn International Music Festival.** This festival features local orchestras from around the country and some international guests. The 1997 festival included the Israeli Philharmonic Orchestra with Zubin Mehta as conductor. Most concerts are at the Rudolfinum. You can buy tickets in advance through the Festival Office, Sekaninova 26, Praha 2 (fax 02/242 7564 or 02/692 7650) or call Ticketpro at ☎ **02/2481 4020.** First 2 weeks of September.

• **Křivoklát Film Festival.** This "Anti-Festival" held at the Gothic fortress 27 miles west of Prague shuns commercially geared flicks and even glossy independents for a raw taste of European experimental cinema. Many films have English subtitles or come with simultaneous translations shown in this medieval setting. Last week of September.

October

• **Mozart in Prague.** This is a monthlong celebration of the composer's works in the city that he said understood him best. Concerts are held in venues throughout Prague. For details, contact Ticketpro (☎ **02/2481 4020;** e-mail: vstupenky@ticketpro.cz; www.ticketpro.cz). Throughout October.

• **Renaissance Days at Křivoklát Castle.** Amid the cold winds and blazing fall colors in the Berounka valley, this Gothic relic of famous Czech lore gets decked out in all the trappings of the 14th and 15th centuries. With merchants, minstrels, and merrymakers filling the fortress grounds, this time-warp event can be fun. See chapter 10 for details. Last weekend in October.

November

• **Anniversary of the Velvet Revolution.** The clash between students and police on Národní street on November 17, 1989, set off the chain of events that eventually brought down the Communist government (many students were injured

Schedule of Events—European City of Culture 2000

How fitting it is that Prague, after spending much of the last century having its cultural brilliance dimmed by power politics, can shine as a truly European city in the last year of the millennium. The European Union has chosen the Czech capital, along with eight other communities on the Old Continent, as European Cities of Culture in 2000. While the others—which include Avignon, Bologna, Brussels, Helsinki, and Krakow—have, by far in most cases, outspent Prague in hosting the yearlong series of events, the eclectic brand of traditional and classical music, avant-garde art, and counterculture oddities to be found here should make this special year memorable.

The best way to stay on top of the schedule, which is expected to be revised throughout the year, is to tap into the Prague Information Service (PIS) Web site at **www.pis.eunet.cz**, where all events are updated in English and Czech.

Among the events expected to be scheduled for the Prague 2000 celebration:

- During all of 2000, each Tuesday, Friday, and Saturday at 8pm, 150 chamber music concerts are planned in Malá Strana's **Nostitz Palace,** while at 9:30pm nightly, jazz concerts will be held at the **Reduta club** near the national theater on Národní street, with domestic and international groups performing.

- January 2000 through January 2001   **The Best of Opera**—weekly Opera Gala at the House at the Stone Bell on Old Town Square.

- March 19, 2000   **North Opera Company** from Leeds in England will perform Bohuslav Martinů's opera *Julietta* at the National Theater.

- March 2000   **"BABA 1932"**—an exhibition presenting Czech purism and functionalism in architecture (site to be announced).

- April 2000   **The Passages of Prague** exhibition in the Jaroslav Fragner Gallery will present countless architectonic curiosities documenting the cultural and social development of Prague from the beginning of the century to the present.

- April 30 through October 31, 2000   **Praga Mystica**—an exhibition presenting the history of the town from primeval ages to the Rudolphian Era, in the underground space under the Old Town Square.

- April through September 2000   **The Italian Influence on Czech Architecture** between the Renaissance and the late-Baroque eras. Exhibition at Belvedere Summer House and the Ball Hall of Prague Castle.

- May 12 to June 3, 2000   **Prague Spring International Music Festival**—55th year.

but none died). Czechs refer to the period since as the Post-November Era, though few commemorate the event (which isn't a national holiday, strangely enough). President Havel usually lays a wreath at the small bronze "free hands" monument hanging on a wall near Národní 20. November 17.

December

- **Christmas in Prague.** This is a festive time in Prague. St. Mikuláš (Nicholas), the Czech version of Santa Claus but dressed in a white bishop's costume, kicks off the season on December 5 by giving sweets to well-behaved children and coal and potatoes to rowdy ones. Just before Christmas, large barrels of live carp are

- May 26 to 28, 2000   **Production 2000—3x Nederlands Dans,** a Dutch dance creation at the State Opera.
- May through September 2000   **The Baroque Principle** exhibition relates the phenomenon of the Czech Baroque and its influence to the genesis of Czech modern art (sites to be announced).
- May through September 2000   Parks and gardens throughout the city will host a series of **dance performances** (sites to be announced).
- July 6 to 9, 2000   **European Folklore Festival** (sites to be announced).
- July 2000   **From Copernicus to NASA**—exhibition of American space technology at Prague Exhibition Grounds.
- July through November 2000   **The Unknown Prague**—exhibition mapping vanished elements of the city, plus dreams and visions that have never materialized, at the Wallenstein Riding Hall.
- August 3 to September 21, 2000   **International Organ Festival** at the Basilica of St. James, every Thursday at 6pm.
- August through September 2000   **WOMAD**—British ethnic music festival under the aegis of Peter Gabriel.
- September 8 to 30, 2000   **Antonín Dvořák and His Prague**—concert project placing emphasis on the composer's relation to Prague and its cultural life (sites to be announced).
- September through December 2000   **Prague 2000—the Optical Globe.** Between September and December, Wenceslas Square will serve as the site of multimedia projections of archival photographs of historic events in Prague's history.
- October 2000   **International Jazz Festival** at Lucerna, Reduta, Žofín, and Nostitz Palace.
- November 17 to 24, 2000   **Four+Four Days in Motion**—festival presenting young, nonconventional European performance artists (sites to be announced).
- December 1 to 3, 2000   **International Festival of Advent and Christmas Music.**
- January 1, 2001   **First Concert of the Third Millennium** by the Prague Philharmonic in the Dvořák Hall of the Rudolfinum.

brought into the city, where the fish are clubbed to death and gutted on demand for families to take home for the traditional Christmas meal. 'Tis the season. December 5 to 26.

- **New Year's Eve.** Unless you are looking for trouble or enjoy dodging missiles, you should stay well away from the center of Prague on New Year's Eve. On the night known as "Silvester," Old Town Square and Charles Bridge become battle zones with indiscriminately fired bottle rockets and other fireworks causing random and often serious injuries. Each year has gotten worse. Best to stay inside one of the many hotel or restaurant galas being offered on that night. December 31.

4 Health & Insurance

VACCINATIONS

Unless you're arriving from an area known to be suffering from an epidemic, no inoculations or vaccinations are required to enter the Czech Republic. Be sure to carry a doctor's prescription for any medication or controlled substance you require. It's best to bring all the medication you'll need on your trip, though Western remedies are now easier to find.

INSURANCE

Most travel agents sell low-cost health, theft, and trip-cancellation insurance. Flight insurance, against damages suffered in the event of a plane crash, is available from self-service counters at most major airports. Some credit-card companies also offer free automatic travel-accident insurance (up to $100,000) when you purchase travel tickets with their cards.

If you fall ill in the Czech Republic and wish the services of an English-language doctor, you'll probably have to pay up front for services rendered (and you should be reimbursed by your insurer if the policy is in order). Check to see if you're covered in foreign countries by your insurance carrier before you purchase additional protection.

In addition to medical insurance, you can protect your travel investment by insuring against lost or damaged baggage and trip cancellation or interruption. This coverage is often combined into a single plan and sold by travel agents or credit-card issuers.

SAFETY

Citizens are reporting more burglaries and violent assaults, and some visitors have been targeted, though Prague remains safe by Western standards. The best strategy is to use common sense. Women especially should avoid walking alone late at night on dark streets, through parks, and around Wenceslas Square—one of the main areas for prostitution. All visitors should be watchful of pickpockets in heavily touristed areas, especially on Charles Bridge, in Old Town Square, and in front of the main train station. Be especially wary on crowded buses, trams, and trains. Don't keep your wallet in a back pocket and don't flash a lot of cash or jewelry.

5 Tips for Travelers with Special Needs

FOR TRAVELERS WITH DISABILITIES

The Czechs have made little effort to accommodate the needs of the disabled. There are few elevators or ramps for wheelchairs, there are only a few beeping crosswalks for the visually impaired, and TTD phones for the hearing impaired are rare.

In the cobblestone streets of downtown Prague, wheelchairs are almost unknown. Only a few hotels (like the Renaissance and the Palace) offer barrier-free accommodations, and most stores, public transport, theaters, and restaurants are inaccessible to wheelchairs. The following metro stations in the city center are accessible: Florenc, Hlavní nádraží, Pankrác, Roztyly, Chodov, Karlovo náměstí, Skalka, and Nádraží Holešovice.

For the most part, attractions don't offer discounts to people with disabilities. There are exceptions, however, so always ask before paying full price.

ORGANIZATIONS   The **Travel Information Service,** Moss Rehab Hospital, 1200 W. Tabor Rd., Philadelphia, PA 19141, serves as a telephone resource for travelers with physical disabilities. Call ☎ **215/456-9600** (voice) or 215/456-9602 (TTY).

The **Society for the Advancement of Travel for the Handicapped,** 347 Fifth Ave., Suite 610, New York, NY 10016 (☎ **212/447-7284;** fax 212/725-8253), can provide information for people with disabilities and for the elderly, as well as listings of specialized tour operators.

One of the best organizations serving the needs of persons with disabilities (especially those assisted by wheelchairs and walkers) is **Flying Wheels Travel,** 143 West Bridge (P.O. Box 382), Owatonna, MN 55060 (☎ **800/525-6790**).

FOR GAY & LESBIAN TRAVELERS

During the Communist regime, homosexuality was met with official silence. However, many Czechs have always had a genuine live-and-let-live attitude. Open hostility toward homosexuals is rare in Prague. Since November 1989, many gays have "come out." Gay sex is legal, with the age of consent at 15. Several bars and nightclubs in Prague cater exclusively to the gay community and are listed in chapter 9.

The **Association of Organizations of Homosexual Citizens (SOHO)** (☎ **02/ 2422 3811**) was founded in 1991 as an umbrella group uniting several smaller gay organizations.

The best information on happenings for gay visitors is in **SOHO Review,** a monthly magazine listing activities and events. It's in Czech but does run some English-language information and personal ads. The *Prague Post* also prints updated gay and lesbian reviews.

PUBLICATIONS   Note that in early 1999 Frommer's Travel published its first guide especially for gay and lesbian travelers, **Frommer's Gay and Lesbian Europe,** which includes Prague among its destinations. These books and others are available from **A Different Light Book Store,** 151 W. 19th St., New York, NY 10011 (☎ **800/343-4002** or 212/989-4850), or **Giovanni's Room,** 1145 Pine St., Philadelphia, PA 19107 (☎ **215/923-2960;** fax 215/923-0813).

Our World, 1104 N. Nova Rd., Suite 251, Daytona Beach, FL 32117 (☎ **904/ 441-5367;** fax 904/441-5604), is a magazine devoted to gay and lesbian travel worldwide; it costs $35 for 10 issues. *Out & About,* 8 W. 19th St., Suite 401, New York, NY 10011 (☎ **800/929-2268;** fax 800/929-2215), has been hailed for its "straight" reporting about gay travel. Aimed at the more upscale gay traveler, it has been praised by everybody from *Travel & Leisure* to the *New York Times.*

TRAVEL AGENCIES   A company called **Our Family Abroad,** 40 W. 57th St., Suite 430, New York, NY 10019 (☎ **800/999-5500** or 212/459-1800; fax 212/ 581-3756), operates escorted tours that include about a dozen European itineraries. In California, a leading option for gay travel arrangements is **Above and Beyond,** 300 Townsend St., Suite 107, San Francisco, CA 94107 (☎ **800/397-2681** or 415/ 284-1666; fax 415/284-1660).

FOR SENIORS

Because Communist equality meant that seniors were no worse off financially than younger persons, Czechs have little experience offering special discounts to pensioners. Several attractions, such as the National Museum, have senior discounts, many times announced only in Czech with the price for *důchodce* (pensioner). Always ask if a markdown applies to you as well, since there's an accepted Czech system of dual pricing for foreigners.

Older travelers are particularly encouraged to purchase travel insurance. When making airline reservations, ask about a senior discount (usually 10%), but also ask if there's a cheaper promotional fare.

ORGANIZATIONS   The **American Association of Retired Persons (AARP)**, 601 E St. NW, Washington, DC 20049 (☎ **202/434-AARP**), is the nation's leading organization for people 50 and older. It serves their needs and interests through advocacy, research, informative programs, and community services provided by a network of local chapters and experienced volunteers throughout the country. The organization also offers members a wide range of special membership benefits, including *Modern Maturity* magazine and the monthly *Bulletin*.

Elderhostel, 75 Federal St., Boston, MA 02110-1941 (☎ **617/426-8056**), arranges numerous study programs around Europe, including the Czech Republic. Most courses, lasting about 3 weeks, represent great value since they include airfare, accommodations in student dormitories or modest inns, all meals, and tuition. The courses involve no homework, are ungraded, and often focus on the liberal arts. They're not luxury vacations, but they're fun and fulfilling. Participants must be 55 or older.

FOR FAMILIES

Prague isn't the easiest place to explore with kids. Only strollers with large wheels can manage the cobblestone streets, and few restaurants have smoke-free areas or cater to the needs of kids. For a selection of family-friendly accommodations and restaurants, see the boxes in chapters 4 and 5. While you should pack medicines or special foods that your children need, you'll find baby food, diapers (including familiar brands), and other sundries available in food stores and pharmacies around town. For special activities, see "Especially for Kids" in chapter 6.

FOR STUDENTS

Students regularly enjoy discounts on travel, theater, and museum tickets. The **International Student Identity Card (ISIC)** is the most readily accepted proof of status and is available from most university travel agents and from the **Council on International Educational Exchange**, 205 E. 42nd St., New York, NY 10017 (☎ **212/661-1450**). To be eligible, you must be enrolled in a degree program. The application must include proof of student status via an official letter from the school registrar or high school principal, a registration fee, and one passport-size photo.

Prague's hostels not only are some of the cheapest places to stay but also are great for meeting other travelers. You don't have to be a card-carrying member of the International Youth Hostel Federation (IYHF) to lodge at them. Since the venerable Charles University is largely a commuter school with buildings scattered throughout the city, central Prague lacks the verve and bustle of a college community.

If you want to make some music or do some magic busking for money, you can do so legally anywhere in the city. If you want to sell something, though, beware that authorities require permits for those who wish to hawk on Charles Bridge and elsewhere.

6 Getting There

BY PLANE
THE MAJOR AIRLINES

About two dozen international airlines offer regularly scheduled service into Prague's Ruzyně Airport. The only U.S. carrier flying direct to Prague is Continental via its New York/Newark hub using a code-sharing arrangement with the Czech national carrier **ČSA Czech Airlines** (☎ **800/223-2365**). ČSA also flies to Prague from Toronto and Montréal. Germany's **Lufthansa** (☎ **800/645-3880**) has frequent connections to Prague with no-smoking flights from New York and San Francisco via their Frankfurt hub.

Other major carriers serving the Czech Republic are **Air France** (☎ **800/ 237-2747**); **Alitalia** (☎ **800/223-5730**); **Austrian Airlines** (☎ **800/843-0002**), **British Airways** (☎ **800/247-9297** in the U.S. or 020/8897-4000 in the U.K.), as well as BA's new **GO** economy short-haul service from London's Stanstead Airport; **KLM Royal Dutch Airlines** (☎ **800/777-5553**); **SAS** (☎ **800/221-2350**); and **Swissair** (☎ **800/221-4750**).

See the box "Cyber Deals for Net Surfers" for the Web sites of these airlines.

PRAGUE AIRLINE OFFICES   To get flight information in Prague or make reservations or changes, contact **Air France,** Václavské nám. 10, Praha 1 (☎ **02/2422 7164**); **Alitalia,** Na Můstku 9, Praha 1 (☎ **02/2419 4150**); **Austrian Airlines,** Revoluční 15, Praha 1 (☎ **02/231 3378**); **British Airways,** Ovocný trh 8, Praha 1 (☎ **02/2211 4444**); **ČSA Czech Airlines,** V celnici 5, Praha 1, next to the Renaissance Hotel (☎ **02/2010 4111** or 02/2010 4620); **GO** airlines (no Prague location yet, but you can phone for info at ☎ **02/9633 3333**); **KLM Royal Dutch Airlines,** Na Příkopě 13, Praha 1 (☎ **02/2421 6950**); **Lufthansa,** Pařížská 28, Praha 1 (☎ **02/ 2481 1007**); **SAS,** Rytířská 13, Praha 1 (☎ **02/2421 4749**); and **Swissair,** Pařížská 11, Praha 1 (☎ **02/2481 2111**).

FINDING THE BEST AIRFARE

Airlines observe three pricing seasons to Prague: low (winter, except for the Christmas season), high (summer), and shoulder (spring and fall). At this writing, the lowest published online round-trip summer fare from New York was $835, from Chicago $938, and from Los Angeles $1,004. During winter, the lowest fare from New York was $677, from Chicago $769, and from Los Angeles $813.

Business-class seats can cost exorbitantly more than the price of coach. Expect to pay about $3,500 from New York and a little more from Chicago and Los Angeles if they're available. ČSA often has good deals that are a lot cheaper than those offered by Delta and other Western carriers, but still it lags in service and cuisine.

Most airlines offer only a handful of expensive first-class seats on Prague flights. The published first-class airfare from New York is about $5,500, from Chicago about $5,800, and from Los Angeles about $6,000. Before buying, see if your airline offers a first-class upgrade with a full-fare business-class ticket.

DISCOUNTED AIRFARES   **Consolidators,** or **bucket shops,** sell tickets at deeply discounted rates—often 20% to 30% lower. For example, in winter from New York, you can buy bucket-shop tickets to Prague on well-known international airlines for as little as $250 each way; the prices rise to about $600 in summer. Remember, however, that it's very difficult to return these tickets and many restrictions apply.

The lowest-priced bucket shops are typically local operations with low profiles and overheads. Look for ads in the travel or classified section of your newspaper. Nationally advertised consolidators are usually not as competitive as smaller local operations, but they have toll-free numbers and are easily accessible. These include **Travac,** 989 Sixth Ave., New York, NY 10018 (☎ **800/TRAV-800** or 212/563-3303).

Charter operators mostly sell seats through travel agents. One reliable company is **Council Charter,** 205 E. 42nd St., New York, NY 10017 (☎ **800/800-8222** or 212/661-0311). Look for round-trip fares from New York as low as $550 (midwinter) and $700 (summer). Before deciding, check the restrictions on the ticket. If you decide on a charter flight, seriously consider purchasing cancellation insurance.

You can also travel to Europe as a **courier.** Companies transporting time-sensitive materials, such as documents for banks and insurance firms, regularly hire couriers. All

Cyber Deals for Net Surfers

It's possible to get some great deals on airfare, hotels, and car rentals via the Internet. So grab your mouse and start surfing before you head to the Czech Republic—you could save a bundle on your trip. The Web sites I've highlighted below are worth checking out, especially since all services are free (but don't forget that time is money when you're online).

Microsoft Expedia (www.expedia.com)   The best part of this multipurpose travel site is the Fare Tracker: You fill out a form on the screen indicating that you're interested in cheap flights to the Czech Republic from your hometown, and, once a week, they e-mail you the best airfare deals. The site's Travel Agent will steer you to bargains on hotels and car rentals, and you can book everything, including flights, right online. This site is even useful once you're booked: Before you go, log on to Expedia for oodles of up-to-date travel info, including weather reports and foreign exchange rates.

Preview Travel (www.reservations.com and www.vacations.com)   Another useful site, reservations.com has a Best Fare Finder that'll search the Apollo computer reservations system for the three lowest fares for any route on any days of the year. Say you want to go from New York to Prague and back between December 6 and 13: Just fill out the form on the screen with times, dates, and destinations, and within minutes, Preview will show you the best deals. If you find an airfare you like, you can book your ticket online—you can even reserve hotels and car rentals on this site. If you're in the preplanning stage, head to Preview's vacations.com site, where you can check out the latest package deals by clicking on Hot Deals.

Travelocity (www.travelocity.com)   This is one of the best travel sites out there. In addition to its Personal Fare Watcher, which notifies you via e-mail of the lowest airfares for up to five destinations, Travelocity will track in minutes the three lowest fares for any routes on any dates. You can book a flight then and there, and if you need a rental car or hotel, they'll find you the best deal via the SABRE computer reservations system (a huge database used by travel agents worldwide). Click on Last Minute Deals for the latest travel bargains.

Trip.Com (www.thetrip.com) This site is really geared toward the business traveler, but vacationers-to-be can also use Trip.Com's valuable fare-finding engine, which will e-mail you every week with the best city-to-city airfare deals on your selected route or routes.

you have to do is give up your checked-baggage allowance and make do with carry-ons. Expect to meet a courier service representative at the airport before departure to get the manifest of the checked items. On arrival, you deliver the baggage-claim tag to a waiting agent. One drawback, besides restricted baggage, is that you have to travel alone. You might contact **Now Voyager, Inc.,** 74 Varick St., Suite 307, New York, NY 10013 (☎ **212/431-1616** daily from 10am to 6pm). Prices change all the time, from low to very low. Flights are booked on a round-trip basis exclusively, though there's often nothing to carry on the way home.

INTRA-EUROPEAN FLIGHTS   If you're flying to Prague from Europe, fares are generally high, except from London, where a fare war has brought prices way down. Some airlines offer special promotions as well as 7- and 14-day advance-purchase fares.

Discount Tickets (www.discount-tickets.com)   Operated by the ETN (European Travel Network), this site offers discounts on airfares, accommodations, car rentals, and tours. It deals in flights between the United States and other countries.

E-Savers Programs   Several major airlines offer a free e-mail service known as **E-Savers,** via which they'll send you their best bargain airfares on a weekly basis. Once a week (usually Wednesday), subscribers receive a list of discounted flights to and from various destinations. Now here's the catch: These fares are available only if you leave the very next Saturday (or sometimes Friday night) and return on the following Monday or Tuesday. It's really a service for the spontaneously inclined and travelers looking for a quick getaway. But the fares are cheap, so it's worth taking a look. If you have a preference for certain airlines (in other words, the ones you fly most frequently), sign up with them first. *Note:* You'll get frequent-flier miles if you purchase one of these fares, but you can't use miles to buy the ticket.

Here's a list of airlines and their Web sites, where you can not only get on the e-mail lists but also book flights directly:

- **ČSA Czech Airlines:** www.csa.cz
- **Lufthansa:** www.lufthansa-USA.com
- **Air France:** www.airfrance.com
- **Alitalia:** www.italiatour.com/alitalia.html
- **Austrian Airlines:** www.aua.at/aua
- **British Airways:** www.british-airways.com
- **GO:** www.go-fly.com
- **KLM:** www.klm.nl
- **Swissair:** www.swissair.com

Epicurious Travel (travel.epicurious.com), another good travel site, allows you to sign up for all these airline e-mail lists at once.

—Jeanette Foster

Jeanette Foster is coauthor of *Frommer's Hawaii from $60 a Day* and *Frommer's Honolulu, Waikiki & Oahu.*

Look in local newspapers or visit a European travel agent to find out about cheaper chartered fares.

Trailfinders (☎ **020/7937-5400**), which sells discounted fares to Prague on a variety of airlines, is a highly recommended company. You may also want to check out bucket shops in London's Earl's Court neighborhood. For your own protection, make sure that the company you deal with is a member of the IATA, ABTA, or ATOL.

BY TRAIN

Train fares in Europe are lower than those in the United States. Czech tickets are particularly inexpensive but are getting more expensive. Because European countries are compact, it often takes less time to travel city-to-city by train than by plane. Prague is about 5 hours by train from Munich, Berlin, and Vienna.

A Taxi Tip

At the airport, shrewd travelers might get an honest ride from one of the taxi drivers that linger in their Škodas and Ladas after dropping off departing passengers at the other end of the terminal. An honest ride should cost no more than 400Kč ($12) to Václavské náměstí (Wenceslas Square).

Direct trains to Prague depart daily from Paris (via Frankfurt) and Berlin (via Dresden). The former takes 10 hours and the round-trip costs about $300 in first class and $200 in second class; the latter takes 5½ hours and costs $42 each way.

The train from London to Prague costs about £215 ($350) for a round-trip ticket in first class and £150 ($250) in second class. The difference is relatively small, a matter of one or two inches of padding on the seats and slightly more leg room.

For information on routes and seat availability, contact the **International Rail Centre** in London's Victoria Station (☎ 020/7834-2345). You can purchase rail tickets to Prague from any "international" ticket window in Victoria Station. And if you need some help planning your rail trip, visit **Wasteels, Ltd.** (☎ 020/7834-7066), opposite Victoria Station's platform 2.

Trains connect Prague and Vienna five times daily; the 5½-hour trip costs $21 each way. Trains connect Prague and Budapest six times daily; the nearly 8-hour trip costs $33 each way. Trains connect Prague and Warsaw two times daily; the 9-hour trip costs $26 each way.

You can also reach Prague from Munich or Frankfurt. The former runs three times daily, with the 7-hour trip costing $56 each way. The latter runs two times daily, with the 7½-hour trip costing $69 each way.

For more information on traveling on Českē dráhy (Czech Railways), see chapter 10.

TRAIN PASSES

The **European East Pass** is good for first-class unlimited rail access in Austria, the Czech Republic, Hungary, Poland, and Slovakia. You must purchase the pass from a travel agent or Rail Europe before you leave for Europe. A pass for any 5 days of unlimited train travel in a 15-day period is $185 for adults and $93 for children 4 to 11. A pass for any 10 days of unlimited train travel in a 1-month period is $299 for adults and $150 for children 4 to 11.

Also available is the **Czech Flexipass,** good for rail travel within the Czech Republic. It costs $69 for 5 days of travel within a 15-day period. However, it's twice as expensive as buying tickets yourself.

Below is a list of European rail passes and their prices. *Note:* These passes are *not* valid in the Czech Republic. You can use the passes to reach the Czech border—Furth im Wald or Schirnding on the German border, Gmünd on the Austrian border—then you can buy your fare between the border and Prague for roughly 340Kč ($10) each way.

Eurailpass: 15 days, $522; 21 days, $678; 1 month, $838; 2 months, $1,188; 3 months, $1,468. First class only, with access to many ferries, steamers, and buses free or at a discount.

Eurail Saverpass: for two or more people traveling together in a 2-month period: 10 days, $524 per person; 15 days, $690 per person. First class only; same privileges as Eurailpass.

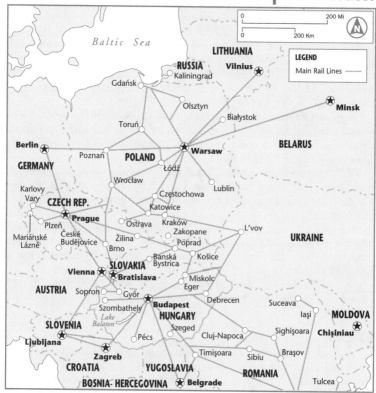

Eastern Europe Rail Routes

Baltic Sea

LITHUANIA
RUSSIA Vilnius ✪
Kaliningrad
Gdańsk
Minsk ✪
Olsztyn
Białystok
Toruń
BELARUS
Berlin ✪
Poznań **POLAND** Warsaw ✪
GERMANY
Łódź
Wrocław
Lublin
Karlovy Vary
Częstochowa
CZECH REP. Katowice
Prague Ostrava Kraków
Plzeň Zakopane **L'vov**
Mariánské Lázně České Budějovice Žilina Poprad **UKRAINE**
Brno
Banská Bystrica Košice
Vienna ✪ **SLOVAKIA**
AUSTRIA Bratislava ✪ Miskolc
Sopron Győr Eger
Szombathely Debrecen Suceava
Lake Balaton **Budapest** Iaşi **MOLDOVA**
HUNGARY Szeged Sighişoara Chişiniau ✪
SLOVENIA
Ljubljana ✪ Pécs Cluj-Napoca
Timişoara Sibiu Braşov
Zagreb ✪ **ROMANIA**
CROATIA **YUGOSLAVIA**
BOSNIA- HERCEGOVINA ✪ **Belgrade** Tulcea

LEGEND
Main Rail Lines ———

0 — 200 Mi
0 — 200 Km

Eurail Flexipass: any 10 days in 2 months, $616; any 15 days in 2 months, $812. First class only; same privileges as Eurailpass.

Eurail Youthpass: for travelers under 26 years. 15 days, $418; 1 month, $598; 2 months, $798. Second class only; same privileges as Eurailpass.

Children under 12 travel for half fare and those under 4 are free with a parent holding a Eurailpass, Eurail Saverpass, or a Eurail Flexipass.

You can buy any of the passes from Rail Europe; call ☎ **800/4-EURAIL** for tickets, information, or brochures.

Many rail passes are available in the United Kingdom for travel in Britain and Europe. However, one of the most widely used of these passes, the InterRail card, isn't valid for travel in the Czech Republic. Passengers under 26 with lots of holiday time sometimes opt for a EuroYouth ticket, which allows unlimited stopovers en route between London and the Czech border, after which it costs the equivalent of £10 to £20 to reach Prague.

BY BUS

Throughout Europe, bus transportation is usually less expensive than rail travel and covers a more extensive area. European buses generally outshine U.S. counterparts. In the Czech Republic, buses cost significantly less than trains and often offer more direct routes. **Europabus,** c/o DER Tours/German Rail, 11933 Wilshire Blvd., Los Angeles, CA 90025 (☎ **800/782-2424** or 310/479-4140), provides information on regular coach service. **Cosmos,** a British operator, specializes in economical bus tours of

Europe that you can book through travel agents in the States. It'll match single travelers who want to share a room to avoid paying a supplement.

If you're coming from London, **Eurolines,** 52 Grosvenor Gardens, London SW1 W OAU (☎ 020/7730-0202), runs regular bus service from London to Prague at about £95 round-trip. Coaches are equipped with toilets and reclining seats, and trips take about 30 hours. By law, drivers are required to stop at regular intervals for rest and refreshment.

Kingscourt Express, Havelská 8, Praha 1 (☎ 02/2423 4583), operates the most popular scheduled bus service between London and Prague, which stops in Prague just across from the Florenc station. The nearly 21-hour trip runs six times weekly, and the one-way cost is 3,350Kč ($98.50).

A daily bus connection between Prague and Vienna takes 4¼ hours and costs $27. Buses connect Prague and Budapest four times weekly, with the 8¼-hour trip costing $25 each way. There's bus service between Prague and Warsaw twice a week for $25 each way.

From Germany, buses connect Prague and Munich four times weekly, and the 7½-hour trip is $30 each way. Buses run between Prague and Frankfurt five times weekly, with the 9¾-hour trip costing $45 each way. The 6-hour trip between Prague and Berlin is $34 each way.

You should make reservations as far in advance as possible. See chapters 10, 11, and 12 for more information on traveling by bus from Prague to other destinations in the Czech Republic.

BY CAR

You definitely shouldn't rent a car to explore Prague. But if you want to see the countryside, driving can be a fun way to travel. Czechs, who learned to drive in low-powered Škodas, still run up your tailpipe before passing, even though many now drive beefier BMWs and Opels. The combination of high-speed muscle cars, rickety East Bloc specials, and smoky cargo trucks crawling along can make driving on two-lane highways frustrating. But a car will make it easier to find a budget hotel or a comfortable spot to camp. You'll find detailed driving directions to the destinations listed in chapters 10, 11, and 12.

Travelers approaching Prague from the west drive through Nürnberg, Germany, before entering the Czech Republic at the Waldhaus/Rozvadov border crossing on a new superhighway that connects to Prague via Plzeň. Drivers from the northwest motor through Chemnitz (formerly Karl-Marx-Stadt), Germany, before entering the Czech Republic at the Reitzenhain/Pohraničí. From the south, Linz, Austria, is a gateway, and from the east, Žilina, Slovakia, is a gateway. Driving distances are from Vienna, 350km (217 miles); from Warsaw, 750km (465 miles); from Munich, 450km (279 miles); and from Berlin, 380km (236 miles).

See "Getting Around" in chapter 3 for information on car-rental firms.

BY FERRY, SEACAT, OR CHANNEL TUNNEL FOR U.K. TRAVELERS

If you're traveling from England and don't want to fly, there are several options for getting to continental Europe. If you want to drive, **P&O Ferries** (☎ 020/8575-8555 or 0304/203-388) is one of the U.K.'s largest drive-on ferryboat operators, carrying cars, passengers, and freight. The company offers daily crossings of the English Channel from Dover to Calais, France, and from Folkestone to Zeebrugge, Belgium. **Brittany Ferries** (☎ 0752/221-321), P&O's largest competitor, offers regular ferry service from Portsmouth to St-Malo and Caen in France.

Another way to cross the channel is by **SeaCat** (a form of high-speed motorized catamaran), which cuts your journey time from the United Kingdom to the Continent. A SeaCat trip can be a fun adventure, especially for first-timers and children, as the vessel is technically "flying" above the surface of the water. A SeaCat crossing from Folkestone to Boulogne, France, is more timesaving to passengers than the Dover to Calais route used by conventional ferryboats. For reservations and information, call **HoverSpeed** at ☎ **0304/240-241.**

You can also go via the Channel Tunnel. The drive-on/drive-off "Chunnel" train runs between Folkestone and Calais, France. Travel time under the water between England and France is just 30 minutes. Train passengers can use the tunnel on direct routes to Paris from London's Waterloo Station. For up-to-the-minute information, call **BritRail** at ☎ **020/7928-5100.**

PACKAGE TOURS

Several tour operators offer escorted and independent tours to Prague and the Czech Republic and are described below. However, using this book you can put together your own itinerary for about one-third less in cost.

Most airlines listed above offer both escorted tours and on-your-own packages—for example, combining airfare and hotel packages departing from major U.S. cities. If you can find round-trip airfare from New York/Newark for $850 or less, you won't be saving any money on package tours. Likewise, the half a dozen add-ons, including walking tours, river cruises, and airport transfers, can all be easily purchased yourself for less money, once you arrive in Prague.

The largest Czech agency **Čedok** has closed its only U.S. office in New York, but English-speaking staff can be contacted through its London or Prague office or through the Internet. In the United Kingdom, the address is 49 Southwark St., London SE1 1RU (☎ **020/7378-6009**), or call the Prague main office for advanced bookings at Na Příkopě 18, Praha 1 (☎ **02/2419 7559**). The Čedok English-language link on its Web site is **www.cedok.cz/en/index.html**.

Isram World of Travel, 630 Third Ave., New York, NY 10017 (☎ **800/223-7460** or 212/661-1193), offers packages to many Eastern European cities, letting you pick which cities you want to visit. The company will arrange hotels, sightseeing tours, and airport/train station transfers. Its Prague package starts at $282 per person, based on double occupancy. If you want to stay in the city center, however, upgrade to the Adria hotel, which costs $367 per person.

Jewish Heritage Tours, 220 71st St., Suite 211, Miami Beach, FL 33141 (☎ **800/ 323-2219** or 305/861-0080), offers both group and independent tours of Prague, including several itineraries that combine a visit to the Czech capital with tours of Vienna, Budapest, Krakow, and Warsaw. A 3-night independent Prague stay includes accommodations, airport transfers, sightseeing tours of both general and Jewish interest, and a visit to the Terezín concentration camp. Its land-only packages begin at $459 per person, based on double occupancy.

3

Getting to Know Prague

by John Mastrini & Hana Mastrini

Prague (Praha in Czech) has long been considered a city of mysterious intrigue, but this chapter should help take some of the mystery out of planning a visit. It will also show you how to navigate its twisting cobblestone streets and unique neighborhoods.

1 Orientation

ARRIVING

BY PLANE

Prague's **Ruzyně Airport** (☎ **02/2011 1111**), 12 miles west of the city center, has completed its long-overdue expansion. Its new, airy, and efficient departure terminal and remodeled arrival terminal have lost the Communist-era feel and have added many amenities. There's a bank for changing money (usually open daily from 7am to 11pm), car-rental offices (see "Getting Around"), and plenty of public phones (most require a card you can buy at newsstands, but some take credit cards for international calls).

GETTING DOWNTOWN   You can make your way from the airport to your hotel by taxi, airport shuttle bus, or city bus.

Official airport taxis are plentiful and line up in front of the arrival terminal. Alas, the Volkswagen Passats queued directly outside the terminal's main exit all belong to the same cartel sanctioned by the airport authority. (See "Getting Around" for details.) The drivers are getting more pleasant but are still often arrogant and dishonest. Negotiate the fare in advance and get it written down. Expect to pay about 500Kč to 600Kč ($14.70 to $17.65) for the 20 or so minutes to the city center, depending on the whims of the syndicate, but don't be surprised if a surly driver barks "Thirty dollars." If you want to save money, find other travelers to share the expense.

CEDAZ operates an **airport shuttle bus** from the airport to nám. Republiky in central Prague. It leaves the airport daily every 30 minutes from 6am to 9pm and stops near the Náměstí Republiky metro station. Going back you can use it from 5:30am to 9:30pm (every 30 minutes). The shuttle costs 90Kč ($2.65) for the 30-minute trip.

Even cheaper is **city bus no. 119,** which brings passengers from the bus stop to the right of the airport exit to the Dejvická metro station (and back). The bus/metro combo costs only 12Kč (35¢), but the bus makes many stops. Travel time is about 40 minutes.

BY TRAIN

Passengers traveling to Prague by train typically pull into one of two central stations: Hlavní nádraží (Main Station) or Nádraží Holešovice (Holešovice Station). Both are on line C of the metro system and offer a number of services, including money exchange, a post office, and a luggage-storage area.

At both terminals you'll find **AVE Ltd.** (☎ **02/2422 3521** or 02/2422 3226), an accommodations agency that arranges beds in hostels as well as rooms in hotels and apartments. It's open daily from 6am to 11pm. If you arrive without room reservations, this agency is definitely worth a visit.

Hlavní nádraží, Wilsonova třída, Praha 2 (☎ **02/2422 3887**), is the grander and more popular of the stations, but it's also the seedier. Built in 1909, this once beautiful four-story art nouveau structure was one of the city's beloved architectural gems before it was connected to a darkly modern dispatch hall in the mid-1970s. From the train platform, you'll walk down a flight of stairs and through a tunnel before arriving in the ground-level main hall, which contains ticket windows, a useful **Prague Information Service** office that sells city maps and dispenses information, and rest rooms. The station's basement holds a left-luggage counter, which is open 24 hours and charges 20Kč (60¢) per bag per day. Though cheaper, the nearby lockers aren't secure and should be avoided. The public showers beneath the main hall are surprisingly clean and a good place to freshen up; they cost just 40Kč ($1.20) and are open Monday to Friday from 6am to 8pm, Saturday from 7am to 7pm, and Sunday from 8am to 4pm. On the second floor is the train information office (marked by a lowercase "i"), open daily from 6am to 10pm. On the top floor is a tattered restaurant we recommend only to the most famished.

After you leave the modern terminal hall, a 5-minute walk to the left puts you at the top of Wenceslas Square and 15 minutes by foot to Old Town Square. Metro line C connects the station easily to the other two subway lines and the rest of the city. Metro trains depart from the lower level, and tickets, costing 8Kč to 12Kč (24¢ to 35¢), are available from the newsstand near the metro entrance. Gouging taxi drivers line up outside the station and are plentiful throughout the day and night but are not recommended.

Nádraží Holešovice, Partyzánská at Vrbenského, Praha 7 (☎ **02/2461 7265**), Prague's second train station, is usually the terminus for trains from Berlin and other points north. Although it's not as centrally located as the main station, its more manageable size and location at the end of metro line C make it almost as convenient.

Prague contains two smaller rail stations. **Masaryk Station,** Hybernská ulice at Havlíčkova (☎ **02/2461 7260**), is primarily for travelers arriving on trains originating from other Bohemian cities or from Brno or Bratislava. Situated about 10 minutes by foot from the main train station, Masaryk is near Staré Město, just a stone's throw from Náměstí Republiky metro station. **Smíchov Station,** Nádražní ulice at Rozkošného (☎ **02/2461 7686**), is the terminus for commuter trains from western and southern Bohemia, though an occasional international train pulls in here. The station contains a 24-hour baggage check and is serviced by metro line B.

BY BUS

The **Central Bus Station–Florenc,** Křižíkova 4–6, Praha 8 (☎ **02/2421 1060**), is a few blocks north of the main railroad station. Most local and long-distance buses arrive here. The adjacent Florenc metro station is on both lines B and C. Florenc station is relatively small and doesn't have many visitor services. Even smaller depots are at **Želivského** (metro line A), **Smíchovské nádraží** (metro line B), and **Nádraží Holešovice** (metro line C).

VISITOR INFORMATION

If you want to arrange accommodations before you come, there are two handy English Web sites from Prague-based **Tom's Travel.** The general site at **www.travel.cz** provides booking for hotels and practical touring information, while at **www.apartments.cz**, you can book a private apartment in a wide range of prices and areas. Once in the city, you can find Tom's Travel near the National Theater at Ostrovní 7 (☎ **02/2499 0983;** fax 02/2499 0999). Especially for those arriving by train or air, **AVE Travel** (☎ **02/2422 3226;** fax 02/5155 6005; e-mail: ave@avetravel.cz; www.avetravel.cz) can arrange accommodations or transfers inside these terminals. It has outlets at the airport, open daily from 7am to 10pm; at the main train station, Hlavní nádraží, open daily from 6am to 11pm; and the north train station, Nádraží Holešvice, open daily from 7am to 9pm.

The city's **Cultural and Information Center,** on the ground floor of the remodeled Municipal House (Obecní dům), náměstí Republiky 5, Praha 1 (☎ **02/2200 2100;** fax 02/2200 2133; www.obecni-dum.cz/ang/default.asp), offers advice, tickets, souvenirs, refreshments, and rest rooms. It's open daily from 9am to 5pm.

The **Prague Information Service,** Na Příkopě 20, Praha 1 (☎ **187** in Prague, 02/544 444 from outside the city; e-mail: tourinfo@pis.cz; www.pis.eunet.cz), near Wenceslas Square, offers tips and tickets for upcoming cultural events and tours. It can also help you find a room. From April to October, it's open Monday to Friday from 9am to 7pm and Saturday and Sunday from 9am to 5pm. During the rest of the year, it's open Monday to Friday from 9am to 6pm and Saturday from 9am to 3pm; closed Sunday. There are also PIS offices inside Old Town Hall and the main train station.

The weekly newspaper the *Prague Post* has a fairly beefy culture section and a special supplement to help visitors. It can be found at most central newsstands.

Čedok, at Na Příkopě 18, Praha 1 (☎ **02/2419 7111;** fax 02/232 1656), was once the state travel bureau and is now a privatized agency. Its entrenched position still gives it decent access to tickets and information about domestic events, and the staff can book rail and bus tickets and hotel rooms. Čedok accepts major credit cards and is open Monday to Friday from 8:30am to 6pm.

Avoid kiosks that look like information points but are really ticket touts for tours and concerts. Asking for directions from a Czech on the street will be more enjoyable (and useful) than the surly response you'll probably get from the usually uninformed kiosk.

CITY LAYOUT

The **river Vltava** bisects Prague and provides the best line of orientation, and you can use **Charles Bridge** as your central point. From the bridge, turn toward **Prague Castle,** the massive complex on the hill with the cathedral thrusting out. Now you're facing west.

Up on the hill is the castle district known as **Hradčany.** Running up the hill between the bridge and the castle is the district known as **Malá Strana** (literally the "Small Side" but known as Lesser Town in English). Turn around and behind you on the right (east) bank is **Staré Město** (Old Town) and farther to the south and east **Nové Město** (New Town). The highlands even farther east used to be the royal vineyards, **Vinohrady,** now a popular neighborhood for expatriates with a growing array of accommodations and restaurants. The districts farther out are where most Praguers live, with few attractions.

MAIN BRIDGES, SQUARES & STREETS   You'll best enjoy Prague by walking its narrow streets, busy squares, and scenic bridges. After **Charles Bridge (Karlův most),** the other two bridges worth walking are **Mánes Bridge (Mánesův most),** which provides a stunning low-angle view of the castle especially at night, and the **Bridge of the Legions (most Legií),** which links the National Theater to Petřín Hill.

On the left bank coming off Charles Bridge is **Mostecká** street and at the end of it sits the cozy square under the castle hill, **Malostranské náměstí.** On the hill outside the main castle gate is the motorcade-worn **Hradčanské náměstí,** on the city side of which you'll find a spectacular view of spires and red roofs below.

On the east side of Charles Bridge, you can wind through most any of the old alleys leading from the bridge and get pleasantly lost amid the shops and cafes. The tourist-packed route through Old Town is **Karlova** street. Like Karlova, most any other route in Old Town will eventually lead you to **Staroměstské náměstí (Old Town Square),** the breathtaking heart of Staré Město. The square is dominated by the black monument to Jan Hus, the martyred Czech Protestant leader. The tree-lined boulevard to the right behind Hus is **Pařížská** (Parisian Boulevard) with boutiques and restaurants; it forms the edge of the Jewish Quarter. Over Hus's left shoulder is **Dlouhá** street, and in front of him to his left is the kitschy shopping zone on **Celetná.** Across the square to Hus's right, past the clock tower of Old Town Hall (Staroměstká radnice), is **Železná** street, which leads to Mozart's Prague venue, the Estate's Theater. Farther to Hus's right is the narrow alley **Melantrichova,** which winds southeast to **Václavské náměstí (Wenceslas Square),** sight of pro-democracy demonstrations in 1989.

FINDING AN ADDRESS Don't worry about getting lost—everyone does temporarily, even lifelong Praguers. If you're pressed for time and can't enjoy an aimless wander, you'll find that street signs are emblazoned on red art nouveau frames, usually bolted to buildings. House numbers generally increase as you get farther from the Vltava or the square from which the street begins.

Note that Prague street names always precede the numbers, like Václavské nám. 25. *Ulice* (abbreviated ul. or omitted) means "street," *třída* (abbreviated tr.) means "avenue," *náměstí* (abbreviated nám.) is "square" or "plaza," *most* is "bridge," and *nábřeží* is "quay."

Prague is divided into 10 postal districts whose numbers are routinely included in addresses. The districts forming the main tourist areas are listed below with their corresponding neighborhoods.

Praha 1 Hradčany, Malá Strana, Staré Město, Josefov, northern Nové Město.

Praha 2 Southern Nové Město, Vyšehrad, western Vinohrady.

Praha 3 Eastern Vinohrady, Žižkov.

Praha 6 Western Bubeneč, Dejvice, Vodovice, Střešovice, Břevnov, Veleslavín, Liboc, Ruzyně, Řepy, Nebušice, Lysolaje, Sedlec, Suchdol.

MAPS A detailed Prague street map is recommended if you want to venture off the main streets or retrace where you think you were during your wandering odyssey. Kartographia Praha produces a series of hiking maps covering the best of the intricately marked footpaths throughout the country; each is called a *turistická mapa* and has a translated key. You can find them at Czech-language bookstores.

Neighborhoods in Brief

Prague was originally developed as four adjacent self-governing boroughs, plus a walled Jewish ghetto. Central Prague's neighborhoods have maintained their individual identities along with their medieval street plans.

Hradčany The Castle District dominates the hilltop above Malá Strana. Here you'll find not only the fortress that remains the presidential palace and national seat of

Prague at a Glance

NEIGHBORHOODS
Castle District ❶
Jewish Quarter ❹
Lesser Town ❸
New Town ⓫
Old Town ❺

INFORMATION
Castle Information Office ❷
Čedok Office ❽

TRANSPORTATION/MAIL
Florenc Bus Station ❼
Main Post Office ❾
Main Train Station ❿
Masaryk Station ❻

DEJVICKÁ Ⓜ
Československé armády
U Prašného mostu
Pod kaštany

HRADČANSKÁ Ⓜ
Badeniho

Milady Horákové

Jelení
Mariánské hradby Chotkovy Sady

Keplerova
U Brusnice U kasáren
HRADČANY ❶
❷ Prague Castle
Chotkova

Nový Svět
Loretánské nám.
MALOSTRANSKÁ Ⓜ

Loretánská
Nerudova
MALÁ ❸ STRANA

Úvoz

Lobkovická Zahrada
Strahovská Zahrada

Karmelitská
Malostr. nábřeží

Strahovská
Seminářská Zahrada

Olympijská Spartakiádni Stadion
Chaloupeckého
Petřínské Sady
Funicular
Újezd
Střeleck Ostro

Jezdecká
Kinského Zahrada

Peškové
Janáčkovo nábřeží

Holečkova
V botanice
Zborovská

Plzeňská
Duškova
Kartouzská

Mozartova
Radlická
ANDĚL Ⓜ
Svornosti

LEGEND
Royal Route ♜ - - - ♜
Metro Ⓜ ━ ━ ━

0 ———————— 1/4 Mi
0 ———————— .25 Km

Ostrovského
SMÍCHOV

32

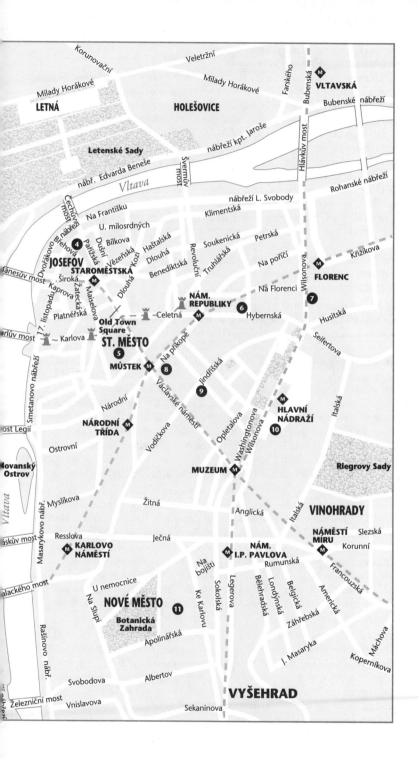

What's All the U-ing About?

Czech establishments have traditionally taken on the name of a distinctive landmark nearby, the name of the house, or the name of the owner of the house. The Czech preposition for *at* is *u*. You'll find that a *u* fronts many pubs, restaurants, hotels, and other businesses, followed by the distinctive name declined to its proper case, such as the Malá Strana restaurant U Malířů (At the Painter's), originally the home of 16th-century artist Šic. Another example is U Fleků (At Flek's), which was Mr. Flek's 1499 home brewery, now a regular stop for German tour buses.

Often the place takes the name of a statue or frieze over the entrance to the building that sets it apart from all others (much more so than just an address number). For example, the frieze above the door of the popular Old Town pub U medvídků tells patrons that they're about to drink "At the Little Bears" house.

---

power but also the Loreto church, Strahov Monastery, and the main national art gallery at the archbishop's palace. You can take a scenic walk down the hill via Nerudova or through the lush Petřín Hill gardens.

Malá Strana (Lesser Town)   Prague's storybook Lesser Town was founded in 1257 by Germanic merchants who set up shop at the base of the castle. Nestled between the bastion and the river Vltava, Malá Strana is laced with narrow, winding lanes boasting palaces and red-roofed town houses (see "Walking Tour 1" in chapter 7). The parliament and government and several embassies reside in palaces here. Kampa Park, on the riverbank just south of Charles Bridge, forms the southeastern edge of Lesser Town, and the riverside Liechtenstein Palace on the park's northern edge was used as the U.S. Embassy in the Tom Cruise version of *Mission: Impossible* (the real U.S. Embassy is a few blocks away). Nerudova is the steep shop-lined alley leading from the town square to the castle. Alternate castle routes for the strong of heart are the New Castle Stairs (Nové zámecké schody), 1 block north of Nerudova, and the Old Castle Stairs (Staré zámecké schody), just northwest from the Malostranská metro station. Tram 22 will take you up the hill if you don't want the heart-pounding hike.

Staré Město (Old Town)   Staré Město was chartered in 1234, as Prague became a stop on important trade routes. Its meandering streets, radiating from Staroměstské náměstí (Old Town Square), are still big visitor draws. Old Town is compact, bordered by the Vltava on the north and west and Revoluční and Národní streets on the east and south. You can wander safely without having to worry about straying into danger. Once here, stick to the cobblestone streets and don't cross any bridges, any streets containing tram tracks, or any rivers, and you'll know that you're still in Old Town. You'll stumble on some of the most beautiful baroque and Renaissance architecture and find some wonderful restaurants, shops, bars, cafes, and pubs. For some direction, see "Walking Tour 3" in chapter 7.

Josefov   Prague's Jewish ghetto, entirely within Staré Město, was surrounded by a wall before it was almost completely destroyed to make way for more modern 19th-century structures. The Old-New Synagogue is in the geographical center of Josefov, and the surrounding streets are wonderful for strolling. Prague is one of Europe's great historic Jewish cities, and exploring this remarkable area will make it clear why. For details, see "Walking Tour 4" in chapter 7.

Nové Město (New Town)   Draped like a crescent around Staré Město, Nové Město is where you'll find Václavské náměstí (Wenceslas Square), the National Theater, and the central business district. When it was founded by Charles IV in 1348, Nové Město was Europe's largest wholly planned municipal development. The street layout has remained largely unchanged, but much of Nové Město's structures were razed in the late 19th century and replaced with the offices and apartment buildings you see today. New Town lacks the classical allure of Old Town and Malá Strana, but if you venture beyond Wenceslas Square into Vinohrady you'll find restaurants, interesting shops, and a part of Prague that feels more like a normal city instead of a tourist attraction.

While violent crime is still relatively rare, you should take caution here at night, especially around Wenceslas Square and nearby Perlová street, where the prostitutes and drug dealers ply their trades.

2 Getting Around

BY PUBLIC TRANSPORTATION

Prague's public transportation network is one of the few sound Communist-era legacies and is still remarkably affordable. In central Prague, metro (subway) stations abound. Trams and buses offer a cheap sightseeing experience but many times also require a strong stomach for jostling with fellow passengers in close quarters.

TICKETS & PASSES   For single-use **tickets,** there are two choices. Tickets for 8 Kč (24¢) allow travel for a maximum of 15 minutes on a bus or tram, without transfers, or for a trip of no more than four stations on the metro. This usually suffices for most visitors looking to move between two sights in the city's old districts. The ticket for 12Kč (35¢) allows for unlimited travel, including transfers, on all forms of municipal transport for 60 minutes during peak periods.

A **1-day pass** good for unlimited rides is 70Kč ($2.06), a **3-day pass** 180Kč ($5.29), a **7-day pass** 250Kč ($7.35), and a **15-day pass** 280Kč ($8.24). The City Council is considering a hike in the fees for longer-term passes in 2000.

You can buy tickets from yellow coin-operated machines in metro stations or at most newsstands marked TABÁK or TRAFIKA. Hold on to your validated ticket throughout your ride—you'll need to show it if a plainclothes ticket collector (be sure to check for his or her badge) asks you. If you're caught without a valid ticket, you'll be asked, and not so kindly, to pay a fine on the spot with all the locals looking on, shaking their heads in disgust. The fine is 200Kč ($5.88) on trams and the metro, double that on buses.

BY METRO   Metro trains operate daily from 5am to midnight and run every 2 to 6 minutes. On the three lettered lines (A, B, and C, color coded green, yellow, and red, respectively) the most convenient central stations are Můstek, at the foot of Václavské náměstí (Wenceslas Square); Staroměstská, for Old Town Square and Charles Bridge; and Malostranská, serving Malá Strana and the Castle District. Refer to the metro map for details.

BY ELECTRIC TRAM & BUS   The 24 electric tram (streetcar) lines run practically everywhere, and there's always another tram with the same number traveling back. You never have to hail trams, for they make every stop. The most popular trams, nos. 22 and 23 (the "tourist trams" and the "pickpocket express"), run past top sights like the National Theater and Prague Castle. Regular bus and tram service stops at midnight, after which selected routes run reduced schedules, usually only once per hour. Schedules are posted at stops. If you miss a night connection, expect a long wait for the next.

Buses tend to be used only outside the older districts of Prague and have three-digit numbers.

A Tram Tip

If you're taking tram no. 22 or 23 to Prague Castle from Národní or anywhere farther from the castle, I recommend you get a 12Kč (35¢) ticket, since you may get caught out beyond the 15-minute limit.

Both the buses and tram lines (which have two digits) begin their morning runs around 4:30am.

BY FUNICULAR   The funicular (cog railway) makes the scenic run up and down Petřín Hill every 15 minutes or so daily from 9:15am to 8:45pm with an intermediate stop at the Nebozízek restaurant in the middle of the hill, which overlooks the city. It requires the same 12Kč (35¢) ticket as other modes of public transport and departs from a small house in the park at Újezd in Malá Strana.

BY TAXI

I have one word for you: *Beware.*

You can hail taxis in the streets or in front of train stations, large hotels, and popular attractions, but many drivers simply gouge visitors. In late 1996, the city canceled price regulations, but instead of creating price competition, it started a turf war between cabbies vying for the best taxi stands. The best fare you can hope for is 17Kč (50¢) per kilometer, but three times that isn't rare. Rates usually aren't posted outside on the door but on the dashboard—once you're inside it's a bit late to haggle. Try to get the driver to agree to a price and write it down before you get in. Better yet, go by foot or public transport.

If you must go by taxi, call reputable companies with English-speaking dispatchers: **AAA Taxi** (☎ **1080** from local phones); **ProfiTaxi** (☎ **1035**); or **SEDOP** (☎ **1087**). Demand a receipt before you start, as it'll keep them a little more honest.

BY RENTAL CAR

Driving in Prague isn't worth the money or effort. The roads are frustrating and slow, and parking is minimal and expensive. However, a car is a plus if you want to explore other parts of the Czech Republic.

RENTAL COMPANIES   Try **Europcar/InterRent,** Pařížská 28, Praha 1 (☎ **02/2481 0039**), open daily from 8am to 8pm. There's also **Hertz,** Karlovo nám. 28, Praha 2 (☎ **02/291 851** or 02/290 122); and **Budget,** at Ruzyně Airport (☎ **02/316 5214**), and in the Hotel Inter-Continental, náměstí Curieových, Praha 1 (☎ **02/2488 9995**).

Local car-rental companies sometimes offer lower rates than the big international firms. Compare **CS Czechocar,** Kongresové centrum (Congress Center at Vyšehrad metro stop on the C line), Praha 4 (☎ **02/6122 2079** or 02/6122 2143), and **SeccoCar,** Přístavní 39, Praha 7 (☎ **02/6671 0602**).

Car rates can be negotiable. Try to obtain the best possible deal with the rental company by asking about discounts. Special deals are often offered for keeping the car longer, for unlimited mileage (or at least getting some miles thrown in free), or for a bigger car at a lower price. You can usually get some sort of discount for a company or an association affiliation. Check before you leave home and take a member ID card with you.

Since extras can send prices into the stratosphere, find out all the charges you're likely to incur; besides the daily or weekly rental, consider a mileage charge, insurance,

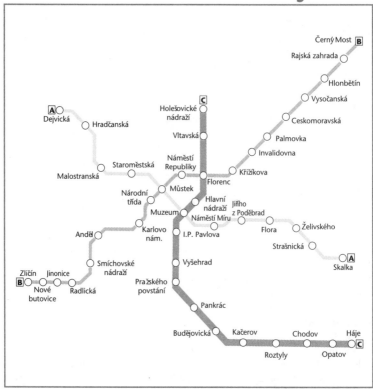

the cost of fuel, and tax on the total rental (22% in Prague). In addition, you may be paying for parking along the way. If you already have collision coverage on your own auto insurance, you're most likely covered when behind the wheel of a rental car; check with your insurance carrier. If you decide on European insurance, be sure it doesn't come with a $1,000 deductible. A collision-damage waiver (CDW) usually costs $7 to $13 per day. Some credit-card companies, including American Express, automatically insure cardholders against collision damage at no extra charge when they rent a car using the company's card.

ROADWAYS & EMERGENCIES Major roadways radiate from Prague like spokes on a wheel, so touring the country is easy if you make the capital your base. The Prague-Brno motorway is the most traveled, but the new Prague-Nürnberg motorway (dálnice) has opened a 2-hour express route into western Germany (though the German side and part of the Czech side isn't yet complete).

Czech roads are often narrow and in need of repair. Add to this drivers who live out their speedway fantasies on these pot-holed beauties and you may want to take the train. The few superhighways that do exist are in good shape, so whenever possible, stick to them, especially at night. If you have car trouble, major highways have **SOS emergency phones** to call for assistance, located about every kilometer. There's also the **ÚAMK,** a 24-hour auto club like AAA that can provide service for a fee. You can summon its bright yellow pickup trucks on the main highways by using the emergency phones. If you're not near an SOS phone or are on a road without them, you can contact ÚAMK at ☎ **123,** or 0123 outside major towns.

Foreign drivers are required to have an **international driver's license** and **proof of international insurance** (a green card issued with rental cars). Czech police are infamous for stopping cars with foreign plates, and the "fines" they exact are often negotiable. If you're stopped, expect to pay at least 750Kč ($22.06) for speeding. Those caught by the police should ask for some type of receipt (*účet* in Czech, pronounced "*oo*-chet"); this can help cut down on overpayment.

GASOLINE   Not only are rentals expensive but also gasoline (*benzín*) in the Czech Republic costs much more than you're accustomed to paying—more than 25Kč (74¢) per liter, or just over 100 Kč ($2.95) per gallon. Filling stations, which used to be difficult to find, are now on all major highways. Most are open 24 hours and many have minimarkets with food and drink as well. If you're leaving the country, fill up near the border, as the price of gas in Austria and Germany is still much higher.

PARKING   Finding a parking spot in Prague can sometimes be even more of a challenge than driving in this maze of a city. Fines for illegal parking can be stiff, but worse are "Denver Boots," which immobilize cars until a fine is paid. If you find your car booted, call the number on the ticket, tell them where you are, then wait for the clamp removers, to whom you will pay 500Kč ($14.70) or more depending on your violation. The city has now installed street parking meters marked with a blue "P" in required zones; they issue slips that you place inside on your dashboard so they're visible through the windshield. These normally run from 20Kč to 30Kč (59¢ to 88¢) per hour for up to 4 hours.

SPECIAL DRIVING RULES   Seat belts are required, you may *not*—repeat *not*— legally make a right turn when a traffic light is red, and autos must stop when a pedestrian steps into a crosswalk (however, they often don't, as you'll find if you remain a pedestrian). Children under 1.5 meters (about 5 ft. tall) can't ride in the front seat. On major highways, the speed limit is 130kmph (80 mph). The yellow diamond road sign denotes the right of way at an unregulated intersection. When approaching an intersection, always make sure who has the right of way, since the "main" road can change several times within blocks on the same street.

BY BIKE

Though there are no special bike lanes in the city center and smooth streets are unheard of, Prague is a particularly fun city to bike in, when the crowds are thin. Vehicular traffic is limited in the center, where small, winding streets seem especially suited to two-wheeled vehicles. Surprisingly, few people take advantage of this opportunity; cyclists are largely limited to the few foreigners who have imported their own bikes. The city's ubiquitous cobblestones make mountain bikes the natural choice. Check with your hotel about a possible rental or try **Cyklocentrum** at Karlovo nám. 29, New Town (☎ and fax **02/294 312;** e-mail: sales@cyklocentrum.cz; www. cyklocentrum.cz).

Fast Facts: Prague

American Express   For travel arrangements, traveler's checks, currency exchange, and other member services, visit the city's sole **American Express office,** at Václavské nám. 56 (Wenceslas Square), Praha 1 (☎ **02/2280 0251**). It's open daily from 9am to 7pm.

Area Code   The area code for Prague is **2.**

Baby-sitters   If your hotel can't recommend a sitter, phone **Affordable Luxuries,** Ječná 1584/39a, Praha 1 (☎ **02/9620 0666**), an American-owned company that provides various child-minding services. Make reservations far in advance. The fee is 180Kč ($5.29) per hour.

Bookstores   The largest English-language bookshops are **The Globe,** Janovského 14, Praha 7 (☎ **02/6671 2610**); **Big Ben Bookshop,** Malá Štupartská 5, Praha 1 (☎ **02/231 8021**); and **U Knihomola,** Mánesova 79, Praha 2 (☎ **02/627 7770**). See chapter 8 for complete information.

Business Hours   Most **banks** are open Monday to Friday from 8:30am to 6pm, but some are also open Saturday from 9am to noon. Business **offices** are generally open Monday to Friday from 8am to 6pm. **Pubs** are usually open daily from 11am to midnight. Most **restaurants** open for lunch from noon to 3pm and for dinner from 6 to 11pm; only a few stay open later. **Stores** are typically open Monday to Friday from 9am to 6pm and Saturday from 9am to 1pm, but those in the tourist center keep longer hours and are open Sunday as well. *Note:* Some small food shops that keep long hours charge up to 20% more for all their goods after 8pm or so.

Currency Exchange   Banks generally offer the best exchange rates, but **American Express** is competitive and doesn't charge commission for cashing traveler's checks, regardless of the issuer. Don't hesitate to use a credit card; We've found that card exchange rates are regularly to our advantage. There's one American Express office in Prague (see above).

Komerční banka has three convenient Praha 1 locations with ATMs accepting Visa, MasterCard, and American Express: Na Příkopě 33, Národní 32, and Václavské nám. 42 (☎ **02/2442 1111,** central switchboard for all branches). The exchange offices are open Monday to Friday from 8am to 5pm, but the ATMs are accessible 24 hours.

Živnostenská banka, Na Příkopě 20, Praha 1 (☎ **02/2412 1111**), has an exchange office open Monday to Friday from 10am to 9pm and Saturday from 3 to 7pm.

Chequepoint keeps the longest hours but offers the worst exchange rates. Central Prague locations are 28.října 13 and Staroměstské nám. 21 (both open 24 hours); Staroměstské nám. 27 (open daily from 8am to 11:30pm); and Václavské nám. 32 (open daily from 8am to 11pm).

Doctors/Dentists   If you need a doctor or dentist and your condition isn't life-threatening, you can visit the **Polyclinic at Národní,** Národní 9, Praha 1 (☎ **02/2207 5120;** for emergencies 02/0600 111; operator 02/140 533), during walk-in hours from 8am to 5pm. Dr. Stránský is an Ivy League–trained straight-talking physician, born to a celebrated Czech émigré family who came back to reclaim property on National boulevard. He turned part of the block into a Western-standard health center that acts as a clinic of record for the U.S. Embassy. You'll be asked to show proof of insurance or pay up front. The **First Medical Clinic of Prague Ltd.,** Vyšehradská 35, Praha 2 (☎ **02/292 286**), provides 24-hour emergency care as well as EKGs, diagnostics, ophthalmology, house calls, and referrals to specialists. Normal walk-in hours are Monday to Saturday from 7am to 7pm.

For **emergency medical aid,** call the **Foreigners' Medical Clinic,** Na Homolce Hospital, Roentgenova 2, Praha 5 (☎ **02/5292 2146,** or 02/5292 2191 after hours).

Electricity   Czech appliances operate on 220 volts and plug into two-pronged outlets that differ from those in America and the United Kingdom. Appliances designed for the U.S. or U.K. markets must use an adapter and a transformer (sometimes incorrectly called a converter). Don't attempt to plug an American appliance directly into a European electrical outlet without a transformer; you'll ruin your appliance and possibly start a fire.

Embassies   The **U.S. Embassy,** Tržiště 15, Praha 1 (☎ 02/5732 0663), is open Monday to Friday from 8 to 11:30am and 2:30 to 4pm. The **Canadian Embassy,** Mickiewiczova 6, Praha 6 (☎ 02/2431 1108), is open Monday to Friday from 8:30am to noon and 2 to 4pm. The **U.K. Embassy,** Thunovská 14, Praha 1 (☎ 02/5732 0355), is open Monday to Friday from 9am to noon. You can visit the **Australian Honorary Consul,** Na Ořechovce 38, Praha 6 (☎ 02/2431 0743), on Monday to Thursday from 8:30am to 5pm and Friday from 8:30am to 2pm. The **Irish Embassy** is at Tržiště 13, Praha 1 (☎ 02/5753 0061).

Emergencies   You can reach Prague's **police** and **fire** services by dialing ☎ 158 from any phone. To call an **ambulance,** dial ☎ 155.

Hospitals   Particularly welcoming to foreigners is **Nemocnice Na Homolce,** Roentgenova 2, Praha 5 (☎ 02/5292 2146, or 02/5292 2191 after hours). The English-speaking doctors can also make house calls. See "Doctors/Dentists," above, for more information. In an emergency, dial ☎ 155 for an ambulance.

Internet Access   One of Prague's trendiest places is the **Terminal Bar** at Soukenická 6 in Old Town near náměstí Republiky (☎ 02/2187 1115; www.terminal.cz), open daily from 11am to 1am. It's a combination Internet cafe, lounge, bookstore, and cinema. Dozens of PCs are available for surfing at 120 Kč ($3.52) per hour. Better-value monthly memberships are 295 Kč ($8.68) and there are also ports to hook up your own laptop. At the bottom of the New Castle Steps in Malá Strana, you can check your e-mail or surf for 2 Kč (6¢) per minute at the closet-like **Internet Café u Zlaté Růže** at Thunovská 21, open daily from 10am to 10pm. The **Internet Café u Pavlánských,** near the funicular train at Újezd 31 in Malá Strana, has about a half-dozen PCs in a pleasant setting for 80 Kč ($2.35) per hour, also open daily from 10am to 10pm.

Language   Berlitz has a comprehensive phrase book in Czech. A clever illustrated **Web tutorial** is found at **www.czechprimer.org**. See Appendix B for basic phrases and vocabulary as well as menu terms.

Laundry/Dry Cleaning   **Laundry Kings,** Dejvická 16, Praha 6 (☎ 02/312 3743), was Prague's first American-style coin-operated self-service Laundromat. Washes cost about 60Kč ($1.76) per load, depending on how much drying power you need. An attendant can do your wash for 50Kč ($1.47) additional, but the service takes at least 24 hours. From Hradčanská metro station, take the Prague Dejvice exit and turn left. Laundry Kings is open Monday to Friday from 6am to 10pm and Saturday and Sunday from 8am to 10pm.

Laundryland, Londýnská 71, Praha 2 (☎ 02/2251 6692), offers dry cleaning as well as laundry service and charges about the same as Laundry Kings. Located 2 blocks from the Náměstí Míru metro station and close to the I. P. Pavlova metro station, it's open daily from 8am to 10pm.

Affordable Luxuries, Ječná 1584/39a, Praha 1 (☎ 02/9620 0666), will pick up your laundry and dry cleaning and return it to your hotel within 48 hours. The charge is 160Kč ($4.71) per load.

Liquor Laws   There's no minimum drinking age in the Czech Republic. Alcohol can legally be sold at any hour, and pubs and clubs can stay open 24 hours.

Lost Property   If you lose something in Prague, it's probably gone for good, but optimists might try visiting the **Lost Property Office,** Karolíny Světlé 5, Praha 1 (☎ **02/2423 5085**).

Luggage Storage/Lockers   The **Ruzyně Airport Luggage Storage Office** never closes and charges 60Kč ($1.76) per item per day. Left-luggage offices are also available at the main train stations, **Hlavní nádraží** and **Nádraží Holešovice.** Both charge 20Kč (59¢) per bag per day and are technically open 24 hours, but if your train is departing late at night, check to make sure someone will be around. Luggage lockers are available in all of Prague's train stations, but they're not secure and should be avoided.

Finally, you can often leave luggage at a fancy, well-located hotel even if you're not a guest. At an average cost of 50Kč ($1.47) per item, your bags can stay at the **Hotel Paříž** (☎ **02/2219 5195**) even if you can't.

Mail   Post offices are plentiful and are normally open Monday to Friday from 8am to 6pm. At press time, the post office was negotiating a postage hike, so check with your hotel for current rates. Mailboxes are orange and are usually attached to the sides of buildings. If you're sending mail overseas, make sure it's marked "Par Avion" so it doesn't go by surface. If you mail your letters at a post office, the clerk will add this stamp for you. Mail can take up to 10 days to reach its destination.

The **Main Post Office (Hlavní pošta),** Jindřišská 14, Praha 1, 110 00 (☎ **02/2113 1111**), a few steps from Václavské náměstí, is open 24 hours. You can receive mail, marked "Poste Restante" and addressed to you, in care of this post office. If you carry an American Express card or Amex traveler's checks, you would be wiser to receive mail care of **American Express,** Václavské nám. 56 (Wenceslas Square), Praha 1 (☎ **02/2280 0251**).

Newspapers/Magazines   The 1995 failure of *Prognosis,* Prague's first English-language newspaper, left the weekly *Prague Post* with a near lock on the local market, though it's being challenged for the business audience by the *Prague Business Journal.* Published each Wednesday, the *Post* is a quick read that usually offers a couple of interesting features, along with updated listings of sightseeing and entertainment happenings. The *Prague Tribune* is a glossy monthly with an excellent mix of news, business, and cultural features.

Přehled, a monthly listings booklet, is probably the best entertainment publication with details on theaters, galleries, concerts, clubs, films, and events around town. It's only in Czech, but the listings aren't too difficult for non-Czechs to understand.

For gays and lesbians, the best information on happenings is in *SOHO Review,* a monthly magazine listing activities and events. It's in Czech but does run some English-language information and personal ads. The *Prague Post* also occasionally updates gay and lesbian offerings.

Newsstands are located inside most every metro station, and good-sized international magazine shops are in major hotels and on most busy shopping streets.

Pharmacies   The most centrally located pharmacy (*lékárna*) is at Václavské nám. 8, Praha 1 (☎ **02/2422 7532**), open Monday to Friday from 8am to 6pm. The nearest emergency (24-hour) pharmacy is at Palackého 5, Praha 1 (☎ **02/2494 6982**). If you're in Praha 2, there's an emergency pharmacy on Belgická 37 (☎ **02/2423 7207**).

Police   In an emergency, dial ☎ **158.**

A Telephone Warning

Be aware that the Czech Republic is going through a massive overhaul of its telephone network, and phone numbers can change overnight without notice. An English-language operator is available for phoning problems at ☎ **0149.**

Radio   You can hear English-language World News on the BBC World Service (101.1 FM). More than a dozen private stations compete with publicly owned news-talk Czech Radiožurnál (94.6 FM). Radio BONTON (99.7 FM) is a rock station that gives Czech bands lots of play. Radio Kiss (98 FM) is an Irish-owned station with a strictly pop-oriented play list. Radio 1 (91.9 FM) plays a world-class assortment of contemporary dance and trance music, mixed with some novelty songs. Radio Free Europe (1287 kHz AM) is an American-funded news-oriented station now based in Prague's Communist-era Parliament building.

Rest Rooms   You'll find plenty of public rest rooms. Toilets are located in every metro station and are staffed by cleaning personnel who usually charge users 3Kč (9¢) and dispense a precious few sheets of toilet paper. Restaurants and pubs around all the major sights are usually kind to nonpatrons who wish to use their facilities. Around the castle and elsewhere, public toilets are clearly marked with the letters WC. For comfort and cleanliness, try lobby-level lavatories in Prague's better-known hotels or the new rest rooms in the Municipal House (Obecní dům), the art nouveau palace next to the Powder Tower in Old Town.

Safety   In Prague's center you'll feel generally safer than in most Western cities, but always take common-sense precautions. Be aware of your immediate surroundings. Don't walk alone at night around Wenceslas Square—one of the main areas for prostitution and where a lot of unexplainable loitering takes place. All visitors should be watchful of pickpockets in heavily touristed areas, especially on Charles Bridge, in Old Town Square, and in front of the main train station. Be especially wary in crowded buses, trams, and trains. Don't keep your wallet in a back pocket and don't flash a lot of cash or jewelry. Riding the metro or trams at night feels just as safe as during the day.

Taxes   A 22% **value-added tax (VAT)** is built into the price of most goods and services rather than being tacked on at the register. Most restaurants also include VAT in the prices stated on their menus. If they don't, that fact should be stated somewhere on the menu. There are not VAT refunds for the Czech Republic.

Telephone/Fax   For **directory assistance** in English, dial (without a charge) ☎ **0149.** For **information on services and rates,** dial ☎ **0139.** Dial tones are continual high-pitched beeps that sound something like busy signals in America. After dialing a number from a pay phone, you might hear a series of very quick beeps that tell you the line is being connected. Busy signals sound similar to dial tones, only quicker.

There are two kinds of **pay phones** in normal use. The first accepts coins and the other operates exclusively with a phonecard, available from post offices and news agents in denominations ranging from 50Kč to 500Kč ($1.47 to $14.70). The minimum cost of a local call is 3Kč (9¢). Coin-op phones have displays telling you the minimum price for your call, but they don't make change, so don't load more than you have to. You can add more coins as the display gets near zero. Phonecard telephones automatically deduct the price of your call from the card. These cards are especially handy if you want to call abroad, as you don't have to

Calling Prague

The **country code** for the Czech Republic is **420,** and the **area code** for Prague is **2** if you're calling from outside the Czech Republic, but **02** if you're calling from within the Czech Republic. To call Prague direct from the United States, dial 011 (international code), 420 (country code), 2 (Prague's area code), and the six-, seven, or eight-digit local number. From Britain, dial 00 (international code), 420 (country code), 2 (Prague's area code), and the local number.

continuously chuck in the change. If you're calling the States, you'd better get a phonecard with plenty of points, as calls run about 42Kč ($1.24) per minute; calls to the United Kingdom cost 25Kč (74p) per minute.

Long-distance phone charges are higher in the Czech Republic than they are in the United States, and hotels usually add their own surcharge, sometimes as hefty as 100% to 200%, which you may be unaware of until you're presented with the bill. Ask before placing a call from a hotel.

Even if you're not calling person-to-person, collect calls are charged with the hotel fees, making them pricey, too. Charging a long-distance call to your phone credit card from a public telephone is often the most economical way to phone home.

You could also find a pay phone that lists its return number, call briefly to dictate the number to your counterpart abroad, and have him or her call you back. This is usually much cheaper than a direct call from this end.

A fast, convenient way to call the United States from Europe is via services like AT&T USA Direct. This bypasses the foreign operator and automatically links you to an operator with your long-distance carrier in your home country. The access number in the Czech Republic for **AT&T USA Direct** is ☎ **00 420 00101.** For **MCI CALL USA,** dial ☎ **00 420 00112,** and for **Sprint Express USA,** call ☎ **00 420 87187.** Canadians can connect with **Canada Direct** at ☎ **00 420 00151,** and Brits can connect with **BT Direct** at ☎ **00 420 04401** or **Mercury Call UK** at ☎ **00 420 04450.** From a pay phone in the Czech Republic, your local phonecard will be debited only for a local call.

Telephone books are printed in two editions: A separate set of white pages contains alphabetical lists of household phone owners, while the yellow pages list businesses according to trade, with an alphabetical listing in more white pages up front. The yellow pages include an English-language index.

You can send **faxes** from the main post office (Hlavní pošta), Jindřišská 14, Praha 1 (☎ **02/2113 1111**). The fax office is open 24 hours and charges 30Kč (88¢) per page, plus the price of the phone call. The best place to receive faxes is the American Express office, Václavské nám. 56 (Wenceslas Square), Praha 1 (☎ **02/2280 0251**).

Television   There are four national broadcast TV stations. ČT1 and ČT2 (channels 1 and 2) are public-service stations often with reruns of Communist-era teleplays and classical music broadcasts. TV Nova is a private commercial station launched by New York cosmetics scion Ronald Lauder, who is in a lengthy lawsuit demanding over $500 million after his Czech partner allegedly cut him out of the station. Nova is loaded with American sitcoms and serials, sensational newscasts, and Western movies all dubbed into Czech. Prima is the upstart nationwide commercial station trying to cut into Nova's dominance with the same tactics. If you're channel surfing after 10pm, note that both Prima and

Nova (which you can find on various channels depending on how your TV is programmed) have very saucy shows often including full frontal nudity. All four stations are off the air sometime between midnight and 2am. Satellite channels at hotels and on cable include Eurosport, MTV, Cartoon Network, CNBC, CNN, and BBC World.

Time Zone Prague is on Continental Europe Time (CET), 2 hours ahead of Greenwich Mean Time (GMT) from April to the end of October and 1 hour ahead from November to the end of March (in both cases 1 hour ahead of London). It's usually 6 hours ahead of U.S. eastern time. Clocks here spring forward and fall back for daylight saving time, but the semiannual rituals follow a slightly different schedule than in the States (about 3 weeks earlier).

Tipping Rules for tipping aren't as strict in the Czech Republic as they are in the United States. At most restaurants and pubs, locals just round the bill up to the nearest few koruny. When you're presented with good service at tablecloth places, a 10% tip is proper. Washroom and cloakroom attendants usually expect a couple of koruny, and porters in airports and rail stations usually receive 25Kč (74¢) per bag. Taxi drivers should get about 10%, unless they've already ripped you off, in which case they should get a referral to the police. Check restaurant menus to see if service is included before leaving a tip.

Transport Information The **Prague Information Service,** near Wenceslas Square on Na Příkopě 20, Praha 1 (☎ **187** in Prague or 02/544 444 outside Prague; www.pis.eunet.cz), can help you find where you are going on local transport (while the travel agencies Čedok, Tom's, and AVE are all good for intercity connections; see "Vistor Information," above). Train timetables for **Czech Rail** are at **www.idos.datis.cdrail.cz/default_e.htm**. All metro stations now have much better maps and explanations in English.

Prague Accommodations 4

by John Mastrini & Hana Mastrini

Arriving in Prague in the wake of the 1989 revolution, a visitor was told not to expect to find a hotel bed easily and certainly not to expect to find a very affordable one. During Communism, rarely were rooms available because the government strictly controlled the number of properties that could be built. This rationing made rooms prohibitively expensive for the casual traveler or reporter on a limited budget. Luckily, John was befriended by a family who offered their hospitality and a room in return for the chance to speak English with a rare species, an American.

However, soon after the revolution, enterprising citizens began to openly court foreigners to stay at their vacant, rent-controlled apartments for hard cash, something officially forbidden during Communism.

While some families have been lucky enough to get to the top of long waiting lists for apartments, others have found ways to acquire second and third rent-controlled apartments, even though many young couples have been waiting for years, since private flats are out of their reach. Czechs, whose average annual declared salary is less than $7,000, rent these extra flats to foreigners. The added income has helped keep the economy afloat, and the government has been reluctant to deregulate rents and crack down on the gray market; however, real estate agents say that the situation is delaying much needed new housing. For Western visitors, though, these flats are a source of inexpensive accommodations.

PRIVATE ROOMS   Rooms in private homes are still more expensive than dorms in student hostels but provide a little more privacy. Since owners spend a lot of time out of Prague at their weekend cottages, the room supply fluctuates constantly. But there are excellent agencies to help you find something to fit your needs. Many, if not most, of these rooms will be in outlying massive concrete housing blocks called *sídliště.* The exteriors are akin to those of prisons, but unlike many Western housing projects, these are relatively safe and well maintained and usually have a basic level of comfort and amenities. Some owners take special care of these rooms, and you may stumble on a homey place with old Bohemian charm. Most of the projects are close to metro stations or tram lines, so getting to the city center shouldn't take longer than 15 to 30 minutes. Expect to pay between 750 and 1,500Kč ($22.05 and $45.11) per person for accommodations in these homes.

A Warning About Two-Tiered Pricing

Some Czech hotels and restaurants have continued a Communist-era practice of two-tiered pricing—giving citizens a cut rate while making foreigners pay more to subsidize the difference. Despite loud screams from foreign visitors about this anarchic system, the government allows it to continue, arguing that it's necessary for the transition to a market economy. However, the market has forced its hand with pressures pushing many places to stop the practice as they compete for a mostly foreign clientele. Some places, especially in the provinces, charge a separate rate for Czechs, many of whom would never pay the prices charged to foreigners.

Better yet, there are **private apartments** offered to tourists for anywhere from 1 night to a long-term stay without having to live with the landlord in the same domicile. These may be the best value around for privacy and location. Expect to pay between 1,500 and 6,000Kč ($45.11 and $176) for a studio apartment for two, depending on location. Larger apartments are also available.

All kinds of private housing are offered by several local agencies. The leader now is Prague-based **Tom's Travel** at **www.travel.cz,** which offers all types of accommodations at their main site, or you can tap their large pictured database of apartments at **www.apartments.cz.** Tom's office is near the National Theater at Ostrovní 7 (☎ 02/2499 0983; fax 02/2499 0999). Another agency, especially for those arriving late by train or air, is **AVE Travel Ltd.** (☎ 02/2422 3226; fax 02/5155 6005; e-mail: ave@avetravel.cz; www.avetravel.cz). It has outlets at the airport, open from 7am to 10pm; at the main train station, Hlavní nádraží, open from 6am to 11pm; and at the north train station, Nádraží Holešovice, open from 7am to 9pm.

HOTELS Full-service hotels have begun to catch up with Western standards in the face of competition, but rooms are still more expensive than those in many European hotels of similar or better quality. The staff, while much more attentive than they were soon after the revolution, still often act as if you were invading their turf. Though diminishing, surliness still rears its ugly head, and at the prices the top hotels charge, it's unforgivable.

The selection is growing, but because there's not much room to build in the historic center, newer properties tend to be farther out, with notable exceptions given below. You can find a few top names, too. Hilton has put its name on the glass-and-fern Hotel Atrium, and the service has improved considerably. Comfortable Renaissance and Marriott hotels are next to the biggest banks, and Vienna International Hotels runs two prime properties, the Palace, just off Wenceslas Square, and the most elegant choice, the Savoy on the far side of Prague Castle in Hradčany. The full service that comes with the full prices at these properties is mostly first class, but other places lack the truly personal attention a luxury hotel should provide.

PENSIONS These guesthouses with few services are cheaper than hotels, but compared with similar Western B&Bs they're still relatively expensive. Some have found a niche, offering a quaint stay in a quiet neighborhood. Note that in most hotel and B&B accommodations, the room rate includes breakfast—usually heavy bread or rolls (*rohlíky*), jam, butter, cheese spreads, and sometimes liver pâté, plus yogurt, cereal, juice, milk, and coffee or tea. Occasionally, slices of Prague ham or smoked pork (*debrecínka*), local cheeses, and fresh fruit will join the buffet, and some offer ham and eggs cooked to order.

HOSTELS If you need simply a dry, cheap place to lay your head, Prague has several relatively clean hostels, especially during the school holiday, when classrooms turn

Which Quarter?

If location is most important, there are really three parts of the city from which you should choose. If you're lucky enough to stay in one of the few rooms on the castle hill in **Hradčany,** you'll feel as if you have a privileged position where princes, potentates, and politburo wonks once roamed. You'll also pay for this privilege. You'll remember your stay in **Malá Strana** because of the quiet old-world atmosphere of this compact quarter, whose red roofs lie in the afternoon shadow of Prague Castle and fight for attention with the dome of St. Nicholas Church. A room in **Old Town (Staré Město)** will put you right in the heart of the largest saturation of shops, theaters, and restaurants. It's certainly the most lively quarter.

Elsewhere, you'll find more affordable options near fine restaurants, cafes, and services in **Vinohrady,** just above Wenceslas Square off the Náměstí Míru metro station. This part of **New Town (Nové Město)** is quickly becoming the trendy part of central Prague, with gentrified First Republic apartment buildings and greener residential neighborhoods. As for staying on **Wenceslas Square,** my advice is to avoid this increasingly rough area, unless you can book a room at the Hotel Esplanade around the corner or if you enjoy living on the edge.

into dorms. These aren't very private but do provide a chance to meet people from around the world. Many hostels are outside the city, but in July and August several emerge in central city schools and conservatories (for details, see below). For the latest, contact **AVE Travel Ltd.** (see "Private Rooms," above).

1 Hradčany

VERY EXPENSIVE

✪ **Hotel Savoy.** Keplerova 6, Praha 1. ☎ **02/2430 2430.** Fax 02/2430 2128. E-mail: savhoprg@mbox.vol.cz. www.hotel-savoy.cz. 61 units. A/C MINIBAR TV TEL. From 9,066Kč ($266) double; from 12,466Kč ($366) suite. Rates include breakfast. AE, DC, MC, V. Tram: 22 or 23.

Prague's finest new hotel (opened in 1994), the Savoy belongs to the company that manages the more venerable Palace on Wenceslas Square, and it has attracted a demanding clientele. Just behind the Foreign Ministry, Černín Palace, a few blocks from the castle, it welcomes you in a modern lobby. The guest rooms are richly decorated and boast every amenity as well as spacious marble bathrooms. The beds are consistently huge, rejecting the frequent central European twin-beds-shoved-together look. As at the Palace, the pleasant staff provides attention to detail a cut above most hotels here.

Dining/Diversions: The Hradčany restaurant is best known for Sunday brunches with a different national cuisine buffet each week. There's also a lobby bar and an elegant library reminiscent of a British men's club. Afternoon tea is served daily except in summer.

Amenities: 24-hour room service, concierge, laundry, massage, hairdresser, business services, "Relaxation" center that includes a small set of exercise machines, sauna, whirlpool.

EXPENSIVE

✪ **Romantik Hotel U raka.** Černínská 10, Praha 1. ☎ **02/2051 1100.** Fax 02/2051 0511. E-mail: uraka@login.cz. www.romantikhotels.com/uraka. 6 units. A/C MINIBAR TV TEL.

Prague Accommodations

 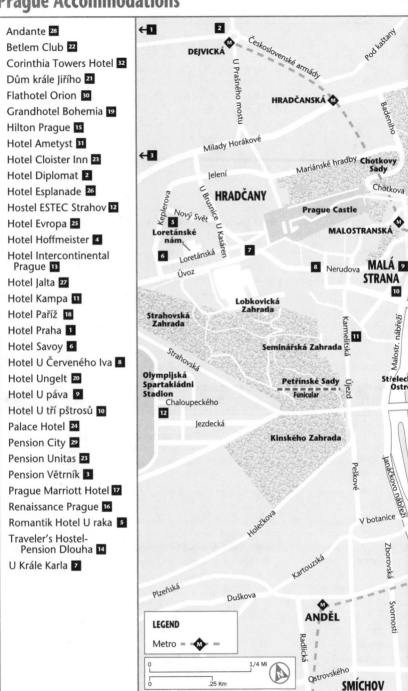

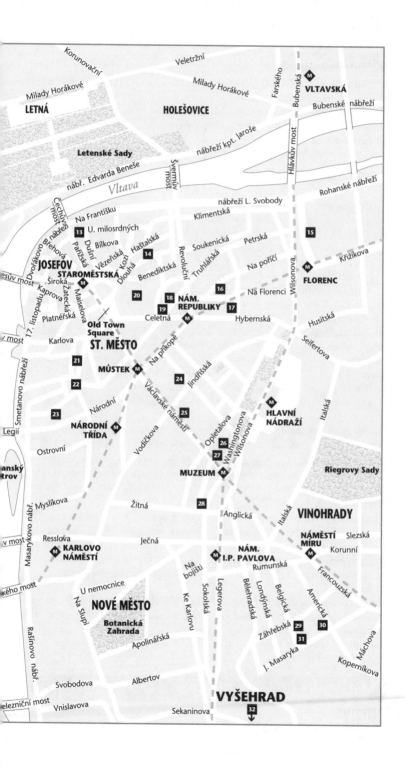

Note on Noisiness

We used to have the **Hotel U Červeného lva,** Nerudova 41 (☎ **02/5753 3832**) as the top pick near Prague Castle, but with ever more tourists walking up Nerudova street, the noise has become prohibitive in the summer season, according to a few Frommer's regulars. Try this place during the colder months when your windows will remain closed.

6,200Kč ($182) double; 7,200Kč ($212) suite. Rates include breakfast. AE, MC, V. Tram: 22 or 23.

Hidden among the stucco houses and cobblestone streets of a pristine medieval neighborhood below Prague Castle is this most pleasant surprise. The Romantik Hotel U raka (At the Crayfish), in a ravine beneath the Foreign Ministry gardens, has been lovingly reconstructed as an old-world farmhouse. This is the quietest getaway you could imagine in the tightly packed city. The rustic rooms have heavy wooden furniture, open-beamed ceilings, and stone walls. The much-sought-after suite has a fireplace and adjoins a private manicured garden, making it a favorite with honeymooners. Water trickles through the Japanese garden landscaping that surrounds the hotel.

The English-speaking owners, the Paul family, approach your stay in a relaxed but attentive manner. A few years ago, the Pauls changed the name to "Romantik Hotel," which connotes to the mostly German clientele a higher standard than the previous "Pension." The Pauls will help you navigate the phalanx of nearby streets. Prague Castle is a 10-minute walk away, and you can catch a tram into the city center by walking up ancient steps at the side of the hotel. Reservations well in advance are recommended.

Dining: Breakfast, coffee, and other drinks and snacks can be taken in the cozy breakfast nook until 7pm, but no lunch or dinner is served.

✪ **U Krále Karla.** Nerudova-Úvoz 4, Prague 1. ☎ **02/5753 2869.** Fax 02/5753 3591. E-mail: Ukrale@tnet.cz. www.romantichotels.cz. 19 units. MINIBAR TV TEL. 6,100Kč ($179) double; 6,700Kč ($197) suite. Rates include breakfast. AE, MC, V. Tram: 22 or 23 to Malostranské náměstí and then up the hill.

This castle hill property does so much to drive home its Renaissance roots, King Charles's heirs should be getting royalties. Replete with period-print open-beamed ceilings and stained-glass windows, the atmosphere is almost Disneyesque in its pretense, but somehow appropriate for this location at the foot of Prague Castle. This is a fun, comfortable choice, with heavy period furniture and colorful angelic accents everywhere.

Dining: Two ornate vaulted dining rooms serve breakfast, lunch, and dinner until 11pm. Evening main courses center on steaks, standard continental cuisine, and Czech favorites, including roast duck with dumplings.

Amenities: Laundry, private limousine hire, limited room service, foreign newspaper stand, solarium.

2 Malá Strana (Lesser Town)

EXPENSIVE

Hotel Hoffmeister. Pod Bruskou 9, Praha 1. ☎ **02/5101 7111.** Fax 02/5101 7120. E-mail: hotel@hoffmeister.cz. www.hoffmeister.cz. 41 units. TV TEL. 5,066–7,582Kč ($149–$223) double; 6,970–13,430Kč ($205–$395) suite. Rates include breakfast. AE, MC, V. Metro: Malostranská.

Money-Saving Tips

Many hotels set their prices depending on the koruna's market rate against the German mark (itself now set by the rate of the euro), so prices change frequently.

Czech hotel reception attendants have little interest in haggling over room rates. Usually they don't have authorization to veer away from the listed rates, and few have been instructed to jiggle the price in order to make a sale. However, times are changing as occupancy rates fluctuate and competition bites. Your best chance for a better rate is calling in advance and getting a very senior manager (preferably the owner) to book your room. Be clear that you're looking at other properties and don't be afraid to say that price *does* matter.

Check with a few other places first before making a final decision. In each case, ask how many rooms they still have available for the night. If it sounds like these are plenty of rooms around town, you're in a great negotiating position. Then find the manager at the place you want and push him or her for a lower rate. You can also seek a deeper discount for a longer stay.

The artsy Hoffmeister opened in 1993, rising out of the ruins of a dilapidated block of buildings. It's one of a kind: a full-service luxury property owned and operated by a Czech who's trying hard to provide friendly customer service. As the hotel is on a busy street used by cars and trams to get to Prague Castle, your stay can be faintly noisy at times, but the rooms are solid, distinctive, and well equipped. Each has a unique color scheme with rich fabrics, matching draperies, and even bed canopies. Conceived by the son of Adolph Hoffmeister, an artist and former diplomat, the hotel strikes you with bold eclectic style and creative use of personal tastes. Sketches by Adolph are hung around the building as tributes to the late artist's friends and acquaintances, including Charlie Chaplin, Salvador Dalí, George Bernard Shaw, and John Steinbeck. At the Hoffmeister, you're greeted by a massive abstract human figure who holds up one corner of the building with its bulbous head and gestures in a way that suggests an Italian-style salute to the wild drivers who pass on their way up the hill. (At least that's what it looks like to us.)

Dining/Diversions: The well-received Czech/continental restaurant Ada serves carefully prepared local favorites like virgin svíčková, tender sirloin in cream sauce, and delicate chicken breast in wine batter. A cafe with terrace seating in good weather covers the quiet side of the building, and there's also a bar.

Amenities: 24-hour room service, concierge, laundry, parking garage, car-rental service.

Hotel U páva. U Lužického semináře 22, Praha 1. ☎ **02/5732 0743.** Fax 02/533 379. E-mail: hotelupava@tnet.cz. www.romantichotels.cz. 11 units. A/C MINIBAR TV TEL. 5,900Kč ($174) double; 6,900Kč ($203) suite. Rates include breakfast. AE, DC, MC, V. Metro: Mal-ostranská.

The U páva (At the Peacock) is a fine B&B in Malá Strana managed by the same group as the King Charles. On the narrow street across from the walled Vojanov gardens, a stone's throw from Charles Bridge, this family-run hotel has the intimacy of a farmhouse and offers room service from its decent kitchen. The best rooms on the top floor facing the front have a fantastic low-angle view of Prague Castle.

Dining/Diversions: The restaurant is gaining a reputation with discreet diplomats. This is a fine choice for a romantic candlelit dinner and then a stroll on the bridge or a promenade in the garden. There's also a small bar.

Amenities: Room service, overnight laundry.

O Hotel U tří pštrosů. Dražického nám. 12, Praha 1. ☎ **02/5732 0565.** Fax 02/5732 0611. E-mail: info@utripstrosu.cz. www.utripstrosu.cz. 18 units. MINIBAR TV TEL. 6,900Kč ($203) double; from 8,850Kč ($260) suite. Rates include breakfast. AE, MC, V. Metro: Malostranská.

The setting is the foot of Charles Bridge on the left bank, with buskers trying to make a living and the shuffling and awestruck conversations of visitors providing the soundtrack. This hotel reopened in 1992, having preserved its painted wooden Renaissance ceilings and some antique furnishings. The rooms are rustic but comfortable. The corner suites offer spectacular views of Charles Bridge and Prague Castle. The small inn is run more like a casual B&B than a professional hotel.

Dining/Diversions: The medieval restaurant makes it worth stomaching the mediocre selection of local fare. The dining room is open from noon to 3pm and 6 to 11pm, and the small Café Bar is open from noon to 11pm.

MODERATE

Hotel Kampa. Vsehrdova 16, Praha 1. ☎ **02/5732 0404.** Fax 02/5732 0262. E-mail: hotel.kampa@mbox.vol.cz. 84 units. MINIBAR TV TEL. 3,550Kč ($104) double (showers only). Rates include breakfast. AE, MC, V. Metro: Malostranská; then the no. 12, 22, or 23 tram to the Hellichova stop.

On the edge of the park where troops once camped along the banks of the Vltava, the Kampa occupies what was a 17th-century armory. It has a choice location on a quiet, winding alley off the park, giving you quick access to Malá Strana and Charles Bridge. The rooms suggest a bit of Communist chintz without much attention to aesthetics, but they're comfortable enough if you don't expect first-class surroundings. The best rooms boast a park view—request when booking or checking in. There's a restaurant, but you'd be better off visiting one of those nearby, like Kampa Park under Charles Bridge.

3 Staré Město (Old Town) & Josefov

VERY EXPENSIVE

Grandhotel Bohemia. Králodvorská 4, Praha 1. ☎ **02/2480 4111.** Fax 02/232 9545. E-mail: grand-hotel-bohemia@austria-hotels.icom.cz. www.austria-hotels.co.at. 78 units. A/C MINIBAR TV TEL. 14,824Kč ($436) double; from 20,740Kč ($610) suite. Rates include breakfast. AE, DC, MC, V. Metro: Náměstí Republiky.

This is one of the most convenient locations on this side of the Vltava, but you pay for it. The Bohemia was reconstructed out of a 1925 art deco building once reputed to have been used frequently by the Communist secret police, the StB. It's now a beautiful Vienna-managed getaway on a back-street off the Celetná shopping zone leading to Old Town Square. The extravagant common areas are filled with porcelain and brass—impressive and quite different from the more contemporary guest rooms. Flowers abound. The cheery accommodations aren't large but are fitted with business-oriented extras. Still, it is somewhat expensive for what you're getting.

Dining/Diversions: The restaurant offers standard European fare, but there are others with much more character nearby. There's also a small cafe.

Amenities: 24-hour room service, concierge, laundry, massage, fax and business services.

O Hotel Intercontinental Prague. Nám. Curieových 43/5, Praha 1. ☎ **02/2488 1111.** Fax 02/2481 0071. E-mail: prague@interconti-com. www.interconti.com. 364 units. A/C MINIBAR TV TEL. From 8,840Kč ($260) double; from 13,600Kč ($400) suite. Rates include buffet breakfast. Children under 19 stay free in parents' room. AE, DC, MC, V. Metro: Staroměstská.

The upper suites have hosted luminaries like Michael Jackson, Madeleine Albright, and, so legend has it, legendary global terrorist Carlos the Jackal. It seems that Michael and Madeleine stayed here for the comfortably reconstructed rooms. Carlos apparently stayed here because it used to be a safehouse with pretty good room and board during the Communist era. The 1970s design has been updated with modern rooms, a glittering fitness center, and an atrium restaurant. The standard guest rooms aren't very large but are comfortable, with decent but not exceptional upholstered furniture, computer ports, and marble bathrooms. A riverside window might give you a glimpse of the castle or at least the metronome at the top of Letná park across the river, where a massive statue of Joseph Stalin stood in the 1950s. When the self-styled "King of Pop" stayed here to kick off his 1996 tour, a giant statue of Jackson was placed on Stalin's old pedestal facing the star's suite—the Cult of Personality lives on.

Dining/Diversions: The penthouse dining room, Zlatá Praha, with huge windows offering sweeping views of the city's spires and rooftops, serves surprisingly delicate Czech and continental cuisine. A more casual restaurant and cafe are on the ground floor for meals and snacks throughout the day.

Amenities: 24-hour room service, concierge, laundry, massage, hairdresser, fax and business services, gift shop/newsstand.

✪ **Hotel Paříž.** U Obecního domu 1, Praha 1. ☎ **02/2219 5195.** Fax 02/2422 5475. E-mail: booking@hotel-pariz.cz. www.hotel-pariz.cz. 93 units. A/C MINIBAR TV TEL. 9,180Kč ($270) double; 12,920Kč ($380) suite. AE, CB, DC, MC, V. Metro: Náměstí Republiky.

At the edge of náměstí Republiky and across from the Municipal House, the Paříž provides a rare chance to put yourself back in the gilded First Republic. Each light fixture, etching, and curve at this art nouveau landmark recalls the days when Prague was one of the world's richest cities. The sinuous banister leading past the reception area is an intricate piece of ironwork, and the lobby is tastefully furnished in the art nouveau style known here as the secese motif. The high-ceilinged guest rooms maintain a purplish theme; they aren't plush but are comfortable and adequately equipped, with more modern furnishings than the lobby would suggest. Still, it's the ground floor that maintains an authentic period elegance. Now that the Municipal House is open again, offering beautiful salons, cafes, restaurants, and concert halls, you can make a 1920s splash without leaving the neighborhood.

Dining/Diversions: The restaurant Sarah Bernhardt, named for the subject of Moravian Alfons Mucha's sumptuous art decoratíf studies, is a beautiful dining room in period style, but the standard continental fare doesn't match the decor. The ground-floor Café de Paris also recalls the period when Mucha wowed Paris and provides a pleasant place to linger with a cup or a glass.

Amenities: 24-hour room service, concierge, laundry, business services.

EXPENSIVE

Hotel Ungelt. Štupartská 1, Praha 1. ☎ **02/2482 8686.** Fax 02/2482 8181. 9 units. MINIBAR TV TEL. 6,330Kč ($186) 1-bedroom suite; 8,640Kč ($254) 2-bedroom suite. Rates include breakfast. AE, MC, V. Metro: Staroměstská or line B to Náměstí Republiky.

In the afternoon shadow of the Týn Church, just off of Old Town Square, you'll find a place not as opulent as the Grandhotel Bohemia but probably a better value. The three-story Ungelt offers full apartments that are airy and spacious. Each unit contains a living room, a full kitchen, and a bathroom. The bedrooms have standard-issue beds and not-too-attractive upholstered couches, but do boast luxurious accents like huge chandeliers and antique dressers; some have magnificent hand-painted ceilings. Because the Ungelt is in a tightly constructed neighborhood behind the church, great exterior views are impossible, but the back rooms look out on a quaint courtyard. My boss and his family raved about the location and spaciousness, especially as they had two small boys in tow.

Dining/Diversions: There's no restaurant, but you're in the middle of Prague's most saturated restaurant district. The small bar offers summer garden seating.

Amenities: Laundry.

MODERATE

Betlem Club. Betlémské nám. 9, Praha 1. ☎ **02/2222 1575.** Fax 02/2222 0580. 22 units. MINIBAR TV TEL. 3,000–3,400Kč ($100–$102) double. Rates include breakfast. No credit cards. Metro: Národní třída.

Protestant firebrand Jan Hus launched his reformation drive at the reconstructed chapel across the street, but the Betlem Club recalls little of those heady 15th-century days, except for the vaulted medieval cellar where breakfast is served. Still, this small hotel offers a great location on a cobblestone square. The rooms are decorated with bland modern pieces but are comfortable and fairly priced. If you come by car, you can park in spots in front of the hotel—a rarity for this parking-deficient city—but book a spot early.

✪ **Hotel Cloister Inn–Pension Unitas.** Bartolomějsk(á) 9, Praha 1. ☎ **02/232 7700.** Fax 02/232 7709. E-mail: cloister@cloister-inn.cz. www.cloister-inn.cz. Hotel: 25 units with ensuite showers. 3,400Kč ($100) double. Pension: 32 units (none with bathroom). 1,200Kč ($35) double. Both rates include breakfast, which is a much more extensive buffet on the hotel side. Hotel: AE, MC, V. Pension: No credit cards. Metro: Národní třída.

Between Old Town Square and the National Theater, this property has been renovated into a good-value mid-range hotel with its hostel-like pension also attracting budget travelers. The original rooms of this unique spot were developed from holding cells used by the Communist secret police, the StB, which themselves were converted from a convent. It sounds ominous, but the Cloister Inn rooms are very inviting while the pension offers sparse, clean accommodations in the old cells at an unbeatable price for the location. Proprietor Jiří Tlaskal has taken over management from the secret police and the Sisters of Mercy (the nuns, not the rock group). George (as he prefers in English) has refurbished and expanded the hotel side with smart colors and comfortable Nordic furniture. For a bizarre treat in the pension, you might like to stay down in Cell P6, once occupied by dissident playwright Václav Havel, a frequent "guest" of the secret police and now president of the country.

There are no meals served other than breakfast, but there are vending machines with snacks. There's dry cleaning and laundry service, and the staff will help arrange tours and rental cars.

INEXPENSIVE

For **Pension Unitas,** see the entry for Cloister Inn–Pension Unitas, above.

Dům krále Jiřího. Liliová 10, Praha 1. ☎ **02/2222 0925.** Fax 02/2222 1707. E-mail: kral. jiri@telecom.cz. 11 units. 2,200Kč ($85) double; 3,300–5,000Kč ($97–$147) suite. Rates include breakfast. AE, MC, V. Metro: Staroměstská.

The "House at King George's" is perched above two pubs on a narrow side street. The recently remodeled rooms have a bit more charm but are still pretty bare. The ceilings are high and the dark wooden furniture is a great leap forward. Charles Bridge is a few dozen steps and a swing to the left from the pension, but this narrow alley has become more like Bourbon Street than the Royal Route. Ask for a room in back if you want to deaden the clamor of the pubs below. Breakfast is served in the wine cellar, which has been recently remodeled without much character. A limited Czech menu is offered to guests from noon to 10pm.

---

① Family-Friendly Accommodations

Private apartments where you can fix your own meals are the most convenient option for families *(see p. 46)*, but if you would prefer more hotel-like service and settings, try:

Flathotel Orion *(see p. 58)*   This affordable apartment-style hotel in Vinohrady has plenty of space for kids as well as kitchens for meals the way they want them.

Corinthia Towers Hotel *(see p. 59)*   The only place in town with its own Western-style bowling alley complete with automatic scoring. Vyšehrad park with playgrounds and beautiful views for picnicking is a short walk away.

Pension Větrník *(see p. 60)*   This country inn has plenty of fresh air and forests for kids to run around in and the biggest lovable St. Bernard to pet. Mom and Dad will like the price and made-to-order meals.

---

4 Nové Město (New Town)

NEAR WENCESLAS SQUARE
VERY EXPENSIVE

✪ **Palace Hotel.** Panská 12, Praha 1. ☎ **02/2409 3111.** Fax 02/2422 1240. E-mail: palhoprg@mbox.vol.cz. www.hotel-palace.cz. 124 units. A/C MINIBAR TV TEL. 9,822Kč ($289) double; 11,900Kč ($350) suite. Rates include breakfast. AE, DC, MC, V. Metro: Můstek.

The Palace has long been the quintessential Prague address for visiting dignitaries and celebrities. It can boast of hosting Josephine Baker, Enrico Caruso, Steven Spielberg, the Rolling Stones, and Britain's Prince Charles. Now surpassed in comfort only by the Savoy in Hradčany, the Palace marks the top central city offering, a block from Wenceslas Square. The 1903 art nouveau building offers a more stoic "Viennese" approach to the era's architectural fashion than the more ornate Paříž and Esplanade nearby. The lobby boasts accents like buttery wood paneling and furniture with subtle flowered upholstery, but the overall effect is that of contemporary wealth tasting the past instead of building a museum to it. The staff remembers your name and uses it in providing excellent service.

The soothing, delicately colored guest rooms are some of the largest luxury accommodations in Prague, each with an Italian marble bathroom. The special Lady Queen suites have luxurious dressing tables to prepare for an elegant night on the Golden City's social circuit. Two handicapped-accessible rooms are available.

Dining/Diversions: Breakfast is a massive buffet of hot and cold delicacies like fresh-baked sunflower-seed rohlíky buns (a memorable simple pleasure). A classical dinner is served in an elegant London-inspired room (coat and tie required). There's also a less imposing art nouveau restaurant as well as a ground-level cafeteria-style restaurant with a salad bar for a quick lunch.

Amenities: 24-hour room service, concierge, laundry, business services.

EXPENSIVE

Hotel Esplanade. Washingtonova 19, Praha 1. ☎ **800/444-7462** in the U.S., 800/181-535 in the U.K., or 02/2421 3696. Fax 02/2422 9306. E-mail: esplanade@esplanade.cz. 74 units. MINIBAR TV TEL. 8,400Kč ($247) double; from 8,950Kč ($263) suite. Rates include breakfast. AE, MC, V. Metro: Muzeum.

Though the Esplanade doesn't get as much attention as the other art deco hotels around Old Town, a recent overhaul has put it into the top class. Constructed during the First Republic, the Esplanade began life as a bank and the offices of an Italian insurance company on a side street at the top of the square. The first owners must've had extravagant tastes, as shown by the ornate accents that remain: An original multi-colored flowered chandelier hangs from an atrium dome in the French restaurant that used to be the bank lobby. Huge oil paintings hang throughout, with intricate ceiling details framing every guest room. Individual private dining salons are available for special luncheons and meetings.

The halls have a musty feel, but the guest rooms are bright and airy, some with standard beds, others with French provincial headboards and tables, and others with extravagant canopies. Suite 101 is packed with antique wooden chairs, intricate inlaid tables, and a fascinating (but busy) embossed wall covering. Top-floor rooms 711 and 712 offer a panorama of Prague. The quality of each room varies, so ask to see what you're offered before you commit. You may be put off by having the main train station across the street, but the honest-looking doorman says that the hotel is solidly safe.

Dining/Diversions: The hotel maintains a moderately priced French restaurant as well as the dining room Est, serving Czech and continental standards. The lobby-level cafe/lounge has rattan chairs clashing with huge oil paintings. A comfortable sidewalk cafe is open in summer.

Amenities: Room service, concierge, laundry.

Hotel Jalta. Václavské nám. 45, Praha 1. ☎ **02/2282 2111.** Fax 02/2421 3866. E-mail: jalta@jalta.cz. www.jalta.cz. 89 units. A/C MINIBAR TV TEL. 8,296Kč ($244) double. Rates include breakfast. AE, DC, MC, V. Metro: Můstek.

Reconstructed after the 1989 revolution, the Jalta has put on a fresh face and a new attitude. The lobby is pretty cold and unwelcome, but the rooms have high ceilings and medium-grade upholstered chairs. The newer hotel furnishings, after an infusion of Japanese investment, are much better than the Communist-issue pieces, which made the Jalta a depressing throwback.

The Jalta is just below the statue of King Wenceslas, where the masses gathered to ring out the Communist government in 1989. The rooms facing the square have balconies, allowing a broad view of the busy square and a chance to imagine the scene on those historic, revolutionary November nights.

Dining: There are two restaurants, including the Tappanyaki, one of the few Japanese menus in Prague. In warm months the lobby-level hotel restaurant has a large front terrace with rattan seats looking out on the square.

Amenities: Room service, concierge, laundry.

MODERATE

✪ **Andante.** Ve Smečkách 4, Prague 1. ☎ **02/2221 1616.** Fax 02/2221 0584. E-mail: andante@netforce.cz. www.andante.cz. 32 units. MINIBAR TV TEL. 4,216Kč ($124) double; 5,576Kč ($164) suite. Rates include breakfast. AE, MC, V. Metro: Muzeum.

A new addition as the best value choice near Wenceslas Square, the understated Andante is tucked away on a dark side street, about 2 blocks off the top of the square. Despite its less than appealing neighborhood, this is the most comfortable property in the price range. It lacks the character of the old Hotel Evropa, but also the neglect. With ensuite bathrooms for every room and higher-grade Scandinavian furniture, you will gain in comfort what you lose in adventure. A close friend of ours, a young businesswoman, said she enjoyed the stay at the Andante, but it was good to have her boyfriend with her, to feel safer at night.

Breakfast, lunch, and dinner are available in the small hotel restaurant but not recommended. Limited room service can be arranged with the reception desk.

INEXPENSIVE

Hotel Evropa. Václavské nám. 25, Praha 1. ☎ **02/2422 8117.** Fax 02/2422 4544. 90 units (20 with bathroom). 1,938Kč ($57) double without bathroom, 3,094Kč ($91) double with bathroom; from 3,944Kč ($116) suite. Rates include continental breakfast. AE, MC, V. Metro: Můstek.

Born in 1889 as the Hotel Archduke Stephan, the Evropa was recast in the early 1900s as an art deco hotel. But this is yet another classical address that has seen much better days. The statue-studded exterior is still one of the most striking landmarks on Wenceslas Square, but unlike other early-century gems, it hasn't been polished and continues to get duller. The rooms are aging and most don't have bathrooms; some are just plain shabby. The best choice is a room facing the square with a balcony, but all are falling into various levels of disrepair. The hotel's famous cafe is another case in point: a wood-encased masterpiece that doesn't shine anymore. Still, this is an affordable chance to stay in one of Wenceslas Square's once-grand addresses, and if by the time you arrive they've cleaned the dining room's skylight, things might be looking up. The Pilsen restaurant is okay for a beer and the cafe is worth a coffee stop to ponder how things used to be.

NEAR NÁMĚSTÍ REPUBLIKY/BANKING DISTRICT
EXPENSIVE

✪ **Prague Marriott Hotel.** V Celnici 8, Praha 1. ☎ **02/2288 8888.** Fax 02/2288 8889. E-mail: praguemarriott@terminal.cz. www.marriotthotels.com. 369 units. A/C MINIBAR TV TEL. 8,058Kč ($237) double; 15,572Kč ($458) suite; 18,428Kč ($542) Executive level. Rates for suites and Executive rooms include breakfast. AE, CB, DC, MC, V. Metro: Náměstí. Republiky.

A major addition to the thin ranks of full-service business hotels in 1999, the Marriott provides just what you would expect—a high-standard space with tasteful, homogenized furniture next to all of the phones, faxes, laptop connections, and services demanded by the virtual salesman. Beyond being newer and slightly better appointed, the Marriott is about 10 paces closer to the Czech central bank than its sister, the Hotel Renaissance, right off náměstí Republiky and around the corner from the headquarters of the largest merchant bank, Komerční banka. This proximity, while not on the attractive end of Old Town, could pay off if you've overslept on that last day of closing the next big post-Communist deal.

Dining/Diversions: The main restaurant is set up to allow for a fairly quick business lunch with prompt service or a more orchestrated dinner. Coat and tie are clearly optional in the casual American atmosphere. The menu ranges from grilled meats to more delicate continental choices. There is also a ground-floor lobby bar and cafe.

Amenities: Along with full concierge service comes a hair salon, valet service with underground parking, a fully equipped business center, and 24-hour room service. The Marriott has a massive fitness center better equipped than the Intercontinental, but still too new to have attracted the buff platoon of regulars seen at the cross-town rival. There is also an indoor swimming pool, saunas, and whirlpools. The hotel complex includes fashionable shops and boutiques.

Renaissance Prague. V Celnici 7, Praha 1. ☎ **02/2182 1111.** Fax 02/2182 2200. www.renaissancehotels.com. 315 units. A/C MINIBAR TV TEL. 6,800Kč ($200) double; from 11,600Kč ($341) suite. AE, CB, DC, MC, V. Metro: Náměstí Republiky.

The Renaissance, opened in 1993 and now run by Marriott, also has the standard comforts of a top-level business hotel, across the street from the Marriott. It's also around the corner from the central bank and caters to conferences and entrepreneurs. Each room is strategically lit, with warm woods and earth tones but without any of the accents found at the Old Town's art nouveau hotels. The top two floors of the eight-level building have rooms with pitched ceilings, adding some variety. Suites on the top floor are spacious and have walk-in closets and sizable bathrooms. A few standard rooms are wheelchair-accessible.

Dining/Diversions: Breakfast and lunch are served in the Pavilion, a buffet of fine foods with a revered Sunday brunch. The Potomac, an American-style steak house, is smaller and brighter with hearty meat and fish dishes. The bar is open until 2am.

Amenities: Room service, concierge, laundry, massage, indoor pool, small exercise room, business center, gift shop.

5 Vinohrady

EXPENSIVE

Hotel Ametyst. Jana Masaryka 11, Praha 2. ☎ **02/2425 4185.** Fax 02/2425 1315. E-mail: mailbox@hotelametyst.cz. www.hotelametyst.cz. 84 units. MINIBAR TV TEL. 4,828–6,052Kč ($142–$178) double. Rates include breakfast. AE, DC, MC, V. Metro: Náměstí Míru.

The most expensive full-service hotel in an affordable part of town, the Ametyst nonetheless provides better value than hotels of similar quality in the older districts. On a quiet back street about 5 blocks from náměstí Míru, it's spotless and decorated in a warm contemporary style. The top-floor rooms are especially bright and cheery, with pitched ceilings and balconies looking out over the peaceful residential neighborhood. The hotel is clearly geared toward attracting German visitors, so you won't find many signs in Czech, much less English. If it weren't for the nearby pensions, the Ametyst would be worth the money, but you can get even better value nearby.

Dining/Diversions: Two restaurants include a contemporary continental dining room, bar, and a woodsy wine cellar.

Amenities: Sauna, solarium, small fitness center.

INEXPENSIVE

✪ **Flathotel Orion.** Americká 9, Praha 2. ☎ **02/2252 1700.** Fax 02/2252 1701. E-mail: oktours@oktours.cz. 19 units. TV TEL. 2,300Kč ($68) 1 bedroom; 3,000–3,900Kč ($88–$115) 2 bedrooms. Breakfast 150Kč ($4.40). Metro: Náměstí Míru.

The best family value close to the city center, the Orion is an apartment hotel with each unit sporting a well-equipped kitchen. All rooms are either one- or two-bedroom flats, sleeping up to six people. In this friendly neighborhood, fruit and vegetable shops and corner grocery stores can be found around náměstí Míru, just up the street. The rooms are comfortable but not very imaginative, bordered in pale blue with black leather armchairs and dark wooden bed frames without much on the walls. The bathrooms are basic white and modern, much like the kitchens. The only extra outside the rooms is a Finnish sauna.

Pension City. Belgická 10, Praha 2. ☎ **02/2252 1606.** Fax 02/2252 2386. E-mail: hotel.city@telecom.cz. www.telecom.cz/hotel.city. 19 units (7 units, each sleeping up to 4, with bathrooms; 12 two-room apt. with shared bathrooms). TV is additional 75Kč ($2.20) per night, TEL 35Kč ($1) per night. 1,550Kč ($46) double in apt.; 2,320Kč ($68) double room with private bathroom. Rates include breakfast. AE, CB, DC, MC, V. Metro: Náměstí Míru.

The City offers clean, characterless rooms, with typical dark wood-veneer furniture and Communist-era Day-Glo orange interiors. The rooms, however, are large and expandable into triples or quads with an extra charge for additional people. TVs cost extra. The best thing about the City is that it's around the corner from the pub Na Zvonařce (see chapter 5).

A Note on Floors

Remember that Europe's floor-numbering system differs from America's. European buildings have a ground floor (the first floor in the States), then a first floor (the second floor in the States), a third floor, and so on.

Warning 1: The prices should remain affordable, but the exact rate depends on the daily koruna/German mark exchange rate. *Warning 2:* The City has been waiting for its phone numbers to change for a while. If you can't get through, check with AVE Travel Ltd. (see the beginning of this chapter) for an update. *Warning 3:* There's a restaurant on site, but we don't recommended it beyond the basic breakfast buffet.

6 Elsewhere in Prague

EXPENSIVE

Corinthia Towers Hotel. Kongresová 1, Praha 4. ☎ **02/6119 1111.** Fax 02/420 684. E-mail: towers@corinthia.com. www.corinthia.com. 570 units. A/C MINIBAR TV TEL. 8,126Kč ($239) double; from 13,226Kč ($389) suite. Rates include breakfast. AE, DC, MC, V. Metro: Vyšehrad.

Opened in the mid-1980s, the Hotel Forum was one of the last "achievements" of Communist central planners. Intended to serve partly as a posh place for delegates attending Party Congress meetings at the Palace of Culture next door (now the Congress Center), the hotel, now sold again and renamed, juts up from a hill with a gorgeous panorama of the city. The rooms are like those in a 1980s upper-middle-range Sheraton.

The hotel is ironically (see "A Warning for American Travelers," p. 60) American in its approach, with an AMF bowling alley in the basement. Though the city center isn't within walking distance, the Vyšehrad metro station is just below the hotel entrance.

Dining/Diversions: The hotel contains a standard continental eatery, a Czech restaurant, and an Internet cafe in the mezzanine. The basement beer pub/bowling alley was popular with the American ex-pat community, until the threat of sanctions kicked in.

Amenities: 24-hour room service, concierge, laundry. Well-equipped fitness center with pool, sauna, exercise machines, refreshment bar, and spectacular city view; beauty salon; game room.

Hilton Prague. Pobřežní 1, Praha 8. ☎ **02/2484 1111.** Fax 02/2484 2378. E-mail: sales_prague@hilton.com. www.hilton.com. 788 units. A/C MINIBAR TV TEL. 7,885Kč ($232) double; from 12,350Kč ($363) suite. Breakfast not included. AE, CB, DC, DISC, MC, V. Metro: Florenc.

The Hilton looks like a huge ice cube outside and a greenhouse inside, built in a 1980s galleria style seemingly out of place in Prague. The guest rooms are relatively cushy and functional, somewhat like an upscale U.S. motel. The building is packed with amenities, including a tennis club, pool, fitness center, and casino. The 700-plus rooms make this place (which the former state travel wonks Čedok launched but Hilton is now running) a natural choice for the largest conferences and conventions. President Bill Clinton and his entourage took over the Atrium during his well-staged 1994 visit. The location of this modern mammoth just outside of center city isn't ideal, but the overpriced hotel Mercedes are ready to take you where you want.

Dining/Diversions: There's an airy cafe/restaurant in the mezzanine, which is the most enjoyable of the six nooks serving food in this behemoth.

A Warning for American Travelers

The Maltese company, which now owns the Corinthia Towers, is itself partly owned by a Libyan state firm on the U.S. State Department's list for trade sanctions. A U.S. citizen staying at this place is technically breaking a federal law, although there are no known cases that have been prosecuted. Check with the U.S. Embassy's consular section if you are concerned about staying here.

Amenities: 24-hour room service, concierge, laundry, tennis club, indoor pool, putting greens, casino, gift shop.

INEXPENSIVE

✪ **Pension Větrník.** U Větrníku 40, Praha 6. ☎ **02/2051 3390.** Fax 02/361 406. E-mail: milos.opatrny@telecom.cz. 6 units. TV TEL. 2,000Kč ($59) double (4 with showers only; 2 with full bathroom). Rates include breakfast. MC. Metro: Line A to Hradčanská station; then tram 1 or 18.

The mostly scenic half-hour tram ride from the center (or metro-tram combo) takes you to a secret country hideaway. After getting off the tram, walk back behind a bunch of large concrete dorms to find a painstakingly restored 18th-century white windmill house. It made the most romantic pension stay for us. Once you buzz at the metal gate (watch to avoid the buzzer for the door to the family residence), Miloš Opatrný will greet you in decent English, along with Arnošt, a huge, lovable St. Bernard known in these parts as spokesdog for a Swiss insurance company. Arnošt will help show you through lush gardens and the tennis court into a quaint guesthouse where a stone staircase will lead to spacious rooms with big beds, open-beamed ceilings, and modern amenities. The plain bedcovers and odd-shaped table lamps could be improved to match the setting, though. The bathrooms are roomy, with huge stand-up showers, and the windows are shuttered and boast flower boxes.

Opatrný, a former foreign-service chef, takes pride in whipping up a traditional Czech country dinner and serving it personally in a small medieval stone cellar with a crackling fire. If the guests don't mind, Arnošt adds atmosphere near the fireplace on a cold night. There's a patio for drinks outside during pleasant weather. You can't get more romantic than this, especially for the price.

7 Hostels

Hostels are most abundant in July and August, the school vacation period when many classrooms are converted into dorms. For the latest, contact **AVE Travel Ltd.** (see the beginning of this chapter).

Hostel ESTEC Strahov. Vaníčková 5, Praha 1 (on Strahov Hill). ☎ **02/5721 0410.** Fax 02/5721 5263. E-mail: estec@jrc.cz. www.hotel.cz/ESTEC_STRAHOV_HOSTEL/. 110 units (20 singles, 75 doubles, 15 triples). 300–500Kč ($8.82–$14.70) per person. AE MC V. From Dejvická metro station, take bus 143, 149, or 217 to Strahov Stadium.

Across from the giant Strahov Stadium on the biggest hill overlooking the castle and city below, this complex of hostels was built to house competitors for Socialist *Spartakiada* exercise festivals that were held before the fall of Communism. Today, these concrete high-rises are a popular choice for backpackers from all over the world. Most rooms are doubles, none has a private bathroom, and all are open 24 hours. Nothing much more than a bed and a place to throw your things in a pretty clean concrete cell, but the price is right. Dinner is served at the nearby student cafeteria for 100 to 150Kč ($2.94 to $4.41).

✪ **Traveller's Hostel-Pension Dlouhá.** Dlouhá 33, Praha 1. ☎ **02/2482 6662.** Fax 02/
2482 6665. E-mail: hostel@travellers.cz. www.travellers.cz. 39 units, expandable from singles
to 6 beds. 550Kč ($16) per person. AE MC V. Metro: Náměstí. Republiky.

This is, by far, the best hostel in the city center. The flagship in the local Traveller's
group of hostels is open year-round, just a few blocks off of Old Town Square a few
floors above the wildest dance club in town, the Roxy. There is a total of 90 beds—
which can be expanded from singles to sextets—on two floors, with all sharing large,
well-equipped bathrooms. This hostel attracts a mix of student backpackers and veteran tourists taking advantage of the clean, affordable, modern setting, renovated in
1997. One single and one double have ensuite bathrooms, but they are saved as a premium for tour group leaders; ask anyway. Traveller's offers other hostels at dormitories
throughout town during the high season. Check their Web site for each season's roster.

8 Near the Airport

Hotel Diplomat. Evropská 15, Praha 6. ☎ **02/2439 4111.** Fax 02/2439 4207. E-mail:
diphoprg@gts.cz. www.diplomat-hotel.cz. 372 units; 5 studios. A/C MINIBAR TV TEL.
5,644–6,970Kč ($166–$205) double; 5,750 Kč ($169) studio; 11,322Kč ($333) suite. Children under 12 stay free in parents' room. Rates include breakfast. AE, CB, DC, MC, V. Metro:
Dejvická.

Prague's primary airport business hotel, the clean and functional Diplomat, isn't next
to Ruzyně but about 15 minutes on the way into town. Another in the Vienna International Hotels group that manages the more fashionable Savoy and Palace in Prague,
the Diplomat achieves what it sets out to do: provide an array of business services and
a room comfortable enough to get things done. Note that the rates are adjusted
according to the daily Czech koruna/German mark exchange rate.

Dining/Diversions: Two restaurants serve Czech and continental-standard food,
and the casual CD-Club restaurant has musical entertainment. There's also a lobby
cafe/bar.

Amenities: 24-hour room service, business services, laundry/dry cleaning, health
club with sauna.

✪ **Hotel Praha.** Sušická 20, Praha 6. ☎ **02/2434 1111.** Fax 02/2431 1218. E-mail:
reserv@htlpraha.cz. www.htlpraha.cz. 124 units. A/C MINIBAR TV TEL. 4,975Kč ($146)
double; from 6,620Kč ($194) suite. Rates include breakfast. AE, DC, MC, V. Metro: Dejvická.

The Forum was the most tasteful of the hotels completed just before the collapse of
Communism, but the Praha is the most grotesque of the central-planners' whims.
During the postinvasion 1970s, this terraced mammoth was built into a prime hill in
the richest part of western Prague as a guesthouse for visiting party bosses, destroying
any romantic notion that Communism was all-for-one and one-for-all. It had all the
brass, chrome, and marble veneer that Brezhnev and Castro could've ever wanted. It
looks like an attempt at kitsch but isn't. However, before you dismiss the Praha as a
relic, you might be interested to know that Tom Cruise and other celebrities have
stayed here while filming in Prague. The draws are the fortresslike setting, massive
guest rooms and bathrooms, private balconies, magnificent views of the city, and proximity to the airport.

5

Prague Dining

by John Mastrini & Hana Mastrini

So you haven't heard much about Czech food? Don't worry—John hadn't either until first coming here. The country's culinary reputation doesn't resound much beyond the borders of Bohemia, but there are still plenty of tasty treats.

Even while neighbors like the Germans and Hungarians haven't garnered much global renown for the fruits of their kitchens, schnitzels, strudels, and goulashes are familiar to almost everyone. Czech cuisine borrows a lot from these countries, but with some fine twists—like tasteful *svíčková na smetaně*, sirloin slices in a baked vegetable–based cream sauce served over tender, spongy, sliced dumplings.

If prepared with care, Czech dishes are as delicious as they are slowly digestible. A few innovative restaurateurs have added character to the generally dull diet of soups, meat, game, potatoes, and dumplings, proving there can be delicacy even in this cuisine. We've listed a selection of the best of these.

But if there's a gastric draw to Bohemia, it's the beer. Pubs are so much of the local life here that eating in them is just something you have to do to go along with the lager. We've included a "Pick of the Pubs" section listing those places that offer decent meals at fantastic prices—and that serve the best brew on earth.

With the influx of postrevolutionary tourism came the inevitable explosion of restaurants catering to every set of taste buds. The majority of better Prague restaurants are now serving either a selection of continental European standbys or more exotic niche cuisine. As a result, you can find anything from Indonesian to Lebanese and Greek to Tex-Mex, a shocking variety when you consider the vacuum there was just a few years ago. Below, we steer you to the finest local cuisine, international standouts, and best budget bets.

CZECH MEALS Whenever we discuss with Czechs the subject of the heaviness of Czech foods, they love to remind us that obesity is much more of a problem in the United States. Statistically they're right. It seems that the walking-hiking-biking lifestyle of Czechs goes a long way toward keeping their waistlines trim compared with the more sedentary U.S. routine. Still, statistics also show that the incidence of heart disease is much greater in the Czech Republic than in the United States, so maybe keeping weight off is just not insurance. Yet most people reading this will be coming for only a few days or weeks. So check your calorie counters at the border, loosen your belts, and sample the best of Bohemia (you'll walk enough to burn some of the extra calories anyway).

Starters, outside the ubiquitous ham rolls and unappetizing gelatin appetizers shoved in your face by waiters, are usually soups, often garlic or onion or beef broth with noodles. The herb soups are often the most piquant part of the meal, but the meat-based broth, be it chicken or beef, is frequently served without filtering the heavy renderings.

As for **main courses,** no respectable Czech restaurant could open its doors without serving at least some version of the three national foods: *vepřo, knedlo, zelo* (pork, dumplings, cabbage). The pork (*vepřové maso*) is usually a shoulder or brisket, baked and lightly seasoned, smoked, or breaded and fried like a schnitzel (*řízek*). Unlike German sauerkraut, the cabbage (*zelí*) is sweetly boiled with a light sugar sauce, and the dumplings are light and spongy, made from flour (*houskové knedlíky*) or dense and pasty and made from potatoes (*bramborové knedlíky*). The VKZ combo cries out for an original Budweiser (Budvar), Kozel, or Pilsner Urquell to wash it down.

Other standard main courses are the above-mentioned *svíčková,* roast beef (*roštěná*), baked chicken (*grilované kuře*), and smoked ham and other spicy cured meats (*uzeniny*). A local favorite of colleagues is *cmunda,* found at the pub U medvídků: a steaming potato pancake topped with sweet boiled red cabbage and spicy Moravian smoked pork. The woodsy Bohemian attitude gives rise to a lot of wild game, like venison, goose, rabbit, and duck, or more exotic bags, like the wild boar goulash served at U modré kachničky, probably the best Czecho-centric restaurant. Czech sauces tend to be heavy and sometimes without character but are more frequently tasted with daring doses of spice.

There's also usually a good selection of indigenous freshwater fish, such as trout, perch, and carp, the Christmas favorite. People worry about the safety of waterways, but most fish served in Prague come from controlled fish farms. Since the country has no coastline, you'll find most seafood at the more expensive restaurants, but a growing selection of sea bass, shark, and shellfish is shipped in on ice.

Side dishes, usually ordered separately, are rice, fries, potato croquettes or potato pancakes, and the stalwart sliced dumplings (sponges for all that sauce on your plate). Many dishes are accompanied by a sour fruit chutney, such as cranberry, to cut through the heaviness on your tongue.

As for a **sweet final course,** try a *palačinka,* a crêpe-thin pancake filled with chocolate, fruit, or marmalade and whipped cream. Some restaurants, such as Vinárna v zátiší, sometimes serve a flaming *sibiřská palačinka,* doused in vodka. A favorite dessert guilt is *ovocné knedlíky,* whole dumplings filled with strawberries, apricots, or cherries, rolled in sweet butter, and topped with powdered sugar.

RESERVATIONS Not long ago, getting reservations at a decent Prague restaurant was as easy as finding a health-conscious meal or a friendly waiter: Fat chance! However, the number of solid restaurants has grown substantially, and the chances of getting a table as a walk-in are much better. If you don't want to gamble, you can generally get a reservation at better places on the same day, by early afternoon. Some popular smaller places need a few days' notice and we've noted these below.

Unfortunately, there still are very few restaurants worth organizing your day around in Prague. So, as with the rest of your touring strategy, let the winding roads take you where they may and don't be afraid to stumble into a cozy-looking pub or restaurant. But don't set your standards too high. Below are some of the best choices depending on the neighborhood into which you've wandered. And you might just find that elusive light meal and an affable waiter.

SERVICE   Czech service is improving proportionally to the growth of competition. Still, many have yet to master the art of nonintrusive service. Waiters barge in at inappropriate moments or are nowhere to be found when you need them. The concept of better tips for better service is catching on, and waiters are generally much more attentive and pleasant in restaurants where they tell you up front that service is not included in the bill.

TIPPING & TAX   Tips of about 10% of the bill's total are becoming more the custom, though just rounding up the bill to a logical point is still more traditional. Tipping was frowned on by the Communists, and waiters, as you might guess, became lazy, looking for reasons to avoid your table and make your stay as long as possible in order to thin the workload. Today, good service, if you should luckily get it, demands a decent tip.

At most restaurants, menu prices include the 22% value-added tax (VAT). When they don't, the menu must say so. It's also common for some restaurants to levy a small cover charge in the evening, usually about 10Kč (29¢) per person, although some places raise it three or five times that, even with no entertainment.

DINING CUSTOMS   Traditional Czech custom is simply to find whatever seats are available without the assistance of a hostess or maître d', but newer restaurants are employing staff to seat you. Barring this, just point at the table you want and nod at a nearby waiter to make sure it's available. Don't be afraid to sit in open seats at the large tables where others are already seated, in many pubs and casual restaurants. However, it's customary to ask *"Je tu volno?"* ("Is this spot free?") before joining a large table. Likewise, don't be surprised if others ask to sit at your table. Just nod or say *"Ano, je"* ("Yes, it's free"), and make some new friends.

1 Restaurants by Cuisine

AMERICAN
Buffalo Bill's (p. 77)
Red Hot & Blues (p. 75)

BAGELS
Bohemia Bagel (p. 71)

CAFES/TEAROOMS
Café Evropa (p. 82)
Café Milena (p. 81)
Dobrá čajovna (p. 82)
Globe Bookstore (p. 83)
Kavárna Medúza (p. 82)
Kavárna Obecní dům (p. 81)
Kavárna Slavia (p. 82)
La Dolce Vita (p. 82)
Velryba (p. 82)

Internet Cafes
Internet Café u Pavlánských (p. 83)
Internet Café u Zlaté Růže (p. 83)
Terminal Bar (p. 83)

CAJUN
Red Hot & Blues (p. 75)

CONTINENTAL
Circle Line Brasserie (p. 69)
Globe Bookstore (p. 83)
Kampa Park (p. 69)
Nebozízek (p. 70)
Osmička (p. 80)

CZECH
Café-Restaurant Louvre (p. 78)
Klub architektů (p. 76)
Metamorphis (p. 72)
Na Zvonařce (p. 76)
Nebozízek (p. 70)
Osmička (p. 80)
Pivnice Radegast (p. 76)
Restaurant U Čížků (p. 78)
U medvídků (p. 76)
U modré kachničky (p. 70)
Vinárna U Maltézských
rytířů (p. 70)

DELI
Cornucopia (p. 79)
Obchod čerstvých uzenin (p. 75)

FAST FOOD/BURGERS

KFC (p. 75)
KFC/Pizza Hut (p. 75)
McDonald's (p. 75)

FRENCH

Brasserie Le Molière (p. 78)
Chez Marcel (p. 76)
Circle Line Brasserie (p. 69)
La Provence (p. 74)
Le Bistrot de Marlene (p. 80)
U Malířů (p. 68)

HEALTH CONSCIOUS

Country Life (p. 75)
Gafrujola (p. 75)

INDONESIAN

Saté Indonesian Restaurant (p. 68)

INTERNATIONAL

Bellevue (p. 71)
Café-Restaurant Louvre (p. 78)
Circle Line Brasserie (p. 69)
Hradčany Restaurant (p. 65)
Klub architektů (p. 76)
Metamorphis (p. 72)
Osmička (p. 80)
Ostroff (p.69)
Ponte (p. 78)
Vinárna V zátiší (p. 72)

ITALIAN

Ambiente Pasta Fresca (p. 74)
Bella Napoli (p. 77)
Il Ritrovo (p. 79)
Ostroff (p. 69)
Ponte (p. 78)

KOSHER

King Solomon Strictly Kosher
Restaurant (p. 74)

LATINO/SPANISH/TEX-MEX/MEXICAN

Buffalo Bill's (p. 77)
Corona Bar & Restaurant (p. 74)
Red Hot & Blues (p. 75)

LEBANESE

Fakhreldine (p. 77)

PIZZA

Pizzeria Rugantino (p. 77)

SANDWICHES

Bohemia Bagel (p. 71)
Cornucopia (p. 79)

SEAFOOD

Kampa Park (p. 69)
Reykjavik (p. 72)
Rybí trh (p. 72)

SPORTS BAR

Cornucopia (p. 79)
Jagr's Sports Bar (p. 79)
Sports Bar Praha (p. 79)

STEAKS

Metamorphis (p. 72)
Reykjavik (p. 72)
U bílé krávy (p. 80)

VEGETARIAN

Country Life (p. 75)
Radost FX Café (p. 80)

WILD GAME

Bellevue (p. 71)
Metamorphis (p. 72)
U modré kachničky (p. 70)

YUGOSLAV

Dolly Bell (p. 80)

---

2 Hradčany

EXPENSIVE

✪ **Hradčany Restaurant.** In the Hotel Savoy, Keplerova 6, Praha 1. ☎ **02/2430 2150.** Reservations recommended. Main courses 510–930Kč ($15–$26.80). AE, DC, MC, V. Daily noon–3pm and 6:30–11pm. Tram: 22 or 23, 2 stops past Prague Castle. INTERNATIONAL.

Matching the crisp English setting of the hotel in which it resides, the Austrian-managed Hradčany is the most elegant choice this side of the castle. The menu lists a set of beef, pork, and fish, including succulent poached salmon and lean sliced veal in

Prague Dining

Bohemia Bagel ⓫
Brasserie Le Molière ㉔
Circle Line Brasserie ❸
Dolly Bell ㉖
Fakhreldine ⓮
The Globe Bookstore ⓭
Hradčany Restaurant ❶
Il Ritrovo ㉒
Internet Café U Pavlánských ❾
Internet Café U Zlaté Růže ❹
Jágr's Sports Bar ⓯
Kampa Park ❻
Kavárna Medúza ㉓
Le Bistrot de Marlene ㉗
Na Zvonařce ㉕
Nebozízek ❿
Osmička ⓴
Ostroff ⓬
Ponte ⓲
Radost FX Café ⓳
Restaurant U Čížků ㉑
Saté Indonesian Restaurant ❷
Sports Bar Praha ⓰
U bílé krávy ⓱
U Malířů ❼
U modré kachničky ❽
Vinárna U Maltézských rytířů ❺

66

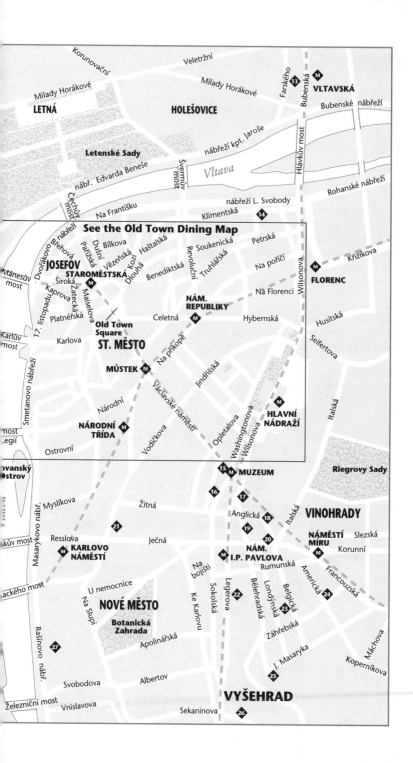

See the Old Town Dining Map

A Few Dining Warnings

Some Czech restaurants are notorious for placing seemingly harmless nuts or olives on the table or offering platters of appetizers or aperitifs that appear to be compliments of the house. They're not. What's worse is that when the bill comes you might find that you're paying the equivalent of $5 for a bowl of stale cashews. Always ask before munching.

Many places, especially in the evening, tack on an extra 30 or 50 koruny per person as a cover charge, even if they don't offer live entertainment. If this charge is mentioned at all, it'll be written discreetly on the menu as *couvert*.

Further, as more Czech restaurants accept plastic, stories of waiters adding a digit or two to the end of your total have increased. One protection is to write out the total in words on the credit-card bill, the way you would on a personal check. Also ask for the carbons and keep a good record of where you've used your card to check against your bank statement to ensure that someone hasn't been using your number. The restaurants below don't seem to engage in these practices, but be on guard, especially if you veer from our suggestions.

---

herb-cream sauce. There are also surprises, such as herb-stuffed tortellini and prawns in avocado mousse. The service sets the standard for Prague, and the new lunch sitting is sure to attract a solid clientele to this jewel beyond the castle gates.

INEXPENSIVE

Saté Indonesian Restaurant. Pohořelec 152/3, Praha 1. ☎ **02/2051 4552.** Main courses 80–200Kč ($2.35–$5.90). No credit cards. Daily 11am–10pm. Tram: 22 or 23. INDONESIAN.

The Saté has made quite a business out of simple Indonesian dishes at simple prices. It's just down the street from the Castle Square (Hradčanské náměstí) and past the massive Černín Palace, great for a postcastle lunch. The unassuming storefront near the Swedish Embassy doesn't scream out to you, so look closely. The pork saté comes in a peanut sauce along with a hearty Migoreng. The casual dining room eagerly welcomes foot-dragging visitors in search of a bite and a rest.

3 Malá Strana (Lesser Town)

VERY EXPENSIVE

✪ **U Malířů.** Maltézské nám. 11, Praha 1. ☎ **02/5732 0317.** Reservations recommended. Main courses 520–1,490Kč ($15.30–$43.80); fixed-price menus 1,190Kč ($35) and 1,490Kč ($43.80). AE, DC, MC, V. Daily 7pm–2am. Metro: Malostranská. FRENCH.

The 1991 rebirth of the vinárna in the Malá Strana house "At the Painter's" shocked the city with the relatively enormous prices charged for what seemed to be a simple bowl of broth, even if it was made by French-trained Czech chef Jaromír Froulík. Though the gourmet fare, by the standard of Western European capitals, wasn't excessively expensive, the owners of U Malířů have given in to the pressure of competition and are offering a more affordable chance to sample the finer attributes of a Parisian kitchen. Surrounded by Romance-age murals and gorgeously appointed tables in three intimate dining rooms, you're faced with some tough choices. Creamy scallops ragout swim in light vanilla sauce, pike perch comes with truffles, rack of lamb is glazed in tarragon, and an exotic set of quail chicks bathe in Armagnac. The crispy breast of duck and a select fillet of beef are safe choices. Some in the diplomatic corps still hiss that they've had better French at the less stuffy Le Bistro de Marlene across the river,

Money-Saving Tips

Stick to the pubs or restaurants with an exclusively Czech menu, and remember that the farther from the castle or Old Town you go, generally the cheaper your meal will be. Imported foods or those prepared in a "foreign" fashion will always be more expensive.

You can also save money by looking for fixed-price menus, two-for-one specials, and deals in the local English-language newspapers. Don't eat anything without first determining its price (see the box "A Few Dining Warnings"). For very cheap meals, try the places covered in the box "Inexpensive Meals on the Run."

---

but if you want a truly old-world evening of elegant romance and French specialties, U Malířů is finally getting to be worth it.

EXPENSIVE

Circle Line Brasserie. Malostranské nám. 12, Praha 1. ☎ **02/5753 0023.** Main courses 295–695Kč ($8.70–$20.40). AE, MC, V. Mon–Fri noon–11pm, Sat–Sun 11am–midnight. Metro: Malostranská. FRENCH/CONTINENTAL/INTERNATIONAL.

The Circle Line has jumped track from a primarily seafood draw to a fuller French-oriented international menu. The setting still has a breezy casual ease despite its frequently buttoned-up clientele from the nearby embassies. Expanding from the cellar to the ground-floor rooms once occupied by its more casual sister restaurant Avalon, the Circle Line has starters that include a rich duck foie gras lightly fried with peaches as well as sautéed oysters and artichokes. Main courses range from straightforward baked chicken in herbs to poached turbot with slices of Prague ham.

☻ **Ostroff.** Střelecký ostrov 336, Praha 1. ☎ **02/2491 9235.** Reservations recommended. Main courses 400–600Kč ($11.80–$17.65). AE, MC, V. Mon–Fri noon–2pm; Mon–Sat 7–11:30pm. Tram: 22, 23, 9, or 6 to Národní divadlo, then walk midway across the bridge (most Legií), down the stairs to the island below (Střelecký ostrov). ITALIAN/INTERNATIONAL.

Nowhere else in Prague is Italian as intricately prepared as at Ostroff, on a river island across from the National Theater. Young Milanese cooks and pastry chefs have brought new twists to northern Italian fare, which is served attentively in a classical vaulted wine cellar with modern Milano chic. Begin with a flaky vegetable flan laden with goat cheese, a wafer-thin sea bass carpaccio, or oysters on the half shell. Follow that with a second plate of tagliatelle in a white-bean sauce or a fine minestrone soup. Meat and fresh seafood top the entrees, including a tender grilled rack of lamb or entrecôte on rosemary. The daily business lunch special, for under 450Kč ($13.25) without wine, is a great value—a selected pasta is followed by a meat or seafood entree with vegetables plus one of the outstanding desserts like a lemon torte. Before or after the meal you can have a cocktail at the riverside bar with a stunning view of the gold-domed National Theater casting a sexy nighttime glow on the Ostroff and your partner.

MODERATE

☻ **Kampa Park.** Na Kampě 8b, Praha 1. ☎ **02/5731 3493.** Reservations recommended. Main courses 365–455Kč ($10.74–$13.38). AE, DC, MC, V. Daily 11:30am–1am. Metro: Malostranská. CONTINENTAL/SEAFOOD.

The best thing about Kampa Park is the summertime riverside view from its patio below Charles Bridge. In high season, the terrace is lively with grills churning out steaks, pork, ribs, halibut, mahimahi, and other barbecued favorites. The desserts have

---

ⓘ **Family-Friendly Restaurants**

Pizzeria Rugantino *(see p. 77)*   A long list of crispy individual pizzas and salads, a rare no-smoking section, and childproof tables make this noisy Old Town stop a staple for families.

Red Hot & Blues *(see p. 75)*   A casual spot for burritos and burgers along with spicier Louisiana treats for parents and a tasty Sunday brunch in the courtyard.

Osmička *(see p. 80)*   Just above the National Museum in Vinohrady, this artful cellar has a huge menu ranging from heavy Czech to numerous chicken dishes and fresh salads, with heavy wooden tables, little smoke, and a pleasant wait staff.

---

won raves from kids, like a creamy parfait and a fresh strawberry soup. During colder weather, this left-bank chalet is more sublime, as candlelit tables provide glimpses of the stone bridge through the windows. Kampa Park boasts solid portions of fresh salmon, beefsteaks, and venison.

Nebozízek. Petřínské sady 411, Praha 1. ☎ **02/537 905.** Reservations recommended. Main courses 160–390Kč ($4.70–$11.47). AE, MC, V. Daily 11am–11pm. Tram: 22 or 23 to Újezd, then take funicular up the hill. CZECH/CONTINENTAL.

Nebozízek relies too much on its unique location to draw crowds and not enough on its food. In its case, the allure is the hillside setting looking east over Prague—not the absolute best vantage point for a city panorama, but pretty nonetheless. You get to this white Victorian house midway up Petřín Hill by taking the funicular to the interim stop (see chapter 3). The standard continental menu has no real standouts, but the pepper steak and roast pork are solid, and the garlic soup gets high marks. The view draws curious tourists, so tables are difficult to get—make reservations early.

✪ U modré kachničky. Nebovidská 6, Praha 1. ☎ **02/5732 0308.** Reservations recommended for lunch, required for dinner. Main courses 300–500Kč ($8.82–$14.70). AE, MC, V. Daily noon–4pm and 6:30–11:30pm. Metro: Malostranská. CZECH/WILD GAME.

The "Blue Duckling," on a narrow Malá Strana street, is our choice for the most innovative attempt at turning Czech food into Bohemian cuisine. This series of small dining rooms with vaulted ceilings and playfully frescoed walls is packed with antique furniture and pastel-flowered linen upholstery. The menu is loaded with an array of wild game and quirky spins on Czech village favorites. Former prime minister Václav Klaus took visiting leaders here when he wanted to prove that Czechs can have unique style. Starters include lightly spiced venison pâté and goose liver in apples and wine. The guláš isn't ordinary pub stew, popping up with various game meats, like wild boar or Fallow deer. The roast rabbit, a favorite of mama from Karlovy Vary, is cooked tender in a creamy herb sauce with cranberries. Other main choices are venison, beef, pork, and chicken, all prepared with imagination. There's also the Malá Strana Templar's Sword, a skewer sampling several meats. Grandma's old risotto recipe was never like this, with tangy cheese and mushrooms. Finally, the ubiquitous palačinky crêpes are thin and tender and filled with fruit, nuts, and chocolate.

✪ Vinárna U Maltézských rytířů (Knights of Malta). Prokopská 10, Praha 1. ☎ **02/536 357.** Reservations recommended. Main courses 350–550Kč ($10.30–$16.17). AE, MC, V. Daily 11am–11pm. Metro: Malostranská. CZECH.

The restaurant on the ground floor and in the cellar of a charming house that was once a Maltese Knights' charity will provide one of the friendliest and most reasonable home-cooked Czech meals in central Prague. Nadia Černíková's apple strudel keeps the regulars coming back. Her husband, Vítězslav Černík, once noticing a hungry and lost American (John), came out to guide him into the restaurant through the scaffolding erected for the reconstruction of this 16th-century burgher house on a narrow Malá Strana side street. The setting makes you feel as if you've been invited into the family's home for a cozy candlelit dinner. The menu offers a fine and affordable chateaubriand for two, thick salmon steak in herb butter, and a breast of duck in cranberry sauce. But save room for the flaky strudel served with egg cognac.

INEXPENSIVE

✪ **Bohemia Bagel.** Újezd 16, Praha 1. ☎ **02/531 002.** Bagels and sandwiches 20–135Kč (58¢–$4). No credit cards. Mon–Thurs 7am–midnight, Fri 7am–2am, Sat 8am–2am, Sun 8am–midnight. Tram: 6, 9, 12, 22, or 23 to Újezd stop. BAGELS/SANDWICHES.

Bohemia Bagel emerged in 1997 at the base of Petřín Hill as the answer to the bagelless morning blues. The roster of golden-brown, hand-rolled, stone-baked bagels is stellar. There's plain, cinnamon raisin, garlic, or onion, providing a sturdy but tender frame for Scandinavian lox and cream cheese or maybe jalapeño-cheddar cheese (on which you can lop Tex-Mex chili for the Sloppy Bagel). There are also turkey club, marinated chicken breast, or egg sandwiches. A Fatouš cucumber or tomato salad, daily quiche, gourmet coffee, and even a Bloody Mary round out the board. The earthy contemporary setting is comfortable.

4 Staré Město (Old Town)

If you're timing walks so that you end up with lunch and dinner, be aware that your best chance to find a table in a good restaurant is around Old Town Square. This picturesque area boasts the largest concentration of dining choices and flat streets just when your hunger beckons and your feet give out.

EXPENSIVE

✪ **Bellevue (formerly Parnas).** Smetanovo nábřeží 18, Praha 1. ☎ **02/2222 1449.** Reservations recommended. Main courses 650–990Kč ($19.11–$29.11); fixed-price menu 1,190–1,290Kč ($35–$37.94). AE, DC, MC, V. Mon–Sat noon–3pm and 5:30–11pm; Sun 11am–4pm and 5:30–11pm. Metro: Staroměstská. INTERNATIONAL/WILD GAME.

Still our perennial top choice of any restaurant in Prague, but followed closely by Ostroff. The artful restaurant, formerly known as Parnas, moved in 1997 to the venerable Bellevue building close to Charles Bridge while its home on the same riverfront street was being renovated. It stayed and kept the Bellevue name. Meanwhile, new owners have opened the old Parnas location near the National Theater, but without nearly the raves given its former operator.

The ambitious Blue Moon Group (which also runs Vinárna V zátiší, Circle Line, and Corona Bar) has put all its energy into the Bellevue's intelligent menus of choice beef, nouvelle sauces, well-dressed fish and game, delicate pastas, and artistic desserts. Poached Norwegian salmon glistens in a light herb sauce and prawns dance on a piquant garlic glaze. Several wild game options are always on the menu, like Fallow deer with oysters and mushrooms or rabbit. For a tamer but extraordinary treat, try the rack of New Zealand lamb. Al dente pastas share a plate with lobster-and-spinach purée, garlic and herbs, or tomatoes and olives. The greens on the side are always fresh and never overcooked. Desserts feature crème brûlée, rich tiramisù, or wild berries in port or cognac painted with brushstrokes from a citrus palette. The consistent food and presentation and the pleasant and perfectly timed service make the Bellevue an evening to remember.

Metamorphis. Malá Štupartská 5 (Týnský dvůr), Praha 1. ☎ **02/2482 6059.** Main courses 300–700Kč ($8.80–$20.60). AE, MC, V. Mon–Fri 9am–1am, Sat–Sun 10am–1am. Metro: Můstek. INTERNATIONAL/CZECH/WILD GAME/STEAKS.

This entry in the reconstructed courtyard behind Old Town's Týn Church is note-worthy only for the breadth of its menu and its cavern home. The wild game stable of boar, duck, venison, and rabbit shares the bill with vegetarian entrees, large salads, and exotic seafood. The food appears ambitious, but the results are uneven and (horror of horrors) the pastas are overcooked. Thankfully, neither the menu nor the motif mimics Kafka's bizarre imagination. Instead, this quirky dungeon looks like a James Bond villain's hideaway: a high-tech medieval maze you enter via a 1689 staircase, scattered with geometric iron tables, pop art, and iron chairs against the stone cellar walls. Metamorphis makes a typical Prague mistake by thinking that loud reproduced pop music adds to the event, but a more sedate jazz combo plays at peak hours. Summer dining in the stone courtyard is pleasant.

Reykjavik. Karlova 20, Praha 1. ☎ **02/2222 1419.** Main courses 500–800Kč ($14.70–$23.53). AE, DC, MC, V. Daily 11am–midnight. Metro: Staroměstská. SEAFOOD/STEAKS.

On one of the busiest pedestrian intersections, Reykjavik is a safe choice just off Charles Bridge. It's decorated inside like a clubby brasserie with plenty of cozy wood and busy curiosities, and the narrow menu is a consistent lineup featuring Icelandic salmon and steaks from the north country. During summer you can dine on a plat-form out in front as the throngs of tourists pass by on Karlova street on their way to Charles Bridge or Old Town Square.

✪ **Rybí trh.** Týn 5, Praha 1. ☎ **02/2489 5447.** Reservations recommended. Main courses 190–1,690Kč ($5.60–$49.70). AE, MC, V. Daily 11am–midnight. Metro: Můstek. SEAFOOD.

That strange smell wafting from deep inside the courtyard behind Týn Church is the most extensive selection of fresh seafood in Prague, served at the "Fish Market." From starters like oysters on the half shell (We're still trying to get our Czech friends to try them) and jumbo shrimp to main choices like monkfish, salmon, eel, shark, and many others, you select your favorite fish and method of preparation at the bright counter near the entrance. You can eat it with the standard pilaf and other accompaniments, in numerous spices and sauces, either in the comfortably modern indoor area or the medieval courtyard during nicer weather. Despite the name, the dining room has the trappings of a modern bistro rather than an old fish market. The waiters seem cocky for what little they do, but otherwise this isn't a bad choice for seafood lovers.

Vinárna V zátiší. Liliová 1, Praha 1. ☎ **02/2222 0627.** Reservations recommended. Main courses 400–600Kč ($11.76–$17.65); fixed-price menu 775–1,075Kč ($22.80–$31.60). AE, DC, MC, V. Mon–Sat noon–3pm and 5:30–11pm; Sun 11am–2pm and 5:30–11pm. Metro: Národní třída. INTERNATIONAL.

Best described as "Bellevue Light," this laid-back version of our riverfront favorite pro-vides much the same quality and similar ingredients, with a few lighter choices like the vegetarian puff pastry pockets filled with eggplant, mushrooms, and spinach. There are several fish and game choices, and the scampi never disappoints. V zátiší (still life) has a casual elegance, like the living room of a beachfront Mediterranean villa, with cushy upholstered wrought-iron chairs and plenty of artfully arranged flora. The dessert selections often echo the Bellevue's, but a flaming vodka-doused Siberian palačinka one snowy Christmas Eve here stands out in our memory. Maybe one of the helpful waiters will convince the chef to do it again.

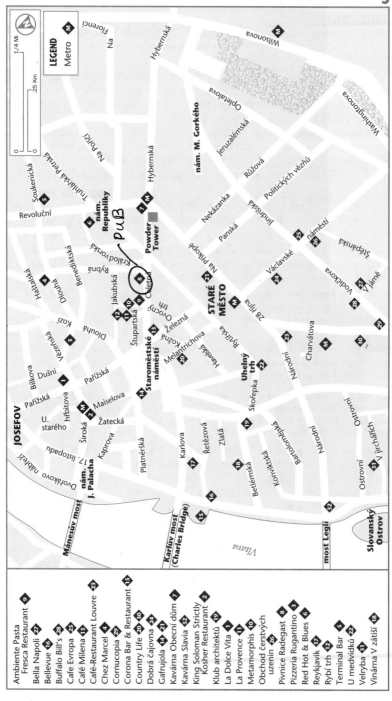

MODERATE

Ambiente Pasta Fresca. Celetná 11, Praha 1. ☎ **02/2423 0244.** Reservation recommended. Main courses 190–280Kč ($5.60–$8.23). AE, MC, V. Daily 11am–midnight. Metro: Můstek. ITALIAN.

We have decided to narrow our previous selection from the Ambiente family of "living restaurants" down to one choice—the pasta joint on the Royal Route, just off Old Town Square. While Ambiente's Vinohrady locations once warranted the trip out of the city center for what used to be the only ribs and Tex-Mex in town, others have since been there and done that. What the outlet on Celetná offers is location, location, location and usually enough tables to satisfy the endless tourist rush hour. In a candlelit basement trattoria, the menu is limited to pastas—albeit served about 50 different ways—salads, a few meaty entrees, and garlic bread if you're still hungry.

✪ **Corona Bar & Restaurant.** Novotného lávka 9, Praha 1. ☎ **02/2108 2208.** Main courses 225–390Kč ($6.62–$11.47). AE, MC, V. Tues–Thurs noon–1am, Fri–Sat noon–3am; full restaurant menu served Tues–Sat 6pm–midnight. Metro: Staroměstská. LATINO/SPANISH.

The Corona opened in 1995 with the feel of a roadside Mexican fruit stand. It attracted hordes with its plates of affordable and tasty food. The real draw was dancing to the salsa rhythms, tipping tequila in a breezy and surreal setting, and looking up from the broad back windows at brightly lit Charles Bridge.

It lasted just a little longer than the Macarena. The management—who certainly knows a thing or two about restaurants since it runs Bellevue and others—decided that the Corona had to go more upscale. So the place was gutted and turned into a beautiful dining room with more romance and class (and two huge bars) but less passion and machismo. The menu is broader, with demanding entrees, more haute than hot. The Corona is still a fun holiday spot with excellent food, but many early regulars, missing the passion, are saying "No más."

✪ **King Solomon Strictly Kosher Restaurant.** Široká 8, Praha 1. ☎ **02/2481 8752.** Reservations recommended. Main courses 300–1,600Kč ($8.82–$47). AE, MC, V. Mon, Thurs, and Sun 11am–11pm, Fri 11am to 90 min. before sundown for the Sabbath, Sat by arrangement only. Metro: Staroměstská. KOSHER.

Under the supervision of the Orthodox Council of Kaschrus, the King Solomon has brought to Prague a truly Kosher restaurant, across from the Pinkas Synagogue. The restaurant's dozen booths are camped under an industrial-esque atrium. Within dining hours, which strictly adhere to the Sabbath, you can choose from a variety of fresh vegetable and meat dishes following Kosher dietary rules. Saturday meals must be arranged separately and paid for before the Sabbath. The broad menu ranges from a vegetable béchamel for 250Kč ($7.35) to a stuffed roast quail for 1,600Kč ($47). Selections of Israeli, American, and Moravian Kosher wine include the restaurant's pride: a Frankovka red from the Aaron Günsberger Moravian cellars in Rakvice.

La Provence. Štupartská 9, Praha 1. ☎ **02/232 4801.** Reservations recommended. Main courses 170–650Kč ($4.41–$19). AE, MC, V. Daily noon–midnight (bar 11am–1am). Metro: Náměstí Republiky. FRENCH.

A French country wine cellar meets urban kitsch in this loud subterranean haunt. Tables have been squeezed in, making this once comfortable setting a little too intimate. Still, the din of the crowd allows you to discuss private matters without too much eavesdropping. A lunch choice of the local banking crowd, La Provence offers a wide array of French provincial dishes, as well as Italian linguine and other spicy pastas, and the spiciest scampi in Prague. Escargots, easily accessible on a tray in drawn butter, are garlicky and surprisingly good. Salads, from Caesar to Niçoise, are large and fresh, with tangy niva and croutons; they come with fresh French bread and garlic

Inexpensive Meals on the Run

Deep in the Rathova passage next to the Myslbek shopping center at Ovocný trh 12 or in its new location inside the U Rotta delicatessen near Old Town Square at Malé nám. 3, **Gafrujola** (☎ **02/2163 7171**), provides a clean, comfortable cafeteria-style lunch in the city center. You'll find numerous salads and vegetarian dishes, lasagna, chicken casseroles, and other concoctions. Food is charged mostly by weight, with a decent-size lunch ranging from 75 to 150Kč ($2.20 to $4.41); it accepts American Express, MasterCard, and Visa and is open Monday to Saturday from 10am to 7pm.

The more Czech-style delicatessen **Obchod čerstvých uzenin,** Václavské nám. 36, Praha 1 (no phone), offers meat, meat, and meat on the ground floor of Wenceslas Square's Melantrich Building. The front of the shop is a take-out deli offering dozens of cooked and smoked meats, sausages, and salami. In the back, it serves goulash, cooked meats, sausages with mustard and a slice of dense bread, and cheap beer. You have to eat standing up, but prices are pure Czech. Expect to pay about 60Kč ($1.76) for a plate of meat and a beer. It's open Monday to Friday from 7am to 7pm and Saturday and Sunday from 9am to 7pm. No credit cards are accepted.

Vegetarians will like **Country Life,** Melantrichova 15, Praha 1 (☎ **02/2421 3366**), and at Jungmannova 1, Praha 1 (☎ **02/5704 4419**), a health-food store run by the Seventh-Day Adventists; it offers a strictly meatless menu also served to go. You'll find tofu, tomato, cucumber, and shredded cabbage salads; zesty wheat bread pizzas topped with red pepper, garlic, and onions; and vegetable burgers served on multigrain buns with garlic-yogurt dressing. Selections are 50 to 75Kč ($1.47 to $2.20). It's open Monday to Thursday from 8:30am to 6pm and Friday from 8:30am to 2:30pm (Melantrichova); Monday to Thursday from 9:30am to 6:30pm, Friday from 10am to 3pm (Jungmannova). Takeout is Monday to Friday from 8:30am to closing (Jungmannova only). No credit cards are accepted.

And in a pinch in Praha 1, there's always numerous **McDonald's,** including two at the top and bottom of Wenceslas Square (nos. 56 and 9), one at Vodičkova 15 just off the square, and one at Mostecká 21 about 100 meters after you get off Charles Bridge in Malá Strana. **KFC** is at Vodičkova 32, Wenceslas Square 56, and Kaprova 14 near Old Town Square. There's a **KFC/Pizza Hut** combo at Na Poříčí 42, next to the Hotel Axa, with a play area for kids upstairs. **Pizza Hut** is at Celetná 10, about 50 paces from Old Town Square on the right.

butter. Weekends often attract drag queens from the Banana Café upstairs for a funky lip-synch floor show, which we doubt the bankers would appreciate at lunch.

Red Hot & Blues. Jakubská 12, Praha 1. ☎ **02/231 4639.** Main courses 99–399Kč ($2.91–$11.74). AE, MC, V. Daily 9am–11pm; Sat–Sun brunch 9am–4pm. Metro: Náměstí Republiky. AMERICAN/CAJUN/MEXICAN.

As a pudgy former resident of the region that inspired Red Hot & Blues, John was skeptical about this early postrevolutionary Prague attempt at Creole/Cajun cooking. And while you won't find a crawfish or chef Paul Prudhomme lurking about, the étoufée is excellent and the spicy Cajun shrimp delivers a punch. Tex-Mex regulars, plus burgers and nachos, round out the menu. Sunday brunch, best taken in the small courtyard, includes tangy huevos rancheros on crispy tortillas. The casual French Quarter feel makes this a family-friendly choice. From 7 to 10:30pm you can hear live jazz.

INEXPENSIVE
THE PICK OF THE PUBS

Besides being the center of extracurricular activity, *hospody* are the best places to get a fulfilling, inexpensive meal and a true Czech experience—not to mention the best brews (some call them "liquid bread"). Selections are typically the same *svíčková, guláš, roštěná na roštu* (see above), or breaded fried hermelín cheese (*smažený sýr*). All can be ordered with fries, rice, potato pancakes (*bramborák*), or boiled potatoes. Reservations aren't usually accepted, though you may see tables reserved for friends of the waiters, for regulars (*štamgast*), or just because the waiter doesn't want to serve more tables (see chapter 1 for tips on pub etiquette).

Below we've listed two top Old Town pub choices and one in Vinohrady based on atmosphere, authenticity, and price. For more pub selections, see chapter 9.

✪ **Na Zvonařce.** Šafaříkova 1, Praha 2. ☎ **02/2425 1990.** Main courses 80–150Kč ($2.35–$4.41). V. Daily 11:30am–11pm. Metro: I. P. Pavlova. CZECH.

The best pub choice outside the city center, the pub at "The Bellmaker's" in Vinohrady has a huge menu—probably the best all-around pub food in town—and super Pilsner Urquell beer. During summer it's hard to get a table on the patio, but it's worth the wait for the beer and grub under the trees.

✪ **Pivnice Radegast.** Templová 2, Praha 1. ☎ **02/232 8237.** Main courses 60–140Kč ($1.76–$4.11). AE, MC, V. Daily 10am–midnight. Metro: Můstek or Náměstí Republiky. CZECH.

The raucous Radegast dishes up Prague's best pub guláš in a single narrow vaulted hall. The namesake Moravian brew seems to never stop flowing from its taps. The Radegast attracts a good mix of visitors and locals and a somewhat younger and upwardly mobile crowd than the pub above.

U medvídků. Na Perštýně 7, Praha 1. ☎ **02/2421 1916.** Main courses 90–250Kč ($2.65–$7.35). AE, MC, V. Daily 11am–11pm. Metro: Národní třída. CZECH.

Bright and noisy, the "House at the Little Bears" serves a better-than-average vepřo, knedlo, zelo with two colors of cabbage. The pub on the right after entering is half as cheap and more lively than the restaurant to the left. It's a hangout mixing locals, German tour groups, and foreign journalists who come for the original Czech Budweiser beer, the genuine article. In high season, an oompah band plays in the beer wagon in the center of the pub.

NONPUB MEALS

Chez Marcel. Haštalská 12, Praha 1. ☎ **02/231 5676.** Main courses 100–250Kč ($2.94–$7.35). No credit cards. Mon–Fri 8am–1am, Sat–Sun 9am–1am. Metro: Staroměstská. FRENCH.

Off a small, secluded Old Town square, this casual French country restaurant is a good option for postcurtain or late dining. On the menu are large portions of salmon and beef tips, tangy soups, cold appetizers like thin marinated salmon, and unique salads. There's also steak and fries for those who don't want to venture onto the chalkboard's daily specials. There's a little more room to breathe here than at La Provence, but the menu isn't as eclectic. Chez Marcel is related to the newly opened Brasserie Le Molière in Vinohrady, which offers an even wider selection of daily specials.

Klub architektů. Betlémské nám. 5a, Praha 1. ☎ **02/2440 1214.** Reservations recommended. Main courses 70–130Kč ($2.10–$3.95). AE, MC, V. Daily 11:30am–midnight. Metro: Národní třída. CZECH/INTERNATIONAL.

Tucked into the alcoves of a 12th-century cellar across the courtyard from Jan Hus's Bethlehem Chapel, this eclectic clubhouse for the city's progressive architects' society is the best nonpub value in Old Town. Among the exposed air ducts and industrial swag lights hovering above the tables in the stone dungeon, you can choose from baked chicken, pork steaks, pasta, stir-fry chicken, and even vegetarian burritos. It's not really spectacular, but the large portions and variety will satisfy a range of tastes. The wicker seating in the courtyard makes a summer night among the torches enjoyable, though the alfresco menu is limited.

✪ **Pizzeria Rugantino.** Dušní 4, Praha 1. ☎ **02/231 8172.** Reservations not accepted. Individual pizzas 100–300Kč ($2.94–$8.82). No credit cards. Mon–Sat 11am–11pm, Sun 6–11pm. Metro: Staroměstská. PIZZA.

Generous iceberg salads front the best selection of individual pizzas in Prague. Wood-fired stoves and handmade dough result in a crisp and delicate crust on which a fresh layer of cheese, vegetables, and meats can be placed. The Diabolo with fresh garlic bits and very hot chiles goes nicely with a salad and a pull of Krušovice beer. The constant buzz, no-smoking area, and heavy childproof wooden tables make this a family favorite.

5 Nové Město (New Town)

MODERATE

Bella Napoli. V jámě 8, Praha 1. ☎ **02/2223 2933.** Reservations not necessary. Main courses 120–400Kč ($3.53–$11.76). No credit cards. Mon–Sat 11:30am–11:30pm, Sun 6–11:30pm. Metro: Můstek. ITALIAN.

This New Town standby never disappoints with its fresh and simple line of predominately northern Italian fare. The antipasti bar includes roasted peppers, calamari rings, marinated mushrooms, and grilled eggplant. A first course of pasta is offered, but the large portions can also stand as the main course. My favorite is the buccatini with chunks of garlic and hot red peppers sautéed in olive oil. The second or traditional main course, ranging from beef to chicken, is highlighted by a tender veal piccata with just a taste of sweetness in the wine sauce. The simple dining room with Italian maps and pictures is warmly lit with stem lamps on each table.

Buffalo Bill's. Vodičkova 9, Praha 1. ☎ **02/2494 8624.** Reservations recommended on weekends. Main courses 150–300Kč ($4.41–$8.82). AE, MC, V. Daily noon–midnight. Metro: Můstek. MEXICAN/AMERICAN.

This cellar cantina near Wenceslas Square is cramped, always full, and about the best you can do in Prague if you're craving fajitas, chimichangas, or burritos. Buffalo Bill's has found its niche among those who have to have a crispy taco fix from time to time and Czechs who want to try their first. Unlike in Warsaw, which has had the fortune (or misfortune) for PepsiCo to install Taco Bells, you still have to pay a premium for a Bohemian taco. Buffalo Bill's also caters the annual July 4 party at the U.S. Embassy, at which Alan Alda said in 1996 while filling his shell in the grub line, "My God, Prague and a taco."

Fakhreldine. Klimentská 48, Praha 1. ☎ **02/232 7970.** Main courses 250–350Kč ($7.35–$10.29). AE, DC, MC, V. Daily noon–midnight. Metro: Florenc. LEBANESE.

This outlet of London's popular Lebanese restaurant delivers a quality exotic menu in a simply elegant dining room. Entrees include charcoal-grilled lamb, marinated veal, and steaks. But you can put together a mix of appetizers, a fantastic variety of tastes, to constitute a meal. These include raw lamb, grilled Armenian sausages, the spicy eggplant dish babaganush, and Lebanese cream cheese. The hummus isn't too pasty as in many Middle Eastern eateries, and meals come with the fresh unleavened naan bread. Three kinds of baklava and cardamom-scented coffee await the final course. Service is sharp and attentive.

✪ **Restaurant U Čížků.** Karlovo nám. 34, Praha 2. ☎ **02/2223 2257.** Reservations recommended. Main courses 170–320Kč ($5–$9.41). AE, MC, V. Daily noon–10pm. Metro: Karlovo náměstí. CZECH.

One of the city's first private restaurants, this cozy cellar cum hunting lodge on Charles Square can now be found by the long line of German tour buses parked outside. The fare is purely Czech, and the massive portions of game, smoked pork, and other meats will stay with you for a while. The traditional *starý český talíř*, with a variety of local meat preparations, dumplings, and cabbage, is about as authentic Czech as it gets. The still excellent value earns this pioneer a star.

INEXPENSIVE

Café-Restaurant Louvre. Národní třída 20, Praha 1. ☎ **02/297 223.** Reservations not accepted. Main courses 60–300Kč ($1.76–$8.82). AE, DC, MC, V. Daily 8am–11pm. Metro: Můstek. CZECH/INTERNATIONAL.

A big, breezy upstairs hall, Café-Restaurant Louvre, previously known as Gany's, is great for coffee, an inexpensive pretheater meal, or an upscale game of pool. A fabulous art nouveau interior, with huge original chandeliers, buzzes with local coffee talk, the shopping crowd, business lunches, and students. Starters include smoked salmon, battered and fried asparagus, and ham au gratin with vegetables. Main dishes range from trout with horseradish to beans with garlic sauce. Avoid the always overcooked pasta dishes and stick to the basic meats and fish. In the snazzy billiards parlor in back you can have drinks and light meals are served.

6 Vinohrady

EXPENSIVE

Brasserie Le Molière. Americká 20, Praha 2. ☎ **02/9000 3344.** Main courses 250–450Kč ($7.35–$13.23). V. Mon–Fri noon–3pm and 7–11pm; Sat 7–11pm. Metro: Náměstí Míru. FRENCH.

The more eclectic French cousin to Chez Marcel, this newcomer opened quietly, and at press time was just building its crowd among the tourist and ex-pat mix in the neighborhood. The bistro, with only a few Parisian banquettes in a classical corner room, was nearly empty the last time we were there. You're greeted by a perky polyglot waitress lugging the chalkboard with the day's specials in French, which constitute the entire menu, and a heavy slate with the wine list. The first courses were foie gras and a transparent smoked salmon that was entirely too bland. The main fare included boiled veal in an onion-carrot mixture with au gratin potatoes and braised chicken leg in herb cream sauce. The cheese plate consisted of a few unspectacular chunks of brie and camembert. While it's not a standout, this restaurant is a nice choice for those staying in the neighborhood.

Ponte. Anglická 15, Praha 2. ☎ **02/2422 1665.** Reservations recommended. Main courses 350–500Kč ($10.29–$14.70). AE, MC, V. Daily 11:30am–11pm. Metro: I. P. Pavlova or Náměstí Míru. INTERNATIONAL/ITALIAN.

Our favorite choice above Wenceslas Square in Vinohrady, Ponte is especially great for shunning the cold of an autumn or winter evening near the roaring fire in the brick cellar dining room. As its name suggests, this place is a bridge between Italian cuisine and other continental foods. Beyond the penne and pesto, you can start with a black-bean soup with bacon and fresh tomato, or a tangy spinach salad with niva chunks.

Sports, Spuds & Suds

The pioneering American-style **Sports Bar Praha** closed at its original location and moved a few blocks further down the street to Ve smečkák 30, Praha 2 (☎ **02/2221 0124**), about 3 blocks off the top of Wenceslas Square. In a more traditional Czech pub environment than its previous storefront is the same big screen, big burgers, and big games—with local prices. A burger and fries plate runs 79Kč ($2.32), while a half-litre of local brew costs as little as 15Kč (44¢). There's a rock music club in the basement and billard tables if the games drag on.

Challenging the Sports Bar Praha on his own home ice is the Pittsburgh Penguins Czech-born hockey star Jaromir Jagr, who has opened **Jagr's Sports Bar** along with Czech partners in the Blanik Passage on Wenceslas Square at Václavské náměstí 56 (☎ **02/2403 2483**). It was just opening as we were going to press, so the local buzz was still high. During the season, Jagr and his mates from the NHL will fill the 35 screens in this glass-and-neon disco-esque space, live and on tape, along with soccer, tennis, and other favorite Czech sports. Since Jagr has brought his own mother over to Pittsburgh to cook Czech specialties, the vepro-knedlo-zelo is recommended, but you might want to forgo anything resembling a burger.

If you're seeking great sandwiches and sports in New Town, ✪ **Cornucopia**, Jungmannova 10, Praha 1 (☎ **02/2494 7742**), offers a fantastic Cajun chicken sandwich alongside the still-solid Reuben and Philly cheesesteak. Home fries are cut fresh, and cases of meats and cheeses allow you to call your shots. Homemade soups and salads are also available. Desserts include gooey chocolate-chip cookies and brownies, and breakfast options include eggs, bacon, pancakes, home fries, and French toast. Seating at this tiny deli–cum–sports bar is limited to only half a dozen booths that come with satellite TVs showing major sporting events and films. Sandwiches are 50 to 90Kč ($1.50 to $2.65). It's open Monday to Thursday from 9:30am to 11pm and Friday to Sunday from 10am to 8pm. No credit cards are accepted.

There are several vegetarian and low-calorie chicken-based selections. Jazz combos play on most nights from a small stage in the corner. When reserving, ask for a table within view of, but not too close to, the fireplace. If you do break a sweat, it's not because of the check, as Ponte provides one of the best values in a full-service restaurant in Prague.

MODERATE

Il Ritrovo. Lublaňská 11, Praha 2. ☎ **02/296 529.** Reservations recommended on weekends. Main courses 120–250Kč ($3.53–$7.35). No credit cards. Daily noon–3pm and 6–11:30pm. Metro: I. P. Pavlova. ITALIAN.

This ristorante, in an old gray-stucco apartment house off the beaten path in a quiet Vinohrady neighborhood, reminds me of my late Italian aunt's house. It's a small, cozy place with modest wooden chairs and familiar Italian maps and repros donning the walls, the trappings of a place run by a family of proud immigrants. The food rarely disappoints. The antipasto bar usually is packed with marinated vegetables, spiced olives, mushrooms, and salad. Il Ritrovo's long list of homemade pasta choices would've embarrassed my aunt. The second plates of veal and beef are but passable. The tiramisù was dense but not as thick as the espresso served with it.

U bílé krávy. Rubešova 10, Praha 2. ☎ **02/2423 9570.** Reservations recommended in high season. Main courses 150–250Kč ($4.41–$7.35). AE, MC, V. Daily 11am–11pm. Metro: I. P. Pavlova. STEAKS.

"At the White Cow" is a Czech version of a French steak house with the pale-faced Charolais beef from Burgundy as the main draw. Decked out as a faux-farmhouse, the setting is woodsy and warm, except for the cow murals peering over your shoulder. The meat portions, while tender and tasty, are smallish, as are the salads, and the vegetables aren't as fresh as they might be. Not a bad price for a good steak though.

INEXPENSIVE

Osmička. Balbínova 8, Praha 2. ☎ **02/2282 6208.** Reservations not necessary. Main courses 60–240Kč ($1.76–$7). MC, V. Mon–Thurs 9am–midnight, Fri 9am–2am, Sat noon–midnight, Sun noon–11pm. Metro: I. P. Pavlova or Náměstí Míru. CONTINENTAL/CZECH/INTERNATIONAL.

Osmička is an interesting hybrid in Vinohrady on a side street a few blocks above the National Museum. At first sight, the "Number 8" reveals a tourist-geared cellar restaurant with tawny eclectic colors, local art for sale on the walls, and a menu dominated by Italian standbys, fresh salads, and a variety of sandwiches. But once a Czech sits down, he or she quickly recognizes the neighborhood secret: This is still a good ol' Bohemian hospoda with *vepřo-knedlo-zelo* and other indigenous fare at local prices— just served on new solid wood furniture by nicer-than-normal staff. Proprietor Libor Nevšímal tries hard to make guests feel welcome, including families, taking the time to negotiate the right combo for our sometimes finicky boys. If you're staying in Vinohrady, Osmička should be on your itinerary. Look closely for the dark metal triangle, marking the location, next to one of the few golf pro shops in town.

✪ **Radost FX Café.** Bělehradská 120, Praha 2. ☎ **02/2251 2035.** Reservations not accepted. Main courses 60–150Kč ($1.80–$4.55). MC, V. Daily 11am–5am. Metro: I. P. Pavlova. VEGETARIAN.

En vogue and full of vegetarian offerings, Radost is a clubhouse for the hip new Bohemians, with plenty of Americans and others lingering, too. The veggie burger is well seasoned and substantial on a grain bun, and the soups, like lentil and onion, are light and full of flavor. Saté vegetable dishes, tofu, and huge Greek salads round out the health-conscious menu. Avoid the poorly crusted pizzas. The dining area is a dark rec room rummage sale of upholstered armchairs, chaise longues, and couches from the 1960s, with coffee tables from which you eat. Too cool.

7 Elsewhere in Prague

MODERATE

Dolly Bell. Neklanova 20, Praha 2. ☎ **02/298 815.** Reservations recommended. Main courses 100–250Kč ($2.94–$7.35). AE, DC, MC, V. Daily 3pm–midnight. Metro: Vyšehrad. YUGOSLAV.

This is the best Yugoslav restaurant in town, memorably set like a surreal library with cluttered upside-down tables fixed to the ceiling above diners' heads. The Serbian food looks and sounds Czech but comes out much more lively and well spiced than northern Slav fare. There's a Balkan moussaka with layers of potatoes and ground beef, topped with béchamel sauce. Excellent appetizers are the flaky cheese and meat pies and thick stews and soups. Main meats are seared or skewered on a spit.

✪ **Le Bistrot de Marlene.** Plavecká 4, Praha 2. ☎ **02/291 077.** Reservations recommended. Main courses 150–530Kč ($4.41–$15.60). AE, MC, V. Mon–Fri noon–2:30pm; Mon–Sat 7–10:30pm. Metro: Karlovo náměstí FRENCH.

Le Bistrot de Marlene, on a residential street near Vyšehrad Park, is packed with locals and visitors in search of the finest casual French cuisine in town. Chef Marlene Salomon has kept the menu short and simple, focusing on high-quality meats and produce. Many starters are recommendable, including *flan aux champignons* (a wonderful mushroom loaf served on parsley sauce) and *terrine de lapin* (rabbit terrine). Of the main courses, roast leg of lamb and steak curry are recommended. Most everything comes with a side of vegetables, simply steamed or baked with layers of cheese.

8 Cafe Society

In their heyday in the late 19th and early 20th centuries, Prague's elegant *kavárny* (cafes) rivaled Vienna's as places to be seen and perhaps have a carefree afternoon chat. But the Bohemian intellectual, much like the Parisian Left Bank philosophers of the 1920s, laid claim to many of the local cafes, turning them into smoky parlors for pondering and debating the anxieties of the day.

Today, most of Prague's cafes have lost the indigenous charm of the Jazz Age or, strangely enough, the Communist era. During the Cold War, the venerable Café Slavia, across from the National Theater, became a de facto clubhouse for dissidents to pass the time, often in the listening range of the not-so-secret police. It's here that Václav Havel and the arts community often kept the flicker of the Civic Society alive.

The eighth anniversary of the Velvet Revolution was the rebirth of an old friend. For on that day, the remodeled **Kavárna (Café) Slavia** (☎ **02/2422 0957**) opened again, saved from the dead after a half decade's absence prolonged by a Boston real estate speculator who apparently was sitting on the property until she could extract a better price. President Havel, once a Slavia regular when it was the dissident hangout, intervened to plead the cafe's case. After a long legal battle, his wish was granted, "a small victory for reason over stupidity," he said in a proclamation read at the gala opening. Prague needs the Slavia again, a familiar place to call home.

New Bohemian haunts have also popped up, now serving better exotic blends of espresso and cappuccino. The gorgeous **Kavárna Obecní dům** has been returned to its pristine splendor. Cafe life may be returning to Prague yet again.

Meanwhile, as post-Communist Prague seeks to keep up with the new times, a swath of Internet cafes have opened (see box below), but only one, **Terminal Bar,** successfully melds Prague's past with its future.

STARÉ MĚSTO (OLD TOWN) & JOSEFOV

Café Milena. Staroměstské nám. 22, Praha 1. ☎ **02/2163 2602.** Light snacks and desserts 60–150Kč ($1.80–$4.41). AE, MC, V. Daily 10am–10pm. Metro: Staroměstská. CAFE FARE.

This quaint cafe managed by the Franz Kafka Society is named for Milena Jesenská, one of the writer's lovers. The best draw is a great view of the Orloj, the astronomical clock with the hourly parade of saints on the side of Old Town Square's city hall.

✪ **Kavárna Obecní dům.** In the Municipal House, náměstí Republiky 5, Praha 1. ☎ **02/2200 2763.** Cakes and coffees around 40Kč ($1.17). AE, MC, V. Daily 7:30am–11pm. Metro: Náměstí Republiky. CAFE FARE.

This is how an afternoon must've been spent back when art nouveau was the fashion not the history. The reopening of the entire Municipal House in the spring of 1997 was a holiday for those who love this style of architecture, and the kavárna might be its most spectacular public room. Witness the lofty ceilings, marble wall accents and tables, altarlike mantle at the far end, and huge windows and period chandeliers. Coffee, tea, and other drinks come with pastries and light sandwiches.

Impressions

Today's opening of Café Slavia, one of the places that played such a fundamental role in my life, I understand as a step toward renovation of the natural structure of Czech spiritual life.

—President Václav Havel's proclamation at the
Slavia's reopening (November 17, 1997)

✪ **Kavárna Slavia.** Národní at Smetanovo nábřeží, Praha 1. ☎ **02/2422 0957.** Coffees and pastries 15–25Kč (44¢–74¢); salad bar and light menu items 40–120Kč ($1.17–$3.53). AE, MC, V. Daily 8am–midnight. Metro: Národní třída. CAFE FARE.

You'll most certainly walk by this Prague landmark, which reopened after a 6-year hiatus (see above) across from the National Theater. The restored crisp art deco room recalls the Slavia's 100 years as the meeting place for the city's cultural and intellectual corps. The Old-New Slavia still has its relatively affordable menu accompanying the gorgeous riverfront panoramic views of Prague Castle.

La Dolce Vita. Široká 15, Praha 1. ☎ **02/232 9192.** Cappuccino 40Kč ($1.18); pastries 30–100Kč (88¢–$2.94). No credit cards. Daily 8:30am–midnight. Metro: Staroměstská. CAFE FARE.

Half a block off Pařížská in Prague's Jewish Quarter, Josefov, is the city's finest Italian cafe. Lively banter, attractive regulars, strong pulls on the espresso machine, and pretty good Italian pastries keep the place humming.

Velryba. Opatovická 24, Praha 1. ☎ **02/2491 2391.** Light meals 50–100Kč ($1.47–$2.94). No credit cards. Daily 11am–2am. Metro: Národní třída. CAFE FARE.

This is the city center's cafe for young intellectuals. Journalists and actors set the mood in this pretty bare basement on a backstreet off of Národní třída, where the emphasis is on good friends and hard talk. Pretty decent pasta dishes are served.

NOVÉ MĚSTO (NEW TOWN)

Cafe Evropa. Václavské nám. 25, Praha 1. ☎ **02/2422 8117.** Coffee 45Kč ($1.32); pastries 50–100Kč ($1.47–$2.94). AE, MC, V. Daily 9am–11pm. Metro: Můstek. CAFE FARE.

Once a grande dame of Wenceslas Square, the Evropa has fallen into disrepair, but its wooden and etched-glass grandeur is still worth a coffee and a look.

Dobrá čajovna. Václavské nám. 14, Praha 1. ☎ **02/2423 1480.** Daily 10am–9:30pm. No credit cards. Metro: Můstek. CAFE FARE.

On the walk toward the National Museum on the right side of Wenceslas Square, there is an island of serenity in the courtyard at number 14. Inside the Dobrá čajovna (Good Tearoom), a pungent bouquet of herb teas, throw pillows, and sitar music welcome the visitor to this very understated Bohemian corner. The extensive tea menu includes green Japanese tea for 55Kč ($1.61) a cup.

VINOHRADY

✪ **Kavárna Medúza.** Belgická 17, Praha 2. ☎ **02/258 534.** Cappuccino 25Kč (74¢); pastries/light meals 25–68Kč (73¢–$2). No credit cards. Mon–Fri 11am–1am, Sat–Sun noon–1am. Metro: Náměstí Míru. CAFE FARE.

With the feeling of an old attic, the Medúza, near several Vinohrady hotels and pensions, has a comfortable mix of visitors and students. The cappuccino comes in bowls, not cups, and the garlic bread hits the spot.

Internet Cafes

One of the most progressive and interesting places to visit in the new Prague is **Terminal Bar** at Soukenická 6 in Old Town near náměstí Republiky (☎ **02/ 2187 1115;** www.terminal.cz), open daily from 11am to 1am. It's a combination cyber space, lounge, bookstore, and cinema, with an eclectic modern but nature-conscious atmosphere and a great mix of Czechs and foreigners. Dozens of PCs are available for surfing at 120Kč ($3.52) per hour. Better-value monthly memberships are 295Kč ($8.68) and there are also ports to hook up your own laptop. A cup of coffee costs 20Kč (58¢).

In Malá Strana, at the bottom of the New Castle Steps, you can check your e-mail or surf for 2Kč (6¢) per minute at the tiny **Internet Café u Zlaté Růže,** Thunovská 21 (☎ **02/5377 004;** e-mail: cafe@internetpoint.cz), open daily from 10am to 10pm. Coffee and tea are 15Kč (44¢); no food is served.

Also in Malá Strana, the **Internet Café u Pavlánských,** at Újezd 31, has about a half dozen PCs in a pleasant setting for 80Kč ($2.35) per hour. It's open daily from 10am to 10pm.

ELSEWHERE IN PRAGUE

Globe Bookstore. Janovského 14, Praha 7. ☎ **02/6671 2610.** Sandwiches and desserts 60–100Kč ($1.76–$2.94). No credit cards. Daily 10am–midnight. Metro: Vltavská. LIGHT FARE.

A mainstay for the younger English-speaking ex-pats, the Globe is split into a fairly well stocked bookstore and a usually crowded literary cafe serving sandwiches, salads, and chewy brownies along with stiff espresso.

6

Exploring Prague

by John Mastrini & Hana Mastrini

While Prague's classical music and the Czech Republic's unmatched beer are among the fine reasons to visit, the primary draw for many is simply walking along the winding cobblestone streets and enjoying the unique atmosphere. Only by foot can you explore the countless nooks and crannies. It would be hard to think of another world capital where there is so much in such a compact area.

Exquisite examples from the history of European architecture—from Romanesque to Renaissance, baroque to art nouveau and cubist—are crammed next to one another on twisting narrow streets. Seen from Charles Bridge, this jumble of architecture thrusts from the hills and hugs the riverbanks, with little of the 20th century's own excesses obscuring this view of grandeur from the past millennium. The most revered areas remain relatively free of the blinding electric Technicolor world—however, splotches of graffiti and seemingly constant reconstruction often taint the mood.

While Prague's leaders have been slow to tap into the city's true potential as a primary European tourist destination, there have been some marked improvements in recent years. The most striking was the 1997 reopening of the city's most beautiful 20th-century edifice, the art nouveau Municipal House (Obecní dům), returned to its near pristine state, with a few extras like a modern information center thrown in.

In 1999, Old Town Square had a face-lift with a pleasant square-side garden with plenty of benches and new trees added so that people have somewhere else to sit and picnic other than at the feet of Jan Hus.

Sightseeing Suggestions

Your itinerary should be a loose one. Prague's most intriguing aspects are its architecture and atmosphere, best enjoyed when slowly wandering through the city's heart. If you have the time and energy, go to Charles Bridge at sunrise and then at sunset to view the grand architecture of Prague Castle and the Old Town skyline. You'll see two completely different cities.

If You Have 1 Day

In order to digest enough of Prague's wonders, do what visiting kings and potentates do on a 1-day visit: Walk the **Royal Route** (or at least part of it). From the top of the castle hill in Hradčany (tram 22, 23, or a taxi is suggested for the ride up, unless you're very fit), tour **Prague Castle** in the morning. The three key sights on the grounds are the towering **St. Vitus Cathedral,** the **Royal Palace,** and **St. George's Basilica,** now an art gallery. Don't miss the tiny houses on **Golden Lane (Zlatá ulička),** also within the castle walls. Then begin your slow descent through the odd hill-bound architecture of **Lesser Town (Malá Strana).**

After lunch, stroll across **Charles Bridge,** on the way to the winding alleys of **Old Town (Staré Město).** You can happily get lost finding **Old Town Square (Staroměstské náměstí),** stopping at private galleries and cafes along the way. In Old Town Square, you can see a performance of the astronomical clock at the top of each hour, climb to the top of the **Old Town Hall** tower for a panoramic view, visit the **Týn** or **St. Nicholas Church,** explore the nearby **Jewish Quarter (Josefov),** or continue to the end of the Royal Route at **Powder Gate,** marking the edge of the Old Town walls. From Old Town it's a short walk to **Wenceslas Square (Václavské náměstí),** site of the demonstrations that led to the Velvet Revolution.

Along the route from Old Town you'll pass near Mozart's Prague venue, the **Estates' Theater.** Dinner and your evening entertainment are all probably within a 10-minute walk from anywhere in this area.

If You Have 2 Days

Spend Day 1 as above. On Day 2, explore the varied sights of **Old Town, Lesser Town,** and the **Jewish Quarter**—what you didn't have time for the day before. Just wander and browse. Throughout Old Town you'll find numerous **shops and galleries** offering the finest Bohemian crystal, porcelain, and modern artwork, as well as top **fashion boutiques, cafes,** and **restaurants.** While the shops aren't that much different than those in other European cities, the setting is. In Josefov, you can visit the astonishing **Old Jewish Cemetery** and the adjacent **Ceremonial Hall,** which displays heart-wrenching sketches by the children held at the Terezín concentration camp during World War II.

From Old Town, it's just a short walk across Charles Bridge to Lesser Town. This once was the neighborhood for diplomats, merchants, and those who served the castle, with narrow houses squeezed between palaces and embassies. The diplomats and merchants remain, while the castle servants are now state bureaucrats all living elsewhere. Visit the **Waldstein Gardens** or get a riverside view of the city and Charles Bridge from **Kampa Park.** The **Lennon Wall,** a symbol of youthful defiance of the Communists depicting the late member of the Beatles, is near Kampa.

The dome of the **Church of St. Nicholas** (same saint, different church), with its gilded baroque interior, dominates the view from **Lesser Town Square (Malostranské náměstí).** As you head up Nerudova, the road leading to the castle, you'll find small **shops and galleries** tucked into every narrow nook.

If You Have 3 Days

Spend Days 1 and 2 as above, except go lighter on touring Prague Castle to begin Day 1 (your ticket for Prague Castle is good for 3 days). On Day 3, after seeing what you held over from the first day at the castle, spend the rest of the day on **Hradčany Hill.** Here you can visit the **National Art Gallery at Šternberk Palace,** the **Military History Museum,** the **Strahov Monastery** with its ornate libraries, and the **Loreto Palace** with its peculiar artwork. Or you can stroll over to **Petřín Hill,** where kids will enjoy the view tower, observatory, and mirrored labyrinth. Try to work in a cruise on the Vltava or pilot your own rowboat ride in the evening.

Impressions

Prague is a priceless asset which surely deserves to be spared from the worst excesses of modern development which have so ravaged the other cities of Europe. The challenge must be to find ways of ensuring . . . that it becomes once again the thriving prosperous heart of Europe, not merely a crumbling museum exhibit.
—Prince Charles to Prague's leaders (May 7, 1991)

If You Have 4 Days or More

Spend Days 1 to 3 as above. Then try touring one of the many other museums or galleries or venturing out of the city center. Visit the old southern citadel over the Vltava, **Vyšehrad,** where you get a completely different view of the city you've just explored. Here you can picnic and stroll among the paths winding throughout the large complex of churches, gardens, and cemeteries.

Beyond Prague's borders are easy day trips, such as an excursion to **Karlštejn Castle,** the most visited attraction outside Prague (see chapter 10 for details). For those with more time to discover Bohemia and even Moravia, see chapters 11 and 12 about visits to the historic towns of **Karlovy Vary, Český Krumlov, Telč, České Budějovice,** and **Brno.**

1 Prague Castle (Pražský Hrad) & Charles Bridge (Karlův most)

The huge hilltop complex known collectively as ✪ **Prague Castle (Pražský Hrad),** on Hradčanské náměstí, encompasses dozens of houses, towers, churches, courtyards, and monuments. (It's described in detail in chapter 7's "Walking Tour 2," with a map on page 121.) A visit to the castle could easily take an entire day or more, depending on how thoroughly you explore it. Still, you can see the top sights—St. Vitus Cathedral, the Royal Palace, St. George's Basilica, the Powder Tower, and Golden Lane—in the space of a morning or an afternoon.

You can also explore the castle complex at night, as it's generally lit until midnight, or make a return trip to see the Gothic art in St. George's Convent. The complex is always guarded and is said to be safe to wander at night, but keep to the lit areas of the courtyards just to be sure.

If you're feeling particularly fit, you can walk up to the castle, or you can take metro line A to Malostranská or Hradčanská or tram 22 or 23.

TICKETS & CASTLE INFORMATION   You can wander the castle grounds for free, but you need to buy a ticket for St. Vitus Cathedral, the Royal Palace, St. George's Basilica, and the Powder Tower; it's valid for 3 days. Entrance to the four main attractions is 120Kč ($3.53) for adults and 60Kč ($1.76) for students without a tour guide or 180Kč ($5.29) for adults and 120Kč ($3.53) for students with an English-speaking guide (guided tours only Tuesday to Sunday from 9am to 4pm). Main attractions are open daily from 9am to 5pm (until 4pm from November to March).

Tickets are sold at the **Prague Castle Information Center** (☎ **02/2437 3368**), a roundish building in the second courtyard after passing through the main gate from Hradčanské náměstí. The center also arranges tours in various languages and sells tickets for individual concerts and exhibitions held on the castle grounds.

You'll find a good selection of guidebooks, maps, and other related information at the entrance to the Royal Palace.

St. Vitus Cathedral

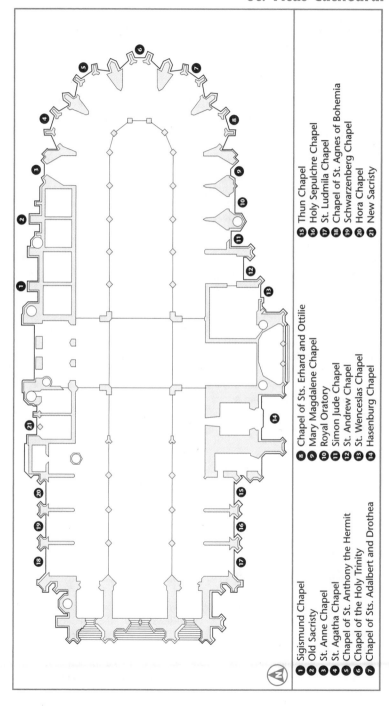

1 Sigismund Chapel
2 Old Sacristy
3 St. Anne Chapel
4 St. Agatha Chapel
5 Chapel of St. Anthony the Hermit
6 Chapel of the Holy Trinity
7 Chapel of Sts. Adalbert and Drothea

8 Chapel of Sts. Erhard and Ottilie
9 Mary Magdalene Chapel
10 Royal Oratory
11 Simon Jude Chapel
12 St. Andrew Chapel
13 St. Wenceslas Chapel
14 Hasenburg Chapel

15 Thun Chapel
16 Holy Sepulchre Chapel
17 St. Ludmila Chapel
18 Chapel of St. Agnes of Bohemia
19 Schwarzenberg Chapel
20 Hora Chapel
21 New Sacristy

The Prague Information Service maintains a listing of current exhibits on its Web site at **www.eunet.cz/pis/praha**.

✪ TOURING ST. VITUS CATHEDRAL (CHRÁM SV. VÍTA)

St. Vitus Cathedral (Chrám sv. Víta), named for a wealthy 4th-century Sicilian martyr, isn't just the dominant part of the castle, it's the most important section historically. In April 1997, Pope John Paul II paid his third visit to Prague in 7 years, this time to honor the thousandth anniversary of the death of 10th-century Slavic evangelist St. Vojtěch. He conferred the saint's name on the cathedral along with St. Vitus's, but officially the Czech state calls it just St. Vitus.

Built over various phases beginning in A.D. 926 as the court church of the Premyslid princes, the cathedral has long been the center of Prague's religious and political life. The key part of its Gothic construction took place in the 14th century under the direction of Mathias of Arras and Peter Parléř of Gmuend. In the 18th and 19th centuries, subsequent baroque and neo-Gothic additions were made. The **Golden Portal** entrance from the third courtyard is no longer used; however, take a look above the arch. The 1370 mosaic *The Last Judgment* has been painstakingly restored with the help of computer-aided imagery provided by American art researchers.

As you enter the cathedral through the back entrance into the main aisle, you may be dazzled by the colored light seeping through the intricate **stained-glass windows** that rise to the Gothic ceiling above the high altar. The center windows, restored in the 2 years after World War II, depict the Holy Trinity, with the Virgin Mary to the left and St. Wenceslas kneeling to the right.

Of the massive Gothic cathedral's 21 chapels, the ✪ **St. Wenceslas Chapel (Svatováclavská kaple)** stands out as one of Prague's few indoor sights that every visitor really must see. Located midway toward the high altar on the right, it's encrusted with hundreds of pieces of jasper and amethyst and decorated with paintings from the 14th to the 16th centuries. The chapel sits atop the grave site of Bohemia's patron saint, St. Wenceslas.

Just beyond this, the **Chapel of the Holy Rood (Kaple sv. Kříže)** leads to the entrance to the underground **royal crypt.** In the early 1900s, the crypt was reconstructed, and the remains of the kings and their relatives were replaced in new sarcophagi. The center sarcophagus is the final resting place of Charles IV, the favorite Bohemian king who died in 1378 and is the namesake of much of Prague. In the back row are Charles's four wives (all in one sarcophagus), and in front of them is George of Poděbrady, the last Bohemian king, who died in 1471.

CONTINUING THROUGH THE CASTLE COMPLEX

For more than 700 years, beginning in the 9th century, Bohemian kings and princes resided in the **Royal Palace (Královský palác),** located in the third courtyard of the castle grounds. Vaulted Vladislav Hall **(Vladislavský sál),** the interior's centerpiece, hosted coronations and is still used for special occasions of state. Here Václav Havel was inaugurated president. The adjacent Diet was where kings and queens met with their advisers and where the supreme court was held. From a window in the Ludwig Wing, where the Bohemia Chancellery met, the Second Defenestration took place (see the box "Beware an Open Window").

St. George's Basilica (Kostel sv. Jiří), adjacent to the Royal Palace, is Prague's oldest Romanesque structure, dating from the 10th century. It also houses Bohemia's

Beware an Open Window:
The Czech Tradition of Defenestration

About 600 years before Prague's popular uprising brought down Communism, the Czech people began a long tradition of what might be considered a unique form of political protest.

In 1402, Jan Hus, a lecturer from Prague University, became the leading voice in a growing condemnation of the Catholic Church. From a pulpit in Old Town's Bethlehem Chapel (later destroyed but reconstructed in the 1950s), Hus gained popular support for his claims that the omnipotent power of the mostly German-dominated clergy had to be bridled. In 1414, he was invited to the Catholic ecclesiastical Council of Konstanz to explain his beliefs. Though the emperor had promised Hus safe conduct, on arriving he was promptly arrested, and a year later he was burned at the stake. The Protestant Hussite supporters declared him a martyr and rallied their calls for change around his death.

On July 30, 1419, a group of radical Hussites stormed the New Town Hall on Charles Square and demanded the release of other arrested pro-reform Hussites. After town councilors rejected the demand, the Hussites tossed them out of third-story windows, killing several. This became known as the First Defenestration, from the Latin for "out of the window." The incident sparked a 15-year battle known as the Hussite Wars, which ended in the defeat of the radical Protestants in 1434.

By the 17th century, the Austrian Catholics who came to power in Prague tolerated little dissent, but the Protestant Czechs continued to become more wealthy and began criticizing the Habsburg monarchy. This bubbled over again on May 23, 1618, when a group of Protestant nobles entered Prague Castle, seized two pro-Habsburg Czechs and their secretary, and tossed them out of the eastern window of the rear room of the Chancellery—the Second Defenestration. In the Garden on the Ramparts below the Ludwig Wing, two obelisks mark where they landed. This act led, in part, to the conflict known as the Thirty Years' War, which ended again in victory in 1648 for the Catholics. The Habsburgs remained in power for another 270 years, ruling over Prague as a provincial capital until the democratic Czechoslovak state was born.

Though Prague's 1989 overthrow of the totalitarian Communist regime gained the name the Velvet Revolution for its nonviolent nature, scattered calls for another defenestration (some serious, some joking) were heard. Contemporary Czech politicians surely know to keep away from open windows.

first convent. No longer serving a religious function, the convent contains a gallery of Gothic Czech art (see "Museums & Galleries," below) that you should see on a separate visit, if you have the time.

Inside the sparse and eerie basilica you will find relics of the castle's history along with a genealogy of those who have passed through it. If you look carefully at the outer towers, you'll notice that they're slightly different from each other. They have an Adam and Eve motif: The wider south tower represents Adam, while the narrower north tower is Eve.

Golden Lane (Zlatá ulička) is a picturesque street of tiny 16th-century houses built into the castle fortifications. Once home to castle sharpshooters, the houses now

---

A Bridge Tale

Why has Charles Bridge stood for so long? One great yarn that has lived through the ages states that when the lovingly cut stones were being laid, the master builders mixed eggs into the mortar to strengthen the bond. One enterprising village, trying to impress the king, seemed to miss the point and sent carts full of hard-boiled eggs to the capital.

---

contain small shops, galleries, and refreshment bars. In 1917, Franz Kafka is said to have lived briefly at no. 22; however, the debate continues as to whether Kafka actually took up residence or just worked in a small office there.

The **Prague Castle Picture Gallery (Obrazárna Pražského hradu)** displays European and Bohemian masterpieces, but few are from the original Imperial collection, which was virtually destroyed during the Thirty Years' War. Of the works that have survived from the days of Emperors Rudolf II and Ferdinand III, the most celebrated is Hans von Aachen's *Portrait of a Girl* (1605–10), depicting the artist's daughter.

The **Powder Tower (Prašná věž a.k.a. Mihulka)** forms part of the northern bastion of the castle complex just off the Golden Lane. Originally a gunpowder storehouse and a cannon tower, it was turned into a laboratory for the 17th-century alchemists serving the court of Emperor Rudolf II.

CROSSING THE VLTAVA: CHARLES BRIDGE

Dating from the 14th century, ✪ **Charles Bridge (Karlův most),** Prague's most celebrated structure, links Prague Castle to Staré Město. For most of its 600 years, the 1,700-foot-long span has been a pedestrian promenade, though for centuries walkers had to share the concourse with horse-drawn vehicles and trolleys. Today, the bridge is filled with folks walking among folksy artists and busking musicians.

The best times to stroll across the bridge are in early morning or around sunset, when the crowds have thinned and the shadows are more mysterious. The 30 statues lining the bridge are explained in detail in chapter 7's "Walking Tour 1."

---

2 Other Top Sights

HRADČANY

Loreto Palace (Loreta). Loretánské nám. 7, Praha 1. ☎ **02/2051 6740.** Admission 80Kč ($2.35) adults, 60Kč ($1.76) students. Tues–Sun 9am–12:15pm and 1–4:30pm. Tram: 22 or 23 from Malostranská.

Loreto Palace was named after the town of Loreto, Italy, where the dwelling of the Virgin Mary was said to have been brought by angels from Palestine in the 13th century. After the Roman Catholics defeated the Protestant Bohemians in 1620, the Loreto faction was chosen as the device for a re-Catholicization of Bohemia. The Loreto legend holds that a cottage in which the Virgin Mary lived had been miraculously transferred from Nazareth to Loreto, an Italian city near Ancona. The Loreto Palace is thought to be an imitation of this cottage, and more than 50 copies have been constructed throughout the Czech lands.

The Loreto's facade is decorated with 18th-century statues of the writers of the Gospel—Matthew, Mark, Luke, and John—along with a lone female, St. Anne, mother of the Virgin Mary. Inside the **Church of the Nativity** are fully clothed remains of two Spanish saints, St. Felicissimus and St. Marcia. The wax masks on the skeletons' faces are particularly macabre.

Inside the **Chapel of Our Lady of Sorrows** is a painting of a bearded woman hanging on a cross. This is St. Starosta, or Vilgefortis, who, after taking a vow of virginity, was forced to marry the king of Sicily. It's said that God, taking pity on the woman, gave her facial hair to make her undesirable, after which her pagan father had her crucified. Thus, Starosta went into history as the saint of unhappily married women. The painting was created in the 1700s. Also on display is a portrait of St. Apolena (or Appollonia), a 3rd-century deacon who had her teeth knocked out as part of a torture for refusing to renounce Christianity. She's often represented in art by a gold tooth or pincer. As the patron saint of dentists, Apolena is sometimes referred to as the "saint of toothaches."

✪ **Strahov Monastery and Library (Strahovský klášter).** Strahovské nádvoří 1, Praha 1. ☎ **02/2051 6671.** Admission 40Kč ($1.17) adults, 20Kč (58¢) students. Tues–Sun 9am–noon and 1–5pm. Tram: 22 or 23 from Malostranská metro station.

The second oldest monastery in Prague, Strahov was founded high above Malá Strana in 1143 by Vladislav II. It's still home to Premonstratensian monks, a scholarly order closely related to the Jesuits, and their dormitories and refectory are off-limits. What draws visitors are the monastery's ornate libraries, holding more than 125,000 volumes. Over the centuries, the monks have assembled one of the world's best collections of philosophical and theological texts, including illuminated manuscripts and first editions.

The ceiling of the 1679 **Theological Hall** is a stunning example of baroque opulence, with intricate leafing blanketing the walls and framing the 18th-century ceiling frescoes. The rich wood-accented **Philosophical Library's** 46-foot-high ceiling is decorated with a 1794 fresco entitled *The Struggle of Mankind to Know Real Wisdom,* by A. F. Maulpertsch, a Viennese master of rococo. Intricate woodwork frames the immense collection of books. Ancient printing presses downstairs are also worth visiting, as are several altars and the remains of St. Norbert, a 10th-century German-born saint who founded the Premonstratensian order. His bones were brought here in 1627, when he became one of Bohemia's 10 patron saints. Paths leading through the monastery grounds take you to a breathtaking overlook of the city.

MALÁ STRANA (LESSER TOWN)

✪ **Church of St. Nicholas (Kostel sv. Mikuláše).** Malostranské nám. 1, Praha 1. ☎ **02/232 2589.** Free admission. Open Tue–Sun 10am–5pm, concerts are usually held at 5pm. Free admission. Metro: Line A to Malostranská.

This church is one of the best examples of high baroque north of the Alps. However, K. I. Dienzenhofer's 1711 design didn't have the massive dome that now dominates the Lesser Town skyline below Prague Castle. Dienzenhofer's son, Kryštof, added the 260-foot-high dome during additional work completed in 1752. Smog has played havoc with the exterior, yet the gilded interior is stunning. Gold-capped marble-veneered columns frame altars packed with statuary and frescoes. A giant statue of the church's namesake looks down from the high altar.

STARÉ MĚSTO (OLD TOWN)

Estates' Theater (Stavovské divadlo). Ovocný trh 1, Praha 1. ☎ **02/2490 1487.** Metro: Line A or B to Můstek.

Completed in 1783 by wealthy Count F. A. Nostitz, the neoclassical theater became an early symbol of the emerging high Czech culture—with the Greek theme *Patriae et Musis* (the Fatherland and Music) etched above its front columns. In 1799, the wealthy land barons who formed fiefdoms known as The Estates gave the theater its current name.

Prague Attractions

Československé armády
Pod kaštany
HRADČANSKÁ M
Badeniho
Milady Horákové
Mariánské hradby
Chotkovy Sady
Jelení
Chotkova
Keplerova
Nový Svět
HRADČANY
U Brusnice
U Kasáren
Loretánské nám.
Loretánská
MALOSTRANSKÁ
MALÁ STRANA
Úvoz
Nerudova
Lobkovická Zahrada
Strahovská Zahrada
Karmelitská
Malostr. nábřeží
Strahovská
Seminářská Zahrada
Olympijská Spartakiádní Stadion
Chaloupeckého
Petřínské Sady
Funicular
Střelecký Ostrov
Jezdecká
Kinského Zahrada
Janáčkovo nábřeží
Peškově
V botanice
Holečkova
Zborovská
Kartouzská
Plzeňská
Duškova
Mozartova
ANDĚL M
Svornosti
Radlická
Ostrovského
SMÍCHOV

LEGEND

Metro — M —

0 _____ 1/4 Mi
0 _____ .25 Km

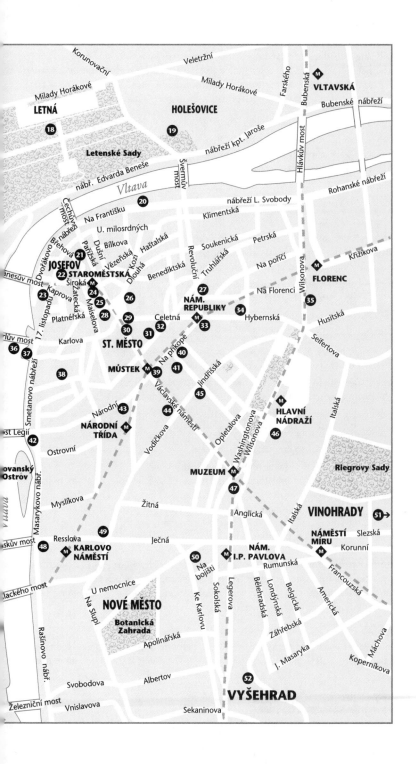

Wolfgang Amadeus Mozart staged the premier of *Don Giovanni* here in 1787 because he said that Vienna's conservative patrons didn't appreciate him or his passionate and sometimes shocking work. They also wanted mostly German opera, but Praguers were happy to stage the performance in Italian. "Praguers understand me," Mozart was quoted as saying.

In 1834, Czech playwright J. K. Tyl staged a comedy called *Fidlovačka,* in which the patriotic song "Kde domov můj?" ("Where Is My Home?") was a standout. It later became the Czech national anthem. In the heady days at the end of World War II in 1945, the Estates' Theater was renamed Tyl Theater, but, when a total reconstruction of the building was completed in 1991, its previous name was reinstated.

Czech director Miloš Forman returned to his native country to film his Oscar-winning *Amadeus,* shooting the scenes of Mozart in Prague with perfect authenticity at the Estates' Theater.

The theater doesn't offer daily tours, but tickets for performances—and the chance to sit in one of the many elegant private boxes—are usually available. Tour events are occasionally scheduled, and individual tours for this and other major monuments can be arranged through the city heritage group **Pražská vlastivěda** (☎ **02/231 1127**). Scheduled tours cost 30Kč (88¢), 20Kč (59¢) for students, plus a 30Kč (88¢) admission cost.

Old Town Hall (Staroměstská radnice) and Astronomical Clock (orloj). Staroměstské náměstí, Praha 1. ☎ **02/2422 8456.** Town Hall tower, 30Kč (88¢) adults; 20Kč (56¢) students, children under 10, and pensioners. Apr–Oct, Mon 11am–6pm, Tues–Sun 9am–6pm; Nov–Mar, Mon 11am–5pm, Tues–Sun 9am–5pm. Metro: Line A to Staroměstská.

Crowds congregate in front of Old Town Hall's Astronomical Clock (*orloj*) to watch the glockenspiel spectacle that occurs hourly from 8am to 8pm. Built in 1410, the clock has long been an important symbol of Prague. According to legend, after the timepiece was remodeled at the end of the 15th century, clock artist Master Hanuš was blinded by the Municipal Council so that he couldn't repeat his fine work elsewhere. In retribution, Hanuš threw himself into the clock mechanism and promptly died. The clock remained out of kilter for almost a century.

It's not possible to determine the time of day from this timepiece; you have to look at the clock on the very top of Old Town Hall's tower for that. This astronomical clock, with all its hands and markings, is meant to mark the phases of the moon, the equinoxes, the season and day, and numerous Christian holidays.

When the clock strikes the hour, a kind of politically incorrect medieval morality play begins. Two doors slide open and the statues of the 12 Apostles glide by, while the 15th-century conception of the "evils" of life—a Death skeleton, a preening Vanity, a corrupt Turk, and an acquisitive Jew—shake and dance below. At the end of World War II, the horns and beard were removed from the moneybag-holding Jew, who's now politely referred to as Greed.

JOSEFOV

Within Josefov, you'll find a community that for centuries was forced to fend for itself, until the horrific purges under Nazi occupation in World War II. Although more than

---

A View with a Warning

It's worth climbing Town Hall's tower for an excellent view over the red rooftops of Staroměstské náměstí and the surrounding area. But be warned: The steps are narrow and steep and quite physically demanding.

The Art of Getting Lost

Prague is popular—too popular, really—and you can find yourself in the middle of a special moment only to have it punctured by an umbrella or the loud voice of a tour guide from Ohio. So my advice to visitors trying to get a peek into the real life of Czechs is simple: Get lost. Get really, really lost.

You won't stray too far, since "tourist Prague" encompasses a relatively small area. And you know the landmarks: the castle, the bridge, the river, Old Town Square. So leave the map behind.

My favorite times to get lost in Prague were early morning and late at night. One foggy morning, I woke up early, grabbed a coffee in the breakfast room of my Communist-era hotel, and headed out. I'm not sure which direction I went—left, I think. I strolled several blocks into unfamiliar territory. I found a wonderful bookshop where I picked up a Czech version of Maurice Sendak's *Where the Wild Things Are*. Then I ducked into an old camera shop in search of film. The shop carried not only the latest German and Japanese cameras but also fascinating, old Eastern European cameras that looked to my American eyes like some discarded cosmonaut space garbage. Next, I discovered a little hut of a church that was dark and wonderful; two old Czech women dusted while I looked around. I'd love to tell you where these memorable places were, but you see, I was lost.

Another great way to get lost is to hop on a tram and let the driver take you where he's going. Get off when you see an intriguing neighborhood, if you're hungry, or if you have to go to the bathroom. Or, if you're adventurous, follow someone. For 40 minutes I trailed an old woman doing her shopping. Wow, did she get me lost! I followed her into a local food shop, not one of the big chains filled with processed foods and produce from Germany, but a little "czecha" shop. I bought some candy, which I still have—for me candy is the best kind of souvenir.

Late in the evening, as you wander aimlessly through Old Town, you'll half expect to see ghosts darting about. The lanterns along the uneven cobblestone streets don't really help you navigate; instead, I'm convinced that their function is to set a mysterious, quiet mood. That peacefulness is occasionally interrupted by the sounds of late-night revelers. You may be tempted to join them for a *pivo* (beer).

Roaming the streets of Prague is like unraveling a big ball of twine. When you get lost, you're likely to find something special, some experience that will make you feel "of" the place, rather than just passing through.

So remember where you are. Then get lost.

—by Bill Boedeker

118,000 Jews were recorded as living in the Czech lands of Bohemia and Moravia in 1939, only 30,000 survived to see the end of the Nazi occupation. Today, the Jewish community in the entire country numbers about 3,000 people, most of whom live in Prague.

Josefov's synagogues have been lovingly regarded as monuments to the survival of Judaism in central Europe, and the Old Jewish Cemetery, with generations buried upon one another, is an odd relic of the cohesion of Prague's ghetto. Prague's Jewish Quarter is described in detail in "Walking Tour 4" in chapter 7.

Prague's Most Powerful Daughter:
The Rise & Surprise of Madeleine Albright

Marie Jana Koerbelová took an unlikely path to becoming the most powerful woman in the world. Born in Prague in 1937, she first learned about the horrors of politics gone wrong at an early age, in 1938 when her diplomat father, Josef Koerbel, fled with the family to London as Hitler invaded Czechoslovakia.

After the war, the family moved to Belgrade, as Josef was appointed Czechoslovak ambassador to Yugoslavia (he also served as a delegate at the founding of the United Nations). The girl was sent to boarding school in Switzerland, where she learned to speak French. Prague's 1948 Communist coup turned the family into refugees again, for Josef feared that his pro-democracy credentials meant that he'd be singled out in the impending totalitarian purges. Eventually the family received asylum in the United States. At age 11, the girl, renamed Madeleine Korbel for American ears, began a new life in Colorado, where her father took a teaching position at the University of Denver.

Her father's fierce devotion to democracy and his interest in world politics influenced Madeleine tremendously, by her own account. After her marriage to New York newspaper scion Joseph Albright (whom she later divorced), Madeleine Albright began to study and forge a career in foreign policy while raising three daughters. Her writings and teachings often focused on the land of her birth and the horrors it had suffered.

After becoming an immensely popular professor at Georgetown University and advising Czech President Havel following the Velvet Revolution, she was picked by U.S. President Clinton as ambassador to the United Nations.

On her first official visit to Prague as ambassador in 1994, she walked into the palatial foreign ministry where her father had once worked. "This is a really

The **Jewish Museum in Prague** (www.jewishmuseum.cz) is the name of the organization managing all the Jewish landmarks in Josefov. It provides guided package tours as part of a comprehensive admission price, with an English-speaking guide. The package includes the Ceremonial Hall, Old Jewish Cemetery, Old-New Synagogue, Pinkas Synagogue, Klaus Synagogue, Maisel Synagogue, and Spanish Synagogue. From April to October, tours leave on the hour starting at 9am with the last tour at 4pm, but there must be at least 10 people in a group. Off-season, the tours leave whenever enough people gather in the same language. The package costs 480Kč ($14.11) for adults and 340Kč ($10) for students.

The Maisel Synagogue now serves as the exhibition space for the **Jewish Museum.** In October 1994, the State Jewish Museum closed; the Torah covers, 100,000 books, and other exhibits once housed there were given to the Jewish community, who then proceeded to return many items to synagogues throughout the country. Much of Prague's ancient Judaica was destroyed by the Nazis during World War II. Ironically, those same Germans constructed an "exotic museum of an extinct race," thus salvaging thousands of objects, such as the valued Torah covers, books, and silver now displayed at the Maisel Synagogue.

✪ **Old Jewish Cemetery (Starý židovský hřbitov).** U Starého hřbitova. ☎ **02/ 2481 0099.** Admission 280Kč ($8.24) adults, 200Kč ($5.84) students. Sun–Fri 9am–6pm. Metro: Line A to Staroměstská.

emotional moment for me," she said to journalists as she entered Černín Palace, fighting back tears. She has since played tour guide for the Clintons in Prague and has dazzled Czechs with her native language, albeit frozen in a girlish tone and vocabulary.

In early 1997, Ambassador Albright became Secretary of State Albright, the first woman ever to serve in such a high government post. "Nothing compares to the feeling of coming to my original home, Prague, as Secretary of State of the United States, for the purpose of saying to you 'Welcome Home,'" she said in both languages in an emotional 1997 speech celebrating the country's invitation to join NATO.

Raised a Catholic, she said she discovered only in early 1997 that her parents hid their Jewish heritage during the war and never told their children of their true background. During that 1997 trip, Albright visited the Pinkas Synagogue, where the names of her paternal grandparents are inscribed on the wall, alongside the thousands of Czech Jews who died in the Holocaust.

Albright's remaining link to Prague is the house U labutí ("At the Swans"), tucked in the corner at 11 Hradčanské náměstí adjacent to the castle, where she lived as a small girl.

Just before his 1977 death, Albright's father had foreshadowed 1989's revolutionary events when he wrote this as the last paragraph of his final book, *Twentieth Century Czechoslovakia*: "The spark is still there. One cannot doubt that it will flicker one day again into flame, and freedom will return to this land that is so essentially humane."

One of Europe's oldest Jewish burial grounds, just 1 block from the Old-New Synagogue, dates from the mid–15th century. Because the local government of the time didn't allow Jews to bury their dead elsewhere, graves were dug deep enough to hold 12 bodies vertically, with each tombstone placed in front of the last. The result is one of the world's most crowded cemeteries: a 1-block area filled with more than 20,000 graves. Among the most famous persons buried here are the celebrated Rabbi Loew (Löw) (d. 1609), who created the legend of Golem (a giant clay "monster" to protect Prague's Jews), and banker Markus Mordechai Maisel (d. 1601), then the richest man in Prague and protector of the city's Jewish community during the reign of Rudolf II.

✪ **Old-New Synagogue (Staronová synagóga).** Červená 2. ☎ **02/2481 0099.** Admission 200Kč ($5.88) adults, 140Kč ($4.11) students. Sun–Thurs 9am–6pm, Fri 9am–5pm. Metro: Line A to Staroměstská.

First called the New Synagogue to distinguish it from an even older one that no longer exists, the Old-New Synagogue, built around 1270, is Europe's oldest remaining Jewish house of worship. The faithful have prayed here continuously for more than 700 years, carrying on even after a massive 1389 pogrom in Josefov that killed over 3,000 Jews. It was interrupted only between 1941 and 1945 because of the Nazi occupation. The synagogue is also one of Prague's great Gothic buildings, built with vaulted ceilings, retro-fitted with Renaissance-era columns.

ELSEWHERE IN PRAGUE

✪ **Vyšehrad.** Soběslavova 1, Praha 2. ☎ **02/296 651.** Tram: 3 or 17 from Karlovo náměstí to Výtoň south of New Town.

This sprawling rocky hilltop complex is the cradle of the Bohemian state. From this spot, legend has it, Princess Libuše looked out over the Vltava valley toward present-day Prague Castle and predicted the founding of a great kingdom and capital city. Vyšehrad was the first seat of the first Czech kings in the Premyslid dynasty before the dawn of the 20th century.

This was also the first Royal Route. Before the kings could take their seat at the more modern Prague Castle, they first had to pay homage to their predecessors on Vyšehrad and then follow the route to Hradčany for the coronation.

Today, the fortifications remain on the rocky cliffs, blocking out the increasing noise and confusion below. Within the confines of the citadel, lush lawns and gardens are crisscrossed by dozens of paths leading to historic buildings and cemeteries. Vyšehrad is still somewhat of a hidden treasure for picnics and romantic walks, and from here you'll see one of the most panoramic views of the city. You can see all four corners of Prague from up here.

Vyšehrad Cemetery (Vyšehradský hřbitov) is the national cemetery within the ancient citadel on the east side of the Vltava. It's the final resting place of some 600 honored Czechs, including composers Antonín Dvořák and Bedřich Smetana and art nouveau painter Alfons Mucha. The complex of churches and gardens is a pleasant getaway from the city crush.

3 Museums & Galleries

Many fine private art galleries showing contemporary work by Czech and other artists are in central Prague, within walking distance of Staroměstské náměstí. Although their primary interest is sales, most welcome browsing. See chapter 8 for information on the city's top art galleries.

As for public museums and galleries, note that many museums are closed on Monday.

NATIONAL GALLERY SITES

The national collection of fine art is grouped for display in the series of venues known collectively as the **National Gallery (Národní Galerie).** Remember this term refers to several locations, not just one gallery.

The most extensive collection of classic European works spanning the 14th to 18th centuries is found at the Archbishop's Palace complex in the **Šternberský palác** across from the main gate to Prague Castle.

Veletržní Palace houses most of the 20th-century art collection, and now also shows the important national revival works from Czech artists of the 19th century. Much of the rest of the national collection is divided between Kinský Palace on Old Town Square and the Gothic collection at St. Agnes Convent near the river in Old Town.

The key Prague sites within the national gallery system are listed below.

HRADČANY

St. Agnes Convent (Klášter sv. Anežky České). U milosrdných 17, Praha 1. ☎ **02/ 2481 0628.** www.ng-ssu.cz. Admission 90Kč ($2.64) adults, 50Kč ($1.47) children. Tues–Sun 10am–6pm. Metro: Line A to Staroměstská.

A complex of early-Gothic buildings and churches dating from the 13th century, the convent, tucked in a corner of Staré Město, was to begin exhibiting much of the

National Gallery's collection of Gothic art in 2000. Once home to the Order of the Poor Clares, it was established in 1234 by St. Agnes of Bohemia, sister of Wenceslas I. The Blessed Agnes became St. Agnes when Pope John Paul II paid his first visit to Prague in 1990 for her canonization. The convent was long home to the National Gallery's collection of 19th- and 20th-century Czech art, but in 1999, the director of the National Gallery decided to move these Czech works from St. Agnes to the modern-art bastion of **Veletržní Palace.**

The museum contains many bronze studies that preceded the casting of some of the city's greatest public monuments, including the equestrian statue of St. Wenceslas atop the National Theater. Downstairs, a Children's Workshop offers hands-on art activities, most of which incorporate religious themes. The grounds surrounding the convent are pretty nice, too. The convent is at the end of Anežka, off of Haštalské náměstí.

St. George's Convent at Prague Castle (Klášter sv. Jiří na Pražském hradě). Jiřské nám. 33. ☎ **02/5732 0536.** www.ng-ssu.cz. Admission 90Kč ($2.64) adults, 50Kč ($1.47) students. Tues–Sun 10am–6pm. Metro: Line A to Malostranská or Hradčanská.

Dedicated to displaying traditional Czech art, the castle convent is especially packed with Gothic and baroque Bohemian iconography as well as portraits of patron saints. The most famous among the unique collection of Czech Gothic panel paintings are those by the Master of the Hohenfurth Altarpiece and the Master Theodoricus. The collections are arranged into special exhibits usually revolving around a specific place, person, or historical time.

○ **Šternberk Palace (Šternberský palác).** Hradčanské nám. 15, Praha 1. ☎ **02/2051 4599.** www.ng-ssu.cz. Admission 90Kč ($2.64) adults, 50Kč ($1.47) students and children. Tues–Sun 10am–6pm. Metro: Line A to Malostranská or Hradčanská.

The jewel in the National Gallery crown (also known casually as the European Art Museum), the gallery at Šternberk Palace, adjacent to the main gate of Prague Castle, displays a wide menu of European art throughout the ages. It features 5 centuries of everything from Orthodox icons to Renaissance oils by Dutch masters. Pieces by Rembrandt, El Greco, Goya, and van Dyck are mixed among numerous pieces from Austrian imperial court painters. Exhibits such as Italian Renaissance bronzes rotate throughout the seasons.

STARÉ MĚSTO (OLD TOWN)

○ **Kinský Palace (Palác Kinských).** Staroměstské náměstí, Praha 1. ☎ **02/2481 0758.** At this writing, the Kinský is scheduled to reopen in spring 2000 after a massive renovation. Metro: Line A to Staroměstská.

The rococo Palace houses graphic works from the National Gallery collection, including pieces by Georges Braque, André Derain, and other modern masters. Pablo Picasso's 1907 *Self-Portrait* is here and has virtually been adopted as the National Gallery's logo. Good-quality international exhibits have included Max Ernst and Rembrandt retrospectives, as well as shows on functional arts and crafts.

Veletržní Palace (National Gallery). Veletržní at Dukelských hrdinů 47, Praha 7. ☎ **02/2430 1111.** www.ngprague.cz. Admission 120Kč ($3.53) adults, 60Kč ($1.76) students; Thurs 6–9pm general admission 40Kč ($1.18). Tues–Sun 10am–6pm (Thurs to 9pm). Metro: Line C to Vltavská or tram 17.

This 1925 constructionist palace, built for trade fairs, was remodeled and reopened in December 1995 to hold the bulk of the National Gallery's collection of 20th-century works by Czech and other European artists. Three atrium-lit concourses provide a comfortable setting for some catchy and kitschy Czech sculpture and multimedia works. Alas, the best cubist works from Braque and Picasso, Rodin bronzes, and many other primarily French pieces have been relegated to the second floor. Other displays

> **❓ Did You Know?**
>
> - Charles University, central Europe's first postsecondary school, opened in Prague in 1348.
> - Albert Einstein was a professor of physics in Prague from 1911 to 1912.
> - The word *robot* was coined by Czech writer Karel Čapek and comes from a Slavic root meaning "to work."
> - Contact lenses were invented by a Czech scientist.
> - The word *dollar* came from the Tolar coins used during the Austrian empire; the coins were minted in the western Bohemian town of Jáchymov from silver mined nearby.

are devoted to peculiar works from Czech artists that demonstrate how creativity flowed even under the weight of the Iron Curtain. The first floor features temporary exhibits from traveling shows.

OTHER MUSEUMS & GALLERIES

HRADČANY

National Military History Museum (Vojenské Historické Muzeum). Schwarzenberg Palace, Hradčanské nám. 2, Praha 1. ☎ **02/2020 2023.** Admission 30Kč (88¢) adults, 15Kč (44¢) students. Apr–Sept, Tues–Thurs and Sat–Sun 10am–6pm. Metro: Line A to Malostranská or Hradčanská.

Adjacent to Prague Castle's main entrance and across from the Šternberk Palace Art Museum is the eye-catching Schwarzenberg Palace with its checkered parquet outer walls. Inside you'll find an extensive collection of ancient guns, ammunition, cannons, and military regalia from Bohemia and Europe. Uniforms, decorations, and explanations of major and minor battles from the first Bohemian armies to the founding of the Czechoslovak state in 1918 are on display.

STARÉ MĚSTO (OLD TOWN)

Bedřich Smetana Museum (Muzeum B. Smetany). Novotného lávka 1, Praha 1. ☎ **02/2422 9075.** Admission 40Kč ($1.17) adults, 20Kč (59¢) students and children. Wed–Mon 10am–5pm. Metro: Staroměstská. Tram: 17 or 18.

Opened in 1936 (in what was the former Old Town waterworks) and jutting into the Vltava next to Charles Bridge, this museum pays tribute to the deepest traditions of Czech classical music and its most patriotic composer, Bedřich Smetana. The exhibits show scores, diaries, manuscripts, and gifts presented to the composer while he was the preeminent man of Prague music in the mid–19th century. Concerts are held here, and you can buy tickets on site or at **Prague Information Service,** Na Příkopě 20, Praha 1 (☎ **187** in Prague or 02/264 022 outside Prague).

NOVÉ MĚSTO (NEW TOWN)

Alfons Mucha Museum (Muzeum A. Muchy). Panská 7, Praha 1. ☎ **02/628 4162.** E-mail: museum@mucha.cz. Admission 120Kč ($3.53). Daily 10am–6pm. Metro: Můstek.

This museum opened in early 1998 near Wenceslas Square to honor the high priest of art nouveau, Alphonse (Alfons in Czech) Mucha. Though the Moravian-born turn-of-the-20th-century master spent most of his creative years in Paris drawing luminaries like actress Sarah Bernhardt, Mucha's influence can still be seen throughout his home country. The new museum, around the corner from the Palace Hotel, combines examples of his graphic works, posters, and paintings and highlights his influence in jewelry, fashion, and advertising. Those who can remember the 1960s and 1970s will flash back to one of Mucha's most famous works, the sinuous goddess of Job rolling papers.

Dvořák Museum (Muzeum A. Dvořáka). Ke Karlovu 20, Praha 2. ☎ **02/298 214.** Admission 30Kč (88¢) adults, 15Kč (44¢) students and children. Tues–Sun 10am–5pm. Metro: Line C to I. P. Pavlova.

The favorite 19th-century Czech composer, Antonín Dvořák, lived here during the golden years of his life. Built in 1712, the two-story rococo building, tucked away on a Nové Město side street, was Dvořák's home for 24 years until his death in 1901. In the 18th century when the building was erected, this part of Prague was frontier land. Czechs willing to open businesses so far from the center were called "Americans" for their pioneer spirit. This building came to be known as America. Opened in 1932, the museum shows an extensive collection, including the composer's piano, spectacles, Cambridge cap and gown, photographs, and sculptures. Several rooms are furnished as they were around 1900. Upstairs, a small recital hall hosts chamber-music performances in high season, with concerts usually at 8pm. Tickets are 220Kč to 395Kč ($6.47 to $11.60). You can buy them on site or at **Prague Information Service,** Na Příkopě 20, Praha 1 (☎ **187** in Prague or 02/264 022 outside Prague).

National Museum (Národní muzeum). Václavské nám. 68, Praha 1. ☎ **02/2449 7111.** www.nm.cz. Admission 70Kč ($2.05) adults, 35Kč ($1.02) students; free for children under 6; free for everyone 1st Mon of each month. May–Sept, daily 10am–6pm; Oct–Apr, daily 9am–5pm; closed 1st Tues each month. Metro: Line A or C to Muzeum metro station.

The National Museum, dominating upper Václavské náměstí, looks so much like an important government building that it even fooled the Soviet soldiers, who fired on it during their 1968 invasion, thinking it was the seat of government. If you look closely on the columns you can still see shell marks. This grandiose statement of nationalist purpose opened in 1893, as the national revival gained momentum. The exterior is rimmed with names of the great and good of the fatherland (albeit with several foreign guests such as astronomer Johannes Kepler). Inside the grand hall on the first floor is the lapidarium with statues depicting the most important figures in Czech history, including the father of the republic, Tomaš Masaryk. Also on the first floor is an exhaustive collection of minerals, rocks, and meteorites from the Czech and Slovak Republics.

The other floor's exhibits depict the ancient history of the Czech lands through zoological and paleontological displays. Throughout the prehistory exhibit are cases of human bones, preserved in soil just as they were found. Nearby, a huge model of a woolly mammoth is mounted next to the bones of the real thing, and half a dozen rooms are packed with more stuffed-and-mounted animals than you could shake a spear at.

ELSEWHERE IN PRAGUE

✪ **Bertramka (W. A. Mozart Museum).** Mozartova 169, Praha 5. ☎ **02/543 893.** Admission 90Kč ($2.65) adults, 50Kč ($1.47) students. Daily 9:30am–6pm. Tram: 4, 6, 7, 9, 10, 14, or 16 from Anděl metro station.

Mozart loved Prague, and when he visited, the composer often stayed at this villa owned by the Dušek family. Now a museum, it contains displays of his written work and his harpsichord. There's also a lock of Mozart's hair, encased in a cube of glass. Much of the Bertramka villa was destroyed by fire in the 1870s, but Mozart's rooms, where he finished composing the opera *Don Giovanni,* have miraculously remained untouched. Chamber concerts are often held here, usually starting at 5pm. Tickets are

350Kč ($10.29) for adults and 230Kč ($6.76) for students, available on site or at **Prague Information Service,** Na Příkopě 20, Praha 1 (☎ **187** in Prague or 02/ 264 022 outside Prague).

✪ **Museum of the City of Prague (Muzeum hlavního města Prahy).** Na Poříčí 52, Praha 8. ☎ **02/2481 6772.** Admission 30Kč (88¢) adults, 15Kč (44¢) students; free for children under 6; free for everyone 1st Thurs each month. Tues–Sun 9am–6pm (to 8pm 1st Thurs each month). Metro: Line B or C to Florenc.

Not just another warehouse of history, where unearthed artifacts unwanted by others are chronologically stashed, this delightfully upbeat museum encompasses Prague's illustrious past with pleasant brevity. Sure, the museum holds the expected displays of medieval weaponry and shop signs, but the best exhibit in the Renaissance building is an intricate miniature model of 18th-century Prague. It's fascinating to see Staré Město as it used to be and the Jewish Quarter before its 19th-century face-lift. A reproduction of the original calendar face of the Old Town Hall astrological clock is also on display, as are a number of documents relating to Prague's Nazi occupation and the assassination of Nazi commander Reinhard Heydrich. The museum is 1 block north of the Florenc metro station.

National Technical Museum (Národní technické muzeum). Kostelní 42, Letná, Praha 7. ☎ **02/2039 9111.** Admission 50Kč ($1.47) adults, 20Kč (59¢) students. Tues–Sun 9am–5pm. Tram: 1, 8, 25, or 26 from Hradčanská metro to Letná Park.

The Czechs are justifiably proud of their long traditions in industry and technology. Before Communism, this was one of the world's most advanced industrialized countries. At the National Technical Museum it's clear why. The depository holds nearly one million articles, but it can show only about 40,000 at a time. The array of machines, vehicles, instruments, and design documents is displayed in awesome detail. You can see the harbingers of radio and TV technology, the development of mechanization, and the golden age of rail service during the Austrian monarchy, when velvet-lined cars were standard, only to be replaced by the frayed vinyl upholstery seen in much of today's Czech Rail.

4 Churches & Cemeteries

CHURCHES
STARÉ MĚSTO (OLD TOWN)

Bethlehem Chapel (Betlémská kaple). Betlémské nám. 4, Praha 1. Apr–Oct, daily 9am–6pm; Nov–Mar, daily 9am–5pm. Admission 30Kč (88¢) adults, 20Kč (59¢) students. Metro: Line B to Národní třída.

This is the site where, in the early 15th century, the firebrand Czech Protestant theologian Jan Hus raised the ire of the Catholic hierarchy with sermons critical of the establishment. He was burned at the stake as a heretic in 1415 at Konstanz in present-day Germany and became a martyr for the Czech Protestant and later nationalist cause. A memorial to Hus dominates the center of Old Town Square. The chapel was completed in 1394 and reconstructed in the early 1950s. In the main hall you can still see the original stone floors and the pulpit from where Hus preached; it's now used as a ceremonial hall for Czech national events.

Church of St. Nicholas (Kostel sv. Mikuláše). Old Town Square at Pařížská, Praha 1. Free admission, except for occasional concerts. Tues–Sun 10am–5pm. Metro: Line A to Staroměstská.

At the site of a former Gothic church begun by German merchants, this St. Nicholas church was designed in 1735 by the principal architect of Czech baroque,

K. I. Dienzenhofer. He's the same Dienzenhofer who designed Prague's other St. Nicholas Church, in Lesser Town (see above). This church isn't nearly as ornate as the other but has a more tumultuous history. The Catholic monastery was closed in 1787, and the church was handed over for use as a concert hall in 1865. The city's Russian Orthodox community began using it in 1871, but in 1920 management was handed to the Protestant Hussites. One notable piece inside is the 19th-century crystal chandelier with glass brought from the town of Harrachov. Concerts are still held here; for details, see the box "Classical Concerts Around Town" in chapter 9.

Týn Church or the Church of Our Lady Before Týn (Kostel paní Marie před Týnem). Staroměstské náměstí, Praha 1, entrance from Štupartská. Metro: Line A to Staroměstská. At this writing it is still impossible to see the interior due to a long, massive reconstruction.

Huge double square towers with multiple black steeples make this church the most distinctive standout of Old Town Square. The "Týn" was the fence marking the border of the central marketplace in the 13th century. The church's present configuration was completed mostly in the 1380s, and it became the main church of the Protestant Hussite movement in the 15th century (though the small Bethlehem Chapel in Old Town where Hus preached is the cradle of the Czech Protestant reformation). The original main entrance to the church is blocked from view when looking from Old Town Square because the Habsburg-backed patricians built in front of it with impunity. A massive reconstruction to fortify the aging church is nearing completion.

   Aside from the church's omnipresent lurch over the square and the peculiar way buildings were erected in front of it, it's well known as the final resting place of Danish astronomer Tycho de Brahe, who died in 1601 while serving in the court of Austrian Emperor Rudolf II. Brahe's tombstone bearing his effigy as an explorer of many worlds is behind the church's main pulpit. The brilliant floodlights washing over the front of the church at night cast a mystical glow over the whole of Old Town Square.

MALÁ STRANA (LESSER TOWN)

Church of Our Lady Victorious—Holy Child of Prague (Klášter Pražského jezulátka). Karmelitská 9, Praha 1. Fee for occasional concerts. Museum of the Infant Jesus 40Kč ($1.17) adults, 20Kč (59¢) students. Mon–Sat 9:30am–5:30pm, Sun 1–5:30pm. Metro: Line A to Malostranská.

This 1613 early baroque home of the Carmelite order is famous mostly throughout Italy and Latino countries for the wax statue of Jesus displayed on an altar in the right wing of the church. The Holy Child of Prague was presented to the Carmelites by the Habsburg patron Polyxena of Lobkowicz in 1628 and is revered as a valuable Catholic relic from Spain. Copies of the Bambino are sold frequently on the Lesser Town streets outside the church, angering some of the faithful.

CEMETERIES

New Jewish Cemetery (Nový židovský hřbitov). Jana Želivského street, Praha 10. Daily dawn–dusk. Metro: Line A to Želivského.

Though it's neither as visually captivating nor as historically important as Prague's Old Jewish Cemetery (see above), the ivy-enveloped New Jewish Cemetery is popular because writer Franz Kafka is buried here. To find his grave, when you first enter the cemetery, turn immediately to your right. Go along the wall about 300 feet and look down in the first row of graves. There you'll find Kafka's final resting place. If you don't have a yarmulke (skullcap), you must borrow one from the man in the small building at the entrance. He's quite happy to lend one, but don't forget to return it. If you only come to see Kafka, you'll find yourself staying longer; it's a soothing and fascinating place.

The Art of Prague's Architecture

Prague's long history, combined with the good fortune of having avoided heavy war damage, makes it wonderful for architecture lovers. Along with the standard must-see castles and palaces comes a bountiful mixture of styles and periods. Buildings and monuments from the Middle Ages to the present are interspersed with one another throughout the city.

The best examples of Romanesque architecture are parts of **Prague Castle,** including St. George's Basilica. In Staré Město you'll see the best examples of the 3-century-long Gothic period: the **Convent of St. Agnes,** Na Františku; the **Old-New Synagogue,** Pařížská třída; **Old Town Hall** and the **Astronomical Clock,** Staroměstské náměstí; **Powder Tower,** Celetná ulice; and **Charles Bridge.** A few Renaissance buildings still stand, including **Golden Lane, Malá Strana Town Hall,** and **Pinkas Synagogue (Široká ulice)** in Staré Město.

Many of Prague's best-known structures are pure baroque and rococo, enduring styles that reigned in the 17th and 18th centuries. Buildings on Staroměstské náměstí and Nerudova street date from this period, as does **St. Nicholas Church,** Malostranské náměstí, in Malá Strana, and the **Loreto Palace,** Loretánské náměstí, in Hradčany.

Renaissance styles made a comeback in the late 19th century. Two neo-Renaissance buildings in particular—the **National Theater,** Národní třída, and the **National Museum,** Václavské náměstí, both Praha 1—have endured and are among Prague's most identifiable landmarks.

An exciting addition to the architectural lineup is the painstakingly refurbished 1911 art nouveau **Municipal House (Obecní dům)** at náměstí Republiky, Praha 1. Every opulent ceiling, sinuous light fixture, curling banister, etched-glass window, and inlaid ceramic wall creates the astonishing atmosphere of hope and accomplishment from the turn of the 20th century. This is Prague's outstanding monument to itself. The music salon, Smetana Hall (home to the Prague Symphony), has a gorgeous atrium roof with stained-glass windows. After World War I, with independence won, the democratic Czechoslovak Republic was declared here by the first National Council (parliament) in 1918. You can arrange private guided tours by calling the building's directors at ☎ **02/2200 2100** well in advance. The city's information center is now located down a ramp from the ground-floor main entrance.

Olšanské Cemeteries (Olšanské hřbitovy). Vinohradská street, Praha 3. Daily dawn–dusk. Metro: Line A to Flora or Želivského.

Olšanské hřbitovy is the burial ground of some of the city's most prominent former residents, including the first Communist president, Klement Gottwald, and Jan Palach, who burned himself to death in protest of the 1968 Soviet invasion. Olšanské hřbitovy is just on the other side of Jana Želivského street from the New Jewish Cemetery.

5 Historic Buildings & Monuments

Education has always occupied an important place in Czech life. Professors at **Charles University**—the city's most prestigious and oldest university, founded in 1348—have been in the political and cultural vanguard, strongly influencing the everyday life of

Other excellent examples of whimsical art nouveau architecture are the **Hotel Evropa,** on Václavské náměstí, and the main rail station, **Hlavní nádraží,** on Wilsonova třída, both in Praha 1.

Prague's finest cubist design, the **House at the Black Mother of God (Dům U Černé Matky boží),** at Celetná and Ovocný trh in Old Town, is worth a look. The building is named for the statuette of the Virgin Mary on its well-restored exterior. It now houses a modern art gallery. You'll also find a full cubist neighborhood of buildings directly under Vyšehrad park near the right bank of the Vltava.

The city's most unappealing structures are the functional socialist designs built from 1960 until the end of Communism. Examples are the entrance and departure hall of **Hlavní nádraží,** Wilsonova třída, Praha 1; the **Máj department store** (now a British Tesco), Národní třída 26, Praha 1; and the **Kotva department store,** náměstí Republiky, Praha 1.

However, the absolute worst are the prefabricated apartment buildings (*paneláky*) reached by taking metro line C to Chodov or Háje, built in the 1970s, when buildings grew really huge and dense, each 20 or more stories tall. Today, half of Prague's residents live in paneláks, which rim the city.

One postrevolution development—the ✪ **Rašín Embankment Building,** Rašínovo nábřeží at Resslova, Praha 2—continues to fuel the debate about blending traditional architecture with progressive design. Known as the Dancing Building, the Prague headquarters of the Dutch insurance group ING opened in 1996.

Co-designed by Canadian-born Frank Gehry, who planned Paris's controversial American Center, this curved twist of concrete and steel has never before been tried in Europe or anywhere else. An abstract Fred Astaire, dusting off his white tie and tails, embraces an eight-story ball-gowned Ginger Rogers for a twirl above the Vltava. The staggered design of the windows gives the structure motion when seen from afar. The only way to get the full effect is from across the river. The kicker is that the building is made out of prefabricated concrete, proving that the Communist panelák apartment houses could have been made more imaginatively. President Havel used to live next door in a modest apartment in the neoclassical building owned by his family.

---

all citizens. During the last 50 years, the university has expanded into some of the city center's largest riverfront buildings, many of which are between Karlův most (Charles Bridge) and Čechův most (Čech's Bridge).

STARÉ MĚSTO (OLD TOWN)

Powder Tower (Prašná brána, literally Powder Gate). Náměstí Republiky, Praha 1. Metro: Line B to Náměstí Republiky.

Once part of Staré Město's system of fortifications, the Old Town Powder Tower (as opposed to the Powder Tower in Prague Castle) was built in 1475 as one of the walled city's major gateways. The 140-foot-tall tower marks the beginning of the Royal Route, the traditional three-fourths-mile-long route along which medieval Bohemian monarchs paraded on their way to being crowned in Prague Castle's St. Vitus Cathedral. It also was the east gate to the Old Town on the road to

Kutná Hora. The tower was acutely damaged during the Prussian invasion of Prague in 1737.

The present-day name comes from the 18th century, when the development of Nové Město rendered this protective tower obsolete; it was then used as a gunpowder storehouse. Early in the 20th century, the tower served as the daily meeting place of Franz Kafka and his writer friend Max Brod. On the tower's west side, facing Old Town, you'll see a statue of King Přemysl Otakar II, under which is a bawdy relief depicting a young woman slapping a man who's reaching under her skirt. The interior of the tower is open from 10am to 6pm, costing adults 30Kč (88¢) and students 20Kč (58¢). You'll see the remains of the original construction on the first floor above the ground.

NOVÉ MĚSTO (NEW TOWN)
Můstek Metro Station. Václavské náměstí, Praha 1. Metro: Line A or B.

It's not the metro station itself, which is 20 years old, that warrants an entry here. But descend to Můstek's lower escalators and you'll see the illuminated stone remains of what was once a bridge that connected the fortifications of Prague's Old and New Towns. In Czech, *můstek* means "little bridge," but the ancient span isn't the only medieval remains that modern excavators discovered. Metro workers had to be inoculated when they uncovered viable tuberculosis bacterium, which had lain here dormant, encased in horse excrement, since the Middle Ages.

Na Příkopě, the pedestrian street above Můstek metro station, literally translates as "on the moat," a reminder that the street was built on top of a river that separated the walls of Staré Město and Nové Město. In 1760, it was filled in. The street follows the line of the old fortifications all the way down to the Gothic Powder Tower at náměstí Republiky.

✪ **National Theater (Národní divadlo).** Národní třída 2, Praha 1. ☎ **02/2490 1448.** Metro: Line B to Národní třída.

Lavishly constructed in the late Renaissance style of northern Italy, the gold-crowned National Theater, overlooking the Vltava, is one of Prague's most recognizable landmarks. Completed in 1881, the theater was built to nurture the Czech National Revival Movement—a drive to replace the dominant German culture with home-grown Czech works. To finance construction, small collection boxes with signs FOR THE PROSPERITY OF A DIGNIFIED NATIONAL THEATER were installed in public places.

Almost immediately on completion, the building was wrecked by fire and rebuilt, opening in 1883 with the premiere of Bedřich Smetana's opera *Libuše*. The magnificent interior contains an allegorical sculpture about music and busts of Czech theatrical personalities created by some of the country's best-known artists. The motto *"Národ sobě"* ("A Nation to Itself") is written above the stage. Smetana conducted the theater's orchestra here until 1874, when deafness forced him to relinquish his post.

The theater doesn't have daily tours, but tickets for performances are usually available (see chapter 9) and tour events are occasionally scheduled. You can arrange individual tours through the city heritage group **Pražská vlastivěda** by calling ☎ **02/2481 6184.**

ELSEWHERE IN PRAGUE
Petřín Tower (Rozhledna). Atop Petřín Hill, Praha 1. Admission 30Kč (88¢) adults, 20Kč (59¢) students and children 6–15. Apr–Aug, daily 10am–7pm; Sept–Oct, daily 10am–6pm; Nov–Mar, Sat–Sun 10am–5pm. Tram: 12, 22, or 23 to Újezd, then ride the funicular to the top.

Modern Memorials

One of the city's most photographed attractions is the colorful graffiti-filled **Lennon Wall,** on Velkopřevorské náměstí. This quiet side street in Malá Strana's Kampa neighborhood near Charles Bridge is across from the French Embassy on the path leading from Kampa Park.

The wall is named after singer John Lennon, whose huge image is spray-painted on the wall's center. Following his 1980 death, Lennon became a hero of freedom, pacifism, and counterculture throughout Eastern Europe, and this monument was born. During Communist rule, the wall, with pro-democracy and other slogans, was regularly whitewashed, only to be repainted by the faithful. When the new democratically elected government was installed in 1989, it's said that the French ambassador, whose stately offices are directly across from the wall, phoned Prague's mayor and asked that the city refrain from interfering with the monument. Today young locals and visitors continue to flock here, paying homage with flowers and candles. Lennon's picture has been repainted, larger and more angelic. It is now surrounded by graffiti more ridiculous than political.

The 1989 revolution over Communism is modestly remembered at the **Národní Memorial,** Národní 16, under the arches, midway between Václavské náměstí and the National Theater. This marks the spot where hundreds of protesting college students were seriously beaten by riot police on the brutal, icy night of November 17, 1989.

Just 5 years later, only about 100 Czechs showed up to commemorate the fifth anniversary of the Velvet Revolution at the place that became the cradle of the rebellion. President Václav Havel laid flowers at the tiny monument, but all around him were examples of how things have changed. A shiny new red Ferrari, with Czech plates, streaked past the group and screeched to a halt about a block farther on. Throwing a blistering U-turn, it sped back. The driver, wearing designer sunglasses, stuck his head out to see that it was just a guy and some flowers. He disappointedly slid back into the car and peeled out back down Národní, as the police shook their heads and said in awe, "What a car."

On the 10th anniversary of the revolution, Havel invited the last "Cold Warriors"—leaders Bush, Thatcher, Kohl, and Gorbachev—to Prague for a walk down "Revolution Lane."

The street has itself become a monument to the country's new capitalism. Where armed police and dogs once lined up outside the rotting Máj department store, people now flock to find bargains at the British-owned Tesco. Fashion boutiques, a plastic surgeon's private office, and sparkling new branches of private banks take spots once occupied by such "businesses" as the Castro Grill at the Cuban Culture Center.

It all obscures a small bronze monument whose peace-sign hands recall the night when Czechoslovakia's bloodless revolution began.

A one-fifth-scale copy of Paris's Eiffel Tower, Prague's Petřín Tower was constructed out of recycled railway track for the 1891 Prague Exhibition. It functioned as the city's primary telecommunications tower until the space-age Emir Hoffman tower opened across town. Those who climb the 195 feet to the top are treated to striking views, particularly at night.

6 Historic Squares

The most celebrated square in the city, ✪ **Old Town Square (Staroměstské náměstí)** is surrounded by baroque buildings and packed with colorful craftspeople, cafes, and entertainers. In ancient days, the site was a major crossroads on central European merchant routes. In its center stands a memorial to Jan Hus, the 15th-century martyr who crusaded against Prague's German-dominated religious and political establishment. It was unveiled in 1915, on the 500th anniversary of Hus's execution, and the monument's most compelling features are the dark asymmetry and fluidity of the figures. Take metro line A to Staroměstská. The square and Staré Město are described in more detail in Walking Tour 3 in chapter 7.

Officially dedicated in 1990, **Jan Palach Square (náměstí Jana Palacha),** formerly known as Red Army Square, is named for a 21-year-old philosophy student who set himself on fire on the National Museum steps to protest the 1968 Communist invasion. An estimated 800,000 Praguers attended his funeral march from Staroměstské náměstí to Olšanské cemeteries (see above). To get to the square, take metro line A to Staroměstská at the Old Town foot of Mánesův Bridge. There is now a pleasant riverside park with benches. Charles University's philosophy department building is on this square; on the lower-left corner of the facade is a memorial to the martyred student: a replica of Palach's death mask.

One of the city's most historic squares, ✪ **Wenceslas Square (Václavské náměstí)** was formerly the horse market (Koňský trh). The once muddy swath between the buildings played host to the country's equine auctioneers. The top of the square, where the National Museum now stands, was the outer wall of the New Town fortifications, bordering the Royal Vineyards. Unfortunately, the city's busiest highway now cuts off the museum from the rest of the square it dominates. Trolleys streamed up and down the square until the early 1980s. Today the half-mile-long boulevard is lined with cinemas, shops, hotels, restaurants, casinos, and porn shops.

The square was given its present name in 1848. The giant equestrian statue of St. Wenceslas on horseback surrounded by four other saints, including his grandmother, St. Ludmila, and St. Adalbert, the 10th-century bishop of Prague, was completed in 1912 by prominent city planner J. V. Myslbek, for whom the new Myslbek shopping center on Na Příkopě was named. The statues' pedestal has become a popular platform for speakers. Actually, the square has thrice been the site of riots and revolutions—in 1848, 1968, and 1989. At the height of the Velvet Revolution, 250,000 to 300,000 Czechs filled the square during one demonstration. Take metro line A or B to Můstek.

Built by Charles IV in 1348, **Charles Square (Karlovo náměstí)** once functioned as Prague's primary cattle market. New Town's Town Hall (Novoměstská radnice), which stands on the eastern side, was the sight of Prague's First Defenestration—a violent protest sparking the Hussite Wars in the 15th century (see the box "Beware an Open Window," above). Today, Charles Square is a lazy park in the center of the city, crisscrossed by tram lines and surrounded by buildings and shops. Take metro line B to Karlovo náměstí.

7 Parks & Gardens

Havel's Market (Havelský trh), on Havelská ulice, a short street running perpendicular to the main route connecting Staroměstské náměstí with Václavské náměstí, is a great open-air place to shop for picnic supplies. Here you'll find seasonal home-grown fruits and vegetables at inexpensive prices. Vyšehrad (see above) is my family's favorite place for a picnic. The market is open Monday to Friday, 8am to 6pm.

HRADČANY

The ✪ **Royal Garden (Královská zahrada)** at Prague Castle, Praha 1, once the site of the sovereigns' vineyards, was founded in 1534. Dotted with lemon trees and sur-rounded by 16th-, 17th-, and 18th-century buildings, the park is consciously and con-servatively laid out with abundant shrubbery and fountains. Enter from U Prašného mostu street, north of the castle complex. It's open daily from 10am to 6pm.

The castle's ✪ **Garden on the Ramparts (Zahrada na Valech),** on the city-side hill below the castle, was reopened again in spring 1995 after being thoroughly refur-bished. Beyond beautifully groomed lawns and sparse shrubbery is a tranquil low-angle view of the castle above and the city below. Enter the garden from the south side of the castle complex, below Hradčanské náměstí. The park is open Tuesday to Sunday from 10am to 6pm.

MALÁ STRANA

Looming over Malá Strana, adjacent to Prague Castle, lush green **Petřín Hill (Petřínské sady)** is easily recognizable by the miniature replica of the Eiffel Tower that tops it (see above). Gardens and orchards bloom in spring and summer. Throughout the myriad monuments and churches are a mirror maze and an observatory (see above). The Hunger Wall, a decaying 21-foot-high stone wall that runs up through Petřín to the grounds of Prague Castle, was commissioned by Charles IV in the 1360s as a medieval welfare project designed to provide jobs for Prague's starving poor. Take tram 12, 22, or 23 to Újezd.

Near the foot of Charles Bridge in Malá Strana, **Kampa Park (Na Kampě)** was named by Spanish soldiers who set up camp here after the Roman Catholics won the Battle of White Mountain in 1620. The park as it is today wasn't formed until the Nazi occupation, when the private gardens of three noble families were joined. It's a fine place for an inner-city picnic, though the lawns are packed in high season.

Part of the excitement of **Waldstein (or Wallenstein) Gardens (Valdštejnská zahrada)** is its location, behind a 30-foot wall on the backstreets of Malá Strana. Inside, elegant gravel paths, dotted with classical bronze statues and gurgling foun-tains, fan out in every direction. Laid out in the 17th century, the baroque park was the garden of Gen. Albrecht Waldstein (or Wallenstein; 1581–1634), commander of the Roman Catholic armies during the Thirty Years' War. These gardens are the back-yards of Waldstein's Palace—Prague's largest—which replaced 23 houses, three gar-dens, and the municipal brick kiln. The gardens are open May to September, daily from 9am to 7pm.

ELSEWHERE IN PRAGUE

The plain above the western side of the Vltava north of Prague Castle is a densely tree-covered swath, maintained as a park since 1858. **Letná Park (Letenské sady)** provides many quiet spaces for a picnic, and a summer beer garden at the north end serves up brew with a view. The garden is connected to two restaurants in a 19th-century neo-Renaissance château (Letenský zámeček), where you can get a pub-style meal or formal dinner. Take tram 1, 8, 25, or 26 from Hradčanská metro station. Further north is the massive nature reserve **Stromovka** (metro: Nádraží Holešovice, then tram 5 or 17). Acres of densely tree-lined paths, mostly flat and paved, comprise a shaded set of corridors for long strolls, the best jogging, and even in-line skating.

My favorite inner-city getaway is ✪ **Vyšehrad Park** above the Vltava south of the city center. This 1,000-year-old citadel encloses a peaceful set of gardens, playgrounds, footpaths, and the national cemetery next to the twin-towered Church of Sts. Peter and Paul, reconstructed from 1885 to 1887. The park provides a fantastic wide-angle view of the whole city. Take metro line C to Vyšehrad or tram 3 or 17 to Výtoň. It is open at all times.

8 Especially for Kids

ON PETŘÍN HILL

Kids will enjoy the funicular ride to the top of Petřín Hill, capped by the **Petřín Tower,** a miniature replica of the Eiffel Tower. Once there, look for the **Labyrinth (Bludiště),** a mirror maze that you walk through. Like the tower replica, the Labyrinth was built for the 1891 Prague Exhibition, an expo that highlighted the beauty and accomplishments of Bohemia and Moravia.

Inside the Labyrinth is a gigantic painting/installation depicting the battle between Praguers and Swedes on the Charles Bridge in 1648, a commemoration of the fighting that ended the Thirty Years' War. In 1892, the building's other historic exhibits were replaced with mirrors, turning the Labyrinth into the fun house we know today. It's open April to August, daily from 10am to 6pm. Admission is 30Kč (88¢) for adults and 20Kč (59¢) for children.

Also in the park is the **Štefánik Observatory,** built in 1930 expressly for public stargazing through a 90-year-old telescope. Open in fall and winter, Tuesday to Friday from 7am to 9pm, Saturday and Sunday from 10am to noon, 2 to 6pm, and 7 to 9pm. In spring and summer it's open Tuesday to Friday 6 to 9pm, Saturday and Sunday 10am till noon and 2 to 9pm. Admission is 30Kč (88¢) for adults and 20Kč (59¢) for children.

The funicular departs from a small house in the park just above the middle of Újezd in Malá Strana; tram 12, 22, or 23 will take you to Újezd.

ELSEWHERE IN PRAGUE

Budding astronomers can try to catch the stars at the **Planetarium** in Stromovka Park (☎ **02/371 746**). There are shows daily under the dark dome, including one where highlighted constellations are set to music and another that displays that night's sky. The shows are in Czech, but the sky is still the same. To reach the planetarium, take tram 5, 12, or 17 to Výstaviště and walk through the park to your left about 350 yards. Admission is 30Kč (88¢) for the morning shows, 60 to 100Kč ($1.76 to $2.94) for the evening shows. It's open Monday to Thursday from 8am to noon and 1pm until the end of the last program, Saturday and Sunday from 9:30am to noon and 1pm until the end of the evening program.

In the Výstaviště fairgrounds adjacent to Stromovka park is ✪ **Křižík's Fountain (Křižíkova fontána).** A massive system of water spigots spout tall and delicate streams of color-lit water in a spectacular light show set to recorded classical and popular music. Small children are especially fascinated. There's also a small amusement park on the fairgrounds. The water/music program (☎ **02/2010 3280**) runs April to October from 7 to 11pm. Admission is 60 to 160Kč ($1.76 to $4.70) for different performances at 7, 8, and 9pm, sometimes 10pm also. Take tram 5, 12, or 17 to Výstaviště.

9 Sightseeing Options

BUS TOURS

Prague streets can often become gridlocked, making any tour by car or bus frustrating. But if you want to take a guided English-language bus tour, among the best are those given by **Prague sightseeing tours** (☎ 02/2481 2766). Its 3½-hour Grand City Tour leaves April to October, daily at 9:30am and 2pm (only 9:30am during winter), from the company's bus stop at náměstí Republiky. The tour is 560Kč ($16.47).

Better for the kids is the green, open-air, electric **Ekotour train** (an electric bus in the shape of a train) leaving usually hourly from behind the Jan Hus monument on Old Town Square. The 300Kč ($8.82) ticket for adults takes you for an hour around the tourist areas of Old Town and up the hill to Prague Castle, with a recorded narration in several languages. Children up to age 12 travel free with their parents.

CRUISE-SHIP TOURS

Tourist cruise ships are the only commercial vessels allowed to pass through the city. This is an enjoyable, low-impact way to view Prague.

Evropská vodní doprava (☎ 02/231 0208), with a four-ship fleet, offers the most interesting sightseeing excursions, from April to October. Several tours, including some serving usually decent inexpensive meals, disembark from Čechův most at the northern turn of the Vltava and sail past all the key riverside sights. A daily lunch tour with smorgasbord and traditional Czech music leaves at noon, travels to the south end of the city, and returns by 2pm. The price, including a meal, is 550Kč ($16.17). A 1-hour tour, without meal, sails to Charles Bridge and back, leaving at 10 and 11am and 2, 3, 4, and 5pm. It costs 200Kč ($5.88). A 2-hour tour, without the meal, leaves at 3pm and costs 350Kč ($10.29). A dinner cruise to the south end of town leaves at 7pm and returns by 10pm. The price, including a meal, is 650Kč ($19.11).

RENTING A ROWBOAT

Many people rent rowboats and paddleboats on the Vltava, which is free from commercial boat traffic. The remarkably romantic (if not sparkling clean) river slowly snakes through the middle of town and gleams beneath the city's spires.

Rent-A-Boat, on Slovanský ostrov (Slavic Island), is the only company at this writing that offers lanterns for evening jaunts. This is an extremely romantic time to row; the amber lights of the city flicker above you. The docks are at the bottom of the steps on the small island 2 blocks south of the National Theater; enter from just behind the National Theater. Rowboat rates are 40Kč ($1.17) per hour during daylight for up to four people or 80Kč ($2.35) with lanterns after dark. Paddleboats are 80Kč ($2.35) per hour. Boats are available March to October (possibly in November if it's pleasant) from 10am to 11pm, weather permitting.

Adjacent to Rent-A-Boat, **Půjčovna Romana Holana,** on Slovanský ostrov (Slavic Island), offers similar watercraft at cheaper rates, but only during the day. Rowboats cost 20Kč (58¢) per hour and paddleboats 30Kč (88¢) per hour. You can rent boats March to September from 10am to sunset, weather permitting.

WALKING TOURS

Sylvia Wittmann's tour company, **Wittmann Tours** (☎ 02/2481 2325), offers daily walks around Prague's compact Jewish Quarter. A thousand years of history are discussed during the 3-hour stroll. Tours led by an English-speaking guide depart Sunday to Friday from Pařížská 28 at 10:30am and 2pm. The tours include entrance fees to sights and cost 530Kč ($15.58) for adults and 400Kč ($11.76) for students. Wittmann Tours also offers a bus tour to the Terezín concentration camp costing 1,150Kč ($33.82) for adults and 850Kč ($25) for students. It leaves from the same spot on Pařížská daily at 10am. See chapter 10 for more on Terezín.

A Turn-of-the-Century Tram Ride

Prague has had a system of tram lines since horses used to pull cars in the mid–18th century. While the Communist-era tram cars aren't very attractive and the new futuristic designs are built for efficiency instead of charm, you'd have to go back to the really old days to have fun in a Prague tram . . . and you can, thanks to the **Historic Tram Tour (Elektrické dráhy DP),** Patočkova 4, Praha 6 (☎ and fax **02/312 3349**).

If you send a fax with details 1 day ahead, the city transport department will arrange a private tour using one of the turn-of-the-century wooden tram cars that actually traveled on regular lines through Prague. Up to 24 people can fit in one car, which sport wooden-planked floors, cast-iron conductors' levers, and the "ching-ching" of a proper tram bell.

It costs 2,940Kč ($86.47) per hour. Up to 60 people can fit into a double car for 3,780Kč ($111.17) per hour. You can also order a cold smorgasbord with coffee, beer, champagne, a waiter to serve, and an accordion player if you wish. You can choose the route the tram takes—the no. 22 route is best.

BY PLANE

The airport **Točná** (☎ **02/402 5406**) is organizing short charter sightseeing flights from a little airstrip on the edge of Prague. The day and time is negotiable, but you have to call 2 days ahead to set it up.

For example, an 18-minute flight above Karlštejn Castle and back costs 1,890Kč ($55.60) per person. The flights can carry up to three passengers.

To get to the airport, take the metro to Kačerov, then bus no. 205 to the last stop "Komořany," and walk 10 minutes through the forest.

10 Staying Active or Just Watching

ACTIVITIES

BIKING   Paul Radovský, of **Central European Adventure Tours,** Pod útesy 8, Praha 5 (☎ and fax **02/232 8879**), will rent touring bikes and arrange whatever transport you need for them. But the best biking is outside Prague, on the tertiary roads and paved paths in the provinces. Paul will suggest routes and provide maps. One-day biking around Karlštejn Castle with a guide costs 680Kč ($20). Call for an appointment.

GOLF   Czechs are rediscovering golf painfully on the new tournament-caliber course with a world-class view at the **Praha Karlštejn Golf Club,** 30 minutes south of Prague. For details and directions, see chapter 10. You can sharpen your game during cold weather at the **Erpet Golf Center,** Strakonická 510, Praha 5 (☎ **02/5732 1229**). Opened in 1994, the renovated innards of a Communist-era sports hall now has a tropical setting of driving platforms, with pitching and putting greens on Astroturf and interactive video simulators. It's open daily from 8am to 11pm. Take metro line B to Smíchovské nádraží. The price is 200Kč ($5.88) per hour, including the use of a well-equipped fitness center.

HEALTH & FITNESS CLUBS   On the 25th floor of the Corinthia Towers Hotel, Kongresová 1, Praha 4, the **Fitness Centrum** (☎ **02/6119 1326**) has weight machines, free weights, exercise bikes, step machines, a small pool, a sauna, and a solarium. The modern facility also offers tanning beds, squash courts, a whirlpool, and massages. It's open to nonguests. A 1-day pass is 500Kč ($14.70). Squash courts can be rented for 400Kč ($11.76) per hour. It's open Monday to Friday from 7am to 10pm and Saturday and Sunday from 9am to 10pm. Take metro line C to Vyšehrad. The **Erpet Golf Center** (Fitness Center), Strakonické 510, Praha 5 (☎ **02/5732 1229**), has modern fitness machines, free weights, electronic rowers, and treadmills. There's also a relaxation center, with a dry sauna and a whirlpool that's usually open to the public and is coed. Using the fitness and the relaxation center costs 200Kč ($5.88) per hour. It's open daily from 8am to 11pm. Take metro line B to Smíchovské nádraží.

JOGGING Prague's sometimes thick smog makes jogging more like smoking, but on clear days—and there are many in summer—the air is bearable. For the most scenic run, jog on the paths atop the **Vyšehrad** citadel; take tram 3 or 17 from Karlovo náměstí. The parks at Kampa and Letná are also good places to run. The paths crisscrossing Petřín Hill offer a challenging uphill route. The best no-traffic, long-distance runs—flat, long, and mostly tree-lined—are found at **Stromovka Park.**

If you want to run through central Prague, use as much of the traffic-restricted walking zones as you can. For an approximately 1½-mile circuit, start at Můstek at the end of Wenceslas Square, run down Na Příkopě through the Powder Tower (Prašná brána) to Celetná street all the way to Old Town Square and around the Hus monument, back to Železná street, past the Estates' Theater on to Rytířská street, and back to Můstek. This route is virtually free of cars, but your feet will be pounding the bricks. Try running in early morning or late evening before the crowds block your way.

SWIMMING Summer doesn't last long in Prague, and when it arrives, many city dwellers are only too happy to cool off in one of the city's many pools. In addition to the serious 25-meter pool at the Axa hotel and other hotel pools listed in chapter 5, there's the **Džbán Reservoir,** in the Šárka nature reserve, Prague 6. Džbán is fronted by a grassy "beach" that can—and often does—accommodate hundreds of bathers along with a special section for nude swimming and sunbathing. To reach Šárka, take tram 26 from the Dejvická metro station.

TENNIS You can play on the courts where Martina Navrátilová and Ivan Lendl trained. The **Czech Tennis Club** at Štvanice Island (☎ **02/232 4601**) offers daily court rental. In the mornings, rates are 300Kč ($8.82) per hour per court; in the afternoon, 500Kč ($14.70). It's best to make a reservation if the weather's nice.

SPECTATOR SPORTS

For information on games, tickets, and times for hockey and soccer games, check the *Prague Post* sports section.

ICE HOCKEY Although Czech stars, like Jaromír Jágr and Dominik Hašek, have left home to play in the NHL, Czech hockey still has a lot of up-and-comers. Prague's team **Sparta Praha** plays their national rivals from mid-September to April at **Sportovní hala,** Za elektrárnou 419, Praha 7 (☎ **02/872 7443**). Admission is 50Kč ($1.47). Take metro line C to Holešovice and then tram 5 or 17 to Výstaviště.

SOCCER **Sparta Praha,** the top local soccer team, has a fanatical following, and games draw rowdy crowds to **Letná Stadium,** Praha 7 (☎ **02/2057 0323**). Tickets for big matches often sell out long before game time, but seats are usually available up to the last moment for lesser matches. Game tickets are usually 60 to 140Kč ($1.76 to $4.11) for a domestic league game, 350 to 800Kč ($10.29 to $23.53) for an international match. Take metro line A to Hradčanská and then tram 1, 8, 25, or 26 to Stadium.

7

Strolling Around Prague

by John Mastrini & Hana Mastrini

Forget bus tours and taxis—walking is really the only way to explore Prague. Most of the oldest areas are walking zones, with motor traffic limited. It would be best to wear very comfortable, preferably flat, shoes. The crevasses between the bricks in the street have been known to eat stiletto heels. As we mentioned at the beginning of chapter 2, you should "train" yourself for all this walking before you leave home.

Below are recommended routes to take, but getting lost among the twisting narrow streets isn't so bad. Let the turns take you where they may, as they'll usually lead to something memorable.

Walking Tour 1— Charles Bridge & Malá Strana (Lesser Town)

Start: Old Town Bridge Tower (Staroměstská mostecká věž).
Finish: Church of St. Nicholas (Kostel sv. Mikuláše).
Time: About 3 to 4 hours.
Best Times: Early morning or around sunset, when crowds are thinner and the shadows most mysterious.
Worst Time: Mid-afternoon, when the bridge is packed.

Dating from the 14th century, Charles Bridge is Prague's most celebrated structure. As the primary link between Staré Město and the castle, it has always figured prominently in the city's commercial and military history. For most of its 600 years, the 1,700-foot-long span has been a pedestrian promenade, as it is today.

The first sculpture, St. John of Nepomuk, was placed in 1683. It was such a hit that the church commissioned another 21 statues, which were created between 1698 and 1713. Since then the number has increased to 30. The location of the statues is shown on the accompanying map.

As you stand in the shadow of the tower on the Old Town side of the bridge, first turn to your right, where you'll find an 1848 **statue in tribute to Charles IV,** who commissioned the bridge's construction between Prague's oldest quarters. Now begin to walk toward the bridge entrance straight ahead, but first look up at the:

1. **Old Town Bridge Tower (Staroměstská mostecká věž),** a richly ornate 1357 design made for Charles IV by Peter Parléř, the architect who drafted the Gothic plans for St. Vitus Cathedral.

Walking Tour 1—Charles Bridge

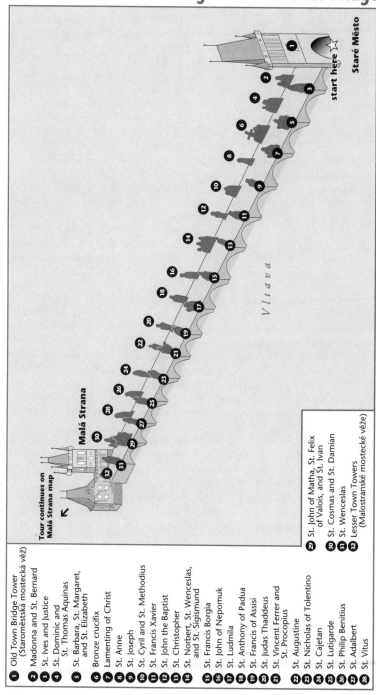

Staré Město

start here ☆

Vltava

Malá Strana

Tour continues on
Malá Strana map.

❶ Old Town Bridge Tower
    (Staroměstská mostecká věž)
❷ Madonna and St. Bernard
❸ St. Ives and Justice
❹ St. Dominic and
    St. Thomas Aquinas
❺ St. Barbara, St. Margaret,
    and St. Elizabeth
❻ Bronze crucifix
❼ Lamenting of Christ
❽ St. Anne
❾ St. Joseph
❿ St. Cyril and St. Methodius
⓫ St. Francis Xavier
⓬ St. John the Baptist
⓭ St. Christopher
⓮ St. Norbert, St. Wenceslas,
    and St. Sigismund
⓯ St. Francis Borgia
⓰ St. John of Nepomuk
⓱ St. Ludmila
⓲ St. Anthony of Padua
⓳ St. Francis of Assisi
⓴ St. Judas Thaddeus
㉑ St. Vincent Ferrer and
    St. Procopius
㉒ St. Augustine
㉓ St. Nicholas of Tolentino
㉔ St. Cajetan
㉕ St. Lutigarde
㉖ St. Philip Benitius
㉗ St. Adalbert
㉘ St. Vitus
㉙ St. John of Matha, St. Felix
    of Valois, and St. Ivan
㉚ St. Cosmas and St. Damian
㉛ St. Wenceslas
㉜ Lesser Town Towers
    (Malostranské mostecké věže)

The original east side of the tower remains pristine, with coats of arms of the Bohemian king and Holy Roman Empire. Shields also depict each territory under the auspices of the Bohemian crown at that time.

Above the east-side arch, seated to the right of the standing statue of St. Vitus, is Charles himself, and on the left is a statue of his ill-fated son, Wenceslas IV (Václav IV), who lost the crown of the empire.

The tower's western side was severely damaged in a battle against invading Swedish troops in 1357. During the Thirty Years' War, the heads of 12 anti-Habsburg Protestants were hung for public viewing from iron baskets on the tower.

The observation platform inside the tower has been recently reopened.

As you pass through the archway, the first statue on the right is of the:

2. **Madonna,** attending to a kneeling **St. Bernard,** flanked by cherubs. Like most of the statues on the bridge, this is a copy; the originals were removed to protect them from weather-related deterioration.

Directly across the bridge is a statue of:

3. **St. Ives,** the patron saint of lawyers, depicted promising to help a person who petitioned him. **Justice,** with a sword on his right, is also portrayed. If you see his outstretched hand holding a glass of beer, you'll know that Prague's law students have just completed their finals.

Cross back again and continue to do so after you view each statue.

4. **St. Dominic** and **St. Thomas Aquinas** are shown receiving a rosary from the hands of the Madonna. Below the Madonna is a cloud-enshrouded globe and a dog with a torch in its jaws, the symbol of the Dominican order.

5. **St. Barbara, St. Margaret,** and **St. Elizabeth** were sculpted by two brothers who worked under the watchful eye of their father, Jan Brokoff, who signed the work as a whole. Franz Kafka has written about the finely sculpted hands of St. Barbara, the patron saint of miners, situated in the center of the monument. To art experts, however, the sculpture of St. Elizabeth (on the left) is the most artistically valuable figure in this group.

6. The **bronze crucifix,** produced for positioning on a bridge in Dresden, Germany, was bought by the Prague magistrate and placed on Charles Bridge in 1657. The statue's gilded Hebrew inscription translates as "holy, holy, holy, God" and is believed to have been paid for with money extorted from an unknown Jew who had mocked a wooden crucifix that formerly stood on this site.

7. The **Lamenting of Christ** depicts Jesus lying in the Virgin Mary's lap, with St. John in the center and Mary Magdalene on the right. Executions were regularly held on this site during the Middle Ages.

8. **St. Anne,** the Virgin Mary's mother, holds baby Jesus and the child embraces the globe in this statue from 1707.

9. **St. Joseph** with Jesus dates from 1854 and was put here to replace another that was destroyed by gunfire 6 years earlier by anti-Habsburg rioters.

10. **St. Cyril** and **St. Methodius** are the Catholic missionaries credited with introducing Christianity to the Slavs.

11. **St. Francis Xavier,** the 18th-century cofounder of the Jesuit order, is depicted carrying four pagan princes on his shoulders—an Indian, a Tartar, a Chinese, and a Moor—symbolizing the cultures targeted for proselytizing. This is widely regarded as one of the most outstanding Czech baroque sculptural works.

12. **St. John the Baptist** is depicted here with a cross and a shell, symbols of baptism.

13. **St. Christopher,** the patron saint of raftsmen, is shown carrying baby Jesus on his shoulder. The statue stands on the site of the original bridge watch-house,

which collapsed into the river along with several soldiers during the Great Flood of 1784.

14. **St. Norbert, St. Wenceslas,** and **St. Sigismund** are patron saints of Bohemian provinces.

15. **St. Francis Borgia,** a Jesuit general, is depicted with two angels holding a painting of the Madonna. Look on the lower part of the sculpture's pedestal, where you'll see the three symbols of the life of the saint: a helmet, a ducal crown, and a cardinal's hat.

16. **St. John of Nepomuk** was thrown to his death in chains from this bridge, and this, the oldest sculpture on the span, was placed here to commemorate him. The bronze figure, sporting a gold-leaf halo, was completed in 1683. The bridge's sole bronze statue, St. John is now green with age and worn from years of being touched for good luck.

17. **St. Ludmila** is pointing to a Bible from which St. Wenceslas is learning to read. In her left hand, St. Ludmila is holding the veil with which she was suffocated. The statue's relief depicts the murder of St. Wenceslas.

18. **St. Anthony of Padua,** dedicated in 1707, depicts the preacher with baby Jesus and a lily. The relief is designed around a motif inspired by the saint's life.

19. **St. Francis of Assisi,** the first Roman Catholic martyr to be incorporated into Bohemian liturgy, is shown contemplatively, between two angels.

20. **St. Judas Thaddeus** is depicted holding both the Gospel and the club with which he was fatally beaten.

21. **St. Vincent Ferrer** is shown boasting to **St. Procopius** of his many conversions: 8,000 Muslims and 25,000 Jews.

22. **St. Augustine,** holding a burning heart and walking on "heretical" books, is a 1974 copy of a 1708 work. On the pedestal is the emblem of the Augustinians.

23. **St. Nicholas of Tolentino** is handing out bread to the poor. Behind him is a house with a Madonna, a mangle, and a lantern on its top-floor balcony. Walk quickly. Legend holds that if the lantern goes out while you're passing by the statue, you'll die within the year.

24. **St. Cajetan** stands here in front of a column of cherubs, while holding a sacred heart. Behind the statue of the saint, a triangle symbolizes the Holy Trinity.

25. **St. Lutigarde,** created in 1710 by 26-year-old M. B. Braun, is widely considered to be the most valuable sculpture on Charles Bridge. St. Lutigarde, a blind nun, is seeing Christ on the cross, in order that she might kiss his wounds.

26. **St. Philip Benitius,** the general of the Servite order, is the only marble statue on the bridge. He's portrayed with a cross, a twig, and a book. The papal tiara is lying at his feet as a symbol of the saint's refusal of the papal see in 1268.

27. **St. Adalbert** (1709), first bishop of Bohemia, is blessing the Czech lands after returning from Rome.

28. **St. Vitus,** attired as a Roman legionary, is standing on a rock between the lions to which he fell victim.

29. **St. John of Matha, St. Felix of Valois,** and **St. Ivan** were commissioned for the Trinitarian order, which rescued Christians from Turkish captivity. In the huge rock is a prison, in front of which there's a dog and a Turk with a cat-o'-nine-tails guarding the imprisoned Christians. With money for their freedom, St. John is standing on the summit of the rock. St. Ivan is seated on the left, and St. Felix is loosening the bonds of the prisoners.

30. **St. Cosmas** and **St. Damian,** the patron saints of physicians, were known for dispensing free medical services to the poor. The saints, which were commissioned

by the medical faculty in Prague, are attired in gowns and holding containers of medicines.

31. **St. Wenceslas** was sculpted in 1858, on a commission by Prague's Klar Institute for the Blind.

Follow the brick path toward the archway at the end of the bridge, but on your way look up at the:

32. **Lesser Town Towers (Malostranské mostecké věže).** The small tower on the left was built in the 12th century before Charles ever began construction on the bridge. It was a plain Romanesque structure, but Renaissance accents were added in the 16th century. The taller tower was built in the 15th century and completed the connection of the archway from the smaller tower built in the early 1400s.

After passing through the tower, you'll enter Mostecká street.

☕ **TAKE A BREAK**   At the first entrance on the left side of the street, at no. 3, is **Café-Cukrárna U Mostecké věže,** a comfortable place to stop right after you get off the bridge. Hot and cold drinks with sweets and ice cream are served in the downstairs restaurant or in the backyard garden with rattan furniture. Coffee and tea are 30Kč (88¢), pancakes 69Kč ($2), and you can have salads, fondue, and steaks as well. It's open daily from 10am to 10pm.

Head back up Mostecká and take the first left to Lázeňská street. At no. 6, on the left, you'll find a graying former hotel and bathhouse:

33. **V lázních (In the Baths).** This was a well-known stop for visitors to Prague in the 1800s. The pub and baths, which once hosted Chateaubriand, were operated on this spot from the earliest periods of Lesser Town.

Just up Lázeňská at no. 11, on the right side, is the hotel:

34. **U zlatého jednorožce (At the Golden Unicorn).** This was another favored stop for honored guests, including Beethoven. A plaque on the front bears the composer's face. The hotel was originally built into the heavy walls that once ringed Malá Strana. On the other side, at the curve of Lázeňská, you come to the:

35. **Church of Our Lady Below the Chain (Kostel Panny Marie pod řetězem).** One of the best Romanesque designs in Prague, this church was built for the Order of the Maltese Knights, replacing the oldest church in Malá Strana after it burned in 1420. You can see remnants of the original inside the church courtyard.

Exiting the church back onto the street, go about 20 steps straight on Lázeňská to:

36. **Maltézské náměstí (Maltese Square).** On the first corner of the square to the left is one of the city's poshest French restaurants packed into a former pub, **U Malířů** or "At the Painter's" (see the listing in chapter 5).

☕ **TAKE A BREAK**   At no. 10 on the square is the **Restaurace Vinárna U vladaře (At the Governor's),** open daily from 11:30am to midnight. You can sit out front on the terrace and order coffee and dessert or a meal from a full Czech-style menu. Inside is a more formal restaurant, on the left, serving traditional Czech food. On the right is what used to be a horse stable, **The Konírna,** with vaulted ceilings, cozy and heavy wooden furniture, and a full menu of hearty Czech food.

Across Maltézské náměstí is the large:

37. **Nostitz Palace (Nostický palác)** representing a grand 17th-century early baroque design attributed to Francesco Caratti. A Prague family who strongly

Walking Tour 1—Malá Strana (Lesser Town)

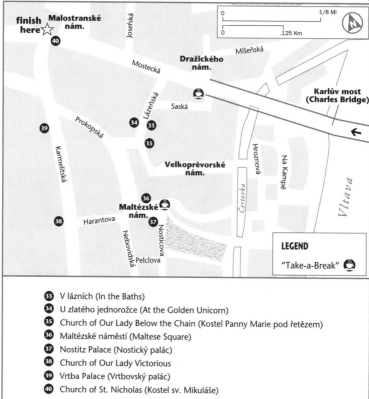

33 V lázních (In the Baths)
34 U zlatého jednorožce (At the Golden Unicorn)
35 Church of Our Lady Below the Chain (Kostel Panny Marie pod řetězem)
36 Maltézské náměstí (Maltese Square)
37 Nostitz Palace (Nostický palác)
38 Church of Our Lady Victorious
39 Vrtba Palace (Vrtbovský palác)
40 Church of St. Nicholas (Kostel sv. Mikuláše)

supported the arts used to own it. Its ornate halls once housed a famed private art collection. You can still hear chamber concerts through its windows. Daily concerts are planned to be held here during the Prague 2000 European City of Culture celebration throughout the year.

Crossing back through the little Maltese Square, you'll enter Harantova street on the way to Karmelitská. After crossing the street and walking another 150 yards, you'll come to the:

38. Church of Our Lady Victorious (Kostel Panny Marie Vítězné). This is the home of the famed wax statue of the baby Jesus, the ***Bambino di Praga,*** seen as an important religious relic in Italian and Latino countries.

From the church entrance, continue up Karmelitská street to see a complex of houses on the left side at no. 25, collectively known as:

39. Vrtba Palace (Vrtbovský palác). In 1631, Sezima of Vrtba seized a pair of Renaissance houses and then connected them to create his palace among the vineyards at the bottom of Petřín Hill. The lush terraced gardens surrounding this complex add to its beauty.

Proceed up Karmelitská, where you'll come finally to Malostranské náměstí. To the left around the uphill side of the square is the imposing dome of the:

40. Church of St. Nicholas (Kostel sv. Mikuláše), the high-baroque gem designed by K. I. Dienzenhofer and completed by his son in 1752. Relax at your walk's end by sitting among the statues and taking in the marble-and-gilt interior. In the square surrounding the church are numerous restaurants and cafes for an afternoon break or your evening meal.

Walking Tour 2—Prague Castle (Pražský Hrad)

Start: The castle's front entrance, at Hradčanské náměstí.
Finish: Daliborka Tower.
Time: Allow approximately 2½ hours, not including rest stops.
Best Times: Weekdays from 9am to 5pm (to 4pm from November to March).
Worst Times: Weekends, when the crowds are thickest.

The history and development of Prague Castle and the city of Prague are inextricably related; they grew up together and it's impossible to envision one without the other. Popularly known as the "Hrad," Prague Castle dates to the second half of the 9th century, when the first Czech royal family, the Premyslids, moved their seat of government here. Settlements on both sides of the Vltava developed under the protection of the fortified castle.

Begin your tour from the castle's front entrance, at Hradčanské náměstí. Walk through the imposing rococo gateway, topped by the colossal Battling Giants statues (1911 copies of 18th-century granite works) to the:

1. **First Castle Courtyard (První hradní nádvoří).** An informal changing of the guard occurs here daily on the hour. It involves only five guards doing little more than some impressive heel clicking and rifle twirling. The guards wore rather drab khaki outfits until 1989, when Václav Havel asked costume designer Theodor Pištěk (who costumed the actors in the film *Amadeus*) to redress them. Their smart new blue outfits are reminiscent of those worn during the First Republic.

   Directly ahead is the:

2. **Matthias Gateway (Matyášova brána).** Built in 1614 as a freestanding gate, it was later incorporated into the castle itself. The gateway bears the coats of arms of the various lands ruled by Emperor Matthias. Once you pass through, you'll see a stairway on the right leading to the state rooms of the president of the republic. They're not open to the public.

   The gateway leads into the **Second Castle Courtyard (Druhé hradní nádvoří).** Ahead, on the eastern side of the square, is the:

3. **Holy Rood Chapel (Kaple sv. Kříže),** constructed in 1763 and redesigned in 1856. The chapel is noted for its high-altar sculpture and ceiling frescoes.

   On the western side of the courtyard is the opulent:

4. **Spanish Hall (Španělský sál),** built in the late 16th century. During 1993 restorations, officials at the castle discovered a series of 18th-century trompe-l'oeil murals that lay hidden behind the mirrors lining the hall's walls.

   Adjoining the Spanish Hall is the:

5. **Rudolf Gallery (Rudolfova galerie),** an official reception hall that once housed the art collections of Rudolf II. The last remodeling of this space—rococo-style stucco decorations—occurred in 1868.

   On the northern side of the square is the:

6. **Picture Gallery of Prague Castle (Obrazárna Pražského hradu).** Containing both European and Bohemian masterpieces, the gallery holds few works from the original Imperial collection, which was virtually destroyed during the Thirty Years' War. Of the works that have survived from the days of Emperors Rudolf II

Walking Tour 2—Prague Castle

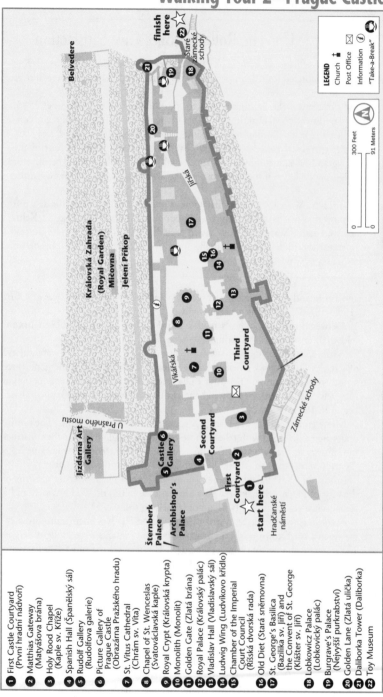

LEGEND

Church †

Post Office ⊠

Information *i*

"Take-a-Break" ●

300 Feet / 91 Meters

1. First Castle Courtyard (První hradní nádvoří)
2. Matthias Gateway (Matyášova brána)
3. Holy Rood Chapel (Kaple sv. Kříže)
4. Spanish Hall (Španělský sál)
5. Rudolf Gallery (Rudolfova galerie)
6. Picture Gallery of Prague Castle (Obrazárna Pražského hradu)
7. St. Vitus Cathedral (Chrám sv. Víta)
8. Chapel of St. Wenceslas (Svatováclavská kaple)
9. Royal Crypt (Královská krypta)
10. Monolith (Monolit)
11. Golden Gate (Zlatá brána)
12. Royal Palace (Královský palác)
13. Vladislav Hall (Vladislavský sál)
14. Ludwig Wing (Ludvíkovo křídlo)
15. Chamber of the Imperial Court Council (Říšská dvorská rada)
16. Old Diet (Stará sněmovna)
17. St. George's Basilica (Bazilika sv. Jiří) and the Convent of St. George (Klášter sv. Jiří)
18. Lobkowicz Palace (Lobkovický palác)
19. Burgrave's Palace (Nejvyšší purkrabství)
20. Golden Lane (Zlatá ulička)
21. Daliborka Tower (Daliborka)
22. Toy Museum

Light It Up: The Rolling Stones Give Satisfaction

Are the lights flickering in Spanish Hall? If they are, someone might be playing with the remote control that operates the lighting. And that someone could be President Václav Havel.

He can control the lighting thanks to the Rolling Stones. In summer 1995, they played to a crowd of more than 100,000 people in their second Prague concert since the Velvet Revolution. After finishing, the Stones gave Havel, a big fan, a bright gift: They paid for a $32,000 overhaul of the lighting in four of the castle's grand halls, including the Spanish Hall and Vladislav Hall. The director and lighting designer of their record-breaking Voodoo Lounge tour managed the project.

The result? Well, it's a somewhat more dignified spectacle than the raucous light show that was part of the mythical Voodooland on stage. Mick Jagger, Keith Richards, Charlie Watts, and Ron Wood presented Havel with a remote control to operate the chandeliers and spotlights, now strategically casting their beams on baroque statues and tapestries.

---

and Ferdinand III, the most celebrated is Hans von Aachen's *Portrait of a Girl* (1605–10), depicting the artist's daughter.

A covered passageway leads to the **Third Castle Courtyard (Třetí hradní nádvoří),** dominated by hulking:

7. **St. Vitus Cathedral (Chrám sv. Víta).** Begun in 1334, under the watchful eye of Charles IV, Prague's most celebrated Gothic cathedral has undergone three serious reconstructions. The tower galleries date from 1562, the baroque onion roof was constructed in 1770, and the entire western part of the cathedral was begun in 1873.

Before entering, notice the facade, decorated with statues of saints. The bronze doors are embellished with reliefs; those on the central door depict the construction history of the cathedral. The door on the left features representations from the lives of St. Adalbert (on the right) and St. Wenceslas (on the left).

Inside the cathedral's busy main body are several chapels, coats of arms of the city of Prague, a memorial to Bohemian casualties of World War I, and a Renaissance-era organ loft (with an organ dating from 1757).

According to legend, St. Vitus died in Rome but was then transported by angels to a small town in southern Italy. Since his remains were brought here in 1355, Vitus, the patron saint of Prague, has remained the most popular saint among the faithful in the country. Numerous Czech Catholic churches have altars dedicated to him.

The most celebrated chapel, on your right, is the:

8. **Chapel of St. Wenceslas (Svatováclavská kaple),** built atop the saint's tomb. A multitude of polished semiprecious stones decorates the chapel's altar and walls. Other spaces are filled in with 14th-century murals depicting Christ's sufferings and the life of St. Wenceslas.

Below the church's main body is the:

9. **Royal Crypt (Královská krypta),** which contains the sarcophagi of Kings Václav IV, George of Poděbrady, Rudolf II, and Charles IV and his four wives. The tomb was reconstructed in the early 1900s, and the remains of the royalty were placed in new encasements. Charles's four wives are together in the same sarcophagus.

Exit the cathedral from the same door you entered and turn left into the courtyard, approaching the:

10. Monolith (Monolit). The marble obelisk measuring over 35 feet tall is a memorial to the victims of the First World War. Just behind it is an equestrian statue of St. George, a Gothic work produced in 1373.

Continue walking around the courtyard. In the southern wall of St. Vitus Cathedral you'll see a ceremonial entrance known as the:

11. Golden Gate (Zlatá brána). The tympanum over the doorway is decorated with a 14th-century mosaic, *The Last Judgment,* which is being carefully restored, bit by bit. The doorway's 1950s-era decorative grille is designed with zodiac figures.

An archway in the Third Castle Courtyard connects St. Vitus Cathedral with the:

12. Royal Palace (Královský palác), which was, until the second half of the 16th century, the official residence of royalty. Inside, to the left, is the **Green Chamber (Zelená světnice),** where Charles IV presided over minor court sessions. A fresco of the court of Solomon is painted on the ceiling.

The adjacent room is:

13. Vladislav Hall (Vladislavský sál), a ceremonial room that has held coronation banquets, political assemblies, and knightly tournaments. Since 1934, elections of the president of the republic have taken place here below the exquisite 40-foot rib-vaulted ceiling.

At the end of Vladislav Hall is a door giving access to the:

14. Ludwig Wing (Ludvíkovo křídlo), built in 1509. Here you'll find two rooms of the Chancellery of Bohemia (Česká kancelář), once the administrative body of the Land of the Crown of Bohemia. When the king was absent, Bohemia's nobles summoned assemblies here. On May 23, 1618, two hated governors and their secretary were thrown out of the eastern window of the rear room. This act, known as the Second Defenestration, marked the beginning of the Thirty Years' War (see the box "Beware an Open Window" in chapter 6).

A spiral staircase leads to the:

15. Chamber of the Imperial Court Council (Říšská dvorská rada), which met here during the reign of Rudolf II. In this room the 27 rebellious squires and burghers who fomented the defenestration were sentenced to death and consequently executed on June 21, 1621, in Staroměstské náměstí. All the portraits on the walls of the chamber are of Habsburgs. The eastern part of Vladislav Hall opens onto a terrace from which there's a lovely view of the castle gardens and the city.

Also located in the palace is the:

16. Old Diet (Stará sněmovna), where the Provincial Court once assembled. It's interesting to notice the arrangement of the Diet's 19th-century furniture, which is all centered around the royal throne. To the sovereign's right is the chair of the archbishop; behind him are benches for the prelates. Along the walls are seats for the federal officials; opposite the throne is a bench for the representatives of the Estates. By the window on the right is a gallery for the representatives of the royal towns. Portraits of the Habsburgs adorn the walls.

Stairs lead down to **St. George's Square (náměstí Svatého Jiří),** a courtyard at the eastern end of St. Vitus Cathedral. If the weather is nice, you might want to:

☕ **TAKE A BREAK   Cafeteria "U kanovníku,"** in the courtyard between St. Vitus and St. George's (nám. Sv. Jiří 3), has a terrace garden with tables under trees, where you can enjoy light fare and hot Czech food. They offer coffee from

37 to 80Kč ($1.08 to $2.35) and great French bread sandwiches for 110Kč ($3.23) daily from 10am to 6pm.

This square is dominated by:

17. **St. George's Basilica (Bazilika sv. Jiří)** and the **Convent of St. George (Klášter sv. Jiří)**, founded in A.D. 973 by Benedictine nuns. In 1967, the convent's premises were acquired by the National Gallery, which now uses the buildings to warehouse and display its collection of Bohemian art from Gothic to baroque periods. See chapter 6 for complete information.

Leave the basilica and continue walking through the castle compound on Jiřská street, the exit at the southeastern corner of St. George's Square. About 200 feet ahead on your right is the entrance to:

18. **Lobkowicz Palace (Lobkovický palác)**, a 16th-century manor that now houses the Permanent History Exhibition of the National Museum, a gallery devoted exclusively to the history of the Czech lands.

Opposite Lobkowicz Palace is:

19. **Burgrave's Palace (Nejvyšší purkrabství)**, now the House of Czech Children, a 16th-century building used for cultural programs and exhibitions aimed toward children.

Walk up the steps to the left of Burgrave's Palace to:

20. **Golden Lane (Zlatá ulička)**, a picturesque street of 16th-century houses built into the castle fortifications. Once home to castle sharpshooters, this charm-filled lane now contains small shops, galleries, and refreshment bars. Franz Kafka supposedly lived or worked at no. 22 for a brief time in 1917.

☕ **TAKE A BREAK** At the top of Golden Lane is the **Bistro Zlatá ulička,** serving sandwiches for 55Kč ($1.62), goulash for 65Kč ($1.91), and cakes, plus coffee, wine, and spirits. There are several cozy tables in the back, but the place is often packed in high season. It's open daily from 9:30am to 6pm.

Turn right on Golden Lane and walk to the end, where stands:

21. **Daliborka Tower (Daliborka)**, part of the castle's late Gothic fortifications dating from 1496. The tower's name comes from Squire Dalibor of Kozojedy, who in 1498 became the first unlucky soul to be imprisoned here.

Turn right at Daliborka Tower, then left, and go through the passageway and down the Jiřská street. There, at no. 6, you can visit the:

22. **Toy museum** (especially appreciated by children), which holds a permanent exhibition of toys. If you make it to Prague soon enough in 2000, you can even see the "40th Anniversary of Barbie" exhibition of Johann Steiger's collection. Going down the old castle steps (Staré zámecké schody) you will reach the Malostranská station on line A of Prague's metro.

Walking Tour 3—Staré Město (Old Town)

Start: Municipal House (Obecní dům), at náměstí Republiky.
Finish: Havel's Market (Havelský trh).
Time: Allow approximately 1 hour, not including any breaks or museum visits.
Best Times: Sunday to Thursday from 9am to 5pm and Friday from 9am to 2pm, when the museums are open.

Walking Tour 3—Staré Město (Old Town)

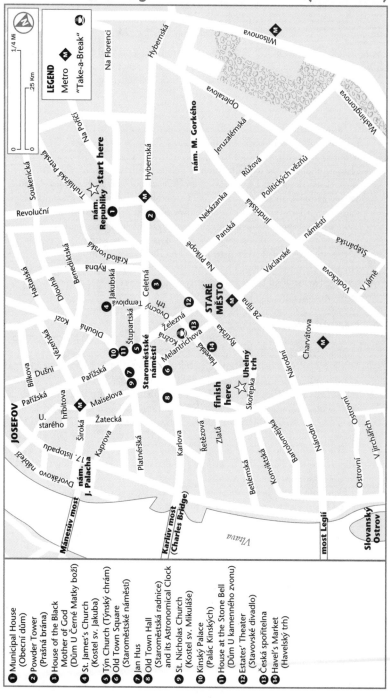

LEGEND
- Metro
- "Take-a-Break"

☆ start here

☆ finish here

1. Municipal House (Obecní dům)
2. Powder Tower (Prašná brána)
3. House of the Black Mother of God (Dům U Černé Matky boží)
4. St. James's Church (Kostel sv. Jakuba)
5. Týn Church (Týnský chrám)
6. Old Town Square (Staroměstské náměstí)
7. Jan Hus
8. Old Town Hall (Staroměstská radnice) and its Astronomical Clock
9. St. Nicholas Church (Kostel sv. Mikuláše)
10. Kinský Palace (Palác Kinských)
11. House at the Stone Bell (Dům U kamenného zvonu)
12. Estates' Theater (Stavovské divadlo)
13. Česká spořitelna
14. Havel's Market (Havelský trh)

125

Worst Times: Weekend afternoons when the crowds are thickest, Monday when the museums are closed, and after 6pm when the market is closed.

Staré Město, founded in 1234, was the first of Prague's original five towns. Its establishment was the result of Prague's growing importance along central European trade routes. Staré Město's ancient streets, most meandering haphazardly around Staroměstské náměstí, are lined with many stately buildings, churches, shops, and theaters.

Although this tour is far from exhaustive, it takes you past some of Old Town's most important buildings and monuments. Begin at the:

1. **Municipal House (Obecní dům),** náměstí Republiky 5, at the metro station. One of Prague's most photographed cultural and historical monuments, the Municipal House was built between 1906 and 1911 with money raised by Prague citizens. In the spring of 1997, it reopened after a long reconstruction, and historians say that it has been returned faithfully to its original grandeur.

From the beginning, this ornate art nouveau building has held an important place as a Czech cultural symbol—the document granting independence to Czechoslovakia was signed here in 1918. The Prague Symphony performs in Smetana Hall, the building's most important room, with a gorgeous stained-glass ceiling. The detail of every piece of decoration tells a story (see chapter 6 for more information).

Inside is a spacious period cafe, a French restaurant, and a Czech pub in the cellar with a fascinating ceramic still-life mural.

With your back to the Municipal House main entrance, walk around to your right under the arch of the:

2. **Powder Tower (Prašná brána, literally Powder Gate).** Once part of Staré Město's system of fortifications, the Powder Tower was built in 1475 as one of the walled city's major gateways. After New Town was incorporated into the City of Prague, the walls separating Old Town from the new section became obsolete. So did the Powder Tower, which was recommissioned as a gunpowder storehouse.

The tower marks the beginning of the **Royal Route,** the traditional path along which medieval Bohemian monarchs paraded on their way to being crowned in Prague Castle's St. Vitus Cathedral.

Continue through the arch down Celetná Street (named after *calt,* a bread baked here in the Middle Ages) to the corner of Ovocný trh, where you'll find the:

3. **House of the Black Mother of God (Dům U Černé Matky boží),** Celetná 34, important not for its contents, but for its cubist architectural style. Cubism, an angular artistic movement, was confined to painting and sculpture in France and most of Europe. As an architectural style, cubism is exclusive to Bohemia.

Constructed in 1921, this house features tall columns sculpted with rectangular and triangular shapes on either side of an ornate wrought-iron gate. The house is named for the Virgin Mary emblem on the corner of the building's second floor that was salvaged from the last building to stand on this site.

With your back to the House of the Black Mother of God, cross Celetná into Templová, walk 2 short blocks, and turn left onto Jakubská. At the corner, on your right, you'll see:

4. **St. James's Church (Kostel sv. Jakuba),** Prague's second longest, containing 21 altars. Enter the church and look up, just inside the church's front door. The object dangling from above is the shriveled arm of a 16th-century thief.

Return to Celetná and continue walking about 300 feet. On the right, below the towering spires, is:

5. Týn Church (Týnský chrám), one of the largest and prettiest of Prague's many churches. Famous for its twin spires that loom over nearby Staroměstské náměstí, the church was closely connected to the 14th-century Hussite movement for religious reform. After the reformers were crushed by the Roman Catholics, many of the church's Hussite symbols were removed, including statues, insignia, and the tower bells that were once known by Hussite nicknames. Note the tomb of Danish astronomer Tycho de Brahe (d. 1601), near the high altar.

Exit the church and continue a few more steps along Celetná, which opens up into:

6. Old Town Square (Staroměstské náměstí). Surrounded by baroque buildings, packed with colorful craftsmen, cafes, and entertainers, Staroměstské náměstí looks like an old European square is supposed to look.

This square has been not just a center of tourist interest but a focal point of Czech history and politics. It has been a meeting place for commerce since the city's inception—from the simple bartering of the Middle Ages to privatization deals of the 1990s.

Old Town Square has also seen its share of political protest and punishment. Protestant Hussites rioted here in the 1400s. In the 1620s, the Catholic Habsburg rulers beheaded 27 Protestants here and hung some of the heads in baskets above Charles Bridge. A small white cross has been embedded in the square near the Old Town Hall for each of the beheaded.

In the 20th century, the square has witnessed a whirlwind of political change. In 1918, the Czechs celebrated the founding of the new sovereign Republic of Czechoslovakia here. But then in 1939, the Nazis celebrated their occupation of the country on the same sight. The Soviets then celebrated kicking the Nazis out of Prague in 1945, only to have their tanks roll through again in their invasion of 1968. In 1948, Klement Gottwald led a celebration in honor of the Communist seizure of power. No wonder the Czechs chose nearby Wenceslas Square to celebrate the return of their government in 1989.

To begin your trip around the square, walk straight toward the massive black stone monument in the center. Here you'll find the statue of:

7. Jan Hus, a fiery 15th-century preacher who challenged the Roman Catholic hierarchy and was burned at the stake for it. The statue's pedestal has been used as a soapbox by many a populist politician trying to gain points by associating himself with the ill-fated Protestant, although today you're more likely to find the international youth holding sway.

The struggle between the supporters of Hus, known as Hussites, set the stage for the religious wars that tore Bohemia apart in the 15th and 17th centuries. The Hussite Church still lives today as the Protestant Czech Brethren, but since Communism its numbers have dwindled. Membership in the Catholic Church has also declined.

From here, turn around and walk left toward the clock tower. Try to time your walk so you can pass the:

8. Old Town Hall (Staroměstská radnice) and its **Astronomical Clock** at the top of the hour. It may be an understated show, but each hour a mechanical parade of saints and sinners performs for the crowd watching below (see chapter 6 for details). If you have time and your knees are up to it, try making the steep and narrow walk up to the top of the tower for a picturesque view of Old Town's red roofs.

Walking past the right side of the clock tower toward the northwest corner of the square, you'll come to:

9. **St. Nicholas Church (Kostel sv. Mikuláše),** a 1735 design of Prague's baroque master architect K. I. Dienzenhofer. The three-towered edifice isn't as beautiful or as ornate inside as his St. Nicholas Church in Lesser Town, but the crystal fixtures are worth a look.

From the front of the church, walk behind the back of the Hus monument, through the square, to the broad palace with the reddish roof and balcony in front. This is:

10. **Kinský Palace (Palác Kinských).** From the rococo balcony jutting from its stuccoed facade, Communist leader Klement Gottwald declared the proletariat takeover of the Czechoslovak government in February 1945. The building was designed by Italian architect Lurago for Count Goltz. It was later taken over by the Habsburg Prince Rudolf Kinský in 1768. It now houses a fine modern art collection in the Czech National Museum complex of palaces (see chapter 6).

Next to this is the:

11. **House at the Stone Bell (Dům U kamenného zvonu).** The medieval Gothic tower was built in the 14th century for the father of Charles IV, John of Luxembourg.

From here, head back toward Old Town Hall, but then about midway to the tower, turn left toward the square's south end and begin walking down Železná. Continue down this car-restricted walking zone about 1,000 feet; then, on the left you'll see the pale green:

12. **Estates' Theater (Stavovské divadlo).** Mozart premiered his opera *Don Giovanni* in this late-18th-century grand hall. More recently, director Miloš Forman filmed many scenes in the story of the composer's life here.

Make sure to walk down Rytířská in front of the theater to get a full view of this beautifully restored building, which just reopened after the revolution.

From the front of the theater, walk about 10 steps back up Železná and take the first left on Havelská.

☕ **TAKE A BREAK** At Havelská 27, you can stop for a tasty pizza, lasagna, gelato, or thick Italian espresso at the **Kogo Pizzeria and Café.** There are tightly packed tables inside, but if the weather is nice, sit in the more comfortable archway.

Continue down Havelská. On the left you'll see:

13. **Česká spořitelna.** The large neo-Renaissance building with statue inlays is, ironically, again the largest Czech savings bank after serving as the museum to late Communist president Klement Gottwald. The building was completed in 1894 as a bank, but after the 1948 coup it was seized by the government and turned into a depository for Communist propaganda. After the 1989 revolution, the building was returned to the bank, which restored the intricate friezes and frescoes depicting bankers' propaganda of early Czech capitalism. It's worth a peek.

Your next destination is the popular street market that overtakes the remainder of Havelská street. Simply continue on to:

14. **Havel's Market (Havelský trh),** a popular local meeting place where you'll find vegetables, fruits, drinks, soaps, toiletries, artwork, and leather goods. Prices here are generally lower than in most shops. Have fun browsing.

The nearest metro is Můstek, line A or B.

Walking Tour 4—Josefov (Jewish Quarter)

Start: Lesser Square (Malé náměstí).
Finish: Café Bar La Dolce Vita.
Time: Allow approximately 2 hours, not including rest stops or museum visits.
Best Times: Sunday to Friday from 9am to 5pm, when the cemetery and sights are open.
Worst Time: Saturday, the Sabbath, when everything is closed.

Josefov, Prague's former Jewish ghetto, is entirely within Staré Město. It was once surrounded by a wall, before that was almost all destroyed to make way for 19th-century structures. Prague is considered one of Europe's great Jewish cities: Jews have been here since the end of the 10th century, and by 1708 more Jews were living here than anywhere else in Europe.

Today, Prague's Jewish community numbers less than 3,000. In 1992, the Jewish community elected Rabbi Karol Sidon as their leader, and he has led a very public fight against anti-Semitism as reported incidents of attacks against Jews and Jewish property have increased. In addition, the government has recently tried to return to Jewish citizens property confiscated by the Nazis and then the Communists. However, many claims are still unresolved.

This tour may seem short, but the sights are gripping and provide much to ponder, so budget your time loosely. Start at:

1. **Lesser Square (Malé náměstí),** adjacent to Staroměstské náměstí. This square can't boast as much history as its larger companion. However, excavations have proven that Malé náměstí was a prime piece of real estate as far back as the 12th century. Archaeologists turned up bits of pottery, evidence of medieval pathways, and human bones from the late 1100s, when developers committed the medieval equivalent of paving over a cemetery to build a shopping mall.

   From Malé náměstí, turn left onto U radnice. One block ahead, in the courtyard across from the Magistrate Building and tucked against St. Nicholas Church, you'll see the:

2. **Franz Kafka Exhibition (Galerie Franze Kafky),** a tribute to the famous writer whose themes at times reflect the life of a Jew in Prague. The small exhibit, on the site of the building where Kafka was born, re-creates the history of his life through words, pictures, and various paraphernalia. The photos and book collection are worth a stop. Unfortunately, it's not as interesting as it sounds—more of a souvenir shop than an in-depth look at the writer. Don't get too caught up about the building itself either—only the gray doorway remains from Kafka's day. The building is open Tuesday to Sunday from 10am to 1pm and 2 to 5pm.

   An unflattering cast-iron bust of Kafka, unveiled in 1965, sits just to the right of the exhibition entrance, at the corner of Maiselova and U radnice. Walk straight ahead onto:

3. **Maiselova Street,** one of the two main streets of the walled Jewish quarter, founded in 1254. As elsewhere in Europe, Prague's Jews were forced into ghettos following a formal Roman Catholic decision that "the Jews" killed Jesus. By the 16th century, Prague's 10,000 isolated Jews comprised 10% of the city's population.

   The ban on Jews living outside the ghetto was lifted in 1848. Eighty percent of the ghetto's Jews moved to other parts of the city, and living conditions on this street and those surrounding it seriously deteriorated. The authorities responded by razing the entire neighborhood, including numerous medieval houses and synagogues. The majority of the buildings here now date from the end of the 19th century; several on this street sport stunning art nouveau facades.

About halfway down the street, on your right, is the:

4. **Maisel Synagogue (Maiselova synagóga),** a neo-Gothic–style temple built on a plot of land donated by Markus Mordechi Maisel, a wealthy inhabitant of Prague's old Jewish town. The original synagogue was destroyed by fire in 1689 but was rebuilt. During the Nazi occupation of Prague, it was used to store furniture seized from the homes of deported Jews. Today, the building holds no religious services; it's home to the Jewish Museum's collection of silver ceremonial objects, books, and Torah covers confiscated from Bohemian synagogues by the Nazis during World War II.

Continue walking down Maiselova and turn left onto Široká. Walk past the former entrance to the Old Jewish Cemetery, through which you can catch a first glimpse of its shadowy headstones, to:

5. **Pinkas Synagogue (Pinkasova synagóga),** Prague's second-oldest Jewish house of worship. After World War II, the walls of the Pinkas Synagogue were painted with the names of more than 77,000 Czech Jews who perished in Nazi concentration camps. The names were subsequently erased by the Communist government, saying that the memorial was suffering from "moisture due to flooding." After the revolution, funds were raised to restore and maintain the commemoration. It's here that U.S. Secretary of State Madeleine Albright came in 1997 to see the proof that her paternal grandparents, Arnošt Koerbel and Olga Koerbelová, were killed in the Holocaust. Albright said that she hadn't been aware of her Jewish ancestry until earlier in 1997. Her father, a Czechoslovak diplomat who fled Prague with his young family twice when Madeleine was a small girl (first from the Nazis, then from the Communists), raised his children as Catholics. See the box "Prague's Most Powerful Daughter: The Rise and Surprise of Madeleine Albright" in chapter 6 for more information.

Backtrack up Široká and turn left onto Maiselova. The pink rococo building on the right side at Maiselova 18 is the:

6. **Jewish Community Center,** an information and cultural center for locals and visitors. It once was the Jewish Town Hall. Activities of interest to Prague's Jewish community are posted here, and the staff provides visitors with details about Jewish tours. Also inside is Prague's only truly kosher restaurant, which, alas, is open only for members.

On the Community Center wall facing the Old-New Synagogue is a clock with a Hebrew-inscribed face. It turns left, counter to what's considered "clockwise."

Continue walking 1 block along Maiselova and turn left onto U Starého hřbitova, heading to the:

7. **Old Jewish Cemetery (Starý židovský hřbitov),** Europe's oldest Jewish burial ground, with the oldest grave dated 1439. Because the local government of the time didn't allow Jews to bury their dead elsewhere, as many as 12 bodies were placed vertically, with each new tombstone placed in front of the last. Hence, the crowded little cemetery contains more than 20,000 graves.

Like other Jewish cemeteries around the world, many of the tombstones have small rocks and stones placed on them—a tradition said to date from the days when Jews were wandering in the desert. Passersby, it's believed, would add rocks to grave sites so as not to lose the deceased to the shifting sands. Along with stones, visitors often leave small notes of prayer in the cracks between tombstones.

Walking Tour 4—Josefov (Jewish Quarter)

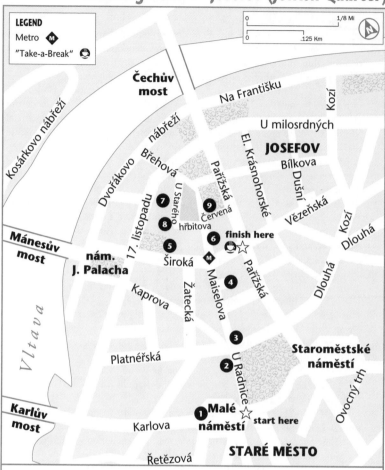

1. Lesser Square (Malé náměstí)
2. Franz Kafka Exhibition (Výstava Franze Kafky)
3. Maiselova street
4. Maisel Synagogue (Maiselova synagóga)
5. Pinkas Synagogue (Pinkasova synagóga)
6. Jewish Community Center
7. Old Jewish Cemetery (Starý židovský hřbitov)
8. Ceremonial Hall
9. Old-New Synagogue (Staronová synagóga)

Buried here is Rabbi Löw, who made from the mud of the Vltava River the legendary Golem, a clay "monster" to protect Prague's Jews. Golem was a one-eyed or three-eyed monster, depending on how you look at him. Legend has it that the rabbi would keep Golem around to protect the residents from the danger of mean-spirited Catholics outside the walls of the Jewish ghetto.

Löw's grave, in the most remote corner opposite the Ceremonial Hall, is one of the most popular in the cemetery; you'll see that well-wishers and the devout cram his tombstone with notes. Across the path from the rabbi is the grave of Mordechai Maisel, the 16th-century mayor of Josefov whose name was given to the nearby synagogue built during his term in office.

As you exit the cemetery you'll pass the:

8. Ceremonial Hall. Inside the hall, where rites for the dead were once held, is a gripping reminder of the horrors of World War II. Displayed here are the sketches of children who were held at the Terezín concentration camp west of Prague (see chapter 10). These drawings, simple and honest, painful in their playful innocence, are of the horrific world where parents and other relatives were packed up and sent to die.

Backtrack along U Starého hřbitova, cross Maiselova, and walk into the small alley called Červená. You're now standing between two synagogues. On the right is the **High Synagogue (Vysoká synagóga),** now an exhibition hall for the Jewish State Museum. On your left is the:

9. Old-New Synagogue (Staronová synagóga). Originally called the New Synagogue to distinguish it from an even older one that no longer exists, the Old-New Synagogue, built around 1270, is the oldest Jewish temple in Europe. The building has been prayed in continuously for more than 700 years, except from 1941 to 1945, during the Nazi occupation in World War II. The synagogue is also one of the largest Gothic buildings in Prague, built with vaulted ceilings and fitted with Renaissance-era columns.

Much of Josefov and Staré Město was often flooded regularly by the Vltava, until a 19th-century planning effort raised the entire area about 10 feet. The Old-New Synagogue, however, has preserved its original floor, which you reach by going *down* a short set of stairs.

You can attend services here. Men and women still sit separately during services, though that's not always rigorously enforced.

Continue to the end of the Červená alley and turn right onto Pařížská (Paris street), Prague's most elegant thoroughfare, built around the turn of the century. Follow Pařížská back toward Staroměstské náměstí, but take the first left and go 1 block. On the left you'll find:

⊙ **WINDING DOWN   La Dolce Vita,** at Široká 15, half a block off Pařížská, one of the city's finest Italian cafes. Its marble interior contains five tables on the ground floor, and 10 tables on a veranda overlook the action below. The cafe offers traditional Italian sandwiches, gelato, and espresso drinks, served by an Italian-speaking Czech waitstaff.

Returning to Pařížská and turning left will lead you back to Staroměstské náměstí.

Prague Shopping

8

by John Mastrini & Hana Mastrini

The rapid influx of visitors, post-Communist wage growth, and new-found consumption habits of the Czech nouveaux riches resulted in expensive boutiques and specialty shops popping up like mushrooms in Prague. Shopping malls now offer everything from designer baby clothes to Bruno Magli shoes. The selection of world-renowned labels is beginning to rival that of many Western European cities, though shops tend to have a tiny inventory compared with the same outlets in Paris or London. Still, since labor and rent make operations cheaper here, you might find a bargain for the same items offered in points farther west.

For those looking more for a piece of Czech handiwork, like some of the world's best crystal and glass, the prices are still often shockingly low. Antiques shops and booksellers abound, and the selection of classical, trendy, and offbeat art is immense at the numerous private galleries. Throughout the city center you'll find quaint, obscure shops, some without phones or advertising.

1 The Shopping Scene

SHOPPING AREAS

The L-shaped half a mile running down from the middle of **Wenceslas Square** around the corner to the right on **Na Příkopě** and to the new Myslbek Center has become Prague's principal shopping street. In this short distance you'll find three new multilevel shopping gallerias, with stores like Britain's **Marks & Spencer, Sergio Tacchini, Kookai, Daniel Hechter,** and **Trussardi.** Between the centers is a wide array of boutiques and antiques shops; in high season there's also a craftsmen's market at the low end of the square.

A handful of fine private art **galleries** is concentrated on the stretch of **Národní třída** running from just east of the National Theater to Wenceslas Square. The wide tree-lined Pařížská, from Old Town Square to the Intercontinental Hotel, is flanked with top-level boutiques and airline offices, as well as eclectic local shops.

In the streets surrounding **Old Town Square,** you'll find a wide contrast of expensive shops like Versace and Mapin & Webb jewelers, with bizarre nooks offering wood carvings, garnets, handmade toys, and typical Czech glass and porcelain.

In **Malá Strana,** you'll find artists and craftspeople selling their jewelry, prints, handicrafts, and faux Red Army surplus on Charles Bridge and the Old Castle Steps (Staré zámecké schody).

HOURS & TAXES

Prague's centrally located shops rely on tourist business and keep fairly long hours. Most are open Monday to Friday from about 9am to 6pm and Saturday from 9am to 1pm, and sometimes much later. Many open on Sunday as well, though usually for a shorter time. Note that some small food shops that keep long hours charge up to 20% more for all their goods after 8pm or so.

Prices for goods in shops include the government's 22% **value-added tax (VAT).** While some European countries encourage visitors to part with their dollars by offering to refund the VAT, the Czech Republic offers no such program.

SHIPPING

Don't trust the post office when it comes to shipping valuable goods. If your package is larger than a bread box, contact **American Rainbow,** Nikoly Tesly 10, Praha 6 (☎ **02/311 9239**), an international shipping company that air freights goods worldwide. You can either bring your packages to them, or they'll pick them up at no extra charge. The minimum price for a package 1 to 30 kg (2.2 to 66 lb.) is 2,600Kč ($76.47) to the U.K. and 3,400Kč ($100) to Washington, D.C., but the price will vary according to the destination.

DHL, Aviatická 12 (Ruzyně airport), Praha 6 (☎ **1030** from Prague only), charges 1,595Kč ($47) for the first half kilogram to the U.K. and 1,800Kč ($53) to the United States.

2 Shopping A to Z

ANTIQUES

If you're shopping for antiques, see "Special Shopping Notes," below.

Antique Andrle Vladimír. Václavské nám. 17, Praha 1. ☎ **02/2400 9166.** Metro: Můstek.

A wide selection of Eastern Orthodox icons marks this shop halfway up Wenceslas Square. The proprietor produces papers showing that each icon was legitimately obtained (despite heavy restrictions in many countries) and legal for export. There's also a large selection of antique watches and other accessories. Open Monday to Saturday from 10am to 7pm and Sunday from 10am to 6pm.

Art Deco Galerie. Michalská 21, Praha 1. ☎ **02/261 367.** Metro: Můstek.

This dandy store sells the trappings of Prague's golden age, filled with colored perfume bottles and clothing from the 1920s and 1930s. Furniture and household items include art deco clocks and lamps. Open Monday to Friday from 2 to 7pm.

✪ **Art Décoratif.** U Obecního domu, Praha 1. ☎ **02/2200 2350.** Metro: Náměstí Republiky.

Another art nouveau throwback, this outlet is housed in the purely authentic hull of the newly refurbished Municipal House, but most things offered aren't originals. Still, there's a fine selection of Alfons Mucha reproductions, jewelry, and lamps from the era. Open daily from 10am to 8pm.

Jiří Vandas. Pařížská 8, Praha 1. ☎ **02/231 3285.** Metro: Staroměstská.

This is a musty market for valuable pieces of Czechoslovak and Czech history. Coins, medals, paper currency, and maps are offered. Vandas, if he's in a good-enough mood, might show you the Order of the White Lion medal, the highest Czechoslovak state

---

Special Shopping Notes

In an effort to keep precious pieces of Czech heritage in the country, the government now requires export permits for a large range of objects, including glass and graphics over 50 years old, miniature art objects valued at more than 3,000Kč ($88), and paintings valued at more than 30,000Kč ($882). Most antiques shops provide export permits; ask for one if necessary.

In many markets, customers are expected to bring their own bags. If you don't have one, ask for a *tašku;* it'll cost a couple of koruny.

---

medal. Only 12 have ever been made; his is priced at 390,000Kč ($11,470). Open Monday to Friday from 10am to 7pm and Saturday from 10am to 6pm.

Vetešnictví Kolesa Jiří. Saská 3, Praha 1. ☎ **02/9004 1985.** Metro: Malostranská.

On a small street under Charles Bridge on the Malá Strana side near Kampa, this feels like your Slavic grandmother's basement, with old cameras, clocks, watches, and copper kitchenware such as milk pitchers. Look for the German sign "Tröder." A first-generation Bohemian phonograph is offered for 5,500Kč ($161). Open daily from 11am to 6pm.

Vladimír Kůrka Antiques. Panská 1, Praha 1. ☎ **02/261 425.** Metro: Můstek.

In a former monastery, this shop specializes in colorful Moravian folk costumes, embroidered tablecloths, and antique textiles. Open Monday to Friday from 10am to 6pm and Saturday from 10am to 2pm.

Zlatá Koruna. Pařížská 8, Praha 1. ☎ **02/231 3285.** Metro: Staroměstská.

Old coins and badges clutter this shop that seems to sell everything from centuries-old silver medallions to Communist-era pins embossed with coup-leader Klement Gottwald. Open Monday to Friday from 10am to 7pm and Saturday from 10am to 6pm.

ART GALLERIES

Central Europe Gallery and Publishing House. Husova 10 and 21, Praha 1. ☎ **02/2422 2068.** Metro: Národní třída or Můstek.

Works of contemporary Czech and other Eastern European artists are priced to sell here. Coffee-table books and catalogs with detailed descriptions in English and color reproductions usually accompany well-planned exhibitions. Open Tuesday to Sunday from 10am to noon and 1 to 6pm.

Galerie Art Praha/Centrum sběratelů. Staroměstské nám. 20, Praha 1. ☎ **02/2421 1087.** Metro: Staroměstská.

A showroom for a collectors' group, this gallery on Old Town Square offers innovative works from some of the more progressive Czech and Slovak artists of the 20th century. Open daily from 10:30am to 7pm.

Galerie Peron–síň Čertovka. U Lužického semináře 12, Praha 1. ☎ **02/5731 7907.** Metro: Malostranská.

This one-room antiques shop has a bit of everything, small that is, but mostly decorative statuettes, vases, oil paintings, and curios from fine Bohemia salons of yesteryear. If you want something easy to pack, there's plenty to fit the bill. Open Monday to Friday from 11am to 7pm, Saturday and Sunday from noon to 6pm.

Prague Shopping

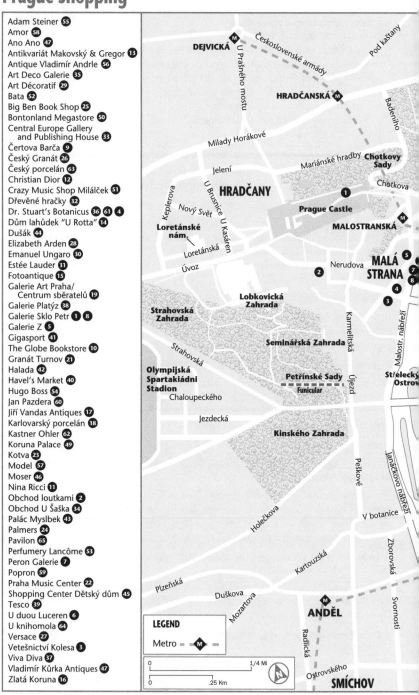

Adam Steiner **55**
Amor **58**
Ano Ano **47**
Antikvariát Makovský & Gregor **13**
Antique Vladimír Andrle **56**
Art Deco Galerie **35**
Art Décoratif **29**
Bata **52**
Big Ben Book Shop **25**
Bontonland Megastore **50**
Central Europe Gallery
   and Publishing House **33**
Čertova Barča **9**
Český Granát **26**
Český porcelán **63**
Christian Dior **12**
Crazy Music Shop Milálček **51**
Dřevěné hračky **32**
Dr. Stuart's Botanicus **36 61 4**
Dům lahůdek "U Rotta" **14**
Dušák **44**
Elizabeth Arden **28**
Emanuel Ungaro **30**
Estée Lauder **31**
Fotoantique **15**
Galerie Art Praha/
   Centrum sběratelů **19**
Galerie Platýz **38**
Galerie Sklo Petr **1 8**
Galerie Z **5**
Gigasport **41**
The Globe Bookstore **10**
Granát Turnov **21**
Halada **42**
Havel's Market **40**
Hugo Boss **54**
Jan Pazdera **60**
Jiří Vandas Antiques **17**
Karlovarský porcelán **18**
Kastner Ohler **62**
Koruna Palace **49**
Kotva **23**
Model **57**
Moser **46**
Nina Ricci **11**
Obchod loutkami **2**
Obchod U Šaška **34**
Palác Myslbek **43**
Palmers **24**
Pavilon **65**
Perfumery Lancôme **53**
Peron Galerie **7**
Popron **59**
Praha Music Center **22**
Shopping Center Dětský dům **45**
Tesco **39**
U duou Luceren **6**
U knihomola **64**
Versace **27**
Vetešnictví Kolesa **3**
Viva Diva **37**
Vladimír Kůrka Antiques **47**
Zlatá Koruna **16**

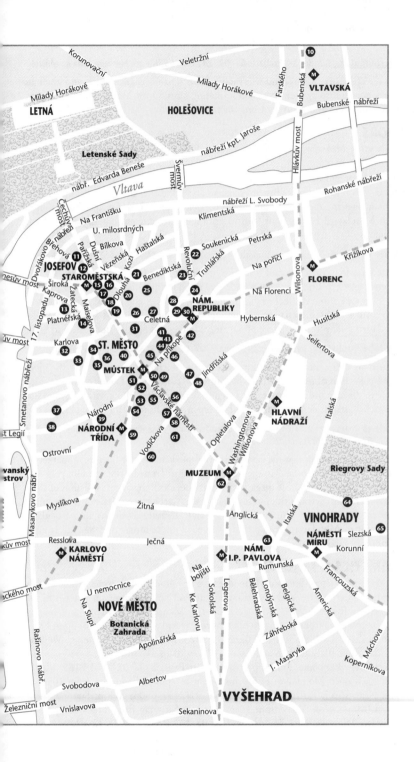

LETNÁ

Korunovační

Milady Horákové

HOLEŠOVICE

Veletržní

Milady Horákové

Farského

VLTAVSKÁ

10

Bubenská

Bubenské nábřeží

Letenské Sady

nábřeží kpt. Jaroše

Hlávkův most

nábř. Edvarda Beneše

Švermův most

Vltava

Rohanské nábřeží

Čechův most

nábřeží L. Svobody

Na Františku

Klimentská

U. milosrdných

Dvořákovo nábřeží

Břehová

Pařížská

Bílkova

Dušní

Vězeňská

Kozí

Haštalská

Revoluční

Soukenická

Petrská

Na poříčí

Wilsonova

Křižíkova

JOSEFOV

STAROMĚSTSKÁ

Široká

Kaprova

Zateckă

17. listopadu

Maiselova

Platnéřská

Benediktská

Truhlářská

22

23

Na Florenci

FLORENC

Čechův most

Na Františku

Dlouhá

21

25

28

24

NÁM.
REPUBLIKY

29 30

Hybernská

Husitská

Seifertova

15

16

17

18 20

19

26 27

31

Celetná

Karlova

Platnéřská

13

14

ST. MĚSTO

41

43

44

42

Na příkopě

46

Jindřišská

32

34

36

40

45

Italská

33

35

MŮSTEK

47

48

HLAVNÍ
NÁDRAŽÍ

51

50 49

52

53 55

56

57

54

58

61

Národní

39

NÁRODNÍ
TŘÍDA

59

Vodičkova

Opletalova

Washingtonova

Wilsonova

Riegrovy Sady

Ostrovní

60

Smetanovo nábřeží

Most Legií

37

38

Myslíkova

Žitná

Anglická

Italská

MUZEUM

62

VINOHRADY

slovanský
ostrov

NÁMĚSTÍ
MÍRU

64

Slezská

65

Masarykovo nábř.

Resslova

KARLOVO
NÁMĚSTÍ

Ječná

NÁM.
I.P. PAVLOVA

63

Korunní

Palackého most

Rašínovo nábř.

U nemocnice

NOVÉ MĚSTO

Na bojišti

Legerova

Sokolská

Rumunská

Belgická

Londýnská

Bělehradská

Francouzská

Americká

Máchova

Na Slupi

Botanická
Zahrada

Ke Karlovu

Apolinářská

Záhřebská

I. Masaryka

Kopernikova

Železniční most

Svobodova

Vnislavova

Albertov

Sekaninova

VYŠEHRAD

137

Galerie Platýz. Národní 37, Praha 1. ☎ **02/2421 0755.** Metro: Národní třída or Můstek.

This eclectic space displays and sells modern Czech paintings, sculpture, and graphics by artists who display their works on a rotating basis. Open Monday to Friday from 10:30am to 7pm and Saturday from 10am to 5pm.

BOOKS

Antikvariát Makovský & Gregor. Kaprova 9, Praha 1. ☎ **02/232 8335.** Metro: Staroměstská.

Czechs are ardent book and map collectors, and this shop near Old Town Square is loaded with fine examples of their cache. You'll find leather-bound works in English, German, French, and Czech, along with decorative and historic maps and graphics. Open Monday to Friday from 9am to 7pm and Saturday and Sunday from 10am to 6pm.

✪ **Big Ben Book Shop.** Malá Štupartská 5, Praha 1. ☎ **02/2482 6565.** Metro: Můstek.

At the far side of the courtyard behind Týn Church near Old Town Square, Big Ben is a good place to find that commemorative or educational book on Prague in English. There are also city tours to take home on videocassette and a wealth of maps to guide you into the hinterlands, plus a good selection of children's literature. Open Monday to Friday from 9am to 6:30pm and Saturday and Sunday from 10am to 5pm.

✪ **Globe Bookstore.** Janovského 14, Praha 7. ☎ **02/6671 2610.** Metro: Vltavská.

Opened in 1993, Prague's first English-language literary hangout boasts the city's largest collection of used paperback literature and nonfiction. The off-campus atmosphere in the adjacent cafe makes for a trendy afternoon read along with stiff espresso, sandwiches, salads, desserts, and a full bar. Open daily from 10am to midnight.

✪ **Mega International Bookstore "U knihomola."** Mánesova 79, Praha 2. ☎ **02/627 7767.** Metro: Jiřího z Poděbrad.

The familiar expat stop "At the Bookworm" has made its bid for the tourist market by adding "Mega International" to the front of its name. Don't let the title fool you—it's not another Barnes & Noble megastore, but it does stock the largest selection of English, French, and German titles in town, as well as Czech classics. There's a cafe in the basement for kava with your Kafka. Its art and literature selections are particularly strong. Open Monday to Friday from 9am to 9pm, Saturday and Sunday from 2 to 9pm.

COSMETICS & FRAGRANCES

The scent of Western life came soon after the revolution, when some of the world's most noted perfumeries and cosmetic boutiques set up as pioneers in Prague. **Elizabeth Arden,** Rybná 2, Praha 1 (☎ **02/232 5471;** Metro: Náměstí Republiky), is open Monday to Friday from 9:30am to 6:30pm and Saturday from 9:30am to 2pm. **Estée Lauder,** Železná 18, Praha 1 (☎ **02/2423 2023;** Metro: Můstek), is open Monday to Friday from 10am to 7pm and Saturday from 10am to 4pm.

Perfumery Lancôme, Jungmannovo nám. 20, Praha 1 (☎ **02/2421 7189;** Metro: Můstek), is open Monday to Friday from 9am to 7pm and Saturday from 10am to 2pm. **Nina Ricci,** Pařížská 4, Praha 1 (☎ **02/2481 0905;** Metro: Staroměstská), is open Monday to Friday from 10am to 6pm, Saturday from 11am to 4pm. At **Christian Dior,** Pařížská 7, Praha 1 (☎ **02/232 7382** or 02/232 6229; Metro: Staroměstská), the Dior line is complemented by fragrances from Christian Lacroix; it's open Monday to Friday from 9am to 7pm and Saturday from 10am to 3pm.

Prague's Best Buys

Blood-red **garnets** are the official Czech national gem, and the ones that you can buy here are among the world's finest, as well as one of the country's top exports. Most garnets are mined near Teplice, about 39 miles northwest of Prague. There are at least five specific kinds. Bohemian garnets are the Pyrope type, an amalgam of calcium and magnesium that's almost always deep red. You can get a small necklace for as little as 660Kč ($19.41) or densely packed broaches or bracelets running more than 33,000Kč ($971), depending on whether they're set in silver or gold. Be warned that fake garnets are common, so purchase your stones from a reputable shop (see below).

Fine **crystal** has been produced in the Bohemian countryside since the 14th century. In the 17th and 18th centuries, it became the preferred glass of the world's elite, drawing royals and the rich to Karlovy Vary to buy straight from the source. The king of Siam made a fabled trip to the west Czech spa town in the 1930s just to choose a setting for his palace. Bohemian factories are responsible for artistic advances in gilding, cutting, and coloring. The quality remains high, and you can still purchase contemporary glass for prices that are much lower than those in the West. In addition to handblown functional pieces, Prague's galleries contain plenty of unusual crystal sculpture. The Museum of Applied Arts often exhibits glass. See below for a list of Prague's most prominent glass retailers.

Antiques and **antiquarian books and prints** are widely available and are distinctive souvenirs, sold by specialist *Antikvariáts*. These antiques shops are located throughout the city, but you'll find many in Old Town and Malá Strana.

Since beer is a little heavy to carry home and the local wine isn't worth it, take home a bottle of **Becherovka,** the nation's favorite herbal liqueur from Karlovy Vary. You'll find the distinctive green decanter in shops around the city, costing about 300Kč ($8.82) per liter.

CRYSTAL & GLASS

Galerie "Z." Letenská 1, Praha 1. ☎ **02/544 048.** Metro: Malostranská.

Sinuous, colorful modern works of handblown glass stand out in this series of shops offering a unique cut above the numerous contemporary glass boutiques in Prague. The offerings come directly from Železný Brod, thanks to students of the country's artistic glass institute. Professor Libinský from the Academy of Creative Arts has designed many of the pieces, like a tall bluish vase, a 1990s update of curvaceous art nouveau designs, for around 13,000Kč ($382). Open daily from 11am to 6pm.

Another showplace for the same group of artists is at **Galerie "Sklo Petr,"** U Lužického semináře 7, Praha 1 (☎ **02/692 3759;** Metro: Malostranská). Open daily 11am to 8pm. There's also **Bílá věž** (White Tower), which you will pass during your castle tour on the Golden Lane (Zlatá ulička). Open from 10am to 6pm.

✪ **Moser.** Na Příkopě 12, Praha 1. ☎ **02/2421 1293.** Metro: Můstek. Second Prague shop is at Malé nám. 11, Praha 1. ☎ **02/2161 1520.** Metro: Můstek.

The Moser family began selling Bohemia's finest crystal in central Prague in 1857, drawing customers from around the world. Even the King of Siam made a special trip to the Karlovy Vary factory in the 1930s to pick out his place settings. Soon after, the Nazis took over and the Jewish Mosers fled. Following the war, the Communists seized the company but kept the Moser name. Surprisingly, the quality and reputation suffered little. The dark-wood showroom upstairs is worth a look if only to get the feeling of Prague at its most elegant. Open Monday to Friday from 9am to 8pm, Saturday and Sunday from 10am to 6pm at Na Příkopě; Monday to Friday from 10am to 7pm, Saturday and Sunday from 10am to 6pm at Malé nám.

U dvou luceren. U Lužického semináře 10, Praha 1. ☎ **02/5731 1678.** Metro: Malostranská.

In this cozy shop you can find art nouveau silver-plated glass vases and plates in limited series or contemporary decorative glass. They also offer ceramics, plates, cups, and jugs and Czech-made jewelry. For those who are taken aback by Prague's architecture, you can actually take the buildings home with you. This shop offers a wide range of miniature versions of the city's most famous buildings and city scenes. Open daily from 10am to 7pm.

DEPARTMENT STORES & SHOPPING MALLS

✪ **Koruna Palace.** Václavské nám. at Na Příkopě 1, Praha 1. ☎ **02/2421 9526.** Metro: Můstek.

At the bottom of Wenceslas Square, the venerable Koruna Building, which used to house Prague's cheapest stand-up buffet, has had its towering passages reconstructed into a series of shops and cafes, including the world's largest **Dunkin' Donuts** (if you're wondering where all the cops are). After a few chocolate eclairs, you can check out the tennis togs at **Sergio Tacchini** or the Parisian men's fashion at **Daniel Hechter.** The basement ✪ **Bontonland Megastore** is Prague's largest record/tape shop, based on the Richard Branson's Virgin concept but without any real savings. Open Monday to Saturday from 9am to 8pm and Sunday from 10am to 6pm.

Kotva. Náměstí Republiky 8, Praha 1. ☎ **02/2480 1111.** Metro: Náměstí Republiky.

Once the symbol of Communist consumer pride (admittedly an oxymoron), Kotva is the country's largest department store, with five floors ("For a Thousand Wishes") and a large supermarket in the basement. The sporting-goods department is well stocked, and you can find most everything expected in a major department store in the space, which has been updated to a more Western style. Open Monday to Friday from 9am to 8pm, Saturday from 9am to 6pm, and Sunday from 10am to 6pm.

✪ **Palác Myslbek.** Na Příkopě 19–21, Praha 1. ☎ **02/2224 5093.** Metro: Můstek.

The first Eastern European entry in Britain's popular **Marks & Spencer** chain anchors this new modern mall in the center of the banking district. Smaller than most of its stores, Prague's "Marks 'n Sparks" still has the same solid-value English clothes and accessories at a fair price. You can also exchange anything bought here at any other outlet in the chain. Open Monday to Friday from 9am to 8pm, Saturday from 9am to 7pm, and Sunday from 10am to 6pm. At the other end of the Myslbek atrium is the ultra-trendy **Kookaï** women's boutique, with **Clinique** cosmetics. Open Monday to Saturday from 9:30am to 7pm and Sunday from noon to 6pm. **Royal Doulton** china and other specialty shops are in between.

✪ **Pavilon.** Vinohradská 50, Praha 2. ☎ **02/2209 7111.** Metro: Náměstí Míru.

This brightly reconstructed town market was central Prague's first high-brow galleria, with boutiques ranging from **Lacoste** to **Diesel** and **Timberland.** There's a **Sony** shop and a **Belgian Butcher,** a decent Italian gelato/espresso shop in the center courtyard, and a fair-priced **grocer** downstairs. Open Monday to Saturday from 9:30am to 9pm and Sunday from noon to 6pm.

Vintage Treasure & Trash

Those looking for acres of antiques and secondhand goods can trek to **Holešovice tržnice** every Saturday from 9am to 5pm. Take the metro to Vltavská, in Prague 7, and follow the signs coming out of the station. People from all over the country come to the capital to unload their attics. Anything from pictures of Soviet leader Josef Stalin to family silver collections can be found here.

✪ **Shopping Centre "Dětský dům."** Na Příkopě, corner of Provaznická. No telephone. Metro: Můstek.

For years before and after the fall of Communism, this corner building down the block from the Estates' Theater was Prague parents' last hope to find jumpers and toys for their tots. After falling into disrepair, the "Children's House" was reopened in 1999 as an upscale kids' mall. The standard stuff is still there, a bit more expensive, and the toy train department still dazzles. An adult clothing store from the Czech textile capital of **Prostějov** has taken the local label uptown on the second floor. Open Monday to Saturday from 9:30am to 8pm, Sunday from 10am to 6pm.

Tesco. Národní třída 26, Praha 1. ☎ **02/2422 7971.** Metro: Národní třída.

In 1996, British retailer Tesco bought the Communist-era Máj department store from the U.S. discount chain Kmart. It has turned the awful Máj into a well-organized modern shopping center. The best reasons to shop at Tesco are the gifts (including fine Leander rose porcelain), snacks on the ground floor (like a Little Caesar's pizza), and a fine grocery store in the basement. Tesco not only kept Kmart's vaunted American junk-food wall full of nachos, microwave popcorn, and peanut butter, but has expanded it with fattening treats from England, too. Open Monday to Friday from 8am to 8pm (food department from 7am), Saturday from 9am to 6pm (food department from 8am), and Sunday from 10am to 6pm (food department from 9am).

FASHION

Adam Steiner. Václavské nám. 24, Praha 1. ☎ **02/2422 0594.** Metro: Můstek.

The tailor-made suits have gone up by about 50% to begin at 15,000Kč ($441) after the *Wall Street Journal* featured Adam as the best value for tailoring in Eastern Europe. You can buy Italian suits and other conservative business clothes, shirts, tops, and underwear off the rack, too. Open Monday to Friday from 9am to 7pm and Saturday from 10am to 4pm.

Ano Ano. Panská 9, Praha 1. ☎ **02/2421 0492.** Metro: Můstek.

Men's and women's designs are by Hugo Boss, Betty Barclay, Sabu, Esquire, and others. Open Monday to Friday from 10am to 6pm.

Emanuel Ungaro. Obecní dům at U Prašné brány, Praha 1. ☎ **02/2200 2330.** Metro: Náměstí Republiky.

Men can find copies of the celebrated Paris designer's suits from about 16,000Kč ($485) off the rack, while women can sample the basic cuts that have made Ungaro a world favorite. Open Monday to Friday from 10am to 7pm and Saturday from 10am to 5pm.

Gianni Versace. Celetná 7, Praha 1. ☎ **02/2481 0016.** Metro: Můstek.

Italy's most famous and flamboyant designer may be gone, but his ferociously unique tastes live on through his worldwide chain of boutiques. The Prague stop offers selections from new lines and off-the-rack repros on the heels of the season's premieres, as well as some of Versace's most daring Italian-villa home furnishings, including gilded vases and gold lamé pillows. Open Monday to Friday from 10am to 7pm and Saturday from 10am to 5pm.

Hugo Boss. Jungmannovo nám. 18, Praha 1. ☎ **02/268 192.** Metro: Můstek.

Germany's king of men's suits, Boss has become a status symbol for the twenty-something stockbrokers who've made a killing on Czech privatization. Expect to pay at least 20,000Kč ($588) for one of his wedge-cut dandies. Open Monday to Friday from 10am to 7pm, Saturday from 10am to 6pm, and Sunday from 11am to 6pm.

Viva Diva. Karolíny Světlé 12, Praha 1. ☎ **02/2423 6728.** Metro: Národní třída.

This very sexy, trendy women's clothing shop specializes in designs by Kookaï. Open Monday to Friday from 10:30am to 7pm and Saturday from 11am to 5pm.

GARNETS
Amor. Václavské nám. 40, Praha 1. ☎ **02/2423 2224.** Metro: Můstek.

Pendants and brooches sold here are some of the most unusual designs in the city. All items are set in 14- or 18-karat gold and range from 500 to about 5,000Kč ($14.70 to about $147). Open Monday to Saturday from 9am to 8pm and Sunday from 10:30am to 8pm.

Český Granát. Celetná 4, Praha 1. ☎ **02/267 410.** Metro: Můstek.

This shop has an excellent reputation for good-quality jewelry at reasonable prices. Traditional, conservative earrings and pendants are spiked with some interesting and unusual designs. Most pieces are set in 24-karat gold or gold-plated silver. Open Monday to Saturday from 10am to 8pm and Sunday from 10am to 7pm.

✪ **Granát Turnov.** Dlouhá 30, Praha 1. ☎ **02/231 5612.** Metro: Náměstí Republiky.

Granát Turnov, the monopoly that controls the Czech Republic's favorite gem industry, is *the* place to visit if you're serious about shopping for garnets. Expect to pay between 750 and 1,500Kč ($22.05 and $45.11) for a mid-priced ring or bracelet. Open Monday to Friday from 10am to 5pm and Saturday from 10am to 1pm.

✪ **Halada.** Na Příkopě 16, Praha 1. ☎ **02/2422 1304.** Metro: Můstek.

Garnets fill the cases of Prague's premier jewelers. Czechs swear by Halada for quality, price, and selection. There is also an outlet of this store among the displays on the ground floor of Tesco. Open daily from 9am to 7pm.

GIFTS & SOUVENIRS
Čertova Barča. U Lužického semináře 7, Praha 1. ☎ **02/9002 8202.** Metro: Malostranská.

Czechs start the Christmas season early with the celebrations of St. Nicholas on December 5, where good kids get oranges, sweets, and toys from St. Nick while the naughty ones get a lump of coal from a little devil. At this "Devilish" shop of Miss Barča, you can cast this entire morality play in wooden toys—planes, trains, automobiles, animals, and almost anything fun from wood. Open daily from 10am to 10pm.

✪ **Český porcelán.** Jugoslávská 16, Praha 2. ☎ **02/2150 5320.** Metro: Nám. Míru or I. P. Pavlova.

Traditional Czech "onion" ("cibulák") china is the calling card for this representative shop of the porcelain factory in Dubí near the German border. The folksy blue-on-bone cobalt onion patterns have become a familiar site in country kitchens around the world. Open Monday to Friday from 9am to 7pm, Saturday from 9am to 2pm, and Sunday from 2 to 5pm.

Dřevěné hracky. Karlova 26, Praha 1. No phone. Metro: Můstek.

Handmade wooden toys are found here, including small jigsaw-cut pigs on wheels and toddler-size rocking horses. Other handicrafts, such as ceramic mugs and candle-holders, are in the back. Open daily from 10am to 8pm.

Dr. Stuart's Botanicus. Mostecká 4, Praha 1. ☎ **02/5731 5089.** Metro: Malostranská.

This chain of natural scent, soap, and herb shops is an amazing Anglo-Czech success story. Started by a British botanist and Czech partners on a farm northeast of Prague, Dr. Stuart's has found 101 ways to ply a plant into a sensuous gift and a lucrative trade. There are five outlets throughout Prague, with this one near Charles Bridge probably most convenient for tourists. You can't miss the heavenly smell of potpourri oozing onto the street. Open Monday to Saturday from 10am to 8pm and Sunday from 10am to 6pm.

Fotoantique. Pařížská 12, Praha 1. No phone. Metro: Staroměstská.

Original photographs by the most famous Czech photographers are sold alongside old cameras, ferrotypes, and magazines and catalogs from the beginnings of photography. Open Tuesday to Friday from 10am to 6pm and Saturday from 9am to 2pm.

✪ **Karlovarský porcelán.** Pařížská 2, Praha 1. ☎ **02/2481 1023.** Metro: Staroměstská.

On display here are some of the best pieces from the 21,000 tons of decorative and domestic porcelain that are produced annually in Karlovy Vary. Open daily from 9am to 7pm.

HATS
Model. Václavské nám. 28, Praha 1. ☎ **02/2421 6805.** Metro: Můstek.

Prague's best haberdasher sells every type of topper, from mink to straw, at prices that are distinctly un-Western. In addition to the hundreds of handcrafted hats on display, the haberdashery can specially produce a hat according to your specifications in just 3 days. Both men's and women's hats are sold. Open Monday to Friday from 9am to 7pm and Saturday from 10am to 5pm.

JEWELRY
✪ **Dušák (Watchmaker and Goldsmith).** Na Příkopě 17, Praha 1. ☎ **02/2421 3025.** Metro: Můstek.

Dušák features Cartier, Gucci, Omega, Rado, and Certina chronographs and does repairs, too. Open Monday to Friday from 10am to 7pm, Saturday from 9am to 6pm, and Sunday from 1 to 6pm.

Halada. Na Příkopě 16, Praha 1. ☎ **02/2422 1304.** Metro: Můstek.

Beyond Garnets, Halada has one of the best arrays of market-priced gold, silver, platinum, and fine gems in this city, which 10 years ago used to ration wedding rings as a subsidized entitlement (no joke). Open daily from 9am to 7pm.

LINGERIE
Palmers. Královodvorská 7, Praha 1. ☎ **02/231 6915.** Metro: Náměstí Republiky.

Luxurious panties, bras, corsets, and Palmer's own other mentionables can be found just a few steps behind the Kotva department store. It's open Monday to Friday from 9am to 6pm and Saturday from 10am to 3pm.

MUSIC

⊙ **Bontonland Megastore** is located in the Koruna Palace (see "Department Stores & Shopping Malls," above).

Crazy Music Shop Miláček. 28.října 8, Praha 1. ☎ **02/2421 8911.** Metro: Můstek.

For Czech rock and pop, visit this hip shop, which also sells the latest Western releases. Open daily from 10am to 7pm.

Popron. Jungmannova 30, Praha 1. ☎ **02/2494 8682.** Metro: Národní třída or Můstek.

This store sells classical to contemporary recordings, with some cuts on vinyl. Open Monday to Friday from 9am to 7:30pm, Saturday from 9am to 7pm, and Sunday from 10am to 6pm.

MUSICAL INSTRUMENTS

Praha Music Center. Revoluční 14, Praha 1. ☎ **02/231 1693.** Metro: Náměstí Republiky.

Bring home an instrument from the land where "every Czech is a musician." Affordable Eastern European–made stringed instruments are sold. Open Monday to Friday from 9am to 6pm.

PHOTOGRAPHY

Jan Pazdera. Vodičkova 28, pasáž ABC, Praha 1. ☎ **02/2421 6197.** Metro: Můstek.

Camera repairs and cheap darkroom equipment make this a Prague snapper's favorite. The bulk of the selection is secondhand cameras, including Russian Smenas and Pentax. You can also find old telescopes, Carl Zeiss microscopes, light meters, and enlargers. Open Monday to Friday from 10am to 6pm.

PUPPETS

Obchod loutkami. Nerudova 47, Praha 1. ☎ **02/5753 2735.** Metro: Malostranská.

Many kinds of puppets are available, including hand, glove, rod, and marionettes, but no ventriloquist dummies, however. Obchod loutkami isn't cheap, but its creations are expertly made and beautifully sculpted. Hundreds of characters from trolls to barmen are available. Open daily from 9:30am to 7pm.

Obchod U Šaska. Jilská 7, Praha 1. ☎ **02/2423 5579.** Metro: Můstek.

High-quality, imaginatively designed clowns, ghouls, witches, and other marionettes are sold, including a good likeness of the Good Soldier Svejk. Open daily from 10am to 8pm.

SHOES

✪ **Bat'a.** Václavské nám. 6, Praha 1. ☎ **02/2421 8133.** Metro: Můstek.

Czechoslovakia's favorite footware émigré, Canadian Tomáš Bat'a has made his post-Communist return with a vengeance, taking a sizable chunk of the market long after the Nazis and then the Communists cut the original Moravian family factory to pieces. His huge outlet on the site where his father started selling shoes earlier this century on Wenceslas Square has been remodeled for modern comfort. Bat'a goods, including travel bags, leather accessories, and sports outfits, are there as well as top-line brands of athletic shoes. Open Monday to Friday from 9am to 8pm, Saturday and Sunday from 10am to 6pm.

pendicular to Melantrichova, between Staroměstské ...ští, **Havel's Market (Havelský trh)**, Havelská ulice, ...t (named well before a Havel became president) fea-...ors selling seasonal home-grown fruits and vegetables ...center. Other goods, including detergent, flowers, and ...n Monday to Friday from 8am to 6pm. Take metro line

...Příkopě 19, Praha 1. ☎ **02/2423 7494.** Metro: Můstek.

...clothes and equipment, Gigasport is Prague's newest ...er. However, the prices aren't much better than what you'd ...pany's overzealous security staff forces you to park all your ...s (you have to have correct change to use them). Open Monday to Satu... ...n 9:30am to 7pm and Sunday from 10am to 6pm.

Kastner Ohler. Václavské nám. 66, Praha 1. ☎ **02/2422 5432.** Metro: Muzeum.

Concentrating on name-brand sports clothing, this outlet of a Europe-wide chain has familiar shoe brands, exercise gear, and accessories. Open Monday to Saturday from 9:30am to 7pm.

WINE & BEER

Budvar and Becherovka are sold in shops all over Prague, but one of the cheapest places to buy these popular drinks is at **Tesco** (see "Department Stores & Shopping Malls," above). Expect to pay about 300Kč ($8.82) for a medium bottle of Becherovka and 150Kč ($4.41) for six bottles of Budvar. They also have a decent selection of domestic and foreign wines.

✪ **Dům lahůdek "U Rotta."** Malé nám. 3, Praha 1. ☎ **02/268 972.** Metro: Můstek.

Probably the best selection of wines in Bohemia, the cellar of this hardware store–turned–gourmet delicatessen claims 1,100 different labels, including a cusp-of-the-war 1939 private-collection Port in the archive under lock and key. Praguers know "U Rotta" as the country's most famous ironmonger, but a property dispute led this Old Town icon to start hocking lots of lox, not loads of lead.

9

Prague After Dark

by John Mastrini & Hana Mastrini

Many Czechs find their best nightly entertainment wrapped in the camaraderie of boisterous discussion and world-class brew at a noisy pub. Visitors with a penchant to blend in with the locals can learn a lot about this part of the world with an evening at the corner *hospoda.* Many find fascination just in a quiet stroll over the ancient city's cobblestones and under the mellow lamps of Charles Bridge and Malá Strana. Others seek the dark caverns of a fine jazz club or the black light and Day-Glo of a hot dance club.

But Prague's longest entertainment tradition, of course, is classical music. Sadly, many visitors leave disappointed at the level of the performances, especially the operas. Some of your choices can be entertaining and others thoroughly disappointing. Government cutbacks amid post-Communist budget realities have forced directors to skimp, while many great young voices have migrated to more lucrative stints abroad or in the rock operas and musicals that have sprung up around town.

A safe bet is Mozart's *Don Giovanni,* presented usually about twice per month in its original 2-centuries-old home, the Estates' Theater. This production, with modern accents, can also be choppy, but the feel of this beautifully restored setting is such that even a mediocre performance is worth it.

Serious music lovers are best steered to the numerous performances of the Czech Philharmonic at the Rudolfinum, the Prague Symphony Orchestra at Obecní dům, or top chamber ensembles at salons and palaces around the city. A bone-jarring pipe organ concert heard while sitting in the pews of one of the city's baroque churches can be inspirational.

For a more daring night, the cutting-edge Laterna Magika has been wowing audiences with its multimedia performance art since the Communists made the surprising decision to allow limited freedom of expression in the 1980s.

TICKETS Events rarely sell out far in advance, except for major nights during the Prague Spring music festival or a staging of *Don Giovanni* in the high season. To secure tickets before arriving, contact the travel bureau **Čedok,** in Prague, at Na Příkopě 18, Praha 1 (☎ **02/2419 7559**); in Britain, at 49 Southwark St., London SE1 1RU (☎ **020/7378-6009**). Or contact the Prague ticket agency

Ticketpro on the Internet at **www.ticketpro.cz** with updated lists of performances and the chance to reserve tickets a few days before your arrival.

Once in Prague, you can get tickets for most classical performances in all the main theaters at the **box office** in the modern **Nová scéna** annex to the **National Theater** at Národní třída 2, Praha 1 (☎ **02/2490 1448**). You can purchase tickets either at theater box offices or from any one of the dozens of ticket agencies. The largest handle most of the entertainment offerings and include a service charge. Ask how much this is before buying, as sometimes rates are hiked substantially. Large, centrally located agencies are **Prague Tourist Center,** Rytířská 12, Praha 1 (☎ **02/2421 2209**), open daily from 9am to 8pm; **Bohemia Ticket International,** Na Příkopě 16, Praha 1 (☎ **02/2421 5031**), open Monday to Friday from 10am to 7pm, Saturday from 10am to 5pm, and Sunday from 10am to 3pm; and **Čedok,** Na Příkopě 18, Praha 1 (☎ **02/2419 7642**), open Monday to Friday from 9am to 7pm and Saturday from 10am to 2pm. You can buy event tickets in person at these computerized outlets.

Ticketpro, Salvátorská 10, Praha 1 (☎ **02/2481 4020;** www.ticketpro.cz), Prague's largest computerized ticket service, sells seats by phone to most events around town. You can purchase tickets using Visa, MasterCard, Diners Club, or American Express, or reserve them on the Web and pay when you arrive.

1 The Performing Arts

Mozart reportedly shocked the Viennese when he once scoffed at his Austrian patrons by claiming simply that "Praguers understand me." His trips to the outpost in the Austrian Empire became the subject of music folklore. His defiant 1787 premiere of *Don Giovanni* is the high-water mark in Prague's cultural history—not that there haven't been fine performances since then. Czech composers Dvořák and Smetana each moved the resurgent nation to tears in the 19th century, while Martinu and Janáček ushered in a new industrial-age sound to classical compositions in the first half of the 20th century. You can still hear many works in grand halls throughout Prague; they're worth a visit just to bathe yourself in the grandeur of the setting along with a bit of musical accompaniment.

OPERA

Even if you're not fond of opera, buying a seat at any of the theaters below is a relatively affordable gamble. Prices range from about 40 to 750Kč ($1.17 to $22) and are often available up to curtain time.

While performances of Mozart's operas at the Estates' Theater are probably the visitor's best overall choices because of the setting, the **National Opera,** performing in the gold-crowned 19th-century National Theater, remains the country's best-loved company. Once the fiefdom of heavy-handed Bedřich Smetana, and then home to soprano Emma Destinová, who sang with the great Enrico Caruso, the National Opera has now fallen on harder times. Yet it still occasionally dazzles with Czech works like Smetana's peppy *Prodaná nevěsta (The Bartered Bride)*. The choreography by Pavel Šmok is fun for the whole family, and explanations of the plot are provided in English. Once in a while, internationally acclaimed soloists stop by. Seasons tend to concentrate on Czech works, though foreign-composed operas are also scheduled.

The **Prague State Opera (Státní opera Praha),** in the aging State Opera House near the top of Wenceslas Square, has reorganized after its 1992 split with the National Opera and now concentrates primarily on Italian classics, though a few Czech favorites

Prague After Dark

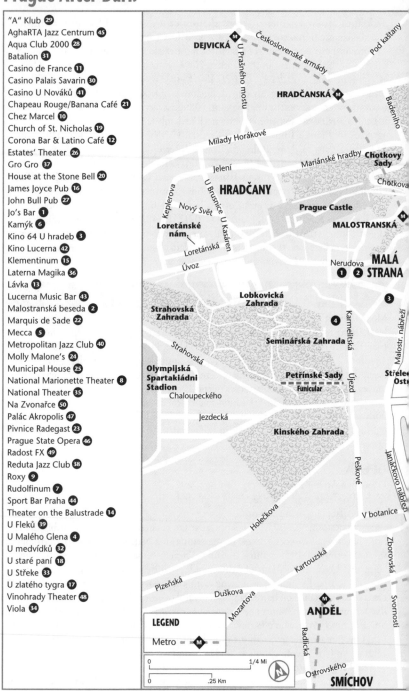

"A" Klub 29
AghaRTA Jazz Centrum 45
Aqua Club 2000 28
Batalion 31
Casino de France 11
Casino Palais Savarin 30
Casino U Nováků 41
Chapeau Rouge/Banana Café 21
Chez Marcel 10
Church of St. Nicholas 19
Corona Bar & Latino Café 12
Estates' Theater 26
Gro Gro 37
House at the Stone Bell 20
James Joyce Pub 16
John Bull Pub 27
Jo's Bar 1
Kamýk 6
Kino 64 U hradeb 3
Kino Lucerna 42
Klementinum 15
Laterna Magika 36
Lávka 13
Lucerna Music Bar 43
Malostranská beseda 2
Marquis de Sade 22
Mecca 5
Metropolitan Jazz Club 40
Molly Malone's 24
Municipal House 25
National Marionette Theater 8
National Theater 35
Na Zvonařce 50
Palác Akropolis 47
Pivnice Radegast 23
Prague State Opera 46
Radost FX 49
Reduta Jazz Club 38
Roxy 9
Rudolfinum 7
Sport Bar Praha 44
Theater on the Balustrade 14
U Fleků 39
U Malého Glena 4
U medvídků 32
U staré paní 18
U Střeke 33
U zlatého tygra 17
Vinohrady Theater 48
Viola 34

LEGEND

Metro — M

0 ——— 1/4 Mi
0 ——— .25 Km

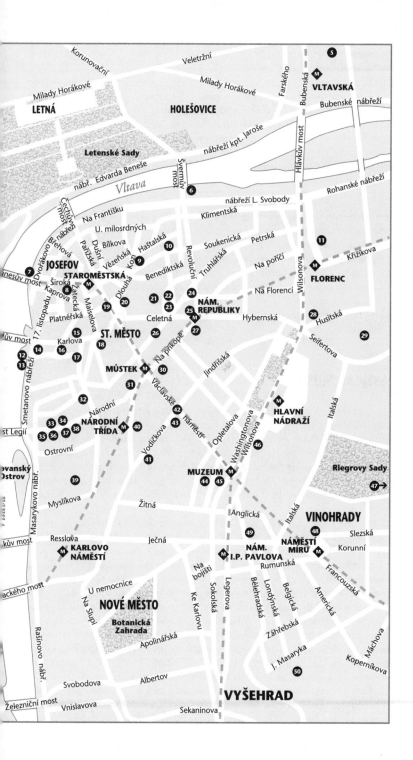

LETNÁ

HOLEŠOVICE

VLTAVSKÁ

Korunovační

Veletržní

Milady Horákové

Milady Horákové

Farského

Bubenské

Bubenské nábřeží

nábřeží kpt. Jaroše

Letenské Sady

nábř. Edvarda Beneše

Švermův most

Hlávkův most

Vltava

Rohanské nábřeží

nábřeží L. Svobody

Na Františku

Klimentská

U. milosrdných

Dvořákovo nábřeží

Břehová

JOSEFOV

STAROMĚSTSKÁ

Bílkova

Dušní

Vězeňská

Haštalská

Kozí

Benediktská

Revoluční

Soukenická

Petrská

Na poříčí

Křižíkova

FLORENC

Pařížská

Široká

Kaprova

Maiselová

Dlouhá

Truhlářská

Na Florenci

Wilsonova

Husitská

Kožná

Maiselová

Platnéřská

Celetná

NÁM. REPUBLIKY

Hybernská

Seifertova

Karlova

ST. MĚSTO

Na příkopě

MÚSTEK

Jindřišská

Václavské

HLAVNÍ NÁDRAŽÍ

Smetanovo nábřeží

Národní

NÁRODNÍ TŘÍDA

Vodičkova

náměstí

Opletalova

Washingtonova

Wilsonova

Italská

Ostrovní

Riegrovy Sady

 slovanský Ostrov

Masarykovo nábř.

Myslíkova

MUZEUM

VINOHRADY

Žitná

Anglická

Italská

Slezská

Resslova

Ječná

NÁM. I.P. PAVLOVA

NÁMĚSTÍ MÍRU

Korunní

KARLOVO NÁMĚSTÍ

Rumunská

Francouzská

Na bojišti

Legerova

Bělehradská

Londýnská

Belgická

Americká

U nemocnice

NOVÉ MĚSTO

Na Slupi

Ke Karlovu

Sokolská

Botanická Zahrada

Apolinářská

Záhřebská

J. Masaryka

Koperníkova

Máchova

Rašínovo nábř.

Svobodova

Albertov

VYŠEHRAD

Železniční most

Vnislavova

Sekaninova

149

Dressing the Part

Czechs are, generally, a casual, live-and-let-live people. President Havel, who has collected an extensive official wardrobe, is etched in everyone's memory as the dissident playwright in the same old frayed sweaters. Journalists still often show up for news conferences with the president or prime minister in T-shirts. But if you plan on attending the opera or theater, **proper evening wear is highly recommended.** There may be no bigger *faux pas* in Bohemia than dressing *Bohemian* for a classical performance. For men: a dark suit, or at least a coat and tie. For women: a mid-length dress or pantsuit.

---

are included each season. Its staging of Puccini's *Tosca* is solid but staid and without sufficient emotion at the tragic ending. Verdi's works like *La Traviata* and *Aïda* have received mixed reviews, mainly because of the cheap sets.

The **Estates' Theater** borrows from the National Opera company for its productions in Prague's most beautiful concert hall. In addition to the quintessential house performance in original Italian of *Don Giovanni,* other works from the master staged here are a Czech version of *The Magic Flute* and *The Wedding of Figaro* in Italian. In between, the theater often stages Czech versions of international classic stage plays or chamber ballets.

See "Landmark Theaters & Concert Halls," below, for detail on the theaters discussed here.

CLASSICAL MUSIC

This small capital boasts three full orchestras, yet all have become financially strapped, so the repertoire tends to be conservative, with most concerts providing popular time-tested works. For information on all three, call ☎ **02/2489 3352.** You can also get information at the ticket agencies listed above. Tickets range from 20 to 600Kč (59¢ to $17.64) during the regular season and up to 2,000Kč ($58.82) for the opening night of the Prague Spring festival. You can find dozens of concerts by the full orchestras or chamber groups each month, but the pickings are thin in July and August, when the musicians are on their holiday. See "Landmark Theaters & Concert Halls," below, for details.

Of the city's three orchestras, the **Czech Philharmonic** is the one that commands a fairly solid international reputation, though it's not considered first-rate. The Philharmonic, which calls the recently restored **Rudolfinum** home, went through turmoil in 1996 with the resignation of its first non-Czech musical director/chief conductor, German-born Gerd Albrecht. Despite acute money problems, the Philharmonic improved under Albrecht's demanding baton. Though many critics delighted in saying that Albrecht had tightened the ensemble and imposed disciplined precision, he had his detractors, including high government officials and orchestra members. In a hail of accusations and counteraccusations of Czech and German nationalism (mostly fanned by the press in both countries), Albrecht resigned, claiming that he'd lost his artistic freedom. He has since been replaced by Vladimir Ashkenazy, a Russian-born pianist who has promised to make the Czech orchestra world-class again.

The **Prague Symphony Orchestra** has positioned itself as the fresher alternative to the Philharmonic, with Gaeton Delogu as chief conductor. It focuses more on 20th-century music but has too often fallen back on Bach. Its freshly remodeled home in the Smetana Hall of the Municipal House (Obecní dům) cries out for a new concert approach, as its bold art nouveau elegance suggests more the power of Shostakovich than the delicacy of Brahms.

Classical Concerts Around Town

When strolling, you'll undoubtedly pick up or be handed lots of leaflets advertising chamber concerts in churches, museums, and other venues. These recitals and choral arrangements usually have programs featuring a classical and baroque repertoire, with an emphasis on pieces by Czech composers. The quality varies, but the results are usually pleasurable. Tickets range from 50 to 350Kč ($1.47 to $10.29) and can be purchased at the churches' entrances or (sometimes) from a hotel concierge.

Because of its extravagant beauty, the **Chapel of Mirrors,** in the Klementinum, Mariánské náměstí, Praha 1 (☎ **02/2166 3111**), is a favorite chamber concert venue. Almost every evening a classical concert highlights strings, winds, or the organ. The varied programs often rely on popular works by Handel, Bach, Beethoven, and Prague's beloved Mozart.

✪ **The Church of St. Nicholas (Kostel sv. Mikuláše),** Staroměstské náměstí, Praha 1 (☎ **02/232 2589**), is one of the city's finest baroque gems. Chamber concerts and organ recitals are popular here, and the acoustics are terrific. There's lots to look at: rich stucco decoration, sculptures of saints, and the crown crystal chandelier.

The **House at the Stone Bell (Dům U kamenného zvonu),** Staroměstské nám. 13, Praha 1 (☎ **02/2481 0036**), across the square from St. Nicholas, regularly hosts chamber concerts and other small gigs, including operatic arias and duets that are often performed here by soloists of the National Theater and State Opera.

The **Prague Radio Symphony Orchestra** is primarily a studio band but does make regular concert appearances. The group plays sufficient versions of classical and contemporary works in the Rudolfinum or Obecní dům.

Two solo Czech violinists to look out for when booking your tickets: the veteran virtuoso Josef Suk, a grandson of Dvořák, who still plays with crisp, if not anal, precision; and his flashier heir apparent, Václav Hudeček, who attacks every stanza with passion and bleeds through his bow.

The city's orchestras all come to life during the ✪ **Spring International Music Festival,** a 3-week series of classical music events each mid-May to early June; they began as a rallying point for Czech culture in the aftermath of World War II. The country's top performers usually participate in the festival, as well as some noted international stars. Tickets for concerts range from 250 to 2,000Kč ($7.35 to $58,82) and are available in advance from Hellichova 18, Praha 1 (☎ **02/2451 0422**).

The younger **Prague Autumn International Music Festival,** in September, hasn't received as much acclaim as the Spring event, but the 1997 appearance of the Israel Philharmonic, with Zubin Mehta at the baton, gave it a much needed boost. Contact Ticketpro (see "Tickets," above) for more information.

DANCE

Of all the musical arts in Prague, dance is the most accessible. From classical ballet to innovative modern dance, you can have several options each week demonstrating an enjoyable mix of grace, beauty, and athleticism. The **National Theater Ballet** troupe has seen most of its top talent go West since 1989, but it still has a deep roster as the country's premier troupe. Beyond the classical favorites at the venerable National

Theater's main stage, the ballet's choreographer, Libor Vaculík, has come up with dance twists on films like *Some Like It Hot* and *Psycho* next door at the modern, comfortable theater in the round, Nová scéna. Vaculík's works are popular, making this one of the most financially secure dance companies in Eastern Europe. Tickets are 30 to 500Kč (88¢ to $14.70); call ☎ **02/2490 1448** for information.

The ✪ **Prague Chamber Ballet** has recently been playing intimate dates at the Estates' Theater, giving the audience the chance to see modern and classical dance in a theater primarily designed for opera. Choreographer Pavel Šmok's fresh takes on Czech spiritual folk music, Latin or Slavic beats, and provocative religious themes are set to recorded music. But the sound system is adequate and the experience above average. Check the *Prague Post* to see what selections are on tap.

LANDMARK THEATERS & CONCERT HALLS

✪ **Estates' Theater (Stavovské divadlo).** Ovocný trh 1, Praha 1. ☎ **02/2490 1448.** Metro: Line A or B to Můstek.

In a city full of spectacularly beautiful theaters, the massive pale-green Estates' ranks as one of the most awesome. Built in 1783, this is the only theater in the world that's still in its original condition. The Estates' was home to the premiere of Mozart's *Don Giovanni*, which was conducted by the composer himself. The building, an example of the late baroque style, was reopened on the 200th anniversary of Mozart's death in 1991, after nearly 9 years of reconstruction.

Simultaneous English translation, transmitted via headphone, is available for plays staged here.

✪ **National Theater (Národní divadlo).** Národní 2, Praha 1. ☎ **02/2490 1448.** Metro: Národní třída.

Lavishly built in the late Renaissance style of northern Italy, the gold-crowned National Theater, overlooking the Vltava River, is one of Prague's most recognizable landmarks. Completed in 1881, the theater was built to nurture the Czech National Revival—a grassroots movement to replace the dominant German culture with that of native Czechs. To finance it, small collection boxes with signs for "the prosperity of a dignified national theater" were installed in public places. Almost immediately on completion, the building was wrecked by fire and rebuilt, opening in 1883 with the premiere of Bedřich Smetana's opera *Libuše*. The magnificent interior contains an allegorical sculpture about music and busts of Czech theatrical personalities created by some of the country's best-known artists. Composer Bedřich Smetana conducted the theater's orchestra here until 1874, when deafness forced him to relinquish his post.

Rudolfinum. Náměstí Jana Palacha, Praha 1. ☎ **02/2489 3111.** Metro: Staroměstská.

Named for Prince Rudolf, the beautifully restored Rudolfinum has been one of the city's premier concert venues since it opened in the 19th century. The Rudolfinum's Small Hall mostly presents chamber concerts, while the larger, more celebrated Dvořák Hall is home to the Czech Philharmonic. Though the acoustics aren't faultless, the grandeur of the hall makes a concert experience here worthwhile.

✪ **Smetana Hall (Smetanova síň).** In the Municipal House (Obecní dům), náměstí Republiky 5, Praha 1. ☎ **02/2200 2100.** Metro: Náměstí Republiky.

Named for the popular composer and fervent Czech nationalist Bedřich Smetana (1824–84), Smetana Hall is located in one of the world's most distinctive art nouveau buildings. Since its 1997 reopening after the building's painstaking reconstruction, the ornate and purely exhilarating Smetana Hall has hosted a series of top-notch events, including a moving speech by U.S. Secretary of State Madeleine Albright speaking of her return to her birthplace to invite the Czechs into NATO, and an eclectic evening during a 1997 forum with Gregory Peck, James Earl Jones, and Lynn Redgrave reciting excerpts from Václav Havel plays.

State Opera House (Státní opera). Wilsonova 4, Praha 2. ☎ **02/2422 7693.** Metro: Muzeum.

First the "New German Theater" and then the "Smetana Theater," the State Opera was built in the 1880s for the purpose of staging Germanic music and drama. Based on a Viennese design, the Renaissance-style theater was rebuilt after suffering serious damage during the bombing of Prague in 1945. Over the years, the auditorium has hosted many great names, including Richard Wagner, Richard Strauss, and Gustav Mahler, whose Seventh Symphony premiered here. In addition to being home to the State Opera, the house stages other music and dance events.

THEATER

Theater has a long tradition in Czech life. Its enormous influence was reconfirmed during the revolutionary events of 1989, when theaters became the focal points and the strategy rooms for the opposition.

Most of the city's theater offerings are in Czech, but a few English-language expatriate troupes have taken root and they stage performances whenever they are ready—or not—at various locations. Check the *Prague Post* for the latest listings.

Czech productions by local and translated authors are staged almost every night. The most highly respected theaters are the gorgeous ✪ **Vinohrady Theater (Divadlo na Vinohradech),** náměstí Míru 7, Praha 2 (☎ **02/2425 7484**), the former workplace of President Havel's wife, Dagmar, who made a final performance as Queen Kristina soon after becoming first lady. The **Theater on the Balustrade (Divadlo Na Zábradlí),** Anenské nám. 5, Praha 1 (☎ **02/2222 2026**), is the place where Havel got his start as a playwright. Tickets, usually costing between 50 and 300Kč ($1.47 and $8.82), should be bought in advance. Simultaneous translation into English is often offered in earphones provided by the theaters, but the translator reads all parts from a script usually without much dramatic verve. Ask when booking if translation is offered.

Laterna Magika, Národní třída 4, Praha 1 (☎ **02/2491 4129**), a performance-art show based in the new wing of the National Theater, plays a range of multimedia productions, from a provocative, racy version of *Odysseus* to a choppy, inconsistent version of *Casanova,* but the stunning presence of the lead Linda Rybová lights up the stage. These are adult themes combining unique uses of dance, music, film, and light and can be very entertaining and easy to follow for audiences of any language. Tickets cost 500Kč ($14.70) and should be bought in advance.

The purpose-built **National Marionette Theatre (Národní divadlo marionet),** Žatecká 1, Praha 1 (☎ **02/232 3429**), is the best of Prague's small handful of puppet theaters. The company's mainstay has been Mozart's *Don Giovanni.* For adults, the best thing about this show is the soundtrack. Tickets cost 490Kč ($14.41), 390Kč ($11.47) for students. The box office is open daily from 10am to 8pm (Wednesday to 7pm). Take the metro to Staroměstská.

2 The Club & Music Scene

The Velvet Revolution had its roots in the underground rock clubs that kept the braver Czech sonic youth tuned in to something more than the monotones of the party during the gray 1970s and 1980s period known as Normalization. The Communists' persecution of the garage band Plastic People of the Universe, named for a Frank Zappa refrain, motivated playwright Václav Havel and his friends to keep the

Prague's Mysterious Nights

If you've never been here, the otherwise uninspired film *Kafka* with Jeremy Irons will give you a fine sense of the dark mystery trapped in the shadows cast over the palace walls and cobblestone streets throughout Old Town and Malá Strana. You'll never forget a slow stroll across Charles Bridge, with its dim lampposts (gas flame until well into the 20th century) cutting the eerie silhouettes from the attending statues. The artfully lit facades of Prague Castle hover above as if the whole massive complex were floating in the darkness. The domes and spires of the skyline leading up to Hradčany have more varied textures and contours than a Dutch master could ever have dreamed of painting. Students howling with a guitar or a single violinist playing his heart out for a few koruny in his hat creates the bridge's ambient sound.

Evenings are also a fine time to walk through the castle courtyards, as the crowds are dispersed and a quiet solemnity falls over the city. From high atop the castle hill, Prague sparkles below.

Across the river, the brightly lit belfries of the Týn Church cast a spine-tingling glow on the rest of Old Town Square, and the mellow lamps around the Estates' Theater provide the light for a memorable walk home after the performance.

human rights heat on the politburo. As president, Havel has paid homage to rock's part in the revolution, keeping company with the likes of Zappa, Springsteen, Dylan, and the Stones, who all have paid tribute to him as the rock-'n'-roll president.

Almost universally, the amps in clubs are turned up to absurd distortion. But while most wanna-be bands playing Prague today lack the political edge of the prerevolution days, some have kept their unique Slavic passion without being overtaken by the urge to sound like Soundgarten. Throughout the rock clubs on any given night you might run into the ascerbic pounding of Psí vojáci (Dog Soldiers) or the no-holds-barred horns of Laura a její tygři (Laura and Her Tigers).

The 1996 neighborhood-enforced death of the original postrevolutionary subterranean hideaway, Bunkr, left a large void on the dance and rock club roster, but some new entries have tried to step in. As for dance tracks, Euro-trash techno-pop dominates most places marked "Disco," but there are a few places where the mix has some imagination and the crowd is a bit older than 16.

ROCK & DANCE CLUBS

Batalion. 28.října 3, Praha 1. ☎ **02/2010 8147.** Cover up to 50Kč ($1.47). Metro: Můstek.

On the side street connecting Národní with the low end of Wenceslas Square, Batalion has become the not-ready-for-prime-time location for up-and-coming Czech rocks bands. Cover and drinks are cheap, and though the usually blaring rock isn't always recommended, it's a quick and easy way to sample the local music scene. The bar is open all day every day; the music starts at 9pm.

Corona Bar & Latino Café. Novotného lávka 9, Praha 1. ☎ **02/2108 2208.** Cover 100Kč ($3.05) Fri–Sat. Metro: Staroměstská.

The nights of salsa and samba have lost some of their raw edge since a 1997 upscale remodeling. Still, the tequila, the spicy food, and the Latin rhythms (live and recorded) will keep you dancing in this warmly decorated place just off Charles Bridge. The Corona is for grown-ups who haven't lost their passion, but you may feel the rumble in your head and stomach well into the next evening. Open Monday to Thursday from 11am to 1am and Friday and Saturday from 11am to 3am.

Lávka. Novotného lávka 1, Praha 1. ☎ **02/2421 4797.** Cover 50Kč ($1.47). Metro: Staroměstská.

Next door to the Corona Bar, Lávka's black light and Day-Glo dance floor stands in stark contrast to the terrace that provides quiet respite from the techno-dance tunes pounding inside. Here you can take advantage of the best riverside outdoor seating during warmer months. The drink prices help pay what has to be a hefty rent for this location. The clientele is a mix of well-heeled locals and visitors. Lávka's always open and music plays from 9:30pm to 5am.

✪ **Lucerna Music Bar.** Vodičkova 36, Praha 1. ☎ **02/2421 7108.** Cover 50–70Kč ($1.47–$2.05). Metro: Můstek.

Big and a bit dingy, this Prague landmark in the belly of the downtown palace that Václav Havel's father built provides the best lineup of Czech garage bands, ex-underground acts, and an occasional reggae or blues gig. The drinks are still cheap for the city center, with a pull of beer still under 15Kč (44¢). The feel of the Lucerna, with its mirrored ball spinning the night away, borrows from disco but is mixed with the funky edginess of the period around the revolution. The crowd is still mostly local. The Lucerna is a frequent stop of Laura and Her Tigers. Open daily from 6pm to 3am, with live music usually beginning at 9pm.

Malostranská beseda. Malostranské nám. 21, Praha 1. ☎ **02/539 024.** Cover 50Kč ($1.47). Metro: Malostranská.

In between hosting random nights of some of the best jazz, the beseda ("meeting place") on the recently restored baroque main square in Malá Strana once acted as the district's town hall. The mix of bands varies, so check the *Prague Post* to see if the beseda is playing your tune. On the second floor, the club consists of little more than two smallish rooms; one holds the bar, the other a stage on which live bands perform most every night. There's more sitting than dancing here. The bar is open daily from 5 to 8pm, but only to ticketholders, and the music usually begins at 9:30pm.

Mecca. U Průhonu 3, Praha 7. ☎ **02/8387 0522.** Cover 50Kč ($1.47). Metro: Vltavská, then tram 1.

For those who don't mind trekking into the depths of Praha 7 to be with some of the trendiest people in town, make your way to Mecca. You don't have to pray to the east to get in, but you'd better be one of the beautiful people, dressed well enough to get through the bouncers at the usually packed entrance. This converted warehouse in a northeast Prague industrial area has become the biggest challenge to the Roxy and Radost for Prague's biggest house parties, with deejay-driven techno, blaring lights, and plenty of sound. Open 11am to 3am daily, longer on weekends.

Palác Akropolis. Kubelíkova 27, Praha 3. ☎ **02/2271 2287.** Cover 50–150Kč ($1.47–$4.41). Metro: Jiřího z Poděbrad.

The eclectic complex in this uptown neighborhood feels like a hip civic center carved out of an old cinema. Pop art dots the rooms and the hip bar, and the concert hall plays host to groups from the Prague underground rock clique. Theater performances start at 7:30pm and deejays play the Theater bar from 11pm. It's a more artsy hangout than a nightclub, serving cheap drinks until 2am.

✪ **Radost F/X.** Bělehradská 120, Praha 2. ☎ **02/2251 3144.** Cover 50–150Kč ($1.47–$4.41). Metro: I. P. Pavlova or Náměstí Míru.

The Radost tries so hard to catch the retro 1960s and 1970s crowd that it has become a cartoon of itself, yet it remains popular with a mixed straight, gay, and model crowd. The rec-room interior of the ground-floor lounge is great for a chat and a drink. The series of downstairs rooms gets filled with rave and techno mixes. The crowd is very attractive and style obsessed, and the bouncers have been known to boot those who don't look the part. Open daily from 10pm to 5am.

A visit to Radost's vegetarian cafe of the same name, upstairs, is usually combined with a trip to the club (see the listing in chapter 5).

Roxy. Dlouhá 33, Praha 1. ☎ **02/2482 6390.** Cover 50–100Kč ($1.47–$2.94). Metro: Náměstí Republiky.

Another reincarnation of a dead cinema, the Roxy pushes the boundaries of bizarre in its dark, stark concrete dance hall down Dlouhá street near Old Town Square. The balcony allows the art-community crowd to try to watch one another amid the candlelight. The club is ultra-deconstructionist. Persian rugs and lanterns soften the atmosphere but don't improve the lousy acoustics. Acid jazz, funk, techno, salsa, and reggae are among the tunes on the play list from the recorded or live acts. The Roxy is the longest late-night romp in town, open from 8pm to 5am.

JAZZ

While Dixieland swing was huge in Prague during the First Republic, urban jazz really made its mark here during the 1960s, when those testing the Communist authority flocked to the smoky caves and wore dark glasses. The chubby Czech songstress Vlasta Průchová grabbed a few hints from Ella Fitzgerald to go with her throaty voice and set the standard for Czech be-bop wanna-bes in the postwar period leading up to the Prague Spring. After defecting, her son Jan Hammer made it big in the United States with his computerized scores, including the theme to *Miami Vice.*

Luckily, most of Prague's ensembles follow Vlasta's lead and not Jan's. There are several good venues for a cool evening with a traditional upright bass, piano, sax, and drum group or occasional shots of fusion and acid jazz. The most publicized gig has been at the Reduta Jazz Club, where Bill Clinton played "Summertime" and "My Funny Valentine" for President Havel and Madeleine Albright during a state visit in 1994.

Look for bookings with the venerable Průchová, who's still belting out the blues along with her Swinging Quartet, or her be-bop heiress apparent, Jana Koubková. The Karel Růžička or Štěpán Markovič quartets are also solid, with surprising doses of soul.

U Malého Glena, listed under "Pubs," below, also offers jazz, fusion, and sometimes funk on most nights in its cellar.

AghaRTA Jazz Centrum. Krakovská 5, Praha 1. ☎ **02/2221 1275.** Cover 80–100Kč ($2.35–$2.94). Metro: Muzeum.

Upscale by Czech standards, the AghaRTA regularly features some of the best music in town, from standard acoustic trios and quartets to Dixieland, funk, and fusion. Hot Line, the house band led by AghaRTA part-owner and drummer Michael Hejuna, regularly takes the stage. Bands usually begin at 9pm. Open Monday to Friday from 5pm to 1am and Saturday and Sunday from 7pm to 1am.

Metropolitan Jazz Club. Jungmannova 14, Praha 1. ☎ **02/2494 7777.** Cover 50Kč ($1.47). Metro: Národní třída.

There never seems to be anyone under 30 in this sophisticated downstairs jazz club, fitted with ceramic-topped tables and red velvet chairs. The small cellar is reached through the courtyard just a few doors down from the McDonald's on Vodičkova. It's home to a house trio that plays several nights a month, and Dixie and swing bands fill the rest of the calendar. Concerts begin at 9pm. Open Monday to Friday from 11am to 1am and Saturday and Sunday from 7pm to 1am.

✪ **Reduta Jazz Club.** Národní 20, Praha 1. ☎ **02/2491 2246.** Cover 120Kč ($3.52). Metro: Národní třída.

Reduta is the most familiar of all of Prague's jazz clubs, and most all of the good Czech acts will make an appearance here sometime during the year. This smoky cavern has cramped seating in fixed metallic boxes with veneer-wood tables, forcing everyone to sit in the same position through most of the night. Drinks are mostly serve yourself from the adjacent bar, though a waitress is known to occasionally show up. But the reason people come here is for the wide range of solid jazz acts that play 6 nights a week, each of them better than the guest sax gig played by that visiting head of state in 1994. Music usually starts around 9pm. Open Monday to Saturday from 9pm to midnight.

U staré paní. Michalská 9, Praha 1. ☎ **02/264 920.** Cover 60Kč ($1.76). Metro: Můstek.

Some of the best bands perform on a small stage that's in the downstairs of an over-priced pension in the middle of Old Town. The jazz is wonderfully close to most every table in this club, which is both visually pleasant and acoustically superior. Karel Růžička and his band play here frequently. Concerts begin at 9pm and usually last until midnight.

Viola. Národní 7, Praha 1. ☎ **02/2422 0844.** Cover 45Kč ($1.32). Metro: Národní třída.

Jazz concerts are scheduled alongside poetry readings and plays on this tiny stage, which has been a favorite haunt of the Prague literary community for decades. A good-size stage and tiered seating are designed for listening, not background music. Strange for a jazz club, but no smoking is permitted here. It makes the experience actually more enjoyable if you're not going through withdrawal. Look for Allen Ginsberg's signature on the lounge wall. The box office is open Monday to Saturday from 4 to 8:15pm. Concerts start at 8pm.

3 Pubs

The chatter and glee of the pubs are Prague's preferred late-evening entertainment. Unlike, British, Irish, or German beer halls, a true Czech pub ignores accoutrement like cushy chairs and warm wooden paneling and cuts straight to the chase—beer. While some Czech pubs do serve a hearty plate of food alongside the suds, it's the brew, uncommonly cheap at usually less than 34Kč ($1) a pint, that keeps people sitting for hours.

Foreign-theme pubs are popping up all over Prague, offering tastes ranging from Irish to Mexican. Still it feels a bit like trying to sell foreign tea in China. Below we've listed the best of the Czech brew stops and then choices whose inspirations come from abroad.

CZECH PUBS

✪ **Na Zvonařce.** Šafaříkova 1, Praha 2. ☎ **02/2425 1990.** Metro: I. P. Pavlova.

Originally the after-work stop for nearby bellmakers, Na Zvonařce has become an institution in Praha 2, especially in the serendipity days of spring and summer, when the large patio is open and the Pilsner Urquel beer really hits the spot. The food is typical Czech, but the preparation is a cut above and the service friendlier than most,

Není Pivo Jako Pivo: There's No Beer Like Beer

This seemingly absurd local proverb makes sense when you first taste the cold golden nectar (*pivo*) from its source and realize that you've never really had *beer* before. While Czechs on the whole aren't religious, *pivo* still elicits a piety unseen in many orthodox countries. The golden Pilsner variety that accounts for most of the beer consumed around the world was born here and has inspired some of the country's most popular fiction, films, poetry, and prayers.

For many Czechs, the corner beer hall (*hospoda* or *pivnice*) is a social and cultural center. Regulars in these smoke-encrusted caves drink beer as lifeblood and seem ill at ease when a foreigner takes their favorite table or disrupts their daily routine. For those wanting to sample the rich, aromatic taste of Czech lagers without ingesting waves of nicotine, dozens of more ventilated pubs and restaurants have emerged since the Velvet Revolution. Alas, the suds in these often cost as much as five times more than those in the standard hospoda.

While always informal, Czech pubs observe their own unwritten code of etiquette:

- Large tables are usually shared with strangers.
- When sitting, you should first ask *"Je tu volno?"* ("Is this place taken?"). If not, put a cardboard coaster down in front of you to show that you want a beer.
- Don't wave for a waitperson—it'll only delay the process when he or she sees you.
- When the waitperson does finally arrive and sees the coaster in front of you, simply nod or hold up fingers for the number of beers you want for you and your companions.
- If there's a choice, it's usually between size—*malé* ("mah-lay") is small, *velké* ("vel-kay") is large—or type—*světlé* ("svyet-lay") is light, *černé* ("cher-nay") is dark.
- The waitperson will pencil marks on a white slip of paper that remains on your table.
- If your waitperson ever comes back for a second round, order enough for the rest of your stay and ask to pay. When he or she returns, say *"zaplatíme"* ("we'll pay") . . . you might not see him or her for a long time.

According to brewing industry studies, Czechs drink more beer per capita than any other people. The average Czech downs 320 pints of brew each year; the average American drinks about 190. Of course, a Czech hospoda regular will drink the year's average for a family of six. Pub regulars do not wonder

albeit sometimes slower in the lazy days of August. Open daily from 11:30am to 10pm.

Pivnice Radegast. Templová 2, Praha 1. ☎ **02/232 8237.** Metro: Můstek.

An Old Town institution under the vaulted ceilings of a smoky, narrow Gothic hall, the Radegast was really the only place to get the tasty beer of the same name shipped in from Moravia. The best pub goulash in town is served here, too. Open daily from 11am to midnight.

why the Czech national anthem is a song that translates as "Where Is My Home?"

Several widely held Czech superstitions are connected with drinking beer. One says that you should never pour a different kind of beer in a mug holding the remnants of another brew. Bad luck is sure to follow. Some believe that the toast—usually *"na zdraví"* ("to your health")—is negated if anyone fails to clink his or her mug with any of the others at your table and then slams the mug on the table before taking the first chug.

Czech beer comes in various degrees of concentration, usually marked on the label or menu. This is not the amount of alcohol, though the higher degree does carry a higher alcohol content. The standard premium 12° brew contains about 5% alcohol, though each label varies. If you want something a little lighter on the head, try a 10°, with 3.5% to 4% alcohol.

The never-ending debate over which Czech beer is best rages on, but here are the top contenders, all readily available in Prague (each pub or restaurant usually will flaunt which is their choice on the front of the building):

- **Pilsner Urquell:** The original Pilsner lager. A bit bitter, but with a smooth texture that comes, the locals say, from the softer alkaline waters that flow under Pilsen. Urquell is mostly packaged for export and often seen at beer boutiques across the Atlantic.

- **Budvar:** The original "Budweiser," this semisweet lager hails from České Budějovice, a town also known by its German name, Budweis. The clash with U.S. giant Anheuser Busch over the "Budweiser" trademark kept the American giant from selling Bud in much of Europe for years. There's little similarity in the taste of the two—you decide. Busch wanted a stake in the Budvar brewery, but the Czech government balked at a deal in 1996.

- **Staropramen:** The flagship of Prague's home brewery is a solid choice and is easiest to find in the capital. Now that Britain's Bass owns Staropramen they're marketing a hybrid called Velvet, a cross between a Czech lager and an Irish ale. It's worth a try.

- **Kozel:** This is a favorite with the American expat community, with a distinctive namesake goat on the label. It has a spicy taste and full body. Light beer this is not.

- **Krušovice:** From a tiny brewery in the cradle of the western hop-growing region, this brew, commissioned by Rudolf II four centuries ago, used to be hard to find in Prague, but no more. Lighter but not fizzy, it has just a glimpse of bitterness.

U Fleků. Křemencova 11, Praha 2. ☎ **02/2491 5118.** Metro: Národní třída.

One of the original microbreweries dating back to 1459, U Fleků is Prague's most famous beer hall, one of the only pubs that still serves only its own beer. It's a huge place with a maze of timber-lined rooms and a large, loud courtyard where an oompah band performs. The ornate medieval-style wood ceilings and courtyard columns are charming but not very old. Tourists come here by the busload, so U Fleků is avoided by disparaging locals who don't like its German atmosphere. But the pub's sweet dark beer is excellent and not available anywhere else; however, the sausages and goulash are overcooked and overpriced. When a band performs in the garden, a cover of 100Kč ($2.94) is charged. Open daily from 9am to 11pm.

✪ **U medvídků (At the Little Bears).** Na Perštýně 7, Praha 1. ☎ **02/2421 1916.** Metro: Národní třída.

This 5-centuries-old pub off Národní třída was the first in town to serve the original Budweiser, Budvar, on tap. It also serves typical Czech pub food, including *cmunda,* potato pancakes topped with sauerkraut and cured meat. It's smoky inside, but it's easier to breathe here than at most local pubs. Be sure to go to the right when you enter; if you don't you'll head into the darker bar, which serves the same food and a wider range of beer choices at close to twice the price. Open daily from 11am to 11pm.

U zlatého tygra (At the Golden Tiger). Husova 17, Praha 1. ☎ **02/2222 1111.** Metro: Staroměstská or Můstek.

One of the most Czech of the central city pubs, this was once the favorite watering hole of Václav Havel and one of his mentors, writer Bohumil Hrabal, who died in 1997. Particularly smoky and not especially visitor friendly, this is a one-stop education in Czech pub culture. Pilsner Urquell is the house brew. Havel and President Bill Clinton joined Hrabal for a traditional Czech pub evening here during Clinton's visit in 1994, much to the chagrin of the regulars. Open daily from 3 to 11pm.

INTERNATIONAL PUBS

James Joyce Pub. Liliová 10, Praha 1. ☎ **02/2424 8793.** Metro: Staroměstská.

Guinness and Kilkenny on tap at authentic Irish prices keep locals to a minimum. Sparsely placed wall hangings make this popular bar closer to the real McCoy than Bennigan's. Juicy burgers and weekend brunches are also available. Open daily from 11am to 1am.

John Bull Pub. Senovážná 8, Praha 1. ☎ **02/269 255.** Metro: Náměstí Republiky.

British and Czech beers are served by the pint in a cozy English pub environment brought to you by the same British corporation that's opening these "neighborhood" pubs around the world. Standard British pub food, including roast beef with Yorkshire pudding, costs just a fraction of the price back home. Open Monday to Saturday from 10:30am to 2am and Sunday from 10:30am to midnight.

✪ **Molly Malone's.** U Obecního dvora 4, Praha 1. ☎ **02/534 793.** Metro: Staroměstská.

This excellent pub evokes the authentic warmth of an old country inn on a rainy Irish night. The farmhouse atmosphere is loaded with old-fashioned sewing-machine tables, green velvet drapes, a roaring fireplace, and turn-of-the-century skivvies hanging on a clothesline. There's plenty of boisterous laughter and Guinness on tap. Pub meals (including huge hamburgers and the best french fries in town) are served daily from noon to 8pm. Open Sunday to Thursday from noon to 1am and Friday and Saturday from noon to 2am.

U Malého Glena. Karmelitská 23, Praha 1. ☎ **02/535 8115.** Metro: Malostranská.

Guinness is served on draft here in this small Malá Strana haunt by the ex-pat American called "Little Glen," who also owns Bohemia Bagel down the street. This place has developed a firm clientele with jazz nights performed in the small cozy cellar. Decent food—soups, salads, and focaccias—are served nightly until 1am. Open daily from 7:30pm to 3am.

Late-Night Bites

Of all the restaurants serving past midnight (see chapter 5 for a complete listing), **Radost FX Café** in Vinohrady is the top late-dining choice, offering its fresh vegetarian dishes and stiff espresso daily until 5am.

At the **Corona Bar & Latino Café** (☎ **02/2108 2208**), they serve the full restaurant menu until midnight and some good appetizers well into the morning. If you're really desperate with the munchies, just down from the Reduta jazz club is the **Gro Gro** kiosk, on the corner of Národní třída and Mikulandská. The "Gro Gro Guy" offers personal grilled-oven pizzas for 40 to 50Kč ($1.17 to $1.47) and a small array of ham-and-cheese baguette sandwiches, chips, sodas, and beer.

---

4 The Bar Scene

The city has acquired a much wider selection of bars in recent years to complement its huge array of beer pubs. The competition has brought out a variety of watering holes—from country to French, from straight to gay to mixed—that would match the offerings in most any major European capital.

Chapeau Rouge/Banana Café. Jakubská 2, Praha 1. No phone. No cover. Metro: Náměstí Republiky.

Hidden on a small Old Town backstreet, this loud and lively New Orleans–esque ground-floor place has twin bars, plank floors, and a good sound system playing contemporary rock. It sells four types of beer on tap and features regular drink specials. It's busy and fun—if you avoid the headache-inducing concoctions from the frozen drink machine. Drag queens often cruise through here, but the crowd is mixed. Open daily from noon to 5am.

Chez Marcel. Haštalská 12, Praha 1. ☎ **02/231 5676.** No cover. Metro: Staroměstská.

This very stylish authentic French cafe looks like it was plucked straight out of Montmartre. Though casual light meals are served, Chez Marcel is best as a cafe/bar and a great place for café au lait. It attracts a good mix of hipsters and suits around sunset and starts to thin out at about 11pm. Open Monday to Friday from 8am to 1am, and Saturday and Sunday from 9am to 1am.

Jo's Bar. Malostranské nám. 7, Praha 1. No phone. No cover. Metro: Malostranská.

The original American backpackers' spot, this fixture is still fun after all these years, but the Mexican food is in need of a gastric overhaul. Open daily from 11am to 2am.

Kamýk. At Švermův Bridge, Praha 1. No phone. No cover. Metro: Náměstí Republiky.

Permanently docked at the foot of Revoluční třída, this small tarp-covered boat is home to one of the liveliest drug scenes in the city. Looking more than just a little bit like a pirate ship, Kamýk is quite an eyeful—and a noseful if the wind is blowing in your direction. It's really smoking after 4pm. Open in summer only from 10am to 4am.

✪ **Marquis de Sade.** Templová 8, Praha 1. No phone. No cover. Metro: Můstek.

In the same neighborhood as La Provence, Chapeau Rouge, and Pivnice Radegast, the Marquis de Sade stands apart from other Czech watering holes because of its huge room with high ornate ceilings that belie the casual wooden furniture and kitschy wall hangings. There's room here to breathe, and the Marquis attracts a solid return business of local ex-pats.

Sport Bar Praha-Zlatá Hvězda. Ve smečkách 12, Praha 1. ☎ **02/2221 0124.** No cover. Metro: Muzeum.

Prague's original jocks-on-the-tube American bar has moved down the street into a more traditional Czech pub setting. Six kinds of Czech beer still flow freely with the games of the week, and the burgers and chicken fingers have outlasted other contenders for the "Sports Bar" title. You can play a good game of pool if the game on TV bores you.

GAY & LESBIAN CLUBS

Prague's small gay and lesbian community is growing in its openness and choices for nightclubs and entertainment. See "For Gay & Lesbian Travelers" in chapter 2 for information or call the **SOHO Infocentrum** at ☎ **02/2422 0327.**

Also see the entry for **Radost FX Café,** above.

"A" Klub. Milíčova 32, Praha 3. No phone. Cover 25Kč (73¢). Metro: Flora, then tram 9.

This sharply decorated lesbian bar is covered with the works of female artists and sports cushy chairs and couches. Fridays are only for women. Men are allowed on other nights, but only in the company of a woman. There's dancing and relaxed chat at this east Prague bar, open daily from 6pm to 6am.

Aqua Club 2000. Husitská 7, Praha 3. ☎ **02/627 8971.** Cover 30Kč (88¢) Mon–Wed, 80Kč ($2.35) Thurs–Sat. Metro: Florenc, then bus 133 to Husitská.

This multiactivity venue attracts a mixed gay and lesbian crowd. This has become Prague's transvestite paradise, with weekend shows touted for their precision and authenticity. On the premises is a sauna, a swimming pool, and a disco. Open daily 6pm to 4am (disco 9pm to 4am, floor shows Monday and Thursday to Saturday).

U Střelce. Karoliny Světlé 12. Praha 1. ☎ **02/2423 8278.** Cover charges vary, usually around 100Kč ($2.95). Metro: Národní třída.

A popular nightclub attracting a mixed gay-straight foreign and local crowd near Charles Bridge, "The Archer's" offers the most extensive cabaret shows in Old Town, with comical drag queens featured during the weekend shows. Open daily from 6pm to 4am.

5 Casinos & Movie Theaters

CASINOS

Prague has many casinos, most offering blackjack, roulette, and slot machines. House rules are usually similar to those in Las Vegas, but there are often slight variations.

Casino Palais Savarin, Na Příkopě 10, Praha 1 (☎ **02/2422 1636;** metro: Můstek), occupying a former rococo palace, is the most beautiful game room in the city. It's open daily from 1pm to 4am. Other recommendable casinos are **Casino de France,** in the hotel Hilton Prague, Pobřežní 1, Praha 8 (☎ **02/2484 1111;** Metro: Florenc), open daily from 2pm to 6am; and **Casino U Nováků,** Vodičkova 30, Praha 1 (☎ **02/2422 2098;** Metro: Můstek), open daily from 1pm to 5am.

MOVIE THEATERS

Unlike neighboring Germany, which has made dubbing such an art that it has become the scourge of the industry, foreign films are generally screened here in their original language, with Czech subtitles. Now, better Czech films are also being screened for visitors with English subtitles. Unlike the prerevolution days, when hardly a decent Western film could be seen, the cinemas (*kinos*) are filled with most first-run films from Hollywood and the independents within a few weeks after their general release.

Many cinemas are on or near Václavské náměstí (Wenceslas Square). Tickets cost 50 to 100Kč ($1.47 to $2.94). Most screenings have reserved seats, and many popular films sell out in advance, so pick your places early. Check the *Prague Post* for listings, or for a more accurate list, look at the billboards outside **Kino Lucerna,** Vodičkova 36, near Wenceslas Square (☎ **02/2421 6972;** Metro: Můstek), or **Kino 64 U hradeb,** Mostecká 21, just off Charles Bridge in Malá Strana (☎ **02/535 006;** Metro: Staroměstská and across Charles Bridge).

Day Trips from Prague

by Alan Crosby

While Prague is the crown jewel of the Czech Republic, it is surrounded by several other gems that you should try to see if time allows. Even with myriad changes throughout the country, the capital still differs from nearby towns; the tourist dollar is just beginning to trickle into some places and has yet to reach others, where crumbling facades and storefront windows harken back to their Communist-era dullness. Prague has been blessed with its golden spires, but the surrounding area is dotted with some of Europe's most beautiful castles, such as the majestic Karlštejn, where you can play a round of golf on a championship course or spend a night in a romantic inn. Also spectacular are the impregnable Český Sternberk, the hunting lodge of Konopiště, and the interior of Křivoklát. Still, for my money, the castle in Orlík overlooking the wide expanse of the Vltava is the nicest of them all.

As much as these sites are a testament to the country's beauty, there are also monuments to reflect its suffering: Lidice, or the remains of what once was a small, sleepy village leveled by Nazi anger; and Terezín (*Theresienstadt* in German), the "model" Jewish ghetto, the so-called Paradise Ghetto, where a cruel trick duped the world and left thousands to die.

Worth exploring is the medieval mining town of Kutná Hora (with the macabre "Bone Church" a mile away in Sedlec; kids will tell friends about it for years). When you tire of touring castles, you can play a round of golf on a championship course in Karlštejn (or Mariánské Lazné if you have the time for a longer trip), sneak away to a cozy inn, or try the next generation of bungee jumping. You can also enjoy a glass of wine at the Renaissance Lobkovic Château, the center of winemaking in the most unlikely of places, Mělník.

Even if you don't have much time, try to spend at least a day or two outside Prague to explore the countryside.

1 Tips for Day Tripping

All the destinations described below are easily accessible from Prague by car, train, or bus. Students should always show ID cards and ask for discounts, which are sometimes available.

GETTING THERE

BY CAR   A liter of gasoline costs about 24Kč (71¢), expensive by North American standards but a little cheaper than in Western

Europe. Gas stations are now plentiful, most equipped with small convenience stores.

Except for main highways, themselves a seemingly endless parade of construction sites, roads tend to be narrow and in need of repair. Add maniacal Czech drivers in BMWs and Mercedes fighting for the limited space alongside the Communist-era Trabant, and you may think that it's a better option to take the train. Especially at night, you should drive only on major roads. For details on car rentals, see chapter 3.

If you experience car trouble, major highways have some emergency telephones where you can call for assistance. There's also the **UAMK,** a 24-hour motor assistance club that can provide service for a fee. They drive bright yellow pickup trucks and can be summoned on main highways by using the SOS emergency phones located at the side of the road every kilometer or so. If you're not near one of these phones or on a road that doesn't have them, you can contact UAMK at ☎ **123** or 0123 outside of major towns. This is a toll-free call.

BY TRAIN Trains run by České dráhy (Czech Railways) provide a good and less expensive alternative to driving, with the fare determined by how far you travel. Every 10 kilometers costs roughly 6Kč (18¢) in second class or 9Kč (26¢) in first class (not usually available, or needed, on shorter trips).

It's important to find out which Prague station your train departs from, since not all trains leave from the main station, though all major stations are on metro lines.

Check when you buy your tickets. Trains heading to destinations in the north, such as Terezín, usually depart from **Nádraží Holešovice,** Vrbenského ulice, Praha 7 (☎ 02/2461 4032), above the Nádraží Holešovice metro stop at the end of the Red metro line (line C). Local trains to the southeast are commonly found at **Smíchovské Nádraží,** Nádražní ulice, Praha 5 (☎ 02/2461 4032), on the Yellow metro line heading west from the center. Most trains to west and south Bohemia and Moravia leave from **Hlavní Nádraží (Main Station),** Wilsonova 80, Praha 1 (☎ 02/2422 3887), at the metro stop of the same name on the Red metro (line C) in the center. Train stations in Prague are now better at providing information, especially in English. There are also timetables for public use that allow you to plan your trips.

BY BUS   Because trains often follow circuitous routes, bus transportation can be a better though slightly more expensive option. A pretty good bus system operates in the Czech Republic. State-run ČSAD buses are still relatively inexpensive and surprisingly abundant, and they offer terrific coverage of the country. Like the train, passengers are charged on a kilometer basis, with each kilometer costing about 75 hellers (three-quarters of a koruna) per kilometer. Make sure, however, that you buy your tickets early, especially on weekends, and get to the proper boarding area early to ensure you get a seat. Reserved seating is not something the state bus company appears to have discovered. Private buses are much better for this, but are also in high demand, so arrive early to be safe.

Prague's main bus station, **Central Bus Station—Florenc,** Křižíkova 5, Praha 8 (☎ 02/2421 1060), is above the Florenc metro stop (line C). Unfortunately, few employees speak English there, making it a bit tricky for non-Czech speakers to obtain schedule information. To find your bus, you can try the large boards just next to the office where all buses are listed. They're in alphabetical order, but sometimes it's tough to find your destination since it may lie in the middle of a route to another place. If you have some time before you depart Prague, your best bet for bus information and tickets is to visit **Čedok,** Na Příkopě 18, Praha 1 (☎ 02/2419 7640; www.cedok.cz), or **Bohemiatour,** at Zlatnická 7, Praha 1 (☎ 02/231 3925; www.vol.cz/win/bohemiatour), and at Jungmannova 4, Praha 1 (☎ 02/2421 6589). Neither agency charges an additional fee for its services, and both are open Monday to Friday from 9am to 6pm.

ORGANIZED DAY TOURS

Once upon a time, taking a day trip from Prague (or any trip in the Czech Republic for that matter) meant one of the worst nightmares known to humankind—dealing with the state monopoly travel agency Čedok. But in the wake of the demise of Čedok's stranglehold on tourist services, dozens of agencies have sprouted up around town offering services for guided tours both in and outside Prague. Though most offer more or less the same services, it pays to shop around. The following agencies are the most reliable.

With a friendly, helpful staff, ✪ **Central European Adventures,** Jáchymova 4, Praha 1 (☎ 02/232 8879), is probably the most imaginative tour service in Prague. Several 1-day guided (in English) adventure tours are offered in the Bohemian countryside from May to September; phone or stop by for complete information. Its bike tour around Karlštejn is fabulous and includes bus transportation from Prague and admission to Koněprusy Cave and costs 700Kč ($21). A canoe tour of a mild 10-mile stretch of the nearby Berounka River departs every Saturday and Sunday and includes life jackets and lunch, costing about 850Kč ($25) per person. Bike tours are offered

A Note on Tours

Though many good organized tours are offered, for the most part I'd recommend going it alone. This gives you the freedom to change plans at the last minute to get in a little more of what you want, not just what the tours provide. Besides, there's more of a sense of accomplishment when you navigate Eastern Europe on your own.

from 8 to 15 days in Bohemia; trips to the Sumava mountains in western Bohemia can be arranged as well. The company also offers guided countryside hikes tailored to your needs and abilities; the hikes include bus transport from and to Prague and light refreshments. If you see a few people thinking about going on the same trip, band together. Groups of four or more receive a 10% discount, enough for several Budvars at your favorite pub.

Martin Tour, Stěpánská 61, Praha 1 (☎ and fax **02/2421 2473;** www. martintour.cz), a less adventurous but just as reliable agency, with four departure points in the center, has been around for several years and offers a couple of worthy tours. The Karlštejn Castle tour is the best they offer and runs Tuesday to Sunday, departing at 10am; it takes 5 hours and is nice because you don't have to wait around for hours until the next general tour at the castle; also included is a typical Czech lunch at a nearby restaurant (diabetics, vegetarians, and babies can be accommodated). The tour with lunch costs 910Kč ($26.75).

Even after maligning it, I have to admit that **Čedok,** Na Příkopě 18, Praha 1 (☎ **02/2419 7640;** www.cedok.cz), in the heart of Prague, still has its advantages. It offers by far the widest array of tours outside of Prague, and the best surprise is no surprise. Don't expect any frills on these trips, just standard tours. On the other hand, Čedok has been doing this so long that it has access to all the important sights and a load of guides speaking several languages. For example, a day trip to Karlovy Vary, lunch, a swim at the Hotel Thermal outdoor pool, and a tour of the Moser glass factory costs 1,450Kč ($42.65), while a journey to the château Konopiště, lunch and tour included, costs 850Kč ($25).

Those looking for real history lessons or authentic Jewish community tours should stop by the **Matana** travel agency in the Jewish Quarter on Maiselova 15, Praha 1 (☎ **02/232 1954;** fax 02/232 1049). Its tours of the Terezín ghetto and Lidice are by far the best way to see these monuments. Matana's guides are experts in Jewish history, and the Terezín tour is a bargain at 1,290Kč ($38) for adults, 990Kč ($29) for students, and 890Kč ($26) for children, considering the fact that you have a walking encyclopedia at your side the entire 8-hour trip. Even lunch at a local restaurant is included. One word of warning: Be mindful of the Jewish Sabbath (Saturday) and the religion's holidays, when tours aren't conducted. On all other days, the tours leave like clockwork at 9:15am.

If you're pressed for time, a good tour is offered by **Prague Sightseeing Tours,** Klimentska 52, Praha 1 (☎ **02/2481 4849** or 02/231 4661), a combination all-day tour of the castles Karlštejn and Konopiště that includes lunch. It's a good way to see both castles without the hassle of negotiating the train and bus stations. However, the price tag is a little steep: 1,660Kč ($49) for adults and 1,360Kč ($40) for children.

If you're not looking for a tour but still want information on trips both near and far from Prague, an official travel information agency, **Česká centrála cestovního ruchu,** Národní třída 37, Praha 1 (☎ and fax **02/2421 1458**), can provide maps, books, and lodging suggestions for almost all areas of the country. Office hours are Monday to Saturday from 9am to 6pm.

2 Karlštejn Castle

18 miles (29km) SW of Prague

By far the most popular destination in the Czech Republic after Prague, Karlštejn Castle is an easy day trip for those interested in getting out of the city. This medieval castle was built from 1348 to 1357 by Charles IV to safeguard the crown jewels of the Holy Roman Empire. Although the castle has been changed over the years, with such additions as late Gothic staircases and bridges, overzealous renovators removed these additions, restoring the castle to its original state.

As you approach, little can prepare you for your first view: a spectacular Disney-like castle perched on a hill, surrounded by lush forests and vineyards. In its early days, the castle's beauty was enhanced by the king's jewels held within. These days, however, it's more spectacular from the outside, since vandalism has forced several of its finest rooms to close. And for some unknown reason, many of the more interesting rooms that have been restored are now kept off-limits, begging the question as to why they were redone at all if nobody will get to see them.

ESSENTIALS

GETTING THERE   The best way to get to Karlštejn is by **train** (there's no bus service). Most trains leave from Prague's Smíchov Station (at the Smíchovské nádraží metro stop) hourly throughout the day and take about 45 minutes to reach Karlštejn. The one-way second-class fare is 22Kč (65¢). It's a short, relaxing trip along the Berounka River. Look hard as you pass through Revnice, Martina Navrátilová's birthplace, to see if a new prodigy is in the making and wait for your first glimpse of the majestic castle. You may even get to see Ondřej Hejma, the lead singer for one of the country's most popular rock bands Žlutý pes (Yellow Dog), who also makes his home there.

You can also **drive** along one of two routes, which both take 30 minutes. Here's the more scenic one: Leave Prague from the southwest along Highway 4 in the direction of Strakonice and take the Karlštejn cutoff, following the signs (and traffic!). The second, much less scenic route follows the main highway leading out of Prague from the west as if you were going to Plzeň. About 20 minutes down the road is the well-marked cutoff for Karlštejn. (You can tell you have missed the cutoff if you get to the town of Beroun. If that happens, take any exit and head back the other way; the signs to Karlstejn are also marked heading toward Prague.)

A trip to Karlštejn can easily be combined with a visit to Křivoklát (see below).

VISITOR INFORMATION   There is no tourist information center per se in Karlštejn, but the ticket/castle information booth can help, as can any of the restaurants or stores.

ORGANIZED TOURS   All of the tour operators listed in "Organized Day Tours," above, offer tours of Karlštejn.

EXPLORING THE CASTLE

The walk up the hill to Karlštejn is, along with the view, one of the few features that make the trip worthwhile. Seeing hoards of visitors coming (an estimated 400,000 were expected in 1997), locals have discovered the value of fixing up the facades of their homes and opening small businesses, even if they have gone a little overboard on the number of outlets selling crystal. Restaurants have also improved tremendously

A Castle-Viewing Tip

Karlštejn is probably best viewed from a distance, so take time to browse in the stores, enjoy the fresh air, and sit out on one of the restaurant patios or down by the riverside. Buy a bottle of the locally grown Karlštejn wine, a vintage started by the king. This is what still makes the castle a worthwhile destination.

since we first visited the castle in the spring of 1990. When you finally do reach the top, take some time to look out over the town and down the Well Tower. You also need to decide if the 120Kč ($3.53) tour is worth the time and money.

If you've decided to take the tour, be prepared: The **Holy Rood Chapel,** famous for the more than 2,000 precious and semiprecious inlaid gems adorning its walls, is closed. And so is the **Chapel of St. Catherine,** Karel IV's own private oratory. What is open are several rooms, most in the south palace. But the tour isn't a total waste of time. Both the **Audience Hall** and the **Imperial Bedroom** are impressive, despite being stripped of their original furnishings.

Admission to the castle is 50Kč ($1.47) for adults and 30Kč (88¢) for children. It's open daily: May, June, and September from 9am to noon and 12:30 to 6pm; July and August from 9am to noon and 12:30 to 7pm.

TEE TIME: KARLŠTEJN'S CHAMPIONSHIP GOLF COURSE

Golfers should take note of Karlštejn's newest addition, a championship 6,370-meter par-72 golf course on the hill just across the river from the castle. Completed in 1995, this North American–designed course at the **Praha Karlštejn Golf Club** is very challenging and offers some pretty castle views. At the elevated tee on the second hole, you'll hit toward the castle. It's a breathtaking place to lose a ball. Try your luck on a course that hosted its first European PGA tour event in 1997, and see if you can match former Masters winner German Bernhard Langer's four-round total of 264 (24 under par).

Karlštejn is one of the few courses in the Czech Republic that really challenges a golfer's ability—narrow fairways, long rough, and greens that are lightning fast. Be prepared to walk uphill between holes. The course is open daily from 8am to sundown, and reservations for weekends should be made a couple of days in advance; call ☎ **0311/684 716.** However, it's a bit expensive, especially for equipment like golf balls and club rentals: Greens fees are 1,000Kč ($29.41) for 18 holes Monday to Friday and 1,800Kč ($53) Saturday, Sunday, and holidays. Motorized cart rentals are 1,000Kč ($29.41) per 18 holes, while a pull cart is 200Kč ($5.88) per round. Club rental is 500Kč ($14.71) per round. There's a driving range to warm up (50Kč per 50 balls), though you can't actually hit your driver there.

To get here by car from Prague, take Highway 116 south through the castle town of Karlštejn. Once you cross the river and a set of train tracks, stay on the road, which veers right and goes up a hill. You'll see the golf course on the left and an entrance soon after.

If you've taken the train here, you can walk to the course through town, but be warned that it's quite an uphill hike. I suggest taking a taxi, which should cost 50 to 70Kč ($1.47 to $2.06).

WHERE TO DINE

The ✪ **Restaurace Blanky z Valois** (no phone), on the main street heading up to the castle, tries for a Provençal feel. While this small and cozy restaurant doesn't exactly take you to France, the covered patio (where all but two of the eight or so tables are

A Romantic Getaway

If the air and noise of Prague start to grate on your nerves or a quiet, romantic overnight trip to a castle in the country sounds like the perfect getaway, head for the ✪ **Hotel Mlýn (Mill Hotel),** 267 27 Karlštejn (☎ **0311/94 194;** fax 0311/94 219).

On the river's edge on the bank opposite the castle, the Mlýn is exactly what its name says—a mill. Recently converted into a hotel, this reasonably priced country inn takes you away from the hustle and bustle of traveling. Its 15 rooms are a little on the small side, but they're quaint and nicely decorated with rustic furniture. At the outdoor patio bar and very good restaurant, you can relax and enjoy the soothing sounds of the river, forgetting what a disappointment the castle tour was. Service here is a cut above what it is at the other hotels in the area. The breakfast is nothing special, so opt out and save the money for some better fare in town.

Rates are 1,000Kč ($29.41) for a double and 1,700Kč ($50) for a suite. Breakfast costs an extra 250Kč ($7.35). Visa and MasterCard are accepted. To get to the hotel, take the bridge across the river that leads to the rail station and turn left at the first street. If you cross the rail tracks, you've gone too far.

located) can be very romantic, especially during an afternoon or evening rain shower. It also remains the village's best food option. The food is a cut above the standard fare, with wild game such as rabbit, boar, and venison the specialty. Main courses are 125 to 400Kč ($3.68 to $11.76); MasterCard and Visa are accepted. The restaurant is open daily from 11am to 10pm. A large wine list includes French and Italian vintages, but I suggest sampling Karlštejn's own. This light, dry wine is surprisingly good considering it's not from Moravia, and it costs less than half the price of the imports.

Also on the main street, the **Hotel Restaurace Koruna** (no phone) is usually busy, especially the terrace tables. The restaurant serves large portions; all of the usual Czech cuisine suspects are on the menu. The real bonus here is the staff: They're used to accommodating families or groups and allow them to spread out over one of the large tables. Main courses are 49 to 199Kč ($1.44 to $5.85); Visa and MasterCard are accepted.

At first glance it may appear as though there's not much difference between **Restaurace U Janů** (no phone) and the Koruna across the road. And there isn't. But prices here are a little lower, and the terrace, shaded by trees, is a little nicer. The menu is basic Czech. Try one of the venison specials as a nice change from the usual meat-and-dumpling meals. Main courses are 40 to 159Kč ($1.18 to $4.68); Visa and MasterCard are accepted. On weekends, live music adds a nice touch.

For a pleasant alternative to heavy sauces and dumplings, try the **U Smĕvavého Buldoka (Smiling Bulldog),** on the main road leading up to the castle. This is also a good place to stop for a quick bite if you don't have the time for a full sit-down meal. The barbecue you see out front is the "kitchen," so be prepared for meat—from hot dogs to pork chops. Main courses are 25 to 120Kč (74¢ to $3.53); no credit cards are accepted.

If you're more inclined for a little nature while you eat, I'd recommend stocking up on a few goodies at the grocery store before leaving Prague and having a picnic along the Berounka, where there are plenty of spots to spread a blanket. If you don't want to drag a heavy bag or two from the city, there's a **grocery store** on the right side of the main street when you're walking up the hill (open Monday to Saturday from 8am to 5pm); here you can buy the bare essentials, but selection isn't one of its strong points. Whatever way you go, pick up a bottle of the local Karlštejn vintage to wash down your meal.

3 Křivoklát

27 miles (43km) W of Prague

Less crowded and much less touristy than its neighbor upstream at Karlštejn, Křivoklát is the perfect destination for a lazy afternoon of touring. A royal castle mentioned as early as the 11th century, Křivoklát is set in the tranquil Berounka River Valley. The fortress was rebuilt several times over the years but still retains its Gothic style. The royal family was one of Křivoklát's frequent visitors, and during the Hussite Uprising, King Zigmund of Luxembourg hid his jewels here. The area surrounding the fortress is protected by UNESCO as a biosphere preservation area, making it an interesting place for a nature walk.

ESSENTIALS

GETTING THERE   This is one of the nicer train rides in the Czech Republic, even though you have to change trains in Beroun. The train winds its way along the Berounka through some wooded areas near Prague. **Trains** run regularly from Prague's Smíchov station to the town of Beroun, where you must change to go on to Křivoklát. The trip takes 1¾ hours; the one-way second-class fare is 38Kč ($1.12).

If you're **driving,** leave Prague on the E50 expressway heading west toward Plzeň and exit at the Křivoklát cutoff. From there, follow Highway 116 as it snakes along the Berounka and turn left on Highway 201, which eventually winds its way around to Křivoklát. It's a 45-minute trip.

VISITOR INFORMATION   There is no tourist information center, but the castle can provide information on the area.

ORGANIZED TOURS   **Prague Sightseeing Tours** offers a combination tour of Karlštejn and Křivoklát; see "Organized Day Tours," above, for details.

EXPLORING THE CASTLE

Often a castle tour fails to live up to expectations (Karlštejn comes to mind), but this is one of the castle tours I like most; it's almost a reverse of Karlštejn. Outside, Křivoklát pales in comparison to Karlštejn's beauty. But inside, Křivoklát blows its rival out of the water. Take time to study the intricate carvings at the altar in the **Royal Chapel.** They're not exactly angelic: Actually, the angels are holding torture toys; Křivoklát was once a prison for political criminals. The **Kings Hall,** a whopping 80 feet long, is the second-largest secular hallway in the country after Prague's Vladislav Hall. In the **Knights Hall** you'll find a collection of fabulous late Gothic art. And the **Furstenberg Picture Gallery** is one of the country's largest castle libraries with some 53,000 volumes on its shelves. Take that, Karlštejn!

A Sightseeing Tip

Křivoklát is near Karlštejn, so consider visiting both in 1 day if you drive or take the train. Both are also close enough to Prague to bike to. The contrast between the bustling Karlštejn and the sleepy Křivoklát is startling.

Admission is 100Kč ($2.94) for adults and 50Kč ($1.47) for children. It's open Tuesday to Sunday: June to August 9am to 5pm, May and September 9am to 4pm, and October to December 9am to 3pm. The tour runs about half an hour, and information in English is available.

WHERE TO DINE

Since Křivoklát is less touristy than Karlštejn, there aren't many restaurants here. But of the few that do exist, **Pension U Jelena** at the bottom of the hill as you approach the castle is your best bet. With six rooms, the pension can be used as an overnight stop if you want to spend a leisurely weekend hiking and biking between Křivoklát and Karlštejn. The restaurant specializes in game—try the venison steak with cranberry sauce and cognac at 260Kč ($7.65) for a sweet twist on a local specialty—and has a great terrace for an afternoon meal or just a drink. Main courses are 69 to 260Kč ($2.03 to $7.65); American Express, JCB, MasterCard, and Visa are accepted. For reservations at the hotel (you won't need them for the restaurant), call ☎ **0313/558 235.** Doubles cost 1,800Kč ($52.94). If you don't want to stop here, you're better off to wait and eat once back in Prague or down the road in Karlštejn.

4 Kutná Hora

45 miles (72km) E of Prague

A medieval town that grew fantastically rich from the silver deposits beneath it, Kutná Hora is also a popular day trip from Prague. Small enough to be seen in a single day at a brisk pace, the town's ancient heart is decayed, making it hard to believe that this was once the second most important city in Bohemia. But the town center is also mercifully free of the ugly Communist-era, functionalist-style buildings that plague many of the country's small towns. Kutná Hora's main draws are the exquisite St. Barbara's Cathedral and the macabre Bone Church (Kostnice), filled with human bones assembled in bizarre sculptures.

ESSENTIALS

GETTING THERE   The 50-minute **drive** from Prague is relatively easy. Take Vinohradská ulice, which runs due east from behind the National Museum at the top of Wenceslas Square, straight to Kutná Hora. Once out of the city, the road turns into Highway 333.

If you don't have a car, your best bet is to go by **bus,** which departs from the terminal at Prague's Želivského metro station and takes about an hour. It costs 39Kč ($1.15).

VISITOR INFORMATION   The **Culture and Information Center (Kulturní a Informační Stredisko),** on Palacého náměstí, provides the most comprehensive information service in town. Check to see if anything special, such as a recital or an exhibition, is in town. The office is open Monday to Friday from 9am to 6pm and Saturday and Sunday from 10am to 4pm.

Across the square, the **Čedok** office (☎ **0327/512 331**), open Monday to Friday from 8am to 4pm, can sometimes be helpful. The town has also posted very useful signs just about everywhere to help visitors get where they're going.

SEEING THE TOWN

The main attraction is the enormous **St. Barbara's Cathedral (Chrám sv. Barbory),** at the southwestern edge of the town. In 1380, Peter Parler began construction of the

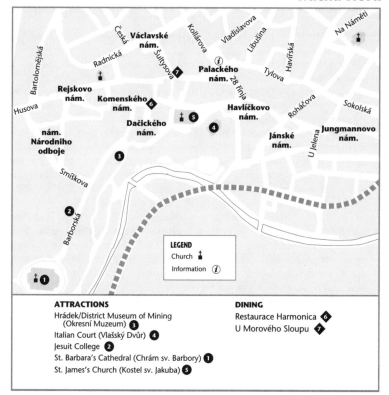

ATTRACTIONS
Hrádek/District Museum of Mining (Okresní Muzeum) ❸
Italian Court (Vlašský Dvůr) ❹
Jesuit College ❷
St. Barbara's Cathedral (Chrám sv. Barbory) ❶
St. James's Church (Kostel sv. Jakuba) ❺

DINING
Restaurace Harmonica ◆6
U Morového Sloupu ◆7

cathedral. Yet the task was so great that it took several more great Gothic masters, including Matthias Rejsek and Benedikt Rejt, close to 200 years to complete the project. From the outside, the cathedral's soaring arches, dozens of spires, and intricate designs raise expectations that the interior will be just as impressive—you won't be disappointed.

On entering (you have to enter from the side, not the front), you'll see several richly decorated frescoes full of symbols denoting the town's two main industries of mining and minting. The ceiling vaulting, with floral patterns and coats of arms, has made many a jaw drop. Admission is 40Kč ($1.18) for adults and 20Kč (59¢) for children. It's open Tuesday to Sunday from 9am to noon and 1 to 5pm.

When you leave the cathedral, head down the statue-lined **Barborská street,** where you'll pass the early baroque **Jesuit College,** built in the late 17th century by Domenico Orsi.

Farther down the road is **Hrádek,** a 15th-century castle that now houses the **District Museum of Mining (Okresní Muzeum).** If you take the tour of Hrádek, you'll actually see little of the building. Instead, you'll tour one of the town's mine shafts. The tour begins in a small room filled with artifacts from the town's mining and minting industries. After a brief speech (guided tours are in Czech only, so ask for a foreign-language handout), it's time to don hard hats and work coats to tour the mine shaft. After a hike of about 300 yards, you'll descend into a narrow corridor of rock and dampness. Children love this half-hour tour almost as much as the bone church; you spend about 15 minutes in the mines. Admission is 50Kč ($1.47) for

The Bone Church in Sedlec

A visit to Kutná Hora isn't complete without a trip to **Kostnice,** the "Bone Church." It's located a mile down the road in Sedlec; those who don't want to walk can board a local bus on Masarykova street. The fare is 8Kč (24¢) and you have to have a ticket before boarding. Tickets are not sold on the bus, but at newspaper stands (*Tabak*).

From the outside, Kostnice looks like most other Gothic churches. But from the moment you enter the front door, you know that this is no ordinary church—all of the decorations are made from human bones. No kidding. František Rint, the church's interior decorator, created crosses of bone, columns of bone, chalices of bone, and even a coat of arms in bone for the Schwarzenberg family, who owned the church.

The obvious questions are where did the bones come from and why were they used for decorations? The first question is easier to answer: The bones came from victims of the 14th-century plague and the 15th-century Hussite wars; both events left thousands of dead, who were buried in mass graves on the church's site. As the area developed, the bones were uncovered, and this was an idea the local monks came up with to put the bones to use.

Admission is a bargain at 30Kč (88¢) for adults and 15Kč (44¢) for children. It's open July and August, daily from 9am to noon and 1 to 5pm; the rest of the year, Tuesday to Sunday from 9am to noon and 1 to 4pm.

---

adults and 25Kč (74¢) for children, and it's open Tuesday to Sunday from 9am to noon and 1 to 5pm.

Once back above ground, go down the hill to **St. James's Church (Kostel sv. Jakuba)** and the **Italian Court (Vlašský Dvůr).** Even though the door is usually closed at St. James's, it's worth trying to open it; perhaps you'll glimpse the baroque paintings on the walls. It's more likely that you'll just have to admire the church from the outside and then head on to the Italian Court.

Constructed in 1300 as a royal mint (what better way for a town to become rich than to print money?), the Italian Court derives its name from its original occupants, who were brought in from Florence to mint coins. The building houses a museum of coins made here between the 14th and 18th centuries, including the Czech *groschen,* the currency of choice in the Middle Ages. Another reason to take the tour is to see the ornate chapels, impressive in their details. Admission is 40Kč ($1.18) for adults and 20Kč (59¢) for children. It's open April to September, daily from 9am to 5pm; October to March, Tuesday to Sunday from 10am to 4pm.

WHERE TO DINE

Despite its popularity, Kutná Hora hasn't developed the infrastructure to handle the masses. Restaurants especially are lacking, except for the local pubs and a couple of cafes that do little to satisfy the palate.

One of the few nice terraces with quick service is the **Restaurace Harmonica** (no phone), Komenského náměstí (to the rear of St. James's Church), making it a decent choice before heading down the road to the Bone Church. The salads are fresh and the soups are hot and hearty, something that isn't all too common in this town. Main courses are 49 to 159Kč ($1.44 to $4.68); no credit cards are accepted. It's open daily from 11am to 10pm.

Two Warnings

The Hrádek mine shaft can be a little claustrophobic (what mine isn't?) and *never* take your hard hat off (low, jagged ceilings can quickly bring about premature balding).

U Morového Sloupu (no phone), Šultyšova 3 (a block west of Palackého náměstí), is located in a 15th-century building that the owner has completely renovated. This remains one of the few places in town that has tried to lure out-of-towners who aren't part of a tour group through its doors. Try to sit in the first room when you walk in; this is a pleasant dining room with dim lighting. In the second room, a decidedly modern look sterilizes whatever ambience there once was. The food on both sides is the same, however, with large portions of tasty pork steaks, schnitzels, and fish. Main courses are 45 to 199Kč ($1.32 to $5.85); American Express, MasterCard, and Visa are accepted. It's open daily from 11am to 11pm.

5 Konopiště

30 miles (48km) S of Prague

A 17th-century castle-cum-hunting lodge built by the Habsburgs, Konopiště was the Club Med of its time. Here emperors and archdukes relaxed amid the well-stocked hunting grounds that surround the castle. In 1887, the castle became the property of the Archduke Franz Ferdinand, who often went hunting, until that fateful day in Sarajevo when he and his wife, Sophie, became the prey.

If you're driving, you can see both Konopiště and Český Šternberk in 1 day (see directions on p. 176).

ESSENTIALS

GETTING THERE   If you're **driving,** leave Prague on the D1 expressway heading south and exit at the Benesov cutoff. From there, turn right at the signs for Konopiště. *Watch out:* The turn kind of sneaks up on you, so start looking for it just after you pass the Benzina gas station on your right. It's a 45-minute trip. Note that the parking lot just outside the castle is your best bet, costing 30Kč (88¢). There aren't any closer lots, and police are vigilant about ticketing or booting cars parked at the side of the road. A minimum fine is 500Kč ($14.71).

If you don't have a car, the bus is the next best option. Several **buses** run daily from Prague's Florenc station and let you off about half a mile from the castle. The 1-hour trip costs 50Kč ($1.47).

It's a little trickier to get here by **train** since the closest station is in nearby Benesov. The trip takes 50 minutes and costs 27Kč (79¢) for a one-way second-class fare. From Benesov you'll have to catch a local bus to the castle for 8Kč (24¢).

EXPLORING THE CASTLE & HUNTING GROUNDS

Since hunting on the grounds is no longer an option, Tour I at Konopiště will have to suffice. You'll know what I mean as soon as you begin the tour: Hundreds of antlers, bears, wild boars, and birds of prey jump off the walls, catching unsuspecting sweaters and dazzling children. The main hall is a testament to the archduke, who reportedly bagged some 300,000 animals—that translates to an incredible 20 animals a day, every day for 40 years. Only 1% of his total hunting collection is on display, and it still ranks as one of Europe's largest collections. Tour I also takes you through the castle's parlors, which have been restored with great attention to detail. Note the handcrafted wooden Italian cabinets with wonderfully detailed inlays and the collection of Meissen porcelain. Tour I is 120Kč ($3.53) for adults and 60Kč ($1.76) for children.

Tour II (for which you must buy tickets separately) takes you through the weapons room, the chapel, and the party room where only men were allowed to let their hair down. This tour is 120Kč ($3.53) for adults and 60Kč ($1.76) for children.

Tour III takes you through Ferdinand's private rooms. But for some reason it costs nearly three times what the other two tours cost: 220Kč ($6.47) for adults and 120Kč ($3.53) for children. While the third tour is interesting, I don't think it's worth the money and may be a little too much. Unless you're a die-hard fan of castle rooms, your time is probably better spent roaming the grounds.

After exploring the castle's interior, wander around the manicured gardens where quails, pheasants, and peacocks roam freely. Children enjoy the moat, home to two bears who wander in circles for hours at a time. Down below the castle is a large pond where some people go swimming, though the water quality is questionable; I'd advise against it. Several large, open areas beg for a blanket, some sandwiches, and a nice bottle of red Frankovka wine. Picnicking isn't forbidden, but stock up before coming since there's no place to get groceries near the castle.

The castle is open Tuesday to Sunday: May to August from 9am to noon and 1 to 5pm, September 9am to noon and 1 to 4pm, and October 9am to noon and 1 to 3pm. The castle grounds are open 24 hours year-round.

WHERE TO DINE

On the castle grounds, **Stará Myslivna** (no phone) is a straightforward Czech restaurant; its interior resembles a hunting lodge. The soups are first rate, and the Czech specialty *svíčková na smetaně* (pork tenderloin in cream sauce) is welcome on a cold day. When the sun is out, sit on the nice terrace around the corner, which usually offers only two meals: pork cutlets and chicken. Both will be cooking on the grill in front of you. Don't bother asking for side orders; they serve only what's on the grill. Main courses are 59 to 199Kč ($1.74 to $5.85); no credit cards are accepted.

If you're touring late in the afternoon and have a little more time or want a little more formal setting, try **Stodola** (☎ **0301/22 732**), at the south end of the grounds. This is similar in menu to Stará Myslivna, but it offers far better-quality meals and a much nicer, though a little too much kitsch, atmosphere. Expect to pay between 89 and 359Kč ($2.62 and $10.56) for hearty meals of grilled meats and traditional Czech specialties like goulash. It's open daily from 6pm to 1am and accepts American Express, Diners Club, JCB, MasterCard, and Visa.

6 Český Šternberk

30 miles (48km) SE of Prague

About 10 miles east of Benešov lies the menacing Český Šternberk, once one of Bohemia's most powerful fortifications. The structure was built in the Gothic style in the first half of the 13th century, during the reign of Wenceslas I. The Habsburgs put in some baroque additions and improved its defenses, leaving few Gothic elements in their wake.

ESSENTIALS

GETTING THERE If you're **driving,** leave Prague on the D1 expressway heading south and exit at the Český Šternberk cutoff. From there, follow Highway 111. It's a

55-minute drive. From Konopiště, take Highway 112 to Highway 111. It's a 25-minute drive.

Several **buses** run daily to and from the castle, but not from the main Florenc station. Instead, you must take the Red metro line (the C line) south to the Roztyly stop. You can buy tickets, costing 24Kč (70¢) each way, at the Florenc station or from the bus driver at Roztyly. The bus takes about 1¾ hours.

SEEING THE FORTRESS

This impressive fortress stands atop a hill, rising above the Sázava River. It's worth taking the 1-hour tour of **Český Šternberk.** The enormous main hall and several smaller salons with fine baroque detailing, elaborate chandeliers, and period art are a testament to the wealth of the Šternberk family.

After the tour, enjoy the grounds and relax among the trees and babbling streams that surround the fortress before heading out. Admission is 100Kč ($2.94) for adults and 50Kč ($1.47) for children. It's open Tuesday to Sunday: June to August from 9am to 6pm, May and September from 9am to 5pm, and April and October from 9am to 4pm. For information, call ☎ **0303/55 101.**

WHERE TO DINE

Inside the castle, the **Vinárna Český Šternberk** (☎ **0303/55 101**) serves standard Czech meat-and-potatoes–type meals, though the quality of food and service is reflected in the prices. Main courses are 45 to 115Kč ($1.32 to $3.38); no credit cards are accepted. Since the restaurant's hours are the same as the castle's, you can't stop in for a quick bite to eat before the first tour or after the last one.

7 Mělník

20 miles (32km) N of Prague

Bohemia isn't known as a wine-making region—this is beer country. Except, that is, for the town of Mělník, where the Vltava and Labe (Elbe) rivers meet. While it's not quite the Loire Valley, Mělník has a decidedly French bent, as the vineyards are stocked with vines that originated in the Burgundy region.

The center of Mělník wine making is the **Renaissance Lobkowicz Château,** owned since 1739 by the family of the same name (except for a 40-year Communist-imposed interruption). The confluence of the rivers provides a stunning backdrop to the château, where another French pastime—sitting on a terrace with a glass of Ludmilla, Mělník's finest, as the afternoon sun slowly fades—can reach an art form.

If you get a chance to visit in mid-September, check out the harvest festival **Mělnické Vinobraní** for the latest vintages.

ESSENTIALS

GETTING THERE   If you're **driving** from the north end of Prague, follow Highway 9, which leads straight into Mělník. It's a 30-minute trip.

Buses leave for Mělník from both Florenc and Holešovice stations in Prague every hour or so. The trip takes about 45 minutes and costs 21Kč (62¢).

VISITOR INFORMATION   Information is available at the castle (☎ **0206/ 622 161**).

TOURING THE CHATEAU & TASTING THE WINE

Mělník's main attraction is the **Renaissance Lobkowicz Château** (☎ **0206/ 622 161**), which only recently opened to the public. The château is a mélange of styles, from its Renaissance balconies and *sgrafitti* to its Gothic touches and baroque southern building. The tour showcases the Lobkowicz's fine taste; in the living quarters, you'll see a barrage of baroque furniture and 17th- and 18th-century paintings. A second tour lets you into the 13th-century wine cellar, where wine tastings regularly occur. (Ask at the gift shop for times of tastings.)

The château tour is 75Kč ($2.21), the wine cellar tour is 50Kč ($1.47), and wine tastings are 75 to 150Kč ($2.21 to $4.41). It's open daily from 10am to 6pm.

WHERE TO DINE

Inside the château are two restaurants: a pricey vinárna and a more realistically priced restaurant, both with stunning views of the river. I prefer the ground-floor **Zámecká Restaurace** (☎ **0206/622 161**), since the food in the vinárna isn't worth the extra money; instead, with my savings I buy an extra bottle of the house wine. Main courses are 75 to 199Kč ($2.21 to $5.85); no credit cards are accepted. The restaurant is open daily from 11am to 11pm.

8　Terezín (Theresienstadt)

30 miles (48km) NW of Prague

Noticing that northwest Bohemia was susceptible to Prussian attacks, Joseph II, the son of Maria Teresa, decided to build ✪ **Terezín** to ward off further offensives. Two fortresses were built, but the Prussian army bypassed the area during the last Austro-Prussian conflict and in 1866 attacked Prague anyway. That spelled the end of Terezín's fortress charter, which was repealed in 1888. More than 50 years later, the fortifications were just what occupying Nazi forces needed.

When people around the world talk of Nazi atrocities in World War II, the name Terezín (Theresienstadt in German) rarely comes up. At the so-called Paradise Ghetto, there were no gas chambers, mass machine-gun executions, or medical testing rooms. Terezín wasn't used to exterminate the Jews, gays, Gypsies, and political prisoners it held. The occupying Nazi forces used it as a transit camp. About 140,000 people passed though Terezín's gates; more than half ended up at the death camps of Auschwitz and Treblinka.

Instead, Terezín will live in infamy for the cruel trick that SS chief Heinrich Himmler played on the world within the walls of this concentration camp north of Prague. On June 23, 1944, three foreign observers—two from the Red Cross—came to Terezín to find out if the rumors of Nazi atrocities were true. They left under the impression that all was well, duped by a carefully planned "beautification" of the camp. Every detail of the visit had been planned by the Germans. The observers saw children studying at staged schools that didn't exist, and store shelves, which had been specially set up, stocked with goods. So the observers wouldn't think the camp was overcrowded, the Nazis transported some 7,500 of the camp's sick and elderly prisoners to Auschwitz. Children even ran up to an SS commandant just as the observers passed; the commandant handed the children cans of sardines to shouts of "What?

Do You Remember?

You may remember Terezín/Theresienstadt from the TV miniseries of Herman Wouk's *War & Remembrance*—Natalie Henry (Jane Seymour); her son, Louis; and her uncle, Aaron Jastrow (Sir John Geilgud) were interned there near the end of the war and forced to participate in the "beautification" scheme.

Only sardines again?" The trick worked so well that the Nazis made a film of the camp, *A Town Presented to the Jews from the Fuehrer,* while it was still "self-governing."

Terezín was liberated by Russian forces on May 10, 1945, 8 days after Berlin had fallen to the Allies. Today, the camp exists as a memorial to the dead and a monument to human depravity.

ESSENTIALS

GETTING THERE   If you're **driving,** Terezín lies directly on the main highway leading north out of Prague, which takes you eventually to Berlin via Dresden. It's a 45-minute drive.

Six **buses** leave daily from Florenc bus station (metro line C). The ride takes about an hour; it costs 29Kč (85¢).

VISITOR INFORMATION   The information center at no. 179 on the main square náměstí Čs, Armády 84, is open Monday to Friday from 9am to 5pm (☎ **0416/ 922 27**). If it's closed, try the Museum of the Ghetto and the Minor Fortress; both have shops that stock materials in several languages.

ORGANIZED TOURS   To arrange a guide at Terezín, contact the Town Information Center on náměstí Čs. Armády 84 (☎ **0416/92 369**). Expect to pay about 50 to 200Kč ($1.47 to $5.88) per person, depending on the length of the tour.

I rarely recommend the tour-group experience, but I must admit that the best way to see Terezín is with the **Matana** travel agency (see "Organized Day Tours" at the beginning of this chapter). Having toured the ghetto three times before, I expected little more than a boring walk around the fortresses hearing the same old thing—wrong! The guides at Matana, which specializes in Czech Jewish community tours, knew an incredible amount of information and put it in a context that relates not only to Terezín but also to the region as a whole. The all-day tour also includes lunch, a documentary, and transportation and is well worth the 1,290Kč ($38) price for adults; slightly reduced prices are available for students and children.

SEEING THE CAMP

The larger of the two fortresses is aptly named the **Main Fortress (Hlavní Pevnost).** Once inside, you'll immediately be struck by its drab plain streets. Just off the main square lies the **Museum of the Ghetto,** which chronicles in great detail the rise of Nazism and life in the camp. Several exhibitions use video, pictures, paintings, and writings. Admission is 50Kč ($1.47) for adults and 25Kč (74¢) for children. A ticket to enter both the Major and Minor fortresses is 100Kč ($2.94) for adults and 50Kč ($1.47) for children. The Major Fortress is open daily from 9am to 6pm.

The **Minor Fortress** is about a 10-minute walk from the Major Fortress over the Ohre River. Just in front of the fortress's main entrance is the **National Cemetery (Národní hřbitov),** where the bodies exhumed from the mass graves were buried. As

---

Impressions

The most brutal thing was that they wanted to show a Terezín where there were nice healthy people. Each person was given a specific role to play. It was arranged beforehand down to the last detail who would sit where and what they would say. Those people looking bad were not to appear at all. They [the Nazis] prepared Terezín so there weren't people looking ill, old, emaciated, or too many of them. They created the illusion of a self-governing normal town where . . . people lived relatively decently.

—Anita Franková, survivor of Terezín

you enter the main gate, the sign above—ARBEIT MACHT FREI ("Work Sets One Free")—sets a gloomy tone. Here you can walk through the prison barracks, workshops, and isolation cells. The Minor Fortress is open daily from 8am to 5:30pm.

WHERE TO DINE

It's understandable that there are few places to eat in Terezín. Indeed, you may not want to stay here much longer than you have to. However, in the main parking lot you'll find a **small stand** where you can buy snacks and drinks. Inside the Major Fortress at Komenského 152, near the museum, is a decent inexpensive **restaurant** with standard Czech fare.

9 Lidice

20 miles (32km) NW of Prague

Two places in central Europe symbolize revenge more than almost anywhere else in the world: Dresden and Lidice. In 1942, when Czech paratroopers stationed in Britain assassinated the highest-ranking officer in the Czech lands, SS Obergruppenfuhrer Reinhard Heydrich, the Nazis focused their anger on this tiny village. As Hitler's main leader in the newly claimed Nazi protectorate of Bohemia and Moravia, Heydrich had ruthlessly and systematically exterminated Jews and intellectuals, while coddling "ordinary" Czechs. The assassination of such a high-ranking official would be dealt with severely. Why did Hitler choose Lidice? No one knows for sure, but this town was rumored to have accommodated the assassins and someone had to pay.

When you get to Lidice, you'll see only a wooden cross and a green field where the town once stood. The Gestapo leveled the town and murdered its men. Women and children were taken to concentration camps, with less than half returning alive. In all, 348 of Lidice's 500 residents were killed. But in 1948, the Czech government, buffeted morally and financially by international outrage at this war crime, created a new town built on neighboring land. Today that town is beginning to get a little run-down, which often makes visitors feel even more melancholy.

ESSENTIALS

GETTING THERE   If you're **driving,** take Highway 7 from the west side of Prague past the airport and head west onto Highway 551. It's a 20-minute drive.

Buses depart for Lidice at the bus stops across the street from the Diplomat Hotel near the Dejvická metro station (last stop on the Green A line). Buses to Kladno don't stop in Lidice, so make sure you're on the right bus by confirming it with the driver. The bus takes about 25 minutes; it costs 19Kč (55¢).

Again, a good way to see Lidice is through the Matana travel agency. The only drawback can be that many of the tours are coupled with a farther jaunt to the spa town Karlovy Vary, so ask ahead of time or be prepared to spend an entire day touring.

Impressions

I am returning, in the name of peace, 82 children to their native place as a warning symbol of the millions of murdered children in the senseless wars of mankind.
    —Marie Uchytilová, in dedicating her 82 sculptures of children ages 1 to 16 who were removed from Lidice and subsequently executed in Poland in 1942

LEARNING ABOUT LIDICE

The **Lidice Memorial Museum** is a sobering monument to the town's martyred residents. In it are pictures of those killed, with descriptions of their fate. You can see a 20-minute English-language documentary on request; otherwise, a Czech version is usually running. There's also a 10-minute cassette that you can listen to as you walk around. Admission is 50Kč ($1.47), and it's open daily from 8am to 5pm. Call ☎ **0312/253 063** for further information.

You're welcome to wander the field where the village once stood. Memorials in the "old" Lidice include a wooden cross marking the spot where the executed men were buried in a mass grave and Lidice's old and new cemeteries (the old one was desecrated by the Nazis, who were looking for gold from the teeth of the dead).

10 Orlík

44 miles (70km) S of Prague

Castles closer to Prague like Karlštejn and Konopiště get all of the oohs and ahhs, but in my opinion ✪ **Orlík Castle** is more deserving of the attention. Set among forests that line the Vltava where it swells from the Orlík Dam, the castle never disappoints me when I visit. It was built in the 13th century but has burned down several times, only to rise like a phoenix from the ashes with new additions and extensions. Inherited by the Schwarzenberg family in 1719 when Maria Ernestina died, the castle was set high up on a hill, overlooking a once vibrant trade route. It stayed that way until 1962, when water trapped by the Orlík Dam downriver flooded thousands of hectares of land, bringing the water level up to the castle's lower walls.

Returned to the Schwarzenberg family in 1992, the castle retains its splendor, while the surrounding area has become one of the most popular lake resorts in the Czech Republic.

Orlík is also one of the nicest swimming areas in the country. It tends to be crowded near the castle, so I recommend taking the **water taxi**—it stops at Orlík throughout the day and costs 30Kč (88¢)—one or two stops. You don't have to decide to get off until the boat stops, so be choosy.

ESSENTIALS

GETTING THERE   By car, this is an easy 1-hour **drive** from Prague. Take Highway 4 heading southwest out of the city. About halfway there, the highway narrows from four lanes to two. Turn right on Highway 19 and then right again into Orlík.

The **Prague-Písek bus** from the Florenc station (as many as six each day) stops near Orlík. Double-check with the driver to make sure you're on the right bus. It's a 75-minute trip that costs 40Kč ($1.18) one way.

VISITOR INFORMATION   There's no real information center in this tiny town, but if you go to the castle gift shop, you can get some basic information.

EXPLORING THE CASTLE

Castle tours explain the history of the Schwarzenberg family and take you through a fine collection of artifacts celebrating the victory over Napoléon at the Battle of Leipzig in 1815. Keep an eye out for the hand-carved wooden ceiling that took over 4 years to complete. Admission is 100Kč ($2.94) for adults and 50Kč ($1.47) for children. Open Tuesday to Saturday: May to August from 9am to noon and 1 to 5pm; April, September, and October from 9am to noon and 1 to 4pm.

Jumping into the Fourth Dimension

If you're looking for a cheap thrill or a holiday pick-me-up, Orlík could be the place for you. While most visitors come for the tranquillity of the castle grounds or for a peaceful nature walk and a day at the beach, the area's newest attraction has a decidedly different flavor.

From high above the river on the Žd'ákovský Bridge, fearless men and women, tethered to two cords, jump off of the 50-meter-high structure to reach the "fourth dimension." That's what the staff from **Hoboe International Organization (HOE),** a worldwide umbrella group for sports like bungee jumping and mountain climbing, call this pastime. Started in April 1995, HOE says that 4-D jumping is better than traditional bungee jumping because it allows you to fall farther before the two cords (each capable of bearing a 2,000kg/4,400-lb. load, I was assured) that tether you start to break your fall.

According to organizers, demand has been so high that a second jump site on the bridge was added to accommodate the large number of thrill-seekers—an average of 60 people a day take the plunge, from an 11-year-old to a 60-year-old Pakistani man, to a Canadian journalist/tour guide writer who swears that while it was an incredible feeling, he'll never do it again! There's even a yearly contest to see which jumper has the lowest pulse rate while jumping. Each jump costs 500Kč ($14.71). Weather permitting, you can take the plunge July and August, daily from 10am to 6pm; April to June, September, and October, Saturday and Sunday from 10am to 6pm. The bridge is on the main highway leading out of town to the southeast (Highway 23).

WHERE TO DINE

Behind the castle gift shop, the ✪ **Restaurace U Toryků (At the Castle)** surprises with its quality, though the portions could be bigger. Unfortunately, the restaurant's biggest lure, polka nights in summer, have been scrapped due to the noise, so leave your dancing shoes in the car and don't worry about leaving room to keep light on your feet. Main courses are 85 to 195Kč ($2.50 to $5.74); no credit cards are accepted. It's open daily from 10am to 8pm (no phone).

The Best of Bohemia   11

by Alan Crosby

The Czech Republic is comprised of two regions: Bohemia and Moravia. The bigger of the two, Bohemia is marked with the triumphs and tragedies of war. Caught between a rock (Germany) and a hard place (the Austrian Empire), Bohemia was almost always in the center of regional conflicts, both secular and religious. But the area also flourished, as witnessed by the wealth of castles that dot the countryside and spa towns that were once the playgrounds of the rich and famous.

Bohemia is slowly returning to that prominence, leaving behind its reputation as a satellite in the former East Bloc and forging a familiar old role as a destination in the center of Europe. Indeed, talk to the people (or, even worse, the politicians) and a look of pain rises with every mention of the East. "This is central Europe, we are west of Vienna!" is a common refrain. While the people may wish to put the past 40 or so years away like a pair of worn trousers, the fact is that they can't. This not only doesn't diminish the splendor of Bohemia's gentle rolling hills and majestic towns but adds to it, giving the area a less-polished, more realistic look.

1 Exploring Bohemia

Though Bohemia has historically been undivided, there are clear-cut distinctions in the region's geography that make going from town to town easier if you "divide" it into sections. After exploring Prague and central Bohemia, decide which area you'd like to see first and then plan accordingly.

WEST BOHEMIA

Home to the country's spa towns, west Bohemia is one of the few places where a full-blown tourist infrastructure is already in place. Its main towns—**Karlovy Vary (Carlsbad), Mariánské Lázně (Marienbad),** and to a lesser extent, **Plzeň**—offer a wide array of accommodations, restaurants, and services to meet every visitor's needs and means.

A relatively inexpensive network of trains and buses covers the region, allowing travel between towns and to and from Prague with a minimum of fuss and confusion. West Bohemia is generally rougher terrain, so only serious bikers should consider seeing the entire area on two wheels.

Bohemia

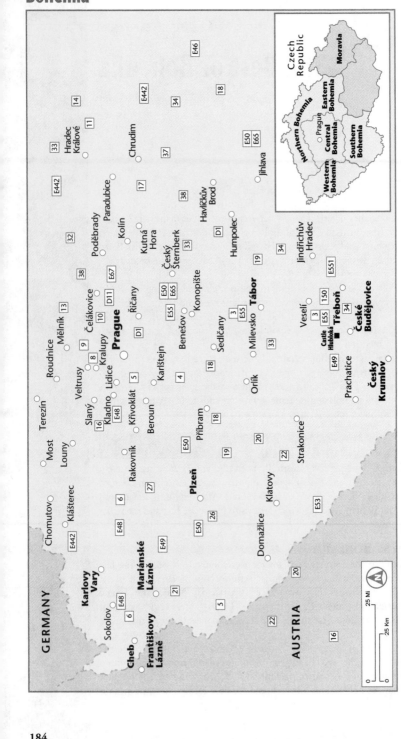

SOUTH BOHEMIA

Once the religious hotbed of the country, south Bohemia was a focal point of the Hussite wars that eventually ravaged many of its towns and villages. Though the days of war took their toll, the region still features fine examples of architecture from every era. Southern Bohemia is also home to the Czech Republic's second-largest castle, **Český Krumlov,** a UNESCO-protected site that dazzles with its Disney-like qualities no matter how many times you visit.

I've found two good approaches for exploring south Bohemia. If you're traveling by train or bus from Prague, make **Tábor** your first stop. It's on a main route, so the arrangements are easy. Then continue heading south, hooking up with **Třeboň, České Budějovice,** and Český Krumlov. If time is of the essence, you may want to set up camp in the area's main city, České Budějovice, and make several day trips since nothing is that far (Tábor, the farthest town, is 37 miles away). In fact, several people I know have taken advantage of relatively cheap taxis and hired drivers to take them to nearby Třeboň for as little as 600Kč ($18). If you split the cost between a couple of passengers, taxis can prove to be an effective way to see the countryside without breaking the bank.

For those who have more time, consider arranging a bike tour. These days, with the possibility of attack from Austria far diminished, south Bohemia is a much quieter setting with a less rugged terrain than west Bohemia. Biking here is much more feasible and you'll find dozens of quaint towns dotting the countryside. ✪ **Central European Adventures,** Jáchymova 4, Praha 1 (☎ **0337/232 8879**), can arrange superb tours that include bike rentals, guides (English-speaking), transportation, and even canoe trips of southern Bohemia at a fraction of what it would cost if you arranged the same trip from home.

2 Karlovy Vary (Carlsbad)

75 miles (120km) W of Prague

The discovery of Karlovy Vary (Carlsbad) by Charles IV reads like a 14th-century episode of the TV show *The Beverly Hillbillies.* According to local lore, the king was out huntin' for some food when up from the ground came a-bubblin' water (though discovered by his dogs and not an errant gunshot). Knowing a good thing when he saw it, Charles immediately set to work on building a small castle in the area, naming the town that evolved around it Karlovy Vary, which translates as "Charles's Boiling Place." The first spa buildings were built in 1522, and before long notables like Albrecht of Wallenstein, Peter the Great, and later Bach, Beethoven, Freud, and Marx all came to Karlovy Vary as a holiday retreat.

Accommodations Tips

Anywhere in the Czech Republic you have the option of staying in hotels or pensions on a town's main square. It's a beautiful sight, but be prepared for the possibility of serious noise, particularly on weekends, as revelers rage on late into the night. Light sleepers may prefer to trade the view for a good night's sleep.

Pensions are less expensive than hotels, and often the best pensions are friendlier, more tasteful, and far more in tune with the surroundings.

You may find that service tends not to be up to Western standards in many places; be warned that desk staff can be surly and unhelpful, and hotels may be woefully understaffed.

After World War II, East Bloc travelers (following in the footsteps of Marx, no doubt) discovered the town, and Karlovy Vary became a destination for the proletariat. On doctor's orders, most workers would enjoy regular stays of 2 or 3 weeks, letting the mineral waters ranging from 43.5°C (110.3°F) to 72°C (161.6°F) from the town's 12 springs heal their tired and broken bodies. Even now, a large number of spa guests are there by doctor's prescription.

But most of the 40-plus years of Communist neglect—they even took out most of the social aspect of spa going and turned it into a science—have been erased as a barrage of renovators is restoring almost all the spa's former glory. Gone is the statue of Russian cosmonaut Yuri Gagarin. Gone are almost all the fading, crumbling building facades that used to line both sides of the river. In their place now stand restored buildings, cherubs, caryatids, and more in the center.

The town is experiencing a renaissance from both its traditional clientele and its newer patrons. Today, some 150,000 people travel annually to the spa resort to sip, bathe, and frolic, though most enjoy the 13th spring—a hearty herb-and-mineral liqueur called Becherovka—more than the 12 nonalcoholic versions. Czechs will tell you that all have medical benefits, and Russians appear to be heeding this advice more and more. In a throwback to Soviet days, many shopkeepers are catering to Russian clientele, so don't be surprised if you're addressed in Russian before English or German, as the Slavic nouveaux riches have once again found a comfortable setting after the backlash they faced soon after the Iron Curtain was drawn.

SPECIAL EVENTS   The **Karlovy Vary International Film Festival** is the place to see and be seen. Each summer (usually in early July), the country's films stars, celebrities, and wealthy folks, supported by a cast of international stars like Lauren Bacall, Michael Douglas, Alan Alda, Mia Farrow, Milos Forman, and Jason Robards, can be spotted taking part in one of Europe's biggest film festivals. Six venues screen more than 200 films, many world premieres, during the 8- to 10-day festival.

Another event that brings out Czech stars, including Karel Gott, the Czech version of Tom Jones and Bert Parks all rolled into one, is the **Miss Czech Republic contest,** held annually in April at the Grand Hotel Pupp.

Karlovy Vary plays host to several other events, including a **jazz festival** and **beer Olympiad** in May, a **Dvořák singing contest** in June, a **Summer Music Festival** in August, and a **Dvořák Autumn Music Festival** in September and October.

For details on the festivals, contact **Kur-Info Vřídelní Kolonáda,** 360 01 Karlovy Vary (☎ **017/322 9312** or 017/322 4097; fax 017/246 67).

ESSENTIALS

GETTING THERE   At all costs, *avoid the train from Prague,* which takes over 4 hours on a circuitous route. If you're arriving from another direction, Karlovy Vary's main train station is connected to the town center by bus no. 13.

Frequent express **buses** make the trip from Prague's Florenc Station to Karlovy Vary's náměstí Dr. M. Horákové in about 2½ hours. Buses leave from platform 21 or 22 five times daily at 7, 9, and 9:40am, noon, and 4pm; tickets cost 49Kč ($1.44). Take a 10-minute walk or local bus no. 4 into Karlovy Vary's town center. Note that you must have a ticket, which costs 8Kč (24¢) to board local transportation. You can buy these tickets at the main station stop or, if you have no change, at the kiosk across the street during regular business hours.

The nearly 2-hour **drive** from Prague to Karlovy Vary is easy. Take Highway E48 from the western end of Prague and follow it straight through to Karlovy Vary. This two-lane highway widens in a few spots to let cars pass slow-moving vehicles on hills.

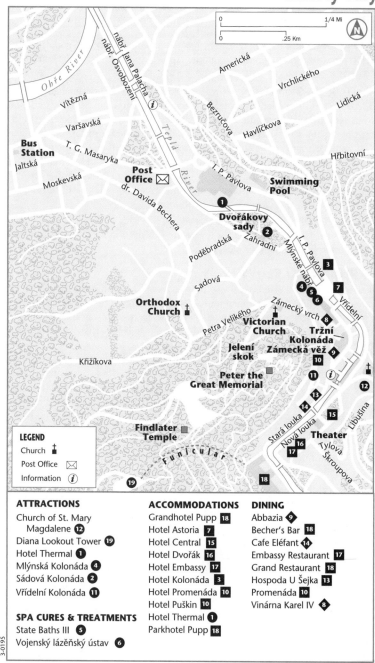

Karlovy Vary

0 — 1/4 Mi
0 — .25 Km

Ohře River
nábř. Jana Palacha
nábř. Osvobození
Vítězná
Varšavská
Americká
Vrchlického
Lidická
Bezručova
Havlíčkova
Bus Station
T. G. Masaryka
Jaltská
Moskevská
Hřbitovní
Post Office ⊠
dr. Davida Bechera
I. P. Pavlova
Swimming Pool
1
Dvořákovy sady **2**
Poděbradská
Zahradní
Sadová
Mlýnské nábř.
I. P. Pavlova
3
4
5
6
7
Orthodox Church †
Petra Velikého
Zámecký vrch
Vřídelní
8
Victorian Church †
Tržní Kolonáda
Jelení skok
Zámecká věž
9
Křižíkova
10
Peter the Great Memorial
11
ⓘ
†
12
13
14
Stará louka
15
Findlater Temple
Nová louka
Theater
Tylova
Škroupova
Libušina
16
17
F u n i c u l a r
18
19

LEGEND
Church †
Post Office ⊠
Information ⓘ

3-0195

ATTRACTIONS
Church of St. Mary Magdalene **12**
Diana Lookout Tower **19**
Hotel Thermal **1**
Mlýnská Kolonáda **4**
Sádová Kolonáda **2**
Vřídelní Kolonáda **11**

SPA CURES & TREATMENTS
State Baths III **5**
Vojenský lázeňský ústav **6**

ACCOMMODATIONS
Grandhotel Pupp **18**
Hotel Astoria **7**
Hotel Central **15**
Hotel Dvořák **16**
Hotel Embassy **17**
Hotel Kolonáda **3**
Hotel Promenáda **10**
Hotel Puškin **10**
Hotel Thermal **1**
Parkhotel Pupp **18**

DINING
Abbazia **9**
Becher's Bar **18**
Cafe Eléfant **14**
Embassy Restaurant **17**
Grand Restaurant **18**
Hospoda U Šejka **13**
Promenáda **10**
Vinárna Karel IV **8**

A Driving Warning

Be warned that Highway E48 from Prague to Karlovy Vary is a popular route for reckless drivers heading to and from the capital. Please take extra care when driving.

VISITOR INFORMATION **Kuri-Info,** inside the Vřídelní Kolonáda (☎ 017/ 322 9312), is open Monday to Friday from 7am to 5pm and Saturday and Sunday from 9am to 3pm. It provides accommodation services, arranges guided tours and spa treatments, and sells tickets for some events. Be sure to pick up a copy of the *Cultural Calendar,* a comprehensive collection of events with a small map of the town center.

There are also two privately run **Info-Centrum** booths: one in the train station and the other in a parking lot at the base of Jana Palacha ulice. Both give away free maps and a brochure of current cultural listings called *Promenáda.* Info-Centrum also books accommodations in private rooms and sells tours.

ORIENTATION Karlovy Vary is shaped like a T, with the Teplá River running up the stem and the Ohre River at the top of the T. Most of the major streets are pedestrian promenades lining both sides of the Teplá.

EXPLORING KARLOVY VARY

The town's slow pace and pedestrian promenades, lined with turn-of-the-century art nouveau buildings, turn strolling into an art form. Nighttime walks take on an even more mystical feel as the sewers, the river, and the many major cracks in the roads emit steam from the hot springs running underneath. It feels like you could meet Vincent Price looming around every corner.

I suggest avoiding the new town, which happens to be conveniently left off most of the small tourist maps. Its only real attraction is a McDonald's and a couple of ATMs (which you can also find in the historic center). If you're traveling here by train or bus, a good place to start your exploration is the **Hotel Thermal,** I. P. Pavlova 11 (☎ 017/ 321 1111), at the north end of the old town's center. Built in the 1970s, it exemplifies how obtrusive Communist architecture can be. Nestled between the town's eastern hills and the Ohre River, the glass, steel, and concrete Thermal sticks out like a sore thumb amid the rest of the town's 19th-century architecture. Nonetheless, you'll find three important places at the Thermal: its pool, the only centrally located outdoor public pool; its upper terrace, boasting a truly spectacular view of the town; and its theater, Karlovy Vary's largest, which holds many of the film festival's premier events. Look at it. Take it all in. And after seeing the Thermal, it's best to keep walking before you remember too much of it.

As you enter the heart of the town on the river's west side, you'll see the ornate, white wrought-iron gazebo named **Sádová Kolonáda** adorning the beautifully manicured park, **Dvořakový Sady.** Continue following the river and about 100 meters later you'll encounter the **Mlýnská Kolonáda.** This long covered walkway houses several Karlovy Vary springs, which you can sample free 24 hours a day. Each spring has a plaque beside it telling which mineral elements are present and what temperature the water is. Bring your own cup or buy one just about anywhere (see the box "Spa Cures & Treatments," below) to sip the waters, since most are too hot to just drink from your hands. When you hit the river bend, you'll see the majestic **Church of St. Mary Magdalene** perched atop a hill, overlooking the **Vřídlo,** the hottest spring. Built in 1736, the church is the work of Kilian Ignac Dientzenhofer, who also created two of Prague's more notable churches—both named St. Nicholas.

Housing Vřídlo, which blasts water some 50 feet into the air, is the glass building where the statue of Soviet cosmonaut Yuri Gagarin once stood. (Gagarin's statue has since made a safe landing at the Karlovy Vary airport, where it greets the waves of Russian visitors who flood the town.) Now called the **Vřídelní Kolonáda,** the structure, built in 1974, houses several hot springs that you can sample for free daily from 7am to 8pm (☎ **017/322 4097**). The building also holds the Kuri-Info information center, where you can find answers to almost all questions.

Heading away from the Vřídelní Kolonáda are Stará and Nova Louka streets, which line either side of the river. Along **Stará (Old) Louka** are several fine cafes and glass and crystal shops. **Nova (New) Louka** is lined with many hotels and the historic town's main theater, built in 1886, which houses paintings by notable artists like Klimt and is currently under reconstruction.

Both streets lead to the **Grandhotel Pupp,** Mírové nám. 2 (☎ **017/310 9111**). The Pupp's main entrance and building have just come out of extensive renovations that have more or less erased the effects of 40 years of Communism (the hotel's name had been changed to the Moskva-Pupp). Regardless of capitalism or Communism, the Pupp remains what it always was: the grande dame of hotels in the area. Once catering to nobility from all over central Europe, the Pupp still houses one of the town's finest restaurants, the Grand, while its grounds are a favorite with the hiking crowd.

If you still have the energy, atop the hill behind the Pupp stands the **Diana Lookout Tower** (☎ **017/322 5677**). Footpaths lead to the tower through the forests and eventually spit you out at the base of the tower, as if to say, "Ha, the trip is only half over." The five-story climb up the tower tests your stamina, but the view of the town is more than worth it. For those who aren't up to the climb just to get to the tower, a cable car runs up every 15 minutes daily from 7am to 7pm.

SHOPPING

Crystal and porcelain are Karlovy Vary's other claims to fame. Dozens of shops throughout town sell everything from plates to chandeliers.

Ludvík Moser founded his first glassware shop in 1857 and became one of this country's foremost names in glass. You can visit the **Moser Factory,** kapitána Jarose 19 (☎ **017/41 61 11**; e-mail: moser@moser-glass.com; bus no. 1, 10, or 16), just west of the town center; it's open Monday to Friday from 7:30am to 3:30pm. There's also a **Moser Store,** on Tržiště 7 (☎ **017/267 94**), right in the heart of new town; it's open Monday to Friday from 10am to 6pm. Dozens of other smaller shops also sell the famed glass and are as easy to find in the old town as spring water.

WHERE TO STAY

Private rooms used to be the best places to stay in Karlovy Vary with regard to quality and price. But this is changing as more and more hotels renovate and raise standards . . . as well as prices. Still, private accommodation can provide better value, but takes a little extra work. If you want to arrange your room, try the **Info-Centrum** (see above) or **Čedok,** Karla IV c. 1 (☎ **017/322 3335**). The office is open Monday to Friday from 9am to 5pm and Saturday from 9am to noon. Expect to pay about 800Kč ($24) for a single and 1,200Kč ($35) for a double.

Some of the town's major spa hotels accommodate only those who are paying for complete treatment, unless for some reason their occupancy rates are particularly low. The hotels I've listed below accept guests for stays of any length.

EXPENSIVE

✪ **Grandhotel Pupp.** Mírové nám. 2, 360 91, Karlovy Vary. ☎ **017/310 9111.** Fax 017/322 4032. www.pupp.cz. 110 units. MINIBAR TV TEL. $165 double deluxe; $215 studio deluxe; $315 apt.; $400 Imperial apt.; $835 Presidential apt. Breakfast $11 extra. A daily exchange rate is used for those who want to pay crowns in cash. AE, DC, MC, V.

Spa Cures & Treatments

Most visitors to Karlovy Vary come for a spa treatment, a therapy that lasts 1 to 3 weeks. After consulting with a spa physician, you're given a specific regimen of activities that may include mineral baths, massages, waxings, mud packs, electrotherapy, and pure oxygen inhalation. After spending the morning at a spa, or sanatorium, you're usually directed to walk the paths of the town's surrounding forest.

The common denominator of all the cures is an ample daily dose of hot mineral water, which bubbles up from 12 springs. This water definitely has a distinct odor and taste. You'll see people chugging down the water, but it doesn't necessarily taste very good. Some thermal springs actually taste and smell like rotten eggs. You may want to take a small sip at first.

You'll also notice that almost everyone in town seems to be carrying "the cup." This funny-looking cup is basically a mug with a built-in straw running through the handle. Young and old alike parade around with their mugs, filling and refilling them at each new thermal water tap. You can buy these mugs everywhere for as little as 50Kč ($1.47) or as much as 500Kč ($14.71); they make a quirky souvenir. *But be warned:* None of the mugs can make the warmer hot springs taste any better.

The minimum spa treatment lasts 1 week and must be arranged in advance. A spa treatment package traditionally includes room, full board, and complete therapy regimen; the cost varies from about $40 to $100 per person per day, depending on season and facilities. Rates are highest from May to September and lowest from November to February.

For information and reservations in Prague, contact **Čedok,** Na Příkopě 18 and at Václavské nám. 24, Praha 1 (☎ **02/2419 7111;** fax 02/2421 3786). Many hotels also provide spa and health treatments, so ask when you book your room. Most will happily arrange a treatment if they don't provide them directly.

If you're coming for just a day or two, you can experience the waters on an "outpatient" basis. The **State Baths III,** Mlynské nábřeží 5 (☎ **017/256 41**), welcomes day-trippers with mineral baths, massages, saunas, and a cold pool. It's open from 7:45am to 3pm: for men on Tuesday, Thursday, and Saturday and for women on Monday, Wednesday, and Friday. Prices range from 500 to 1,000 Kč ($14.71 to $29.41). Next door, the **Vojenský lázeňský ústav,** Mlynské nábřeží 7 (☎ **017/222 06**), offers similar services and costs about 750Kč ($22) per day. They're open to all Monday to Saturday from 7:30am to 3pm. Go as early as possible or phone ahead, since these are two of the busiest spas in town.

Well known as one of Karlovy Vary's best hotels, the Pupp, built in 1701, is also one of Europe's oldest. Its public areas boast the expected splendor and charm, as do the guest rooms, which have been recently renovated. The best rooms tend to be those facing the town center and are located on the upper floors; these have good views and sturdy wooden furniture.

Dining/Diversions: The Pupp's two restaurants, Becher's Bar and the Grand, provide you with a stark choice—dress up or dress down. But after that, things get easier. The Grand serves up as grand a dining room as you'll find, with the food to match. Becher's is more informal but just as thoughtful with its menu of international cuisine and American-style finger foods. See "Where to Dine," below, for fuller reviews of these restaurants. The hotel also has a stylish casino (open midnight to 4am).

Amenities: Room service (6am to midnight), same-day laundry, limousine/taxi, valet parking. Fitness club, 650-seat concert hall, pool hall, hair salon, tennis courts, casino.

MODERATE

Hotel Astoria. Vřídelní 23, 360 01 Karlovy Vary. ☎ **017/322 8224-8.** Fax 017/322 4368. 99 units. TV TEL. 1,500–2,400Kč ($44–$71) double. AE, MC, V.

In the heart of the historic town, the Astoria mainly caters to spa guests, but, unlike many of its competitors, it is big enough to usually have several rooms available for nontreatment visitors. The staff can be a little gruff at times, but the rooms are big, with satellite TV an added bonus. The restaurant serves standard Czech fare, with a lot of vegetable dishes as well, though I'd recommend trying one of the other places in town for a less bland experience.

Hotel Central. Divadelní nám. 17, 360 68 Karlovy Vary. ☎ **017/318 2111.** Fax 017/322 9086. 65 units. TV TEL. 2,550–2,890Kč ($75–$85) double; 3,400–3,910Kč ($100–$115) suite. AE, MC, V.

The hotel certainly is central, located next to the theater. It looks unassuming yet provides good value, with rooms that aren't overly spacious but adequate. Though the Central lacks facilities (avoid the restaurant except for breakfast), the rooms on the upper floors provide a great view of the Kolonáda for far less a price than many of the neighboring hotels, like the Dvořák.

Hotel Dvořák. Nová Louka 11, 360 21 Karlovy Vary. ☎ **017/322 4145.** Fax 017/ 322 2814. www.hotel-dvorak.cz. 79 units. MINIBAR TV TEL. DM140–203 ($74–$107) double; DM240 ($126) suite. A daily exchange rate is used for those who want to pay crowns by cash. AE, DC, MC, V.

Now part of the Vienna International hotel/resort chain, the Dvořák has improved immensely over the past year or two, especially in terms of service. This hotel is within sight of the Pupp, but people who've stayed here say that it's far beyond Karlovy Vary's vaunted hotel, especially price-wise. If the Pupp has the history and elegance, they say, the Dvořák has the facilities. The rooms are spacious and the staff is very attentive. Business travelers will take heart in the hotel's business facilities.

The ground-floor cafe isn't as stylish as the Cafe Eléfant across the way, but its service and selection of coffee and desserts are on a par. Alas, if there's a weakness at the hotel, it's the rather bland restaurant that serves a fine breakfast buffet but fails to impress after that with uncreative meals.

There's also a fitness center, hair salon, indoor pool, sauna, casino, and tennis.

Hotel Embassy. Nová Louka 21, 360 01 Karlovy Vary. ☎ **017/322 1161-5.** Fax 017/322 3146. 20 units. TV TEL. 2,788–3,468Kč ($82–$102) double; 3,060–3,740Kč ($90–$110) double deluxe; 3,570–4,420Kč ($105–$130) suite. AE, V.

On the riverbank across from the Pupp, the Embassy has well-appointed rooms, many with an early-20th-century motif, in a historic house. The staff is what really helps make this worthy of consideration, as does the proximity to the pub on the first floor, which serves up some of the best goulash and beer in the city.

Hotel Kolonáda. I. P. Pavlova 8, 360 01 Karlovy Vary. ☎ **017/322 3258** or 017/322 2472. Fax 017/322 8045. 70 units. TV TEL. 1,800–2,682Kč ($55–$81) double; 2,700–3,400Kč ($79–$100) triple; 3,000–3,800Kč ($88–$112) suite. AE, MC, V.

The Kolonáda, with its lovely facade, was formed by a merger of the Otava and Patria hotels. As the name suggests, it's across from the Kolonáda. The hotel's interior is modern and renovated, as are the rooms, the best of which look out over the real Kolonáda.

Hotel Promenáda. Tržiště 31, 360 01 Karlovy Vary. ☎ **017/322 5648.** Fax 017/322 9708. 16 units. TV TEL. 2,350–2,850Kč ($69–$84) double. AE, MC, V.

Next door to the Puškin, Promenáda is the newest addition to the Karlovy Vary accommodation scene. Opened in 1999, the hotel faces the Kolonáda and has a beautiful view of the center. Rooms on the lower floors are more spacious than those on the upper levels, but all have an elegant decor highlighted with wrought-iron bed frames and large windows.

Hotel Puškin. Tržiště 37, 360 90 Karlovy Vary. ☎ **017/322 2646.** Fax 017/322 4134. 20 units. TV TEL. 2,275Kč ($67) double; 2,850Kč ($84) triple. No credit cards.

Named for the great Russian poet we know as Pushkin, this hotel occupies an intricately ornamented 19th-century building that has just been renovated. It has a terrific location, close to the springs. The rooms are rather basic, but they're comfortable enough; ask for one that has a balcony facing St. Mary Magdalene Church and enjoy one of the nicest views in the old town.

Hotel Thermal. I. P. Pavlova 11, 360 01 Karlovy Vary. ☎ **017/321 1111** or 017/322 8391. Fax 017/322 6992. 200 units. TV TEL. 3,400Kč ($100) double; 7,200Kč ($212) suite. AE, MC, V.

What better way to feel what it was like to stay in Karlovy Vary under Communism? All kidding aside, the Thermal also qualifies as a possibility because of its location, services, and size. Don't expect anything exciting, but do take a picture of yourself in the Star Trek seats in the lobby bar.

✪ **Parkhotel Pupp.** Mírové nám. 2, 360 91 Karlovy Vary. ☎ **017 310 9111.** Fax 017/ 32 240 32. 255 units. MINIBAR TV TEL. 3,400Kč ($100) double; 4,420Kč ($130) apt. Breakfast 272Kč ($8). AE, DC, MC, V.

Part of the Pupp complex, these are basically the rooms in the part of the hotel that doesn't quite measure up to the grand standards of its brother. But the rooms are still nice and functional, if not quite as cozy and elegant. Personally, I'd stay in one of these rooms and use the money I saved on a nice meal and a couple of Karlovy Vary kisses (Becherovka in a frozen glass).

WHERE TO DINE
EXPENSIVE

Embassy Restaurant. Nová Louka 21. ☎ **017/322 1161.** Reservations recommended. Soups 45–85Kč ($1.32–$2.50); main courses 145–895Kč ($4.26–$26.32). AE, V. Daily noon–11pm. CZECH/CONTINENTAL.

Here you'll find many traditional Czech dishes with a slight twist to make them interesting. The grilled loin of pork covered with a light, creamy green-pepper sauce is a nice change from the regular roast pork most Czech restaurants serve. The spicy goulash reminds one more of the piquant flavor found in Hungarian cuisine than that of bland Czech fare.

✪ **Grand Restaurant.** In the Grandhotel Pupp, Mírové nám. 2. ☎ **017/310 9111.** Reservations recommended. Soups 50–150Kč ($1.47–$4.41); main courses 240–1,100Kč ($7.06–$32.35). AE, V. Daily noon–3pm and 6–11pm. CONTINENTAL.

It's no surprise that the Grandhotel Pupp has the nicest dining room in town: an elegant eatery with tall ceilings, huge mirrors, and glistening chandeliers. A large menu gives way to larger portions of salmon, chicken, veal, pork, turkey, and beef in a variety of heavy and heavier sauces. Even the trout with mushrooms is smothered in butter sauce but still mouthwatering.

Promenáda. Tržiště 31. ☎ **017/322 5648.** Reservations highly recommended. Soups 30–39Kč (88¢–$1.15); main courses 139–498Kč ($4.09–$14.65). AE, V. Daily noon–11pm. CZECH/CONTINENTAL.

This cozy, intimate spot may not be as elegant as the Grand Restaurant, but it remains one of the better places to dine and serves creative meals. Across from the Vřídelní Kolonáda, the Promenáda offers a wide menu with generous portions. The daily menu usually includes well-prepared wild game, but the mixed grill for two or the chateaubriand, both flambéed at the table, are the chef's best dishes. The wine list features a large selection of wines from around Europe, but don't sell short the Czech wines, especially the white Ryslink and the red Frankovka. An order of crêpes Suzette, big enough to satisfy two, rounds out a wonderful meal.

MODERATE

Abbazia. Vřídelní 51. ☎ **017/322 5648.** Reservations recommended. Main courses 99–399Kč ($2.91–$11.74). AE, V. Daily 11am–3pm and 5:30–10pm. CZECH/CONTINENTAL.

From the outside, the second-floor Abbazia is easy to miss, but it's worth finding. Near the Vřídelní Kolonáda, it has a wooden interior dominated by huge tables, making it one of the few places where large groups are always welcome. The large menu offers a wide assortment of Czech and international meals at reasonable prices. This is one of the few places in the Czech Republic where I'd recommend the scampi; order it as an appetizer to share with your dining partner(s). That way, you can also sample one of the tasty entrees as well. If there's a drawback, it's that the restaurant isn't open at more convenient times.

Becher's Bar. In the Grandhotel Pupp, Mírové nám. 2. ☎ **017/310 9111.** Appetizers 55–180Kč ($1.62–$5.29); pastas 125–200Kč ($3.68–$5.88); other meals 100–380Kč ($2.94–$11.18). AE, MC, V. Daily noon–1am. CONTINENTAL.

One of the city's best pubs, the Radegast, is gone. But much to my relief, it has been replaced with a slightly upscale cocktail lounge that calls out for Tom Jones (or his Czech equivalent, Karel Gott) to pick up a mike and begin crooning and gyrating. The menu is part roadhouse, part pub, and overall a pleasant change from the regular heavy meals offered around town. And despite the potential to gouge, the management has resisted the urge—even the Becher is only 40Kč ($1.18).

✪ **Vinárna Karel IV.** Zámecký vrch 3. ☎ **017/322 7255.** Reservations recommended. Soups 19–80Kč (56¢–$2.35); main courses 115–290Kč ($3.38–$8.53). AE, MC, V. Daily noon–1am. CZECH/CONTINENTAL.

Perched high above the Vřídelní Kolonáda, this former hunting lodge of Karel IV, built in the early 1600s, is the perfect place to sit outside on a warm summer night as you try to figure out the rhyme and reason of the menu. But who cares if the lightly baked trout in lemon is listed under the "From the Meat" section or that vegetarian meals come from the "Dungeon" or that the shrimp come from "Under the Draw-bridge." The fact is, this is one of the most romantic and satisfying restaurants in Vary. An ample wine list does its best to keep up with the menu, and again, local wines compete well with their imported, expensive cousins.

INEXPENSIVE

Cafe Eléfant. Stará Louka 32. ☎ **017/322 3406.** Cakes and desserts 20–90Kč (59¢–$2.65). Daily 9am–10pm. DESSERTS.

Who needs to travel all the way to Vienna? Since this is a cafe in the true sense of the word, all you'll find is coffee, tea, alcoholic and nonalcoholic drinks, desserts, and enough ambience to satisfy the hoards of Germans who flock to this landmark. (Be prepared to hear more German and Russian than Czech, as this is a see-and-be-seen haunt for foreigners.) The Eléfant is widely known for its belle époque style and is famous for its freshly baked cakes. Its many outdoor tables overlook the pedestrian promenade.

Hospoda U Šejka. Stará Louka 10. No phone. Soups 25Kč (76¢); main courses 99–214Kč ($3–$6.48). MC, V. Daily 11am–11pm. CZECH.

A new addition to the pub scene in town, U Šejka plays on the tried-and-true touristy Good Soldier Svejk theme. Luckily, the tourist trap goes no further, and once inside, you find a refreshingly unsmoky though thoroughly Czech atmosphere. Locals and tourists alike rub elbows while throwing back some fine lager and standard pub favorites such as goulash and beef tenderloin in cream sauce.

3 Mariánské Lázně (Marienbad)

29 miles (46km) SW of Karlovy Vary, 100 miles (160km) W of Prague

When Thomas Alva Edison visited Mariánské Lázně in the late 1800s, he proclaimed: "There is no more beautiful spa in all the world."

Mariánské Lázně now stands in the shadow of the Czech Republic's most famous spa town, Karlovy Vary, but it wasn't always that way. First mentioned in 1528, the town's mineral waters gained prominence at the end of the 18th and beginning of the 19th centuries. Nestled among forested hills and packed with romantic and elegant pastel hotels and spa houses, the town, commonly known by its German name, Marienbad, has played host to such luminaries as Göethe (where his love for Ulrika von Levetzow took root), Mark Twain, Chopin, Strauss, Wagner, Freud, and Kafka. England's Edward VII found the spa resort so enchanting that he visited nine times and even commissioned the building of the country's first golf club.

SPECIAL EVENTS   One of the few places in central Europe not to claim Mozart as one of its sons, Mariánské Lázně has instead chosen to honor one of its frequent visitors, Chopin, with a yearly festival devoted entirely to the Polish composer. The **Chopin Festival** usually runs for 8 to 10 days near the end of August. Musicians and directors from all over the world gather to play and listen to concerts and recitals. In addition, several local art galleries hold special exhibits. Tickets range from 50 to 750Kč ($1.47 to $22).

Each June, the town plays host to a **classical music festival** with many of the Czech Republic's finest musicians, as well as those from around the world. For more details or ticket reservations for either event, contact **Infocentrum KaSS** (see "Visitor Information," below).

Patriotic Americans can show up on **July 4** for a little down-home fun, including a parade and other flag-waving special events commemorating the town's liberation by U.S. soldiers in World War II.

Sports-minded travelers can play one of the country's best golf courses and see how they measure up to the likes of Seve Ballesteros, Bernhard Langer, and Sam Torrance, who all played there at the first European PGA tour event, the Czech Open.

ESSENTIALS

GETTING THERE   The express **train** from Prague takes just over 3 hours. Mariánské Lázně train station, Nádražní nám. 292 (☎ **0165/625 321**), is south of the

---

The Spa Treatment

For a relaxing mineral bubble bath or massage, make reservations through the **Spa Information Service,** Mírové nám. 104, 353 29 (☎ **0165/655 555** or 0165/ 655 550; fax 0165/655 500). Also ask at your hotel, since most provide spa treatments and massages or can arrange them. Treatments begin at 300Kč ($8.82).

---

town center; take bus no. 5 into town. The one-way fare costs 165Kč ($4.85) first class or 110Kč ($3.24) second class.

The **bus** from Prague takes about 3 hours and costs about 120Kč ($3.53). The Mariánské Lázně bus station is adjacent to the train station on Nádražní náměstí; take bus no. 5 into town.

Driving from Prague, take Highway E50 through Plzeň to Stříbro—about 22 kilometers past Plzeň—and head northwest on Highway 21. The clearly marked route can take up to 2 hours.

VISITOR INFORMATION   Along the main strip lies **Infocentrum KaSS,** Dům Chopin, Hlavní 47, 353 01, Mariánské Lázně (☎ and fax **0165/622 474**). In addition to dispensing advice, the staff sells maps and concert tickets and can arrange accommodations in hotels and private homes. It's open Monday to Friday from 7am to 7pm and Saturday and Sunday from 9am to 6pm.

ORIENTATION   Mariánské Lázně is laid out around **Hlavní třída,** the main street. A plethora of hotels, restaurants, travel agencies, and stores front this street. **Lázeňská Kolonáda,** a long, covered block beginning at the northern end of Hlavní třída, contains six of the resort's eight major springs.

TAKING THE WATERS

When walking through the town, it's almost impossible to miss the **Lázeňská Kolonáda,** just off Skalníkovy sady. From Hlavní třída, walk east on Vrchlického ulice. Recently restored to its former glory, the eye-catching colonnade of cast iron and glass is adorned with ceiling frescoes and Corinthian columns. It was built in 1889 and connects half a dozen major springs in the town center; this is the focal point of those partaking in the ritual. Bring a cup to fill or, if you want to fit in with the thousands of guests who are serious about their spa water, buy one of the porcelain mugs with a built-in straw that are offered just about everywhere. Do keep in mind that the waters are used to treat internal disorders, so the minerals may act to cleanse the body thoroughly. You can wander the Kolonáda any time; water is distributed daily from 6am to noon and 4 to 6pm.

LEARNING ABOUT THE CITY'S PAST

There's not much town history, since Mariánské Lázně officially came into existence only in 1808. But engaging brevity is what makes the two-story **City Museum (Muzeum Hlavního Města),** Goetheovo nám. 11 (☎ **0165/622 740**), recommendable. Chronologically arranged displays include photos and documents of famous visitors. Güethe slept here, in the upstairs rooms in 1823, when he was 74 years old. If you ask nicely, the museum guards will play an English-language tape that describes the contents of each of the rooms. You can also request to see the museum's English-language film about the town. Admission is 20Kč (59¢), and it's open Tuesday to Sunday from 9am to 4pm.

HIKING OR GOLFING

If the thought of a spa treatment fails to appeal, you can find relaxation in Mariánské Lázně through one of the simpler things in life: a walk in the woods. The surrounding **Slavkovský les (Slavkov Forest)** has about 70 kilometers of marked footpaths and trails through the gentle hills that abound in the area.

If you're a die-hard golfer or just looking for a little exercise, the **Mariánské Lázně Golf Club** (☎ 0165/624 300), a 6,195-meter par-72 championship course, lies on the edge of town. The club takes pay-as-you-play golfers, with a fully equipped pro shop that rents clubs. Greens fees are 1,200Kč ($35.30) and club rental is 300Kč ($8.82). Reservations are recommended on weekends.

WHERE TO STAY

The main strip along Hlavní třída is lined with hotels, many with rooms facing the Kolonáda. If you feel comfortable about doing this, I suggest walking the street and shopping around for a room; most hotels charge from 2,000 to 3,500Kč ($59 to $119) for a double in May to September. Off-season prices can fall by as much as half.

For private accommodations, try Paláckého ulice, running south of the main spa area.

EXPENSIVE

Hotel Golf. Zádub 55, 353 01 Mariánské Lázně. ☎ **0165/622 651.** Fax 0165/2655. 96 units. MINIBAR TV TEL. 2,278–3,604Kč ($67–$106) double; 4,318–5,576Kč ($127–$164) suite. Rates include breakfast. AE, DC, MC, V.

One of the more luxurious hotels in town, the Golf isn't actually in town but across from the golf course about 2 miles down the road leading to Karlovy Vary. This hotel is busy, so reservations are recommended. The English-speaking staff delivers on their pledge to cater to every wish. The rooms are bright and spacious, with an excellent restaurant and terrace on the first floor. Not surprisingly, given the hotel's name, the staff can help arrange a quick 18 holes across the street. The hotel has also recently opened its own spa center to pamper guests a little more.

Dining/Diversions: The restaurant has one menu but several areas that all have a different feel: The front room is a formal dining room with ornate chandeliers dripping with crystal. The back room has more of a warmer, informal appeal, with a bar to sit at and a fireplace to cozy up to. Between the two is a less-ornate dining room that leads to a beautiful terrace overlooking the grounds.

Amenities: Room service (6am to 11pm), laundry, golf, tennis, spa center, sauna, fitness club.

Hotel Villa Butterfly. Hlavní třída 72, 353 01 Mariánské Lázně. ☎ **0165/626 201.** Fax 0165/626 210. 94 units. MINIBAR TV TEL. 2,100–3,300Kč ($62–$97) double; 3,250–5,400Kč ($96–$159) suite; 4,500–7,200Kč ($132–$212) apt. Rates include breakfast. AE, DC, MC, V.

One of the many hotels on the main street to undergo extensive renovation and expansion recently, the Butterfly has upgraded its 26 rather ordinary rooms into 94 first-rate bright and spacious ones. In fact, from the front hall to the fitness room and even all the way to its new underground parking, the Butterfly has really taken off. Oddly enough, the renovations, which must've cost a lot, have had a reverse effect on the rates, now a good 15% lower. An English-speaking staff and a good selection of foreign-language newspapers at the reception area are added bonuses.

Dining/Diversions: The Fontaine is one of the town's largest restaurants, yet it remains a quiet place to eat top-rate Czech and international cuisine. The Cafe de Paris offers a wide assortment of dishes at its buffet, ranging from poached salmon to goulash. If you're waiting for someone or have some time to kill, the Lobby Bar is one of the few places in town that mixes a proper cocktail.

MODERATE

Hotel Bohemia. Hlavní třída 100, 353 01 Mariánské Lázně. ☎ **0165/623 251.** Fax 0165/622 943. 77 units. MINIBAR TV TEL. 1,800–2,400Kč ($53–$71) double; 2,550–3,100Kč ($75–$91) suite. AE, DC, MC, V.

In the middle of the action on Hlavní, the Bohemia has several rooms with balconies that look out to the Kolonáda. Though not as upscale as the other hotels listed, rooms at the Bohemia tend to be a little larger, and for those looking for location, you can't get more central.

Hotel Cristal Palace. Hlavní třída 61, 353 44 Mariánské Lázně. ☎ **0165/620 169.** Fax 0165/625 012. 94 units. 2,750–3,300Kč ($81–$97) double; 3,800Kč ($112) triple; 4,200–4,500Kč ($124–$132) suite. AE, DC, MC, V.

This hotel emerged from a chrysalis of scaffolding recently to take a serious run at the Butterfly just down the street. Despite the immediate reaction of "Did I just walk onto a set for *Miami Vice?*" upon seeing its pastel colors, the hotel still enjoys an enviable location just a few minutes south of the town center. Alas, the rooms are outfitted with sterile though decent furniture. The restaurant, cafe, wine room, and brasserie also have been redone, much for the better. All are now bright and cheery, pleasant for a quick coffee or drink.

Hotel Excelsior. Hlavní třída 121, 353 01 Mariánské Lázně. ☎ **0165/622 705.** Fax 0165/625 346. 64 units. MINIBAR TV TEL. 1,900–3,100Kč ($56–$91) double; 2,750–3,800Kč ($81–$112) triple; 2,990–4,200Kč ($88–$124) suite. AE, DC, MC, V.

Across from the Nové lázně (New Bath), the Excelsior has benefited inside and out from a post-Communist face-lift. Several rooms have ornate balconies overlooking the park that leads up to the Kolonáda. There are two restaurants, including the Churchill, one of the best watering holes on the strip. The hotel staff is also more attentive than those at some other hotels in town.

Hotel Palace. Hlavní třída 67, 353 01 Mariánské Lázně. ☎ **0165/622 222.** Fax 0165/624 262. 45 units. MINIBAR TV TEL. 1,370–2,680Kč ($40–$79) single; 2,150–3,570Kč ($63–$105) double; 2,810–5,100Kč ($83–$150) suite. AE, DC, MC, V.

The 1920s Palace is a beautiful art nouveau–style hotel 300 feet from the Kolonáda. The rooms are extremely comfortable, with high ceilings and large bay windows giving an airy effect. In addition to a good Bohemian restaurant with a lovely terrace, the hotel contains a cafe, a wine room, and a snack bar.

Hotel Zvon. Hlavní třída 68, 353 01 Mariánské Lázně. ☎ **0165/622 015.** Fax 0165/623 245. 79 units. MINIBAR TV TEL. 1,720–4,720Kč ($51–$139) double; 2,370–8,460Kč ($70–$249) suite. AE, DC, MC, V.

Next door to the Palace, the Zvon lacks a bit of the panache that its smaller neighbor has, but it still ranks as one of the town's nicer hotels and sits in a prime spot, directly across from the Kolonáda. The rooms at the front are brighter and much larger than those facing the back (and come at a price), which fail to receive much sun.

INEXPENSIVE

Hotel Garni San Remo. Zeyerova 161, 353 01 Mariánské Lázně. ☎ **0165/622 239.** Fax 0165/622 058. 24 units. MINIBAR TV TEL. 1,500–1,980Kč ($44–$58) double. AE, MC, V.

On the hill above the Cristal, the San Remo has some great views of the town. The rooms are bright and clean, but the beds are a little soft. The staff here tries hard to make up for the lack of amenities, which counts for a lot.

Family Fun

If you're looking for a weekend break with the family and want to have an enjoyable experience outdoors, book a weekend at the ✪ **Koliba,** Dusíkova 592 (☎ **0165/ 625 169**), and try out the mini–ski hill. Two tows at the foot of the hotel take you up a 150-metre hill perfect for children learning to ski. There are also dozens of kilometers of cross-country ski trails through the local forests that are always in top condition. A book of 25 lift tickets costs 150Kč ($4.41). The après-ski atmosphere of the lodge, with a giant fireplace and lots tables at which to sit and relax, provides the perfect respite from a hectic week. At night the flames of the open grill roasting all different sorts of game will ease the pain of all those bumps and bruises. In the summer, the trails are ideal for hiking, though be careful—many of the paths lead through the golf course, and while golf is gaining in popularity in the Czech Republic, the skill level is still at a point where you need to beware of errant golf balls.

✪ **Hotel Koliba.** Dusíkova 592, 353 01 Mariánské Lázně. ☎ **0165/625 169.** Fax 0165/ 763 10. 10 units. MINIBAR TV TEL. 1,200–1,470Kč ($35–$43) double. AE, MC, V.

Away from the main strip but still only a 7-minute walk from the Kolonáda, the Koliba is a rustic hunting lodge set in the hills on Dusíkova, the road leading to the golf course and Karlovy Vary. The rooms are warm and inviting, with the wooden furnishings giving the feel of a country cottage. The hotel provides a wide array of spa and health treatments, which cost extra.

Pacifik. Mírové nám. 84, 353 29 Mariánské Lázně. ☎ **0165/651 111.** Fax 0165/651 200. 80 units. TV TEL. 950–1,250Kč ($28–$37) double. AE, V.

Facing straight down the main strip, the Pacifik looks like a grand hotel. Well, looks can be deceiving, but it's still not a bad place given its prices. Not as comfortable or nicely appointed as most of the other hotels in the area, the Pacifik is a relatively inexpensive way to stay where the action is. The surly staff will remind you of a bygone era. Ask for a room that faces the street, where the view will take your mind off of the receptionist who thoroughly aggravated you on check-in.

WHERE TO DINE
MODERATE

Churchill Club Restaurant. Hlavní třída 121. ☎ **0165/622 705.** Soups 20Kč (59¢); main courses 150–400Kč ($4.41–$11.76). AE, MC, V. Daily 11am–11pm. CZECH.

Don't let the name fool you—the food is traditional Czech, not British, with few surprises, which is both good and bad. A lively bar with a good selection of local and imported beer makes the Churchill one of the few fun places to be after dark in this quiet town. Try the Winston steak platter if you're really hungry for a slab of nicely cooked beef.

✪ **Hotel Koliba Restaurant.** Dusíkova 592. ☎ **0165/625 169.** Reservations recommended. Soups 20Kč (59¢); main courses 85–385Kč ($2.50–$11.32). No credit cards. Daily 11am–11pm. CZECH.

Every time I'm in town, I make a point of stopping here for a meal. Like the hotel it occupies, the Koliba restaurant is a shrine to the outdoors. The dining room boasts a hearty, rustic atmosphere that goes perfectly with the restaurant's strength: wild game. Check the daily menu to see what's new or choose from the wide assortment of specialties *na rostu* (from the grill), including wild boar and venison. The Koliba also has an excellent selection of Moravian wines that you can order with your meal or at its wine bar, which has dancing with a Gypsy band from 7pm to midnight (except Monday).

Restaurant Fontaine. In the Villa Butterfly, Hlavní třída 72. ☎ **0165/626 201.** Soups 30–60Kč (88¢–$1.76); main courses 90–300Kč ($2.65–$8.82). AE, DC, MC, V. Daily 6–11pm. CZECH/INTERNATIONAL.

The restaurant has undergone a major transformation for the better. The dining room is very large but remains quiet, though a little too well lit. Bow-tied waiters serve traditional Bohemian specialties, like succulent roast duck, broiled trout, and chateaubriand, as well as some inventive variations. Try the duck in oranges with baked apples for an interesting mix of sweet and sour.

INEXPENSIVE

Classic Cafe/Restaurant. Hlavní třída 102. No phone. Salads 35–120Kč ($1.03–$3.53); main courses 69–149Kč ($2.03–$4.38). AE, MC, V. Daily 10am–11pm. CZECH.

A nice place to stop for a light bite, the Classic offers a large assortment of good fresh salads. The open and airy cafe/restaurant has one of the friendliest staffs in town. A few more tables out front would be welcome. It also brews a mean espresso.

Piccolo. Hlavní třída 88. No phone. Pastas 35–75Kč ($1.03–$2.21); pizzas 40–130Kč ($1.18–$3.82). No credit cards. Daily 11am–11pm. ITALIAN.

In the arcade on Hlavní, Piccolo has a big patio that caters to families with its quick service. The pizzas are a better choice than the pastas, many of which appear to use ketchup as a main ingredient. If you need a pasta fix, the lasagna isn't too bad, with lots of cheese making up for a smallish portion.

4 Plzeň (Pilsen)

55 miles (88km) SW of Prague

Some 400 years ago, a group of men formed Plzeň's first beer-drinking guild, and today beer is probably the only reason you'll want to stop at this otherwise industrial town. Unfortunately for the town, its prosperity and architecture were ravaged during World War II, leaving few buildings untouched. The main square, náměstí Republiky, is worth a look, but after that there's not much to see.

SPECIAL EVENTS   If you're an American or speak English, being in Plzeň in May is quite an experience. May 8 marks the day when General George S. Patton was forced to halt his advance after liberating the area, thanks to an Allied agreement to stop. The Russians were allowed to free Prague, becoming its successor superpower as decided in Yalta in 1944. Forty years of Communist oppression, however, means that the town now celebrates **Liberation Day** with a vengeance. You'll be feted and praised into the wee hours, as the city's people give thanks to the forces that ended Nazi occupation.

Anxious to capitalize on its beer heritage and always happy to celebrate, Plzeň started its own Octoberfest, called **Pivní slavnosti.**

In mid-August it hosts a modest music festival called **Jazz on the Streets,** highlighted with several concerts by top-name Czech musicians.

For more details on festivities for all events, contact the City Information Center Plzeň (see "Visitor Information," below).

ESSENTIALS

GETTING THERE   It's more comfortable taking the train to Plzeň than the bus, though the latter is a much quicker (65 min.) trip now that Prague is joined by the

---

Plzeň's Claim to Fame

Founded in 1295 by Václav II, Plzeň was and remains western Bohemia's administrative center. King Václav's real gift to the town, however, wasn't making it an administrative nerve center but granting it brewing rights. So more than 200 microbreweries popped up in almost every street-corner basement. Realizing that the brews they were drinking had become mostly plonk by the late 1830s, rebellious beer drinkers demanded quality, forcing the brewers to try harder. "Give us what we want in Plzeň, good and cheap beer!" became the battle cry. In 1842, the brewers combined their expertise to produce a superior brew through what became known as the Pilsner brewing method. If you don't believe it, look in your refrigerator. Most likely, the best beer in there has written somewhere on its label "Pilsner brewed."

---

new highway. A fast **train** from Prague whisks travelers to Plzeň in just under 2 hours without having to watch the mayhem caused by Czech drivers. Trains between the two cities are just as plentiful and fit most every schedule. The train costs 111Kč ($3.26) first class or 74Kč ($2.18) second class. To get from the train station to town, walk out the main entrance and take Americká street across the river and turn right onto Jungmannova, which leads to the main square.

The **bus** from Prague is quick, but tends to be cramped. It costs 59Kč ($1.74) one way. If you do take the bus, head back into town along Husova to get to the square.

Thanks to the government's highway-building scheme, Plzeň has moved closer to Prague—or at least it seems that way. A once treacherous 2-hour **drive** on a narrow two-lane highway has been replaced by an easy 45-minute cruise on the new Highway E50, which leaves Prague from the west. Spare a thought for the Trabant that once held you up for kilometers as you blow its doors off.

VISITOR INFORMATION   Realizing it has to be as visitor-friendly as possible, the **City Information Center Plzeň,** náměstí Republiky 41, 301 16 Plzeň (☎ **019/ 723 6535;** fax 019/722 4473), is packed with literature to answer your questions.

ORIENTATION   Plzeň's old core is centered around náměstí Republiky. All of the sites, including the brewery, are no more than a 10-minute walk from here.

TOURING THE BEER SHRINES

Plzeňské Pivovary (Pilsner Breweries), at U Prazdroje 7, will interest anyone who wants to learn more about the brewing process. The brewery actually is comprised of several breweries, pumping out brands like Pilsner Urquell and Gambrinus, the most widely consumed beer in the Czech Republic. The 1-hour tour of the factory (which has barely changed since its creation) includes a 15-minute film and visits to the fermentation cellars and brewing rooms. Tours can be taken at the brewery between 8am and 3pm. For groups of six or more, the tour starts immediately, for others, they wait until there are enough people (six or more). It costs 30Kč (88¢) Monday to Friday and 50Kč ($1.47) on Saturday; the price includes a dozen beer-oriented postcards and a tasting of some freshly brewed beer (for details on other available tours, call ☎ **019/ 706 2017**).

If you didn't get your fill of beer facts at the brewery, the **Pivovarské Muzeum (Beer Museum)** is a block away on Veleslavínova (☎ **019/722 4955;** fax 019/723 5574). Inside this 15th-century house you'll learn everything there is to know about beer but were afraid to ask. In the first room, once a 19th-century pub, the guard winds up an old German polyphone music box from 1887 that plays the sweet, though somewhat scratchy, strains of Strauss's *Blue Danube*. Subsequent rooms display a wide collection of pub artifacts, brewing equipment, and mugs. Most displays have English captions, but ask for a more detailed museum description in English when you enter. Admission is 30Kč (88¢). It's open Tuesday to Sunday from 10am to 6pm.

EXPLORING PLZEŇ

Safely full of more knowledge than you may want about the brewing process, proceed to the main square to see what's hopping (sorry, I couldn't resist). Dominating the center of the square is the Gothic **Cathedral of St. Bartholomew,** with the tallest steeple in the Czech Republic at 333 feet. A beautiful marble Madonna graces the main altar. The church is open from about 7am to 8pm daily.

You'll see an Italian flair in the first four floors of the 16th-century **Town Hall** and in the *sgraffito* adorning its facade. Later on, more floors were added, as well as a tower, gables, and brass flags, making the building appear as though another had fallen on top of it. The Town Hall is open Monday to Friday from 8am to 6pm, Saturday from 9am to 1pm. In front of the town hall, a **memorial** built in 1681 commemorates victims of the plague.

Just west of the square on Sady pětatřicátníků lies the shattered dreams of the 2,000 or so Jews who once called Plzeň home. The **Great Synagogue,** the third largest in the world, was built in the late 19th century. The facade has been painstakingly restored, but, sadly, its doors remain locked, with the building undergoing urgent repairs.

WHERE TO STAY

For private rooms that are usually outside of the town center but a little cheaper, try **Čedok,** Sedláčkova 12 (☎ **019/723 7419;** fax 019/722 3703), open Monday to Friday from 9am to noon and 1 to 5pm (to 6pm in summer) and Saturday from 9am to noon. Expect to pay about 500 to 1,000Kč ($14.71 to $29.41) for a double.

Hotel Central. Náměstí Republiky 33, 305 28 Plzeň. ☎ **019/722 6059.** Fax 019/722 6064. 50 units. TV. 1,250Kč ($36.76) double. AE, MC, V.

This rather sterile building is across from St. Bartholomew's Church. The surly staff notwithstanding, the hotel is surprisingly quiet despite being in the center of everything. Ask for one of the rooms facing east, giving a nice view of the church as the sun rises.

Hotel Slovan. Smetanovy sady 1, 305 28 Plzeň. ☎ **019/722 7256.** Fax 019/722 7012. 110 units. TV. 1,290Kč ($37.94) double. AE, MC, V.

An elegant turn-of-the-century staircase graces the entrance foyer to this venerable hotel. But after that, the rooms fall into the same 1970s-modern decor that, hard as it is to believe, was once in fashion. Nonetheless, it remains one of the few quality hotels in the city with laundry facilities and a lively bar on the main floor. The square is only about 2 blocks north.

Interhotel Continental. Zbrojnická 8, 305 34 Plzeň. ☎ **019/723 6479.** Fax 019/722 1746. 55 units (10 with shared shower/bathroom, 20 with private shower only, 25 with private bathroom). TV TEL. 850Kč ($25) double without bathroom; 1,590Kč ($46.76) double with shower only; 2,150Kč ($63.24) double with bathroom; 3,700Kč ($108.82) deluxe double. AE, MC, V.

About a block from the old town square, the modern Continental is considered by locals one of the best in town, though I have to say that it's far from the lap of luxury. Still, velvet-covered furniture and blue-tiled bathrooms (in the rooms with facilities) greet you in rooms bigger than in most of the other hotels in the area. Downstairs, the casino stays open late if you're feeling lucky or just thirsty.

WHERE TO DINE
MODERATE

Grill Restaurant 106.1. Bezrucova 20, Plzeň. ☎ **019/722 2371.** Soups 15–29Kč (44¢–85¢); main courses 75–215Kč ($2.21–$6.32); fondues 260–399Kč ($7.65–$11.74). MC, V. Mon–Sat 11am–midnight. CZECH/CONTINENTAL.

Near náměstí Republiky, this small restaurant named after a local radio station excels at grilled meats and poultry. It also has a bit of a sense of cuisine, serving appetizers such as mozzarella slices with tomatoes and olive oil, something rarely found in a city devoted to the beer culture. The fondues are a little pricey, but not a bad alternative if you have someone to share with.

Pilsner Urquell Restaurant. U Prazdroje 1 (just outside the brewery gates). No phone. Soups 22–32Kč (65¢–95¢); main courses 65–220Kč ($1.95–$6.65). AE, MC, V. Mon–Sat 10am–10pm. CZECH.

This isn't a visitor-oriented pub; literally in the same building that houses the brewery's management, the pub has remained true to those who supply it with beverages by cooking hearty, basic Czech meals, though it has become a little pricey recently.

Restaurace Na Spilce. U Prazdroje (just inside the brewery gates). ☎ **019/706 2754.** Soups 17–20Kč (50¢–60¢); main courses 32–195Kč (95¢–$5.90). AE, MC, V. Mon–Thurs 11am–10pm, Fri–Sat 11am–11pm, Sun 11am–9pm. CZECH.

The Na Spilce looks like a 600-seat tourist trap, but the food is quite good and reasonably priced. The standard řízký (schnitzels), goulash, and svíčková na smetaně (pork tenderloin in cream sauce) are hearty and complement the beer that flows from the brewery. If you've got a big appetite or just can't decide, try the Plzeňska Bašta, with ample servings of roasted pork, smoked pork, sausage, sauerkraut, and two kinds of dumplings.

INEXPENSIVE

Městařská Beseda. Smetanovy sady 13. ☎ **019/723 6667.** Soups 10–20Kč (29¢–59¢); main courses 39–149Kč ($1.15–$4.38). MC, V. Sun–Thurs 10am–11pm, Fri–Sat 10am–midnight. CZECH/CONTINENTAL.

The Beseda is down the street from the Slovan and from the same era. The high ceilings and wall murals help add elegance to this large restaurant visited by the theater crowd. The prices are very reasonable for the center, but the meals are unimaginative. It's a great place to stop for a late evening coffee and strudel or nightcap.

Pivnice Na Parkánu. Veleslavínova 4. ☎ **019/722 4485.** Soups 12–19Kč (35¢–56¢); main courses 45–120Kč ($1.32–$3.53). No credit cards. Daily 10:30am–10pm. CZECH.

A typical Czech pub located next to the Brewery Museum. There's nothing flashy here, even though it preys upon the tourist crowd that has built up a thirst looking at all that brewing paraphernalia. Wooden benches and tables provide the setting for large pork schnitzels, hearty goulash, and creamy svíčkova na smetaně.

U Salzmannu. Pražská 8. ☎ **019/723 5855.** Soups 20–30Kč (59¢–88¢); main courses 85–175Kč ($2.50–$5.15). AE, MC, V. Daily 10am–11pm. CZECH.

The oldest pub in Plzeň, dating back to 1637, it recently underwent a face-lift that has brought out the beauty of this Jugendstil building, which somehow adds to the flavor of the fresh beer served behind its doors. The food is a little disappointing in its standard appearance and taste—one would expect a little flair given the edifice. But if you want to stay near the main square and don't want to make the long walk back across the river and up the hill to the brewery pubs, this will fulfill your needs admirably.

5 Cheb (Eger) & Františkovy Lázně

105 miles (168km) W of Prague, 25 miles (40km) SW of Karlovy Vary

Few people who travel through Cheb actually stop and take a look around. From the outside, that's understandable, but it's too bad, since the center of Cheb is one of the more architecturally interesting places in west Bohemia. Its history is fascinating as well.

A former stronghold for the Holy Roman Empire on its eastern flank, Eger, as it was then known, became part of Bohemia in 1322. Cheb stayed under Bohemian rule until it was handed to Germany as part of the 1938 Munich Pact. Soon after the end of World War II, it was returned to Czech hands, when most of the area's native Germans, known as Sudeten Germans, were expelled for their open encouragement of the invading Nazi army. You can see this bilingual, bicultural heritage in the main square, which could be mistaken for being on either side of the border if it weren't for the Czech writing on windows. These days, the Germans have returned, but only for a few hours at a time, many for the town's thriving sex trade and cheap alcohol. Don't be surprised to see women around almost every corner opening. Still, Cheb is worth exploring for its mélange of architectural styles, the eerie Jewish Quarter Špalíček, and the enormous Romanesque Chebský Hrad (Cheb Castle).

Only about 20 minutes up the road from Cheb is the smallest of the three major Bohemian spa towns, **Františkovy Lázně.** Though it pales in comparison to Karlovy Vary and Mariánské Lázně, Františkovy Lázně has taken great strides in the past few years to erase the decline it experienced under Communism. There's not much to see save for the **Spa Museum,** which holds an interesting display of bathing artifacts, but it's a much quieter and cleaner place to spend the night than Cheb. I've listed places to stay and dine in both Cheb and Františkovy Lázně.

To get to Františkovy Lázně from Cheb by **car,** take Highway E49. The trip takes about 20 minutes. You can also take a taxi; just agree with the driver before you get in that the fare shouldn't be more than 200Kč ($5.88). As with everywhere in the Czech Republic, it's probably better to negotiate the fare before getting into the cab, when you can end up at the mercy of some of the world's most criminal fares.

ESSENTIALS

GETTING THERE   Cheb is located on the E48, one of the main highways leading to Germany. If you're **driving** from Prague, take the same route as you would to Karlovy Vary, which eventually brings you to Cheb. The drive takes about 2 hours.

Express **trains** from Prague usually stop in Cheb, as do several trains daily from Karlovy Vary. Cheb is on a main train route of the Czech Republic, so it's easy to catch many international connections here. The train takes 3½ hours and costs 195Kč ($5.74) first class and 130Kč ($3.82) second class.

Cheb is a long **bus** ride from Prague, and I suggest avoiding it if possible. It's more manageable to take the bus from Karlovy Vary or Mariánské Lázně.

VISITOR INFORMATION   You'll find maps, guidebooks, lodging, and even a currency exchange (at a fairly steep price, so use it only if you're desperate) at the **Informační Centrum Goetz & Hanzlík,** náměstí Premysla Otakara II 2 (☎ **0166/ 459 480;** fax 0166/459 291).

ORIENTATION   At the center of the old town lies the triangular náměstí Krále Jiřího z Poděbrad. Most of the main sights you'll want to see lie either directly on the square or on one of the many streets leading off it.

EXPLORING CHEB

The main square, **náměstí Krále Jiřího z Poděbrad,** attracts most of the attention and is a good place to begin a stroll of the old town. Though it has been overrun with tourist shops and cafes that serve mediocre German fare, the square still shines with Gothic burgher houses and the baroque **old town hall (stará radnice).** At its south end, the **statue of Kašna Roland,** built in 1591 and a former symbol of capital punishment, reminds people of the strength that justice can wield. At the other end of the square stands the **Kašna Herkules,** a monument to the town's former strength and power. Next to it is a cluster of 11 timber houses, called **Špalíček.** These used to be owned by Jews in the early 14th century, but a fervently anti-Semitic clergy in the area incited such hatred that the Jews were forced up Židská ulice (Jews street) and into an alleyway called ulička Zavražděných (Murder Victim's lane), where they were unceremoniously slaughtered in 1350.

Across from Špalíček is the **Cheb Museum** (☎ **0166/222 46**), where another murder took place almost 300 years later—that of Albrecht von Wallenstein in 1634. On the upper level, a display vividly depicts the assassination. The museum's first floor displays many 20th-century paintings, from which you can trace the town's slow demise. Admission is 25Kč (74¢), and it's open Tuesday to Sunday from 9am to noon and 1 to 5pm.

The old town is also packed with several churches. The most interesting is **St. Nicholas,** around the corner from the museum. It's a hodgepodge of architectural styles: Its Romanesque heritage is reflected in the tower windows, while a Gothic portal and baroque interior round out the renovations over the years. The church is open daily from 9am to 6pm.

TOURING CHEB CASTLE

An excellent example of Romanesque architecture in the northeast part of the old town is **Cheb Castle.** Overlooking the Elbe River, the castle, built in the late 12th century, is one of central Europe's largest Romanesque structures.

The castle's main draws are its **Chapel of Sts. Erhard and Ursala** and the **Černá věž (Black Tower).** The two-tiered early-Gothic chapel has a somber first floor where the proletariat would congregate, while the emperor and his family went to the much cheerier and brighter second floor with its Gothic windows.

Across the courtyard from the chapel stands the **Černá věž (Black Tower).** From its 60-foot-high lookout, you'll see the best views of the town. The tower seems dusty and smeared with pollution, but its color isn't from the emissions of the Trabants and Skodas that drive through the streets. Rather the tower is black because the blocks from which it is made are actually lava rocks taken from the nearby Komorni Hůrka volcano (now dormant).

Alas, there are no tours of the castle, and the English text provided at the entrance does little to inform you. Admission is 50Kč ($1.47). It's open Tuesday to Sunday: June to August from 9am to noon and 1 to 6pm, May and September from 9am to noon and 1 to 5pm, and April and October from 9am to noon and 1 to 4pm.

WHERE TO STAY
IN CHEB

Hotel Hvězda (Hotel Star). Náměstí Krále Jiřího z Poděbrad 4, 350 01 Cheb. ☎ **0166/ 422 549.** Fax 0166/422 546. 44 units. TV TEL. 1,150Kč ($33.82) double. AE, MC, V.

Overlooking the rather noisy main square, the Hvězda is a lone star in the Cheb hotel universe. The rooms are small, but most look out onto the square, and the staff tries to make your stay comfortable. If you can't stay in Františkovy Lázně and don't want to drive farther, this is really the only hotel I'd recommend in town.

In Františkovy Lázně

Hotel Tři Lilie (Three Lilies Hotel). Jiráskova 17, 351 01 Františkovy Lázně. ☎ **0166/ 942 350.** Fax 0166/942 970. 32 units. TV TEL. 3,250Kč ($95.59) double; 4,700Kč ($138.24) suite. AE, MC, V.

In 1808, Göethe stayed here, and he knew what he was doing. The Three Lilies is worth the extra money since it's the only luxury hotel in the area. Cheb needs a nice hotel like this. You can relax here; at night, you can block out noise in the spotless, spacious rooms outfitted with satellite television. The staff are very attentive and can arrange spa treatments, massages, and other health services. On the main floor is a nice, though pricey, bar and restaurant.

Interhotel Slovan. Národní třída 5, 351 01 Františkovy Lázně. ☎ **0166/942 841.** Fax 0166/942 843. 25 units. TV TEL. 1,150–1,490Kč ($33.82–$43.82) double. AE, MC, V.

This hotel isn't as elegant as the Three Lilies just down the main street, but it's a nice place nonetheless. The rooms are a little plain and small, but for the money, this is one of the better bets in town. The only drawback is a staff that at times forgets that you're paying for service as well as a bed.

WHERE TO DINE
In Cheb

Kavárna Špalíček. Náměstí Krále Jiřího z Poděbrad. ☎ **0166/225 68.** Soups 15–25Kč (44¢–74¢); main courses 79–199Kč ($2.32–$5.85). No credit cards. Daily 10am–11pm. CZECH.

This is better for a coffee stop than for a full meal. Take a place on the terrace and watch the people, but the real charm of Špalíček lies inside the building, which sits like an island in the middle of the square. This special place is a piece of living history.

Restaurace Fortuna. Náměstí Krále Jiřího z Poděbrad 29. ☎ **0166/221 10.** Soups 15–29Kč (44¢–85¢); main courses 79–185Kč ($2.32–$5.44). No credit cards. Daily 10am– 2am. CZECH.

If you need to have one last schnitzel before leaving, this is as good a place as any. The food has improved in recent years, with most Czech specialties accounted for. It's one of the only restaurants open late, and a terrace right on the main square lends to its appeal.

Staročeská Restaurace. Kamenná 1. No phone. Main courses 69–190Kč ($2.03–$5.59). No credit cards. Daily 10am–10pm. CZECH/CHINESE.

This restaurant serves much the same fare as all of the other restaurants on or around the square, but what catches the eye are a few Chinese dishes. The Kuře Kung-Pao (kung pao chicken) was a good spicy alternative to the sausages and meat and dumplings most of the other diners were having. The chicken with mushrooms is also a nice light choice if you have had your fill of heavy meals.

Zlaté Slunce (Golden Sun). Náměstí Krále Jiřího z Poděbrad 38. No phone. Soups 15–20Kč (44¢–59¢); main courses 78–255Kč ($2.29–$7.50). MC, V. Restaurant, daily 11am–3pm and 5–11pm; grill/bar, daily 11am–11pm. CZECH/CONTINENTAL.

Two restaurants in one allow the sun to shine for almost all tastes in this medieval cellar. On one side, the restaurant serves up Czech specialties, while the grill/bar (as the name suggests) barbecues steaks, chicken, and pork. For those who can't decide, try the grill mix, which puts all three on a plate.

IN FRANTIŠKOVY LÁZNĚ

Hotel Tří Lilie (Three Lilies Hotel). Jiráskova 17. ☎ **0166/942 350.** Main courses 105–475Kč ($3.09–$13.97). AE, MC, V. Daily 10am–midnight. CZECH/CONTINENTAL.

Just as its hotel is the cream of the local crop, so too is the Three Lilies restaurant. A little upscale in appearance, though the service fails to keep pace, this restaurant does very well with creative game dishes that combine Czech basics with European flair.

Restaurace Interhotel Slovan. Národní třída 5. No phone. Main courses 69–210Kč ($2.03–$6.18). No credit cards. Daily 8am–10pm. CZECH.

Be prepared for more heavy central European cuisine, with all four Czech food groups—meat, potatoes, dumplings, and cabbage—well represented. The fish tend to be a lighter meal than the pork cutlet smothered in cheese and ham, but both proved to be excellent choices. Oddly, the service at the restaurant is markedly better than at the hotel.

6 České Budějovice

92 miles (147km) S of Prague

This fortress town was born in 1265, when Otakar II decided that the intersection point of the Vltava and Malse rivers would be the site of a bastion to protect the approaches to southern Bohemia. Although Otakar was killed at the battle of the Moravian Field in 1278 and the town was subsequently ravaged by the rival Vítkovic family, the construction of České Budějovice continued, eventually taking the shape originally envisaged.

In the 15th century, the Hussite revolution swept across southern Bohemia, with one exception—České Budějovice, which, with its largely Catholic population, remained true to the king. Passing the loyalty test with flying colors, it developed into one of Bohemia's wealthiest and most important towns, reaching its pinnacle in the 16th century. This rise made České Budějovice an architecturally stunning place. As the town prospered, older Gothic buildings took on a Renaissance look. A new town hall was built and the flourishing old market (Masné Krámy) was rebuilt. Towering above it all was a new 72-meter-tall turret, the Black Tower. Sadly, the Thirty Years' War (1618–48) and a major fire in 1641 ravaged most of the town, leaving few buildings unscathed. But the Habsburg Empire came to the town's rescue in the 18th century, building baroque-style edifices that stand to this day.

Today, České Budějovice, the hometown of the original Budweiser brand beer, is now more a bastion for the beer drinker than a protector of Bohemia. But its slow pace, relaxed atmosphere, and interesting architecture make it a worthy stop, especially as a base for exploring southern Bohemia or for those heading on to Austria.

SPECIAL EVENTS Each August, České Budějovice hosts the largest **International Agricultural Show** in the country.

If you're passing through in the late fall or winter and want to see Czechs become emotional, head out to a match of the **Czech Extraliga hockey** league at the Winter Stadium (Zimní stadion) on ulice F. A. Gerstnera, where the local team does battle. Arguably some of the best hockey in the world is played in the Czech Republic, which you can see for a fraction of the price—about 40Kč ($1.18)—you'd pay to see players of a similar caliber in Western countries. The games are never sold out. The box office (☎ **038/651 21**) opens 1 hour before the game. The local newspapers, tourist information center, and posters pasted around the town will tell you what time the next match is.

ESSENTIALS

GETTING THERE   If you're **driving,** leave Prague to the south via the main D1 expressway and take the cutoff for Highway E55, which runs straight to České Budějovice. The trip takes about 1½ hours.

Daily express **trains** from Prague make the trip to České Budějovice in about 2½ hours. The fare is 165Kč ($4.85) first class or 110Kč ($3.24) second class. Several express **buses** run from Prague's Florenc station each day and take 2 hours; tickets cost 89Kč ($2.62).

You can take a **taxi** for 500Kč ($15) each way to Třeboň, but as always, be warned; taxi drivers have probably the poorest reputation in all of Europe, and they didn't get it unfairly. Always negotiate a fare like this in advance. If possible, get a Czech speaker from your hotel to haggle for you.

VISITOR INFORMATION   **Tourist Infocentrum,** náměstí Přemysla Otakara II 2 (☎ and fax **038/635 9480**), provides maps and guidebooks and finds lodging.

ORIENTATION   České Budějovice's circular Staré Město (Old Town) centers around the Czech Republic's largest cobblestone square, náměstí Přemysla Otakara II.

EXPLORING THE TOWN

You can comfortably see České Budějovice in a day. At its center is one of central Europe's largest squares, the cobblestone **náměstí Přemysla Otakara II**—it may be too large, as many of the buildings tend to get lost with all the open space. The square contains the ornate **Fountain of Sampson,** an 18th-century water well that was once the town's principal water supply, plus a mish-mash of baroque and Renaissance buildings. On the southwest corner is the **town hall,** an elegant baroque structure built by Martinelli between 1727 and 1730. On top of the town hall, the larger-than-life statues by Dietrich represent the civic virtues: justice, bravery, wisdom, and diligence.

One block northwest of the square is the **Černá věž (Black Tower),** which you can see from almost every point in the city. Consequently, its 360 steps are worth the climb to get a bird's-eye view in all directions. The most famous symbol of České Budějovice, this 232-foot-tall 16th-century tower was built as a belfry for the adjacent **St. Nicholas Church.** This 13th-century church, one of the town's most important sights, was a bastion of Roman Catholicism during the 15th-century Hussite rebellion. You shouldn't miss the church's flamboyant white-and-cream 17th-century baroque interior.

The tower is open daily from 10am to 7pm; admission is 10Kč (30¢). The church is open daily from 9am to 8pm.

TOURING A BEER SHRINE

On the town's northern edge sits a shrine to those who pray to the gods of the amber nectar. This is where **Budějovický Budvar,** the original brewer of Budweiser beer, has its one and only factory. Established in 1895, Budvar draws on more than 700 years of the area's brewing tradition to produce one of the world's best beers.

Four trolleybuses—nos. 2, 4, 6, and 8—stop by the brewery; this is how the brewery ensures that its workers and visitors reach the plant safely each day. The trolley costs 8Kč (24¢) to the brewery. You can also hop a cab from the town square for about 100 to 150Kč ($2.94 to $4.41).

Tours can be arranged by phoning ahead, but only for groups. Contact Budvar n.p., Karolíny Světlé 4, České Budějovice (☎ **038/770 5340**). If you're traveling alone or with only one or two other people, ask a hotel concierge at one of the bigger hotels (we suggest the Zvon or Hotel Malý Pivovar) if he or she can put you in with an already scheduled group. Failing that, you may want to take a chance and head up to the brewery, where, if a group has arrived, another person or two won't be noticed.

Once you're inside the brewery, the smell may cause flashbacks to some of the wilder frat parties you've attended. This is a traditional brew, and not much has changed at the brewery over the past hundred years or so. The room where everything moves along conveyer belts and goes from dirty old bottles to boxed cartons is fascinating, if you haven't seen this before.

WHERE TO STAY

Several agencies can locate reasonably priced private rooms. Expect to pay about 500Kč ($14.71) per person, in cash. **Tourist Infocentrum,** náměstí Přemysla Otakara II 2 (☎ and fax **038/635 2589**), can point you toward a wide selection of conveniently located rooms and pensions.

Hotel Bohemia. Hradební 20, 370 01 České Budějovice. ☎ and fax **038/731 1381.** 12 units. TV TEL. 1,220Kč ($35.88) double. AE, V.

The Bohemia really isn't a hotel but a small pension in the center, and you'll find this out when you walk into the lobby and think that you've stepped into someone's house. The staff make you feel like one of the family with attentive service, and the rooms are pleasant despite being a little small.

Hotel Gomel. Třída Míru 14, 370 01 České Budějovice. ☎ **038/731 1390.** 180 units. MINIBAR TV TEL. 1,950Kč ($57.35) double; 3,200Kč ($94.11) suite. Rates include breakfast. AE, DC, MC, V.

Not known for its ambience (even die-hard Communists would find the place drab), the 18-floor Gomel has a straightforward approach and offers comfortable, clean rooms with either a tub or a shower and few other frills. Views from the upper floors can't be beat; ask for one that faces into town. Located just off the main road entering the city from the north, the Gomel is hard to miss—it's the tallest building around—and is only a few minutes' walk from the historic old town.

✪ **Hotel Malý Pivovar (Small Brewery).** Ulice Karla IV 8–10, 370 01 České Budějovice. ☎ **038/636 0471.** Fax 038/636 0474. E-mail: budvar.hotel@cbu.pvtnet.cz. 28 units. MINIBAR TV TEL. 1,890–2,450Kč ($55.59–$72.06) double; 1,690–2,750Kč ($49.71–$80.88) suite. Rates include breakfast. AE, CB, DC, MC, V.

Around the corner from the Zvon, a renovated 16th-century microbrewery combines the charms of a B&B with the amenities of a modern hotel. Management here is a rarity in the Czech tourism industry; they work hard to help out. The rooms are bright and cheery, with antique-style wooden furniture and exposed wooden ceiling beams providing a farmhouse feeling in the center of town. It's definitely worth consideration if being directly on the square (you're only 30 meters from it) isn't a problem. This is also one of the best places to arrange for a trip to the brewery.

Hotel U solné brány. Radniční ulice 11, 370 01 České Budějovice. ☎ **038/635 4121.** Fax 038/635 4120. 11 units. MINIBAR TV TEL. 1,790Kč ($44) double; 2,000Kč ($61) suite. Rates include breakfast. MC, V.

Another of the growing numbers of conveniently located hotels just off of the main square, U solné brány is one of the products of post-Communism: a bright renovated hotel with a friendly management. It almost feels like a pension. Most rooms have balconies, making a cold Budvar from the minibar almost mandatory in the early evening or as a nightcap.

Hotel Zvon. Náměstí Premysla Otakara II 28, 370 42 České Budějovice. ☎ **038/731 1384.** Fax 038/731 1385. www.hotel-zvon.cz. 75 units. MINIBAR TV TEL. 1,450–2,900Kč ($42.65–$85.29) double; 1,800–3,800Kč ($52.94–$111.76) suite. AE, DC, MC, V.

Keeping Up with the Schwarzenbergs: Visiting a 141-Room English Castle

Only 8 kilometers north of České Budějovice lies **Hluboká nad Vltavou** (☎ 038/965 045). Built in the 13th century, the castle has undergone many face-lifts over the years, but none that left as lasting an impression as those ordered by the Schwarzenberg family. As a sign of the region's growing wealth and importance in the mid–19th century, the Schwarzenbergs remodeled the 141-room castle in the neo-Gothic style of England's Windsor Castle. Robin Leach would be proud, as no expense was spared in the quest for opulence. The Schwarzenbergs removed the impressive wooden ceiling from their residence at Český Krumlov and reinstalled it in the large dining room. Other rooms are as equally garish in their appointments, making a guided tour worth the time, even though only about a third of the rooms are open to the public.

To complete the experience, the **Alšova Jihočeská Galerie (Art Gallery of South Bohemia)** in the riding school at Hluboká houses the second-largest art collection in Bohemia, including many interesting Gothic sculptures from the area.

The castle and gallery are open April to October, Tuesday to Sunday from 10am to 5:30pm. Tours in English run at 11am and 2 and 4pm and cost 75Kč ($2.21), which includes the gallery.

The distance from České Budějovice is short enough to make a pleasant bike trip from the city or a quick stop either on the way to or coming from Prague, Třeboň, or Tábor. The tourist information office can help with bike rentals.

If you're driving to Hluboká from České Budějovice, take Highway E49 north and then Highway 105 just after leaving the outskirts of České Budějovice. For cyclists or those driving who prefer a slower, more scenic route, take the road that runs behind the brewery; it passes through the village of Obora.

Location is everything to the city's most elegant hotel, which occupies several historic buildings on the main square. In fact, pretty soon the hotel and its accompanying businesses will occupy nearly one-quarter of the addresses in the area. The upper-floor rooms have been renovated and tend to be more expensive, especially those with a view on the square. Others are relatively plain and functional. The views from those in front, however, can't be topped, and since the square is so big, noise is rarely a problem. Try to avoid the smaller rooms, usually reserved for tour groups. There's no elevator, but if you don't mind the climb, stay on the fourth floor. One of the biggest changes here in recent years has been the staff, which appear to be learning that guests deserve respect and quality treatment.

WHERE TO DINE

✪ **Masné Krámy (Meat Shops).** Krajinská 29. ☎ **038/633 7957.** Main courses 85–180Kč ($2.50–$5.29). No credit cards. Daily 10am–11pm. CZECH.

If you've pledged not to go to any "tourist traps," rationalize going to this one by reminding yourself that it's also a historical building. Just northwest of náměstí Přemysla Otakara II, labyrinthine Masné Krámy occupies a series of drinking rooms on either side of a long hall and is a must for any serious pub-goer. The inexpensive and filling food is pure Bohemia, including several pork, duck, and trout dishes. Come for the boisterous atmosphere or what's possibly the best goulash in the Czech Republic. The last time I was there, my dinner guest had three plates of it.

U paní Emy. Široká 25. No phone. Main courses 69–200Kč ($2.03–$5.88). No credit cards. Daily 10am–3am. CZECH/INTERNATIONAL.

Usually crowded, U paní Emy has a good selection on the menu, with reasonable prices for both food and beverages. The chicken and fish dishes are the most popular. The pan-fried trout tastes very light, not oily as most Czech restaurants tend to make it. A wine bar here stays open to the wee hours.

U staré pípy. In the Hotel Malý Pivovar, ulice Karla IV 8–10. ☎ **038/636 0471.** Soups 16–25Kč (47¢–74¢); main courses 69–190Kč ($2.03–$5.59). AE, CB, DC, MC, V. Daily 10am–11pm. CZECH.

This typical Czech-style pub serves up hearty food at reasonable prices. If you're looking for adventure, try the *grilovaná veprová kolena* (grilled pig knee). This is a meal that I rarely eat, and only when I know it's prepared correctly. I never hesitate to order it here. The restaurant has also come up with numerous complete menu selections for all price ranges.

7 Český Krumlov

12 miles (19km) SW of Ceské Budêjovice

If you have time on your visit to the Czech Republic for only one excursion, seriously consider making it ✪ **Český Krumlov.** One of Bohemia's prettiest towns, Krumlov is a living gallery of elegant Renaissance-era buildings housing charming cafes, pubs, restaurants, shops, and galleries. In 1992, UNESCO named Český Krumlov a World Heritage Site for its historic importance and physical beauty.

Bustling since medieval times, the town, after centuries of embellishment, is exquisitely beautiful. In 1302, the Rozmberk family inherited the castle and moved in, using it as their main residence for nearly 300 years. You'll feel that time has stopped as you look from the Lazebnický Bridge, with the waters of the Vltava below snaking past the castle's gray stone. At night, by the castle light, the view becomes even more dramatic.

Few deigned to change the appearance of Český Krumlov over the years, not even the Schwarzenbergs, who had a flair for opulence. At the turn of the 19th century, several facades of houses in the town's outer section were built, as were inner courtyards. Thankfully, economic stagnation in the area under Communism meant little money for "development," so no glass-and-steel edifices, like the Hotel Thermal in Karlovy Vary, jut out to spoil the architectural beauty. Instead, a medieval sense reigns supreme, now augmented by the many festivals and renovations that keep the town's spirit alive.

SPECIAL EVENTS   After being banned during Communism (a little too feudalistic for Gottwald), the **Slavnost pětilisté ruže (Festival of the Five-Petaled Rose)** has made a triumphant comeback. It's held each year at the summer solstice. Residents of Český Krumlov dress up in Renaissance costume and parade through the streets. Afterward, the streets become a stage with plays, chess games with people dressed as pieces, music, and even duels "to the death."

Český Krumlov also plays host to a 2-week **International Music Festival** every August, attracting performers from all over the world. Performances are held in nine spectacular venues. For details or ticket reservations, contact the festival organizer, **Auviex,** Obrovského 10, 141 00, Praha 4 (☎ **0337/767 275** or 0337/769 443; fax 0337/2768 881, or 0337/4275 3350 in Český Krumlov).

Český Krumlov

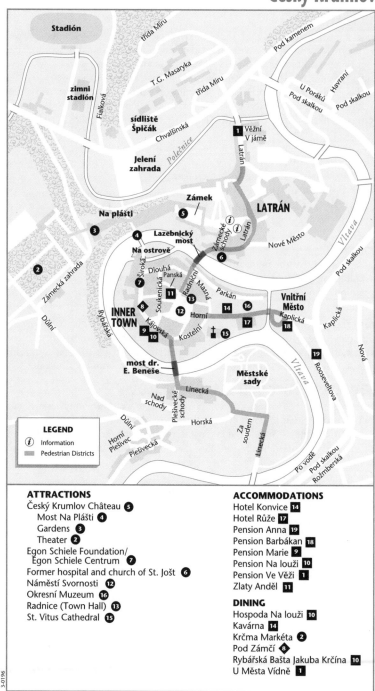

ATTRACTIONS

Český Krumlov Château **5**
   Most Na Plášti **4**
   Gardens **3**
   Theater **2**
Egon Schiele Foundation/
  Egon Schiele Centrum **7**
Former hospital and church of St. Jošt **6**
Náměstí Svornosti **12**
Okresní Muzeum **16**
Radnice (Town Hall) **13**
St. Vitus Cathedral **15**

ACCOMMODATIONS

Hotel Konvice **14**
Hotel Růže **17**
Pension Anna **19**
Pension Barbákan **18**
Pension Marie **9**
Pension Na louži **10**
Pension Ve Věži **1**
Zlaty Anděl **11**

DINING

Hospoda Na louži **10**
Kavárna **14**
Krčma Markéta **2**
Pod Zámčí **8**
Rybářská Bašta Jakuba Krčína **10**
U Města Vídně **1**

3-0196

ESSENTIALS

GETTING THERE   From České Budějovice, it's about a 45-minute **drive** to Krumlov, depending on traffic. Take Highway 3 leading from the south of České Budějovice and turn onto Highway 159. The roads are clearly marked, with several signs directing traffic to the town. From Prague, it's a 2-hour drive.

The only way to reach Český Krumlov by **train** from Prague is via České Budějovice, a slow ride that'll deposit you at a station relatively far from the town center. It takes 3½ hours; the fare is 180Kč ($5.29) first class or 120Kč ($3.53) second class.

The nearly 3-hour **bus** ride from Prague usually involves a transfer in České Budějovice. The fare is 149Kč ($4.38), and the bus station in Český Krumlov is a 15-minute walk from the town's main square.

VISITOR INFORMATION   Right on the main square, the **Information Centrum,** náměstí Svornosti 1, 381 00 Český Krumlov (☎ and fax **0337/711 183**), provides a complete array of services, from booking accommodations to ticket reservations for events, as well as a phone and fax service. It's open daily from 9am to 6pm.

Be warned that the municipal hall is in the same building, and it's crowded with weddings on weekends. If someone holds out a hat, throw some change into it, take a traditional shot of liquor from them, and *blahopřát* (congratulate) just about everyone in the room.

ORIENTATION   Surrounded by a circular sweep of the Vltava River, Český Krumlov is easy to negotiate. The main square, **náměstí Svornosti,** is at the very center of the Inner Town. The bridge that spans the Vltava a few blocks away leads to a rocky hill and Latrán, above which is the castle, **Český Krumlov Château.**

STROLLING THROUGH ČESKÝ KRUMLOV

Bring a good pair of walking shoes and be prepared to wear them out. Český Krumlov not only lends itself to hours of strolling, but its hills and alleyways demand it. No cars, thank goodness, are allowed in the historic town, and the cobblestones keep most other vehicles at bay. The town is split into two parts—the **Inner Town** and **Latrán,** which houses the castle. They're best tackled separately, so you won't have to crisscross the bridges several times.

Begin your tour at the **Okresní Muzeum (Regional Museum)** (☎ **0337/ 711 674**) at the top of Horní ulice. Once a Jesuit seminary, the three-story museum now contains artifacts and displays relating to Český Krumlov's 1,000-year history. The highlight of this mass of folk art, clothing, furniture, and statues is a giant model of the town that offers a bird's-eye view of the buildings. Admission is 20Kč (59¢), and it's open Tuesday to Sunday from 10am to 12:30pm and 1 to 6pm.

Across the street is the **Hotel Růže (Rose),** Horní 153 (☎ **0337/711 141**), which was once a Jesuit student house. Built in the late 16th century, the hotel and the prelature next to it show the development of architecture—Gothic, Renaissance, and rococo influences are all present. If you're not staying at the hotel, don't be afraid to walk around and even ask questions at the reception desk.

Continue down the street to the impressive late Gothic **St. Vitus Cathedral.** Be sure to climb the church tower, which offers one of the most spectacular views of both the Inner Town and the castle across the river. The church is open daily from 8am to 8pm.

As you continue down the street, you'll come to **náměstí Svornosti.** Few buildings show any character, making the main square of such an impressive town a little

A Crowd Alert

Consider yourself warned: Word has spread about this town. Summer season can be unbearable, as thousands of visitors blanket its medieval streets. If possible, try to visit in the off-season, when the crowds recede, the prices decrease, and the town's charm can really shine. Who knows, you may even hear some Czech!

disappointing. The **Radnice (Town Hall),** at náměstí Svornosti 1, is one of the few exceptions. Open daily from 9am to 6pm, its Gothic arcades and Renaissance vault inside are exceptionally beautiful in this otherwise run-down area. From the square, streets fan out in all directions. Take some time to just wander through the streets.

One of Český Krumlov's most famous residents was Austrian-born artist Egon Schiele. He was a bit of an eccentric who on more than one occasion raised the ire of the town's residents (many were distraught with his use of their young women as his nude models), and his stay was cut short as residents' patience ran out. But the town readopted the artist in 1993, setting up the **Egon Schiele Foundation and the Egon Schiele Centrum** in Inner Town, Široká 70–72, 381 01, Český Krumlov (☎ **0337/ 711 224;** fax 0337/711 191). It documents his life and work, housing a permanent selection of his paintings as well as exhibitions of other 20th-century artists. Admission depends on the exhibitions being displayed. It's open from 10am to 6pm.

After the museum, cut down Panenská ulice to Soukenická 39 and stop in at **Galerie u rytíře Krystofa,** Panenská 6, where you can try on the latest in body armor! This place is like the wardrobe room at a theater, and most everything is for sale. It's open Monday to Saturday from 10am to 6pm, Sunday from 1 to 6pm.

For a different perspective on what the town looks like, take the stairs from the **Městské divadlo (Town Theater)** on Horní ulice down to the riverfront and rent a rowboat from **Maláček boat rentals** at 40Kč ($1.18) per hour. Always willing to lend his advice, the affable Pepa Maláček will tell you what to watch out for and where the best fishing is (no matter how many times you say that you don't want to fish!).

You might want to grab a light lunch at one of the many cafes in Inner Town before crossing the river.

As you cross the bridge and head toward the castle, you'll see immediately to your right the former **hospital and church of St. Jošt.** Founded at the beginning of the 14th century, it has since been turned into apartments. Feel free to snoop around, but don't enter the building.

EXPLORING THE CHÂTEAU

Reputedly the second-largest castle in Bohemia (after Prague Castle), the **Český Krumlov Château** was constructed in the 13th century as part of a private estate. Throughout the ages, it has passed to a variety of private owners, including the Rožmberk family, Bohemia's largest landholders, and the Schwarzenbergs, the Bohemian equivalent of the TV show *Dynasty*'s Carrington family.

Follow the path for the long climb up to the **castle.** Greeting you is a round 12th-century **tower,** with its Renaissance balcony. You'll pass over the moat, now occupied by two brown bears. Next is the **Dolní Hrad (Lower Castle)** and then the **Horní Hrad (Upper Castle).**

Perched high atop a rocky hill, the château is open from April to October only, exclusively by guided tour. Visits begin in the rococo **Chapel of St. George,** continue through the portrait-packed **Renaissance Hall,** and end with the **Royal Family Apartments,** outfitted with ornate furnishings that include Flemish wall tapestries and European paintings. Tours last 1 hour and depart frequently. Most are in Czech or German, however. If you want an English-language tour, arrange it ahead of time by calling ☎ **0337/711 465** (fax 0337/711 687).

The tour costs 100Kč ($2.94) for adults and 50Kč ($1.47) for students. The castle hours are Tuesday to Sunday: May to August from 7:45am to noon and 12:45 to 4pm, September from 8:45am to noon and 12:45 to 4pm, and April and October from 8:45am to noon and 12:45 to 3pm. The last entrance is 1 hour before closing.

Once past the main castle building, you can see one of the more stunning views of Český Krumlov from **Most Na Plášti,** a walkway that doubles as a belvedere to the Inner Town. Even farther up the hill lie the castle's riding school and gardens.

WHERE TO STAY

With the rise of free enterprise after the fall of Communism, many hotels have sprouted up or are getting a "new" old look. PENSION and ZIMMER FREI signs line Horní and Rooseveltova streets and offer some of the best values in town. For a comprehensive list of area hotels and help with bookings, call or write to the Infocentrum listed above in "Visitor Information."

EXPENSIVE

Hotel Dvořák Radniční 144. 381 01 Český Krumlov. ☎ **0337/711 020.** Fax 0337/ 711 024. E-mail: dvorak@ckmbox.vol.cz. 20 units. 2,800–3,500Kč ($82.35–$102.94) double; 3,400–4,300Kč ($100–$126.47) suite; 4,300–7,800Kč ($126.47–$229.41) luxury suite. Rates include breakfast. AE, MC, V.

The newest addition to the hotel scene in Krumlov, the Dvořák is a welcome one for those looking for something extra. The views are spectacular, the service top-notch. Rooms are thoughtfully decorated, bright, and airy. A little pricey compared to the rest of the hotels in town, but if you don't mind paying a little more, you get a lot more.

Hotel Růže (Rose Hotel). Horní 153, 381 01 Český Krumlov. ☎ **0337/711 141** or 0337/ 2245. Fax 0337/711 128. 53 units. MINIBAR TV TEL. 1,530–3,420Kč ($45–$100.59) double; 1,800–4,230Kč ($52.94–$124.41) small suite; 2,700–4,950Kč ($79.41–$145.59) large suite. Rates include breakfast. AE, MC, V.

Once a Jesuit seminary, this stunning Italian Renaissance building has been turned into a well-appointed hotel. Comfortable in a big-city kind of way, it's packed with amenities and is one of the top places to stay in Český Krumlov. But for all of the splendor of the building, you may find the Růže a bit of a disappointment. The rooms contain no period pieces, but look as though they were furnished from a Sears warehouse. They're clean and spacious, but the promise of a Renaissance stay dissipates quickly. For families or large groups, the larger suites, which have eight beds, provide good value. For the adventurous or those with the right haircut, try one of the cells, where the Jesuit monks used to stay.

MODERATE

Hotel Konvice. Horní ul. 144. 381 01 Český Krumlov. ☎ **0337/711 611.** Fax 0337/ 711 327. 10 units. 1,300Kč ($38.24) double; 1,600–2,500Kč ($47.06–$73.53) suite. Rates include breakfast. No credit cards.

The rooms at the Konvice are on the small side, with rustic furniture. But the real lure for this hotel is the view. If you can get a room with a view out the back, take it immediately. As you overlook the river and the castle on the opposite bank, you'll wonder why anyone would stay at the Růže just a few doors up.

✪ **Pension Anna.** Rooseveltova 41, 381 01 Český Krumlov. ☎ **0337/711 692.** 8 units. 800–1,000Kč ($23.53–$29.41) double; 1,100–1,300Kč ($32.35–$38.24) suite. Rates include breakfast. No credit cards.

A Renaissance Pub Endures

Most visitors don't come this far up the castle during the day, let alone at night. That's their loss, for I've had what's been one of my finest dining experiences in the Czech Republic at **Krčma Markéta,** Latrán 67 (☎ **0337/711 453**).

To get here, walk all the way up the hill through the castle, past the Horní Hrad (Upper Castle) and past the Zámecké divadlo (Castle Theater). Walk through the raised walkway and into the Zámecká zahrada (Castle Garden), where you'll eventually find this Renaissance pub.

When you go inside, you'll feel as if you've left this century. There's no need for plates here, as meals are served on wooden blocks. Drinks come in pewter mugs. Unfortunately, one of the pub's main draws, former owner Robin Kratochvíl, is gone. But while the new owners have traded in Kratochvíl's big-enough-to-turn-a-Volkswagen tongs for a set of racks where the meat cooks, little else has changed under the new proprietorship. There's still no menu. Just go up to the fire and see what's roasting; usually there's a wide variety of meats, including succulent pork cutlets, rabbit, chickens, and pork knees, a Czech delicacy. When the plate comes, don't wait for the vegetables. But don't worry, vegetarians can now be accommodated.

Before the night is over, you'll probably find yourself talking to someone else at the pub's large wooden tables and forgetting that you still have to walk all the way back down the hill to get to your lodging. Time seems to stand still here. I know I didn't want to go home.

Krčma Markéta is open daily from 6 to 11pm. Reservations are recommended. Soup costs 20Kč (59¢), and main courses are 75 to 155Kč ($2.21 to $4.56). No credit cards are accepted.

Along "pension alley," this is a comfortable and rustic place. What makes this pension a favorite is the friendly management and homey feeling you get as you walk up to your room. Forget hotels—this is the kind of place where you can relax. The owners even let you buy drinks and snacks at the bar downstairs and take them to your room. The suites, with four beds and a living room, are great for families and groups.

Pension Barbákan. Horní 26, 381 01 Český Krumlov. ☎ **0337/5017.** 8 units. 1,800Kč ($52.94) double; 2,100Kč ($61.76) triple. Rates include breakfast. No credit cards.

After a change in management, the Barbákan, across from the theater, has spruced itself up, inside and out. The new owners have redone the inside of the pension completely, putting in new bathrooms in all the rooms and generally keeping the premises spotless. Take breakfast out in the back garden on warm summer mornings and watch Pepa Maláček argue with his customers down below at the riverbank.

Pension Marie. Kájovská 68, 381 01 Český Krumlov. ☎ and fax **0337/711 844.** 6 units. 1,100Kč ($32.35) double. No credit cards.

Next door to Na louži, the facade of this new pension has been completely restored. But inside, the plain furniture fails to rival the charm of its neighbor's. On the other hand, the beds are longer for the vertically gifted.

Pension Na louži. Kájovská 66, 381 01 Český Krumlov. ☎ and fax **0337/712 880.** 5 units. 1,000Kč ($29.41) double; 1,200Kč triple ($35.29); 1,400Kč ($41.18) suite. No credit cards.

Smack-dab in the heart of the Inner Town, the small Na louži, decorated with early-20th-century wooden furniture, is a charming change from many of the bigger, bland rooms found in other nearby hotels. The only drawback is beds with footboards that can be a little short for those over 6 feet.

✪ **Pension Ve Věži (In the Tower).** Latrán 28, 381 01 Český Krumlov. ☎ **0337/ 711 742.** 4 units (all with shared bathroom). May–Sept, 1,400Kč ($41.18) double; 1,800Kč ($52.94) quad. Oct–Apr, 750Kč ($22.06) double; 1,200Kč ($35.29) quad. Rates include breakfast. No credit cards.

A private pension in a renovated medieval tower just a 5-minute walk from the castle, Ve Věži is one of the most magnificent places to stay in town, and the only one I would recommend on the Latrán side. It's not the accommodations themselves that are so grand; none has a bathroom and all are sparsely decorated. Instead, what's wonderful is the ancient ambience. Reservations are recommended.

Zlatý Anděl (Golden Angel). Nám. Svornosti 10–11, 381 01 Český Krumlov. ☎ **0337/ 712 310.** Fax 0337/712 927. E-mail: zlatandel@iol.cz. 32 units. 1,350–1,750Kč ($39.71– $51.47) double; 1,900–2,450Kč ($55.88–$72.06) suite. Rates include breakfast. AE, MC, V.

The Golden Angel has emerged from a chrysalis with new wings. After a long reconstruction and renovation of its rooms, including new furniture, the Golden Angel has shed its Communist furbishings for more stylish fittings right down to the marble bathrooms. A piano bar and small pub add to the fact that this is now the best place on the square.

WHERE TO DINE
MODERATE

Kavárna. In the Hotel Konvice, Horní ul. 144. Main courses 79–210Kč ($2.32–$6.18). AE, MC, V. Daily 8am–10pm. CZECH.

If weather permits, eat outside overlooking the river at the Kavárna. Try the boned chicken breast smothered in cheese or any of the steaks and salads. Portions are big, and the view, again, spectacular. If this place is full, **U písaře Jana** next door has similarly priced meals with almost the same view.

Restaurace Na Ostrově (On the Island). Na ostravě 171. ☎ **0337/711 699.** Main courses 60–245Kč ($1.76–$7.21). No credit cards. Daily 11am–11pm. CZECH.

In the shadow of the castle, and, as the name implies, on an island, this restaurant is best on a sunny day when the terrace overflows with flowers, hearty Czech food with plenty of chicken and fish dishes, and lots of beer. The staff are very friendly, which helps with your patience since there are usually only two waiters working a shift, making service on the slow side. A great place to relax and enjoy the view.

Rybářská Bašta Jakuba Krčína. Kájovská 54. ☎ **0337/712 692.** Reservations recommended. Main courses 110–340Kč ($3.24–$10). AE, MC, V. Daily 7am–11pm. CZECH.

One of the town's most celebrated restaurants, this place specializes in freshwater fish from surrounding lakes. Trout, perch, pike, and eel are sautéed, grilled, baked, and fried in a variety of herbs and spices. Venison, rabbit, and other game are also available, along with the requisite roast beef and pork cutlet dinners.

INEXPENSIVE

Hospoda Na louži. Kájovská 66. No phone. Main courses 49–129Kč ($1.44–$3.79). No credit cards. Daily 10am–10pm. CZECH.

The large wooden tables encourage you to get to know your neighbors in this Inner Town pub, located in a 15th-century house. Still, the atmosphere is fun and the food above average. If no table is available, stand and have a drink; tables turn over pretty quickly and the staff are accommodating. In summer, the terrace seats only six, so dash over if a seat empties.

Pod Zámčí (Under the Castle). Široká 42. Main courses 80–195Kč ($2.35–$5.74). No credit cards. Daily 11am–11pm. CZECH.

This is a no-nonsense cellar restaurant that sticks to the basics and does it well. The pork cutlet in mushrooms surprised me when it arrived—the mushrooms were actually fresh, not canned. This alone makes it worth a reference. The restaurant also has one of the better wine lists I've seen in the town.

U Města Vídně. Latrán 78. No phone. Main courses 40–99Kč ($1.18–$2.91). No credit cards. Daily 10am–10pm. CZECH.

This locals' kind of pub is not only a good restaurant but also one of the best hangouts in town. Traditional meat-and-dumplings–style food is augmented by a few egg-based vegetarian dishes. Natives swear by the pub's locally brewed Českokrumlovské beer, which is a little creamier than most other Czech brews.

8 Třeboň

15 miles (24km) E of České Budějovice

Just a 30-minute bus ride east of České Budějovice—or a 500Kč ($15) taxi ride one way—Třeboň is a diamond in the rough, a walled city that time, war, and disaster have failed to destroy. Surrounded by forests and ponds, the town slowly grew from the 12th to the mid-14th century, when four of the Rozmberk brothers (also known as the Rosenbergs) took over, making Třeboň a home away from home (their official residence was down the road in Český Krumlov). Třeboň quickly flourished, attaining key brewing and salt customs rights. Adding to the town's coffers were more than 5,000 fish ponds built by fish master Štěpánek Netolický, and his successor, Mikuláš Rathard.

Though war and fires in the 17th and 18th centuries razed most of the town's historic Renaissance architecture, a slow rebuilding process eventually restored nearly every square meter of the walled town to its original state. Under Communism, Třeboň was awarded spa rights, which kept money flowing in and buildings in good repair.

Some consider Třeboň to be the poorer sister to Český Krumlov, but I strongly disagree. Sure it's not as breathtaking, but Třeboň hasn't been completely overrun by tourists who trample everything in their wake. Instead, Třeboň exists with or without visitors. Many of my Czech friends stay here on a regular basis, but few of my foreign friends do. This alone makes me recommend Třeboň as the small town to stay in overnight when traveling in the region or for those just looking for some peace and quiet.

Watch for posters or ask at the information center about the historic knight tournament, which, if it occurs, can be a lot of fun. Unfortunately, there's no set date for it and it isn't an annual event.

ESSENTIALS

GETTING THERE Buses leave from the České Budějovice bus station every hour or so and cost about 90Kč ($2.65).

By **train,** the town is a stop on the Prague–Tábor–Vienna route. Trains and buses also regularly leave for Třeboň from Jindrichuv Hradec and Tábor. From Prague the train takes 1¼ hours; the fare is 129Kč ($3.79) first class or 86Kč ($2.53) second class.

Driving from Prague, take Highway E55 through Tábor and turn left onto Highway 150 just past the town of Veselí nad Lužnicí. The trip takes at least 1½ hours. From České Budějovice, take Highway E551 east to Třeboň. This last route is particularly good for bikers, as there are very few hills to climb and several nice villages along the way.

VISITOR INFORMATION   **Informační Středisko** is in the heart of the old town at Masarykovo náměstí 102, 379 01 Třeboň (☎ **0333/721 169;** fax 0333/721 356). The staff is excellent, speaking several languages (especially German), and they provide maps, guidebooks, and information on tours and lodging. Open daily from 9am to 6pm.

ORIENTATION   There are only three ways to penetrate Třeboň's old town walls, short of pole vaulting. To the east is the **Hradecká brána (Castle Gate);** on the southern edge of town lies the **Svinenská brána;** and from the west is **Budějovická brána.** Once you're inside any of these gates, the six or so streets that comprise the old town can be easily navigated.

EXPLORING TŘEBOŇ

City officials, quick to notice that helping visitors helps them, have placed signs guiding visitors to almost every nook and cranny of the center. Since the walled city is relatively small, there's no wrong place to begin a tour, but I prefer to start at the southern gate by the **Svinenská brána,** the oldest of the three, for reasons that'll become immediately apparent. Just outside the gate and to the right stands the **Regent Brewery,** founded in 1379. Locals will tell you that their brew is every bit as good as Budvar, and they're not lying. On entering the old town, continue straight through Žižkovo náměstí and you'll arrive at **Masarykovo náměstí,** where the beautifully colored Renaissance facades look as though they were built just yesterday.

To the left lies the entrance to Třeboň's showpiece, **Zámek Třeboň (Třeboň Castle).** The castle's history is similar to the town's. The original Gothic castle was destroyed by fire and reconstructed several times, most recently in 1611. Rather ordinary-looking from the outside, it has splendidly decorated rooms that show 16th-century furnishings at their best. An exhibition on pond building fascinates most children. A large part of the castle now houses regional archives. Admission is 30Kč (88¢), and it's open May to September, Tuesday to Sunday from 9am to noon and 1 to 5pm; April and October, Saturday and Sunday and holidays from 9am to noon and 1 to 5pm.

Walk out the castle gate and straight along Březanova street to the **Augustinian monastery** and the 14th-century **St. Giles Church** next to it. Inside the church are replicas of some of the finest Gothic works in central Europe; the originals have been moved to the National Gallery in Prague. The church and monastery are open Monday to Saturday from 9am to 7pm and Sunday from 9am to 6pm.

To the south of the old town lies **Rybník Svět,** a large pond that locals flock to on hot afternoons. Several locations around the pond rent Windsurfers, bikes, and other outdoor equipment to enjoy the surrounding areas. On the southeast shore of the pond is **Schwarzenberská hrobka (Schwarzenberg Mausoleum).** Built in 1877, this neo-Gothic chapel and crypt is the resting place for most members of the Schwarzenberg family.

WHERE TO STAY

Bílý Koníček (White Horse). Masarykovo nám. 97, 379 01 Třeboň. ☎ and fax **0333/ 721 213.** 10 units. TEL. 850Kč ($25) double; 1,100Kč ($32.35) triple; 1,250Kč ($36.76) suite. MC, V.

A Farm Stay

With the collapse of Communism and the system of collective farming that went along with it, many farms have been returned to their original owners in a state of disrepair. But slowly, some are being reconstructed back to the state of prosperity they enjoyed before World War II. One such farm, ✪ **Holenský Dvůr,** Kardašový Řečice (☎ **0331/382 376;** fax 0331/383 445), has just opened its refinished doors to guests, offering a comfortable stay with an early European rural charm. Set among the gently rolling hills and fishponds of south Bohemia near Třeboň, this pension is a relaxing alternative to the hustle and bustle of more touristed spots such as Český Krumlov or Karlovy Vary. Rent a mountain bike or go horseback and tour the countryside, or hike through the meadows and clean your lungs from the days of smog inhalation that come with a trip to Prague.

The pension's 10 rooms and two apartments are bright, clean, and refreshingly well appointed, with some of the cleanest and most spacious bathrooms in the country. The owners have promised a swimming pool for the summer of 2000, and given the amount of work they have put into the premises so far, there is little doubt that it will happen on time.

Rooms are rented by the week Saturday to Saturday, but management will tailor stays to fit your needs. Doubles are 2,680 to 3,350Kč ($79 to $99) per person; apartments are 2,870 to 3,590Kč ($84 to $106) per person. Mountain bikes rent for 50Kč ($1.47) per day. To get there take the E55 highway south out of Prague toward České Budějovice. About 12 miles south of Tábor, head east on Route 23 toward Jindřichův Hradec to Kardašový Řečice.

Across from the Zlatá Hvězda, the Bílý Koníček has plain but tidy rooms and a friendly staff. However, the rooms tend to be a little noisier here, because the one road that cars use to go through town passes by. For the most part, though, the streets are pretty quiet and the restaurant downstairs is a good bet for a quick bite.

Hotel Bohemia and Hotel Regent. Lázeňská ulice, Třeboň. ☎ **0333/721 394.** Fax 0333/ 721 396. 82 units. 1,400Kč ($41.18) double; 1,750–2,550Kč ($51.47–$75) suite. AE, MC, V.

These two hotels share everything from a parking lot to a receptionist. If you don't want to stay in the center of town, either of these may be your ticket. Located down by the "beach" area, they stick out like a sore thumb due to their Communist-era functional look. But the rooms are clean and affordable, and the tennis courts and proximity to the pond are a plus.

Hotel Zlatá Hvězda. Masarykovo nám. 107, 379 01 Třeboň. ☎ **0333/757 200** or 0333/757 111. Fax 0333/757 300. 42 units. TV TEL. 850–1,900Kč ($25–$55.88) double; 1,300–2,100Kč ($38.24–$61.76) suite. Rates include buffet breakfast. AE, DC, MC, V.

Despite having rather Spartan rooms, the Zlatá Hvězda is the most upscale hotel in town and its location on Masarykovo náměstí can't be beat. An added plus is that the friendly staff can help arrange brewery tours, fishing permits, horseback riding, bike rentals, and several other outdoor activities.

Pension Siesta. Hradební 26, 379 01 Třeboň. ☎ and fax **0333/752 324.** 7 units. 600Kč ($17.65) per person. No credit cards.

If all the pensions in the Czech Republic showed up for a contest to see which was the friendliest, this one might win. Just outside and to the right of the Hradecká brána, the Siesta is a small but quiet and clean alternative to the hotels on the square. What makes it special is Petr Matějů and his wife, who go out of their way to take care of their guests. The pension also has a pleasant terrace in front by the stream, where you can enjoy an afternoon drink and snack.

WHERE TO DINE

Bílý Koníček. Masarykovo nám. 97. ☎ **0333/721 213.** Main courses 59–179Kč ($1.74–$5.26). V. Daily 10am–11pm. CZECH.

Located in the hotel with the same name, Bílý Koníček has a standard Czech menu of meat, dumplings, and potato dishes that are reasonably priced. In summer, its terrace is a great place to sit and cool off while grabbing a snack; the building's shadow keeps you out of the direct sun. The beer from just down the road is always fresh and cold.

Pizzeria Macado. Březanova 20. No phone. Pizzas 59–149Kč ($1.74–$4.38). No credit cards. Tues–Sat 11:30am–10pm, Sun 11:30am–8pm. ITALIAN.

If you're tired of fish and can't face another dumpling, Macado makes decent affordable pizzas that are filling. They seem to have shed the customary ketchup for real tomato sauce, marking a definite turn for the better. The salads are also fresh, and there's probably the town's widest selection of cocktails on the beverage menu.

Restaurace Beseda. Masarykovo nám. 102/1. No phone. Main courses 45–239Kč ($1.32–$7.03). No credit cards. Sun–Thurs 10:30am–10pm, Fri–Sat 10:30am–11pm. CZECH.

Head through the passage next door to the information center and you'll find a large outdoor terrace with a small restaurant behind it. As with many places in the area, the fish here is a good choice. But watch out: The prices on the menu are for the first 150 grams, and if the fish weighs more than that (and it always does), you'll be charged an extra 5Kč (15¢) per 10 grams.

9 Tábor

55 miles (88km) S of Prague, 37 miles (59km) N of České Budějovice

The center of the Hussite movement following religious leader Jan Hus's execution in Prague, Tábor was officially founded in 1420 and named by the Hussites after the biblical Mount Tábor. They had come to receive Christ on his return to earth and forsook property as he had himself. The group of soldiers leading Tábor, some 15,000 in all, felt that they had been commanded by God to break the temporal power of the Catholics at that time.

Legendary warrior Jan Žižka led the Táborites, as this sect of Hussites were known. Time and time again, Žižka rallied his troops to defeat the papal forces, until he was struck down in battle in 1424. For 10 more years the Hussites battled on, but their loss at Lipany signaled the end of the uprising, and an agreement was reached with Emperor Sigmund of Luxembourg of the Holy Roman Empire. Later, the town submitted to the leadership of Bohemia's Jiří z Poděbrad (George of Poděbrad) and blossomed economically, creating the wealth needed to construct the Renaissance buildings now found in the historic Old Town.

SPECIAL EVENTS In mid-August the **Táborská Setkání (Tábor Meeting)** takes place. Each year, representatives from towns worldwide named after Mount Tábor congregate for some medieval fun—parades, music, and jousting. The 4-day event even reenacts the historic battle of Tábor, with brilliantly colored warriors fighting one another "to the death."

For more details on the Tábor Meeting and summer cultural events, contact **Infocentrum města Tábor** (see "Visitor Information," below).

ESSENTIALS

GETTING THERE   If you're **driving,** leave Prague by Highway D1 and turn off at the E55 exit (signs Benešov, České Budějovice). Highway E55 runs straight into the city of Tábor. It's a 1-hour drive.

Tábor is about 90 minutes by express **train** from Prague or close to an hour from České Budějovice. The train station has a baggage check, and you can get to the center of town by taking bus no. 11, 14, or 31. The fare is 60Kč ($1.80) second class.

The **bus** trip to Tábor lasts about 1½ hours from Prague and costs 66Kč ($2.15). To get to the center, it's about a 20-minute walk; go through the park and then bear right at its farthest corner to walk along třída 9.května into town.

VISITOR INFORMATION   Next to the Hussite Museum, **Infocentrum města Tábor,** Žižkovo nám. 2, 390 01, Tábor (☎ **0361/252 385;** fax 0361/253 339), is stocked with information of all types, from maps, film, and postcards to advice about lodging, restaurants, and the best place for ice cream. The center's staff has volumes of pamphlets, phone numbers, and good advice. It's open May to September, Monday to Friday from 8:30am to 7pm, Saturday from 9am to 1pm, and Sunday from 1 to 5pm; October to April, Tuesday to Friday from 9am to 4pm.

ORIENTATION   Outside the historic town, there's little to see in Tábor besides factories and the ubiquitous *paneláky* (apartment buildings) that ring most every big Czech town and city.

Staré město (Old Town) is situated around Žižkovo náměstí, site of the town church and the Hussite Museum. Medieval walls surround the entire Old Town core. The Kotnov Castle, now one of the town's museums, is at the southwest corner.

EXPLORING TÁBOR

Most of the city's sights are on or around **Žižkovo náměstí.** If you find that, as you leave the square, roads twist, turn, and then end, the Táborites have caught you exactly as planned—the town was designed to hold off would-be attackers with its maze of streets.

On the square's west side is the **Museum of the Hussite Movement** (☎ **0361/254 658**). The late-Gothic former town hall now chronicles the movement that put Tábor on the map and in the history books. In front of the building lie stone tables where Hussite ministers gave daily communion. Leading from the museum's entrance, twisting and turning 650 meters underneath the square, is a labyrinth of **tunnels** dating back to the 15th century. After visiting the museum, take one of the guided tours that snake through the underground maze, which has housed everything from beer kegs to unruly women, imprisoned for such dastardly things as quarreling with men. The tunnels also doubled as a way to sneak under enemy guards if the town ever fell, allowing Hussite soldiers to launch an attack from behind. Admission to the Hussite Museum is 40Kč ($1.18), to the tunnels 25Kč (74¢). They're open April 1 to October 31 daily 10am to 6pm. From November 1 to March 31, weekends 10am to 6pm.

When you emerge from the tunnels, you'll be on the opposite side of the square, facing the **Church of Transfiguration of Our Lord,** with its vaulting impressive stained-glass windows and Gothic wooden altar. Climb the tower for one of the best views of the town. Open daily from 8am to 6pm.

You can pay homage to the Hussite military mastermind Žižka at his **statue** next to the church. For a wondrous avenue of Renaissance buildings, stroll down **Pražská ulice,** off the southeast corner of the square. From here you can turn down Divadelní and head along the Lužnice River toward **Kotnov Castle** (no phone). If your feet aren't up to the walk, you can take a more direct route to Kotnov by heading straight down Klokotská ulice, which runs away from the square next to the Hussite Museum.

A 14th-century castle that forms the southwest corner of the town wall, **Kotnov Castle** is most recognizable for its round **tower,** where you can get another great view of the town. Inside the castle is a well-organized collection on the Middle Ages, with old farming tools, armor, weapons, uniforms, and other artifacts. Admission is 40Kč ($1.18), and it's open Tuesday to Sunday from 8am to 4:30pm.

WHERE TO STAY

Tábor's lack of quality hotels gives you the perfect chance to "go local" and stay in a private pension. Expect to pay about 500 to 1,000Kč ($14.71 to $29.41) per person. The information center next to the town hall at Zizkovo nám. 2 can provide a list of recommendations or call and book a room for you.

The same service is also provided by a private tourist agency on náměstí Frantiska Křižika (☎ **0361/253 401**), open daily from 10am to noon and 1 to 6pm.

Hotel Bohemia. Husovo nám. 591, 390 01 Tábor. ☎ **0361/252 828.** 30 units (21 with bathroom). TV TEL. 1,550Kč ($45.59) double. No credit cards.

What a difference ownership makes! A perfect case study of how indifferent Communist management can ruin a place, the Bohemia has changed into private hands with incredible results. Once a drab, run-down train station hotel, the Bohemia has been spruced up right down to the staff and is worth the walk if you can't find anything closer to the historic town.

Hotel Kapitál. Třída 9.května 617, 390 01 Tábor. ☎ **0361/256 096.** Fax 0361/252 411. 24 units. TV TEL. 1,600Kč ($47.06) double; 1,950Kč ($57.35) suite. AE, MC, V.

Smaller and quieter than the Palcát, the recently renovated Kapitál has a little more character than its bigger neighbor down the street. The rooms are big, and the Kapitál seems to have a helpful staff, who also speak English. The restaurant serves large if unimaginative meals.

Hotel Palcát. Třída 9.května 2467, 390 01 Tábor. ☎ **0361/252 901.** Fax 0361/252 905. E-mail: ivanded@mbox.vol.cz. 68 units. TV TEL. 1,500Kč ($44.12) double; 1,995Kč ($58.68) suite. MC, V.

Since there are few quality hotels in Tábor, the Palcát, a modern but clean place, slips in as one of the town's finest. Though you may be left cold by its Communist-era furnishings, the rooms are spacious if not unforgettable. The higher floors have great views of the town, so working your way up makes your stay much more enjoyable.

WHERE TO DINE

Bowling Club. Třída 9.května 678. Soups 15–25Kč (44¢–74¢); main courses 69–210Kč ($2.03–$6.18). No credit cards. Daily 11am–midnight. CZECH.

Yes, really. There's a bowling alley here, too. The pub upstairs serves good Czech food and beer all day, and since there's not too much to do in town at night, you may want to go bowling downstairs (bowling hours from 6pm to 2am). Don't worry—they serve beer downstairs as well—you can't have one without the other.

Hotel Palcát. Třída 9.května 2467. ☎ **0361/252 901.** Soups 15–29Kč (44¢–85¢); main courses 58–165Kč ($1.71–$4.85). MC, V. Daily 11:30am–2:30pm and 4:30–11pm. CZECH.

Begrudgingly, I have to admit that the Palcát remains one of the better restaurants in town, though the decor looks as though it hasn't been changed since the 1960s. The soups are first-rate, and the fish and beefsteak are fresh and tasty. Beware of the pizza—I swear it's Heinz ketchup (or a derivative thereof) moonlighting as sauce. For a nightcap, the bar/disco is open Tuesday to Saturday until 3am and is one of the few places rockin' in town.

Restaurace Beseda. Žižkovo nám. 8. No phone. Main courses 75–159Kč ($2.21–$4.68). No credit cards. Daily 10am–10pm. CZECH.

The only restaurant with a terrace on the square, Beseda is a good place to stop after slinking through the tunnels and climbing the tower at the Church of Transfiguration of Our Lord. You've probably seen this menu in just about every town so far, but the food is above average if not new. On hot summer days, the patio is great for people-watching while drinking a cold Budvar. Too bad no food is served alfresco, or this place would move up a notch.

Zlatý Drak (Golden Dragon). Žižkovo nám. 14. No phone. Soups 25–60Kč (74¢–$1.76); main courses 90–229Kč ($2.65–$6.74). AE, MC, V. Daily 11:30am–2:30pm and 4:30–11pm. CHINESE.

I've always been wary of a Chinese restaurant that serves french fries, but the Golden Dragon can provide a nice change from heavy Czech cuisine. The chicken dishes tend to outshine their tougher beef counterparts.

12

The Best of Moravia

by Alan Crosby

Bohemia may be the land of monetary riches in the Czech Republic, but Moravia's wealth can be found not in its factories but in its people. Amalgamated with Bohemia more than 1,000 years ago, Moravia has managed to keep its rich culture and tradition despite always being lumped together with its more densely populated cousin to the west. Because of this lack of wealth, Moravia saw far fewer castles built; far less attention paid to its capital, Brno; and in turn, now gets far fewer visitors than Bohemia. So Brno isn't Prague.

Yet Moravia still has many features that make it a worthwhile destination, especially the smaller towns that maintain real Moravian character with lively song and dance and colorful traditional costumes that seem to have fallen by the wayside in Bohemia. Even the food is a little different: The bland goulash in Prague becomes a little spicier in Moravia, owing to the Hungarian influence that has seeped through from neighboring Slovakia. And replacing beer as a staple is wine, especially to the south, where wine making is taken as seriously as it is in most other European grape-growing regions. Many wine bars throughout Moravia serve the village's best straight from the cask. The Bohemians have the sweet taste of Becherovka to sip at meals; Moravians have the sharp taste of slivovice (plum brandy) to cleanse the palate (sometimes for hours on end if it's *domaci*—home brewed).

Having seen its fair share of history, Moravia conjures up a different image than Bohemia: a sort of kinder, gentler central Europe where material wealth is replaced by a rich folklore and more pastoral setting. Here, too, castles and picture-perfect town squares exist. But the people and slower lifestyle set Moravia apart.

1 Brno: The Region's Capital

140 miles (224km) SE of Prague, 80 miles (128km) N of Vienna

An industrial city with an industrial-strength image as boring, Brno suffers a fate that many second cities around the world endure—no respect. Sure, as you approach from the highway, the sight of dozens of concrete apartment buildings may give you cause for second thoughts. But bear with the Communist-inspired urban sprawl—the bad rap is undeserved. In fact, Brno is a vibrant and interesting city with a panache all its own.

Since Brno came of age in the 19th century on the back of its textile industry, the city's architecture, for the most part, lacks the

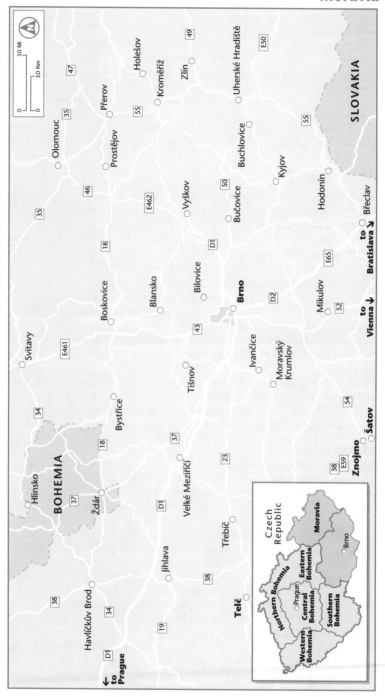

Accommodations Tips

Anywhere in the Czech Republic you have the option of staying in hotels or pensions on a town's main square. It's a beautiful sight, but be prepared for the possibility of serious noise, particularly on weekends, as revelers rage on late into the night. Light sleepers may prefer to trade the view for a good night's sleep.

Pensions are less expensive than hotels, and often the best pensions are friendlier, more tasteful, and far more in tune with their surroundings.

You may find that service tends not to be up to Western standards in most places; be warned that desk staff can be surly and unhelpful, and hotels may be understaffed.

Renaissance facades and meandering alleys of other towns. Indeed, the main square, náměstí Svoboda, bears this out. But spend a day or two here, and the beauty of the old city center will become apparent. Empire and neoclassical buildings abound. Quirky sights like the Brno Dragon and the Wagon Wheel add character. Špilberk Castle and the Gothic cathedral of Saints Peter and Paul give historical perspective. And lush streets and parks make aimless wandering a pleasure.

SPECIAL EVENTS Usually when the words *special events* and Brno are mentioned in the same sentence, the phrase *trade fair* isn't too far behind. Many fairs held at Brno's BVV exhibition grounds are world-class displays of technology, industrial machinery, and even well-groomed pets.

Brno celebrates music as well, hosting the **Janáček Music Festival** each June and the **Brno International Music Festival (Moravský Podzim)** in September and October.

However, probably the most attended event occurs each August when the **Motorcycle Grand Prix** tour rolls into town to tackle the Masaryk Okruh (Masaryk Ring).

For details on all events and a list of fairs at the BVV fairgrounds, contact **Informační Služba** (see "Visitor Information," below).

ESSENTIALS

GETTING THERE **Driving** to Brno is a trade-off. Take the E50—also named the D1—freeway that leads from the south of Prague all the way. The drive shouldn't take more than 2 hours. But the scenery is little more than one roadside stop after another.

Brno is the focal point for train travel in Moravia and most points east, making it an easy 3¼-hour trip from Prague. **Trains** leave almost every hour; the majority go from Hlavní nádraží (Main Station). The fare is 195Kč ($5.74) first class or 130Kč ($3.82) second class. *Watch out:* If the train is marked EuroCity or Intercity (usually on its way to Vienna or Poland), you'll pay a supplement of 36Kč ($1.06).

Nonstop **buses** run from Prague's Florenc station to Brno as often as trains do. The trip takes 2½ hours. Several bus companies have set up their own services along the Prague–Brno corridor to compete with the inefficient former state-owned ČSAD. Probably the best deal is **Český Národní Express** (☎ **02/6679 7186**), where 69Kč ($2.03) will get you a seat on the exact same type of bus ČSAD runs. CNE buses depart across from the Florenc bus station at the underpass behind the McDonald's. Reservations are recommended during peak hours, and do it early because Czechs have taken to this form of capitalism like fish to water. To reserve you have to go to the office itself, so don't try to phone ahead—it just won't work.

Brno

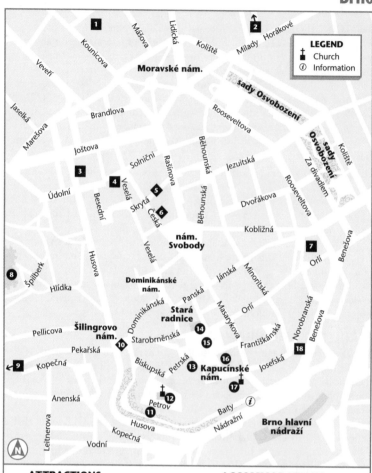

LEGEND
- ✝ Church
- ⓘ Information

ATTRACTIONS
Cathedral of Saints Peter and Paul ⑫
Denisovy sady ⑪
Kapucínský Klášter
 (Capuchin Monastery) ⑰
Kostel Náležení svatého Kříže ⑰
Moravian Museum ⑬
Old Town Hall ⑭
Parnas Fountain ⑮
Reduta Divadlo ⑯
Špilberk Castle ⑧
Zelný trh (Cabbage Market) ⑮

ACCOMMODATIONS
Grandhotel Brno ⑱
Holiday Inn ⑨
Hotel Astoria ⑦
Hotel Boby ②
Hotel Continental ①
Hotel International ③
Hotel Slavia ④
Hotel Voroněž ⑨

DINING
La Braseria ⑨
Modrá Hvězda ⑩
Pivnice Pegas ⑤
Stopková Plzeňska Pivnice ⑥
U Královny Elišky ⑨
Zahradní Restaurace ⑱

3-0198

227

VISITOR INFORMATION   Informační Služba, Radnická 4–10, Brno (☎ **05/ 4221 0758** or 05/4221 1090), provides a plethora of information on accommodations, plus what's on in Brno and how to see it. It's open daily from 9am to 6pm.

You'll find the ubiquitous blue **Čedok Travel** sign at four locations in Brno. The conveniently located office across from the train station provides currency exchange but little else. A better bet is the office at Masarykovo 37, Brno (☎ **05/4221 0942;** fax 05/4221 1562). This office can help arrange accommodations in hotels and private rooms. It's open May to September, Monday to Friday from 9am to 6pm and Saturday from 9am to noon; October to April, Monday to Friday from 9am to 5pm and Saturday from 9am to noon.

ORIENTATION   Brno is a large rambling city, but most sights are concentrated in its inner core. At the center is **Náměstí Svobody (Freedom Square),** connected to the train station by Masarykova ulice. Just west of Masarykova is **Zelný trh (Cabbage Market),** the largest square in town. Cars can't pass through the Old Town, but tram no. 4 barrels through with little regard for the pedestrians in its way.

The city is small enough for walking. All hotels, restaurants, and sights are close enough together that you do not have to take public transportation. The only exception is for those staying at the Holiday Inn or Voronez. If you want to take a tram, walk east (toward the town center) around the edge of the fairgrounds until you get to the New Gate where trams 1 and 10 have stops headed to the center. Get off at the stop Hlavní nádraží (train station).

STROLLING AROUND BRNO

The Old Town holds most of the attractions you'll want to see, so it's probably best to start at the former seat of government, the **Old Town Hall** on Radnická 8. To get there, walk from the train station along Masarykovo and make a left at Orlí street; if you're coming from náměstí Svobody, head toward the train station and turn right on either Panská or Orlí.

Brno's oldest secular building, from the 13th century, the Old Town Hall is a hodgepodge of styles—Gothic, Renaissance, and baroque elements meld together to show the development of Brno through the ages. Almost everything in the building has a story or legend attached to it, beginning with the front door and its crooked Gothic portal. Designed by Anton Pilgram, who lists Vienna's vaunted St. Stephen's Church on his résumé, the door was completed in 1510. But town officials supposedly reneged on their original payment offer, and a furious Pilgram took revenge by bending the turret above the Statue of Justice. On the second floor, a modest collection of armor, coins, and photos is displayed in the same room where town councilors met from the 13th century right up until 1935. Climb the stairs of the tower for an interesting, if not beautiful, city view; smokestacks and baroque buildings battle for attention.

Before leaving Old Town Hall, examine two of Brno's most beloved attractions— the **Brno Dragon** and the **Wagon Wheel.** The "dragon" hanging from the ceiling is actually not a dragon, but an alligator given to the city by Archprince Matayás in 1608. Here also stands the Wagon Wheel, a testament to Brno's industrious image. Local lore has it that a carpenter named Jiří Birek from nearby Lednice wagered with locals that he could chop down a tree, fashion a wheel from it, and roll it the 40 kilometers to Brno all in a single day. Well, he managed to do it, but the townspeople, certain that one man couldn't do so much in 1 day, decided that Birek must've had some assistance from the devil. With this mindset, they refused to ever buy his works again.

A Telephone Warning

As in Prague and some other cities, the antiquated telephone lines of Brno are being replaced. All phone numbers are subject to change, except those with eight digits, which are new digital lines.

Just south of the Old Town Hall is **Zelný trh (Cabbage Market),** a farmers' market since the 13th century. You can still buy a head or two of the leafy vegetable at the market today as entrepreneurs sell their wares under the gaze of the **Hercules,** depicted in the **Parnas Fountain** in the square's center. The fountain used to be a vital part of the market; quick-thinking fishermen let their carp swim and relax in the fountain until the fish were chosen for someone's dinner.

At the southern corner of **Zelný trh** lies the 17th-century **Reduta Divadlo,** a former home of Mozart. Another block closer to the train station, on Kapučínské náměstí, is the **Kostel Náležení svatého Kříže** and the **Kapučínský Klášter (Capuchin Monastery).**

The Capuchin Monastery is famous for its catacombs, which hold many of Brno's most famous citizens. Among those interred here are Moritz Grimm, who was responsible for rebuilding the cathedral in the 18th century, and Austrian army colonel František Trenck, who in intervening years lost his head to vandals. A unique ventilation system preserves the bodies, displayed in open coffins. This display is slightly morbid; skin and clothing are slowly decaying. Parents may want to look ahead or get a brochure to make sure children are up to seeing the coffins. Admission is 20Kč (59¢), and it's open Tuesday to Saturday from 9am to noon and 2 to 5pm and Sunday from 11 to 11:45am and 2 to 5pm. No phone.

Dominating **Zelný trh** at its southwest corner is the **Moravian Museum,** housed in the Dietrichstein Palace. Completed in 1620, the palace was used by Russian Marshal Kutuzov to prepare for the battle of Austerlitz. These days, the museum displays a wide array of stuffed birds and wild game, as well as art, coins, and temporary exhibits. Admission is 35Kč ($1.03), and it's open Tuesday to Sunday from 9am to 6pm. The museum itself doesn't have a phone, but you can call the Culture and Information Center across the square at Radnická 4–10 (☎ **05/4221 1090**).

From the museum, head up Petrská street to the **Cathedral of Saints Peter and Paul.** Perched atop a hill overlooking the city, the cathedral was built in the late 11th and early 13th centuries. In 1743, it was rebuilt in a baroque style, only to be re-Gothicized just before World War I. This melding of styles gives the cathedral its unique character of a Gothic structure with baroque touches. The cathedral is open Monday to Wednesday and Friday and Saturday from 6:30am to 6pm, Thursday from 6:30am to 7:30pm, and Sunday from 8:30am to 6pm.

Take a break at **Denisovy sady,** the park behind the cathedral, and prepare to climb the hill to get to Špilberk Castle. If you're not up for it, tram no. 6, 9, 14, or 17 goes near the castle, but you'll still have a short but strenuous walk from there. The fare is 8Kč (24¢). If you want to walk all the way, head along Biskupská, where interesting houses provide a nice foreground to the bustling city. Make a left on Starobrněnská to Husova and then on to Pellicova. At Pellicova 11 is a fine example of František Uherka's cubist architectural vision.

But the real reason for this climb is **Špilberk Castle.** If there's one building in the Czech Republic that's ready to be overrun by visitors, Špilberk is—and it's had practice. It was built in the 13th century, and the Hussites controlled the castle in the

---

What Time Is It?

If you're touring the cathedral in the late morning, you may think that you've switched time zones. Don't worry: The cathedral bells strike noon an hour early in remembrance of a quick-thinking bell ringer who, seeing that the city was on the verge of attack by the Swedes during the Thirty Years' War, found out that the army was planning to take the city by noon. If not successful by then, Swedish commander General Torstenson was said to have decided the attack would be called off and the army would beat a hasty retreat. The bell ringer, sensing that the town couldn't repel the Swedes, rang the cathedral bells an hour early at 11am, before the army could attack. True to his word, Torstenson packed up and went home.

15th century. The Prussians saw the castle's position as an excellent lookout when they occupied it in the early 17th century. And the Nazis turned it into a torture chamber during their stay, executing some 80,000 people deep inside the dungeons.

Renovated in 1994, Špilberk can be conquered without a guide. Wander through the seemingly endless corridors beneath the bastions to get a feel for what those who perished here saw. It's open Tuesday to Sunday: June to September from 9am to 6pm, April and May from 9am to 5pm, and March and October from 9am to 4pm; Špilberk is closed November to February.

SHOPPING & SOCCER

SHOPPING   Once back in the city center, take some time for a quick meal and browse along the **pedestrian shopping zone,** which unfolds between náměstí Svobody and the train station. Prices for goods are often cheaper here than in Prague, so you may find a better price for the crystal vase or pair of earrings you were thinking of buying.

SOCCER   Sports fans can partake in a Sunday ritual as dear to Czechs as football is to Americans by taking the 20-minute walk north from the main square to Brno stadium, where first league **soccer team Boby Brno** plays its home games. Grab a beer and a sausage and cheer along with the Boby faithful. Tickets—beginning at 30Kč (88¢)—are always plentiful and can be bought at the stadium on game day.

WHERE TO STAY

Note that even high-season prices often double or triple without warning for major trade fairs and the Motorcycle Grand Prix.

EXPENSIVE

Grandhotel Brno. Benesova 18–20, 657 83 Brno. ☎ **05/4251 8111.** Fax 05/4221 0345. austria-hotels.co.at/grandhotel-brno. 110 units. MINIBAR TV TEL. 1,450–2,250 Austrian Schillings ($107–$166) double; 3,500 Austrian Schillings ($259) suite. Daily exchange rate used to calculate cost in koruny. AE, DC, MC, V. Parking 150Kč ($4.41).

Ever since it was taken over by the Austrian chain Austrotel in the mid-1990s, the Grandhotel has lived up to its name. Its rooms are spacious and well appointed, though some located at the front get a little noisy due to the major street running past with its never-ending stream of trams; ask for a room that has windows facing north, away from the commotion. The buffet breakfast is an added bonus, with lots of fresh fruit, breads, and Moravian cakes to get you going.

Dining/Diversions: The hotel has two excellent restaurants, a nightclub, and a casino. The Garden Restaurant is a little more upscale and quiet, concentrating on Moravian and international cuisine. Alas, it has dropped one of its better segments—

Chinese food. The Grill Bar is more informal and concentrates on grilled meats. The casino is worth a look if only for the chandeliers with their fine cut crystal. With little action and a tacky disco decor, the nightclub best serves as a stop for a nightcap.

Amenities: Room service (7am to 3am), 24-hour laundry.

MODERATE

Holiday Inn. Křížovského 20, 603 00 Brno. ☎ **05/4312 2111.** Fax 05/4115 9081. 205 units. MINIBAR TV TEL. DC. 3,300Kč ($97) standard double; 3,600Kč ($106) executive double; 3,400–4,300Kč ($100–$126) suite. AE, MC, V. Parking 150Kč ($4.41) a day.

Yes, that's right. The best surprise is no surprise—even in Brno. The very modern Holiday Inn Brno, on the fairgrounds, caters mainly to the trade fair crowd. Everything, from the rooms to the restaurant and bars, looks eerily similar to other Holiday Inns around the world. Still, the beds are more comfortable than most, and the rooms are spotless, with large writing desks and showers that have no problems with water pressure. The staff is very friendly and speaks at least some English.

Hotel Boby. Sportovní 2a, 602 00 Brno. ☎ **05/727 2111.** Fax 05/4121 2015. E-mail: hotel@boby.cz. 141 units. MINIBAR TV TEL. 3,650–4,100Kč ($107–$121) double; 4,800Kč ($141) suite. AE, JCB, MC, V.

The Bob, as many refer to it, is one of Brno's newest luxury hotels, just north of the city center. It often attracts guests who never leave the hotel. Inside and on the surrounding grounds you'll find a health center, a bowling alley, a shopping mall, tennis courts, squash courts, a pool, a roller-skating rink, a soccer stadium, several bars and restaurants, and even a car wash. The rooms are very comfortable. The walk from the center is a nice 25-minute stroll through long parks. The only drawback can be the bland surroundings and the tackiness of some of the facilities, such as the sex-show bar or the velvety disco in the entertainment complex.

Hotel Continental. Kounicova 20, 662 21 Brno. ☎ **05/4121 2806.** Fax 05/4121 1203. 228 units. TEL. 1,900Kč ($58) double. AE, DC, MC, V.

This is another Communist-era hotel trying to make it in the free market. The rooms still have that Communist hangover of being a little on the small side and a little too modern for those expecting an old-world European experience. The very helpful staff is approachable for advice on how to get to the sights. The Continental is north of the city center, so you'll get some cleaner air and a nice short walk into the center.

Hotel International. Husova 16, 659 21 Brno. ☎ **05/4212 1111.** Fax 05/4221 0843. E-mail: hotelinter@traveller.cz. 262 units. MINIBAR TV TEL. 2,490–3,100Kč ($73.24–$91.18) double; 4,700Kč ($138.24) suite. AE, DC, MC, V.

Just on the edge of the city center, the International has joined the Best Western chain of hotels, which basically has translated into a huge improvement in the quality of service. From the outside, it looks like a dressed-up Communist-era apartment building, and looks this time aren't deceiving. But the rooms have enough space to keep you from feeling claustrophobic. The bar on the main floor is usually crowded with both locals and visitors, making for interesting people watching.

Hotel Slavia. Solniční 15, 662 16 Brno. ☎ **05/4221 5080.** Fax 05/4221 1769. E-mail: hotel.slavia@io1.cz. 81 units. MINIBAR TV TEL. 1,800–2,000Kč ($53–$59) double; 2,200Kč ($65) suite. AE, DC, MC, V.

The Slavia, just on the edge of the pedestrian zone under the castle, falls short of being the upscale hotel it's trying to be, but it is one of the best deals in the center and a nice area to walk through either day or night. Rooms are Spartan, with bland furniture, but clean. The rooms are not uniformly sized, so take a look at a couple before choosing if possible.

Hotel Voroněž. Křížovského 47, 603 73 Brno. ☎ **05/4314 1111.** Fax 05/4321 2002. www.voronez.cz. E-mail: accom@voronez.cz. 376 units. MINIBAR TV TEL. 1,990–2,830Kč ($59–$83) double; 2,700–4,500Kč ($79–$132) suite. AE, CB, DC, MC, V. Parking 150Kč ($4.41) per day.

The Voroněž has added conference rooms and a pool and renovated its restaurants. But for all the new glitz, it still is basically a Czech *panelák* (housing complex) dressed up as a hotel trying hard to shed its Communist-era image—and furniture. It's across from the fairgrounds, making it convenient for those on business. The hotel is split into two sections: a four-star hotel that is housed in the main building with the conference rooms, and a smaller three-star annex next door. The rooms, however, are similar in each. In many of the medium-size rooms, 1970s Naugahyde furnishings have been replaced with light pastel-and-wood beds, desks, and chairs, and these redone rooms now cut the mustard. Except during the busiest times, you can always find a room here.

INEXPENSIVE

Hotel Astoria. Novobranská 3, 662 21 Brno. ☎ **05/4232 1302.** Fax 05/4221 1428. 89 units. TEL. 1,110Kč ($32) double. AE, DC, MC, V.

The Astoria, formerly the Morava, has basic small rooms, but the staff are kinder than most other nearby hotels in this class. Ask to see the room first as some are much brighter and cheerier than others. It's very close to the city center and the train station.

Hotel Brno. Horní 19, 639 00 Brno. ☎ **05/4321 4046.** Fax 05/4321 5308. 90 units. TV TEL. 1,250Kč ($37) double. AE, DC, MC, V.

Once a run-down dive, the Brno has been given a face-lift and a new lease on life. Near the city center, the hotel even has its own tennis courts, but the main attraction is a quiet place to lay down your head at the right price.

WHERE TO DINE
MODERATE

✪ **La Braseria.** Pekřská 80. ☎ **05/4323 2042.** Reservations recommended. Soups and antipastas 40–240Kč ($1.18–$7.06); primi piatti 50–155Kč ($1.47–$4.56); secondi 75–350Kč ($2.21–$10.29); pizzas 50–150Kč ($1.47–$4.41). AE, DC, MC, V. Daily noon–midnight. ITALIAN.

They say that when in Rome, do as the Romans do. So when in Brno, follow this saying and do what the Romans do—come here. Authentic Italian cuisine that (I'm sorry, dumpling aficionados) has too much zest to pass up. Try the chicken in green peppercorn sauce for a delicate change or the spicy penne arrabiata to bring some life to your taste buds. If there is a drawback, as in most Czech restaurants, much of the seafood—except some local fish—can be a disappointment since it's frozen at best. It's located between the fairgrounds and the center, about a 10-minute walk from either.

Modrá Hvězda (Blue Star). Šilingrovo nám. 7. ☎ **05/4221 5292.** Soups 25–50Kč (74¢–$1.47); main courses 79–240Kč ($2.32–$7.06). MC, V. Daily 11am–1am. CZECH.

Recommended to me by a friend who used to live in Brno, the Blue Star is one of the few moderately priced restaurants where you can get good-quality food well into the night. The mixed grill for two remains my choice, served with fresh (not canned) vegetables. The pepper steak is another favorite, and as you can tell, anything from the grill is your best bet.

U Královny Elišký. Mandlovo nám. 1. ☎ **05/4321 2578.** Soups 25–60Kč (74¢–$1.76); main courses 120–320Kč ($3.53–$9.41). AE, MC, V. Daily 7pm–3am. CZECH.

If you're looking for the quintessential Moravian experience, look no further. Nestled in the back wall of the castle where the stables used to be, this never-ending maze of cellars and alcoves oozes Moravian charm. Browse through a menu loaded with pork, chicken, fish, and beef dishes as a Gypsy band wanders the premises. An extensive wine list complements the wide variety of meals. *One warning:* The tray of appetizers wheeled up to your table can cost anywhere from 30 to 100Kč (88¢ to $2.94), so don't be shy to ask how much your choice will set you back.

Zahradní Restaurace (Garden Restaurant). In the Grandhotel Brno, Benešova 18–20. ☎ 05/4232 1287. Reservations recommended. Soups 40–60Kč ($1.18–$1.76); main courses 90–350Kč ($2.65–$10.29). AE, DC, MC, V. Daily 11:30am–3am. CZECH/INTERNATIONAL.

When you enter this restaurant, you'll expect to pay a lot more than you do. The setting is first-rate, with fountains and lots of plants and background music that doesn't intrude. This used to be one of Eastern Europe's finest Chinese restaurants, but now the menu is conspicuous for the absence of Asian dishes. For a taste of local cuisine, try the Moravian plate piled with pork, duck, smoked meat, sauerkraut, and two kinds of dumplings.

INEXPENSIVE

Pivnice Pegas. Jakubská 4. No phone. Main courses 39–120Kč ($1.15–$3.53). No credit cards. Daily 9am–midnight. CZECH.

Set 'em up and knock 'em down. This is a pub and nothing but. Come here for a beer and a quick meal during the day rather than for a formal dinner at night. The Pegas is one of the few pubs in the city center where locals and visitors mix. Hearty goulash and dumplings are always a good choice, as is the fried cheese, though your arteries may not agree.

Stopková Plzeňská Pivnice. Česká 5. No phone. Soups 10–29Kč (29¢–85¢); main courses 42–175Kč ($1.24–$5.15). No credit cards. Daily 10am–midnight. CZECH.

Located just off the main square, Stopková is a classic Czech pub: uncomfortable long wooden benches with little light making it through the two front windows. Equally as classic are the meals—goulash and schnitzels that are filling and tasty. The only thing this place is missing, thank God, are the clouds of smoke billowing from table to table. Some traditions are better left out.

BRNO AFTER DARK

While it may lack the energy Prague has, Brno still has plenty to offer at night. A strong cultural program dominates evenings, with the local theater and symphony offering world-class entertainment. The information agency (see above) has a list of what is going on at all major venues and sells some tickets.

For the young at heart, or those with little hearing left to blow, the **Boby disco** at the Boby hotel is the place to dance, dance, and dance. The music is endless, as is the line if you don't get there early enough. Otherwise, be Czech and go to any number of local pubs, located on nearly every street corner. Start out at the **Stopkova Pivnice** just off the main square and from there just wander the streets. I guarantee you'll go no more than 2 minutes in any direction before another pub greets you.

2 Telč

93 miles (149km) SE of Prague, 54 miles (86km) W of Brno

As you pass through towns on your way to Telč and approach its outskirts, you may be tempted to pass up another "small town with a nice square." Don't. Those who make the trip to Telč strike gold. Telč is one of the few towns in Europe that can boast of not being reconstructed since its original edifices were built. It now enjoys the honor of being a United Nations (UNESCO) World Heritage Site. Its uniformly built houses and castle give it an almost too perfect look, as though no one ever really lived here.

Due to its small size, you can explore Telč in a day. Those traveling by car to Brno or Vienna should stop on their way. I recommend spending the night to admire the illuminated castle and square, especially if there's an evening recital or concert at the castle. You can also combine a stop here with a visit to Znojmo; see below.

SPECIAL EVENTS   Although no one special event occurs in Telč, the **Telčské Kulturní Léto (Telč Cultural Summer)** season of concerts, recitals, and fairs runs from the beginning of June to the end of September. For details, contact the **Telč Informační Středisko** (see "Visitor Information," below).

ESSENTIALS

GETTING THERE   Located about halfway between České Budějovice and Brno, Telč can be reached by taking Highway 23. **Driving** from Prague, take Highway D1 in the direction of Brno and exit at Jihlava, where you pick up Highway 38 after going through the town. Then head west on Highway 23. You can leave your car in the large parking lot near the town's north gate. It's a 2-hour drive from Prague.

Train connections to Telč aren't great, so be patient. A second-class fare costs 98Kč ($2.88). The town lies on the Tábor-Jindřichův Hradec line; you'll have to change at Kostelec u Jihlavy. Once you get there, you'll find about nine trains departing daily to Telč. The train station offers storage, though its hours aren't the most dependable.

I recommend taking the more direct route by **bus**, costing 125Kč ($3.68). Buses leave from Prague's Florenc bus station daily and take about 3 hours. The castle and town square are a 10-minute walk from the bus station. To get to town, exit through the station's back entrance, turn right on Tyršova, and then turn left on Rudnerova. Follow this street as it bears left and turn right at the second small alley. This will guide you to the main square.

VISITOR INFORMATION   Since UNESCO gave its backing to Telč in 1992, services for visitors have blossomed, and none more so than the information center on the main square. At the **Telč Informační Středisko,** náměstí Zachariáše z Hradce (☎ **066/962 233;** fax 066/962 557; e-mail: info@telc-etc.cz), you'll find a wealth of information concerning accommodations, cultural events, guided tours, and even hunting; brochures are in Czech, German, and English. The staff is eager to arrange reservations. The small white Telč guidebook that costs 75Kč ($2.20) is worth the price, filled with minute details about almost every edifice in town. Open daily from 10am to 6pm.

ORIENTATION   Telč's historic center is shaped like a trapezoid and is surrounded by lakes on three sides. At the center is a very large square named after the town's former owner, Zachariáše z Hradce.

EXPLORING TELČ

Start with a tour of **Telč Château** (☎ **066/962 821**) at the northwest end of the main square. Zacharias of Neuhaus, whose name now graces the main square, was so enamored of the Renaissance style rampant in Italy that in 1553 he commissioned Antonio Vlach, and later Baldassare Maggi de Ronio, to rebuild the château, originally a 14th-century Gothic structure. The castle's exterior, however, cannot prepare you for its interior—hall after hall of lavish rooms with spectacular ceilings.

Highlights inside the castle include the **Africa Hall,** with rhino heads, tiger skins, and other exotica from expeditions that Karel Podstatky, a relative of the castle's last owner, accumulated in the early 1900s. The **Banquet Hall's** *sgrafitti* seems to mock those who overindulge, and the **Marble Hall of Knights** boasts a wood ceiling decorated with bas-reliefs from 1570, plus a fine collection of armor. In the **Golden Hall,** where balls and ceremonies once took place, 30 octagonal coffers with mythological scenes stare down at you from the ceiling.

A 1-hour guided tour of the castle halls is 100Kč ($2.94). To see the apartments, take the additional 45-minute tour, which costs the same. The castle is open Tuesday to Sunday: May to August from 9am to noon and 1 to 5pm; April, September, and October from 9am to noon and 1 to 4pm; the castle is closed November to March.

Next to the castle is the **Church of St. James (Kostel sv. Jakuba),** its walls adorned with late 15th-century paintings. Next to St. James is the baroque **Jesuit Church of the Name of Jesus.**

After strolling the castle grounds, head back to the main square, where a sea of soft pastel facades awaits. If you find yourself wondering how the entire square could be so uniform, you're not alone. After rebuilding the castle, Zacharias realized that the rest of the place looked, well, out of place. To rectify the situation, he promptly rebuilt the facade of each building on the square, though Gothic columns belie what once was. Of particular note is the building referred to as **House 15,** where a round oriel and *sgrafitti* portraying the crucifixion, Saul and David, Christopher, and faith and justice jut out onto the street corner. And watching over it all are the cherubs on the Marian column, built in 1718.

WHERE TO STAY

If you haven't arranged lodging ahead of time, head straight to the information center in the main square, where the staff have a complete list of what's available. For hotels, expect to pay around 1,250Kč ($36.76) for a double.

Private accommodations are also available, and for the most part, these rooms are comparable to hotel rooms (if not better and less expensive), though there are far fewer amenities. The information center staff will call and arrange for you to meet the room's owner so you can check out the place. Several rooms located directly on the square are available. Expect to pay about 500Kč ($14.70) per person. On slow days, owners will usually negotiate a better price.

Hotel Celerin. Náměstí Zachariáše z Hradce 43, 588 56 Telč. ☎ **066/724 3477.** Fax 066/ 721 3581. 12 units. 1,400–1,800Kč ($41–$53) double. Rates include continental breakfast. AE, DC, MC, V.

The most upscale hotel on the square, the Celerin has medium-size rooms, the best ones overlooking the square. Looking out over the square at night when it's bathed in light will remind you why this town is so treasured by the United Nations. If you're looking for location, this is the place to stay. Disabled travelers will find the staff here helpful, with some rooms fully equipped.

Hotel Černý Orel (Black Owl Hotel). Náměstí Zachariáše z Hradce 7, 588 56 Telč. ☎ and fax **066/724 3221.** 30 units. 1,100Kč ($32) double. AE, MC, V.

On the main square overlooking the Marian column, the Black Owl is a favorite among visitors. The rooms are Spartan but clean. Ask for a view of the square; the staff will usually accommodate this request if a room is available. A lively restaurant downstairs serves good Czech fare.

Hotel Telč. Na Můstku 37, 588 56 Telč. ☎ **066/724 3109.** Fax 066/722 3887. 15 units. 1,150Kč ($34) double. AE, DC, MC, V.

Just off the main square, the Telč has rooms with a spacious feel because of the high ceilings. The park next to it adds to the effect and provides a sense of being out in the country if you've had enough of staying on squares where noise can sometimes be a problem. Rooms facing the street are brighter but louder than those to the rear. The all-wood furnishings add some ambience, but the bathrooms are cramped.

WHERE TO DINE

Senk pod Věží. Palackého 116. ☎ **066/724 3889.** Soups 15–30Kč (44¢–88¢); main courses 70–135Kč ($2.05–$3.97). No credit cards. Daily 10am–midnight. CZECH.

This place can get a little loud when the disco in the building starts to crank it up at around 10pm, but in the afternoon the terrace provides a peaceful spot for a quick meal. The food is filling and hearty if not exciting.

U Černého Orla (At the Black Owl). Náměstí Zachariáše z Hradce 7. ☎ **066/724 3221.** Reservations recommended. Soups 14–30Kč (41¢–88¢); main courses 45–120Kč ($1.32–$3.53). No credit cards. June–Sept, daily 7am–10pm; Oct–May, Tues–Sun 7am–10pm. CZECH.

If it looks as though every visitor in town is trying to get in here, it's because they are. The Black Owl is worth the effort. This is one of the few restaurants in Telč that can be trusted to serve good food consistently. Crowd in at any free space and enjoy a wide range of Czech meals. The trout is always fresh, and I've never heard a complaint about it or the *řízek* (pork schnitzel). The hearty soups are especially welcome on days when the sun isn't shining. When it is, get a table on the terrace out front—though the service, which is quick if you're inside, usually slows down considerably.

3 Znojmo

119 miles (190km) SE of Prague, 40 miles (64km) S of Brno

Most travelers blow through Znojmo, the wine and pickle capital of the Czech Republic, at about 60 miles per hour, tired of getting caught behind trucks and buses that make the trip to Vienna a long 4-hour haul. But it wasn't always that way.

Znojmo was settled as far back as the 7th century, and the town gained prominence in the 9th century, when the Great Moravian Empire took control. In the 11th and 12th centuries, Prince Bretislav I constructed a fortress; in 1226, the town was granted rights from the king—even before the Moravian capital of Brno. Znojmo's position on the border made it a natural location as a trading center, and Czech kings always ensured the town was taken care of, using it as a lookout over the Austrian frontier. Alas, the original town hall was destroyed during World War II, and the Communist-inspired sprawl that followed has taken away some of Znojmo's character. But the old center remains vibrant, with many religious buildings still intact.

Why do the pickles here taste so good? They're made from the best cucumbers the country has to offer. And when put into a spicy sauce, as they are in *Znojemské gulaš*, they really taste great. These sweet-and-sour pickles are also special because the town really plays them up. You'll get pickle fever, too, I promise. When you do, and want to buy some, you'll notice just how many shops proudly display the Znojmo pickle.

And then there's the wine. If you're looking for the region's best vintages, look no further than Frankovka (a smooth, full-bodied red) or Ryzlink (a light, dry white), with Znojemské (from Znojmo) or Mikulov on the label. These superb wines are available almost everywhere; a liter costs no more than 75 or 125Kč ($2.21 or $3.68). Wine bars often serve the best vintages straight from the cask; you can also fill up—with both wine and fuel—at a gas station.

To best enjoy the town's wine and pickles, you should at least spend a few hours here, or stay overnight if you've got some time. Znojmo's location on the Prague–Vienna route makes it a natural place to stop. An added bonus is its proximity to Telč; you can see both in 1 day if you want.

SPECIAL EVENTS   In late August and early September, residents of Znojmo celebrate one of their most famous commodities at the **Znojmo Wine Festival.** Taste vintages, eat pickles, and listen to traditional Moravian music late into the usually tranquil night. For details, contact **Informační Středisko** (see "Visitor Information," below).

ESSENTIALS

GETTING THERE   Znojmo is most easily reached by **car** and is especially convenient for those heading to or from Vienna or Telč. Take Highway D1 from Prague and exit at Highway 38 in the direction of Jihlava. As you enter the town you're already on the right highway, so just pass by the town center and follow the signs. From Prague, the trip should take about 2½ hours.

Several **trains** leave Brno throughout the day, though some require a quick change in Hrušovany. The ride takes about 2 hours and costs 120Kč ($3.53). From Prague, it's a 4-hour trip total; halfway, you must change in Jihlava. The train is 180Kč ($5.29) first class, 120Kč ($3.53) second class.

You can also take one of three **bus** trips from Prague's Florenc station, but this 3-hour trip is more cramped and less fun. The one-way fare is 155Kč ($4.56). On the plus side, there's no transferring. From Brno, the trip is much quicker and less painful. Almost as many buses run between the two places as do trains.

VISITOR INFORMATION   In the center of the main square in Znojemská beseda, **Informační Středisko,** náměstí T. G. Masaryka 22, Znojmo (☎ **0624/224 369**), can help with accommodations, maps, and directions. Ask what's on in town, and they can book tickets for you on the spot. The office is open Monday to Friday from 8am to 8pm and Saturday from 8am to noon.

ORIENTATION   Znojmo's main square is **náměstí T. G. Masaryka,** and pretty much all you'll want to see is on or near it. **Zelenářská street,** which runs off of the square's northwest corner, leads to the castle and St. Nicholas Church.

STROLLING THROUGH ZNOJMO

A walking tour of Znojmo takes about 2 or 3 hours. Begin at **Masaryk Square,** where the **Art House (Dům umění)** holds a small collection of coins, plus temporary exhibitions. Admission is 25Kč (74¢). The southern end of the square is one of the few historic areas that hasn't been maintained well; the dilapidated **Capuchin Monastery (Kapučinský klášter)** and **Church of St. John the Baptist** show few signs that they were once focal points for the town.

Impossible to miss is the **Town Hall Tower,** the only remaining piece of what was once referred to as Moravia's prettiest town hall. The actual town hall met misfortune during World War II, but the late-Gothic 70-meter-high tower still stands guard. For 20Kč (59¢), climb up to the lookout, which offers a picturesque view of the castle and the Dyje River. Try not to let the nondescript department store that occupies the spot where the town hall once stood wreck the picture. The tower is open daily: May to September from 8:30am to 4pm and October to April from 9am to 3:30pm.

Directly north of the tower on Obrokova ulice is the entrance to the **Znojemské podzemí (Znojmo Underground),** where almost 30 kilometers of tunnels used to store everything from pickles to munitions are accessed. If there's a tour just leaving or

The Painted Cellar of the Šatov Vineyard

Wine, art, and history aficionados unite! The painted cellar of Šatov, one of the region's most proliferate vineyards, awaits. But this isn't an ordinary tour of a vineyard or just a historic place—it's both.

The town of Šatov lies just before the Austrian border, about 6 miles south of Znojmo. So close to the border, in fact, is Šatov, that it was once part of Austria. The town and its surrounding vineyards have long produced some of the country's finest Moravian wines. The excellent soil conditions and continental climate make it perfectly suited for grapes.

You'll find several cellars here, and during late autumn Moravian hospitality opens the doors to just about anyone who knocks. Few, however, knock on the door of Josef Kučera, who can give a different sort of tour. Mr. Kučera, who once patrolled the border to ensure that the vices of capitalism didn't breach the country, will happily lead you down a hidden path for about half a mile until you get to a small, unassuming house. Try to keep up, for Kučera sometimes gets so excited about showing newcomers the cellar that he literally talks and walks a mile a minute!

The house's cellar was most likely carved out in the late 19th century for reasons still a mystery today, but it took on its current form when a one-armed man named Max Appeltauer took to the tunnels and began his work there in 1934. As you enter the cellar and descend about 20 yards, a musty odor envelops you and you wonder how Appeltauer could've spent so much time here. But as you look around the 22-yard tunnel, you'll be thankful he did. Not an artist by trade, Appeltauer set to carving and then painting into the sandstone walls an eclectic set of scenes portraying everything from Prague Castle to Snow White and the

a few people waiting, arrange to join them, since the tours (which are in Czech) are given only to groups of more than six. Admission is 40Kč ($1.18). It's open daily: May to September from 8:30am to 4pm and October to April from 9am to 3:30pm. No phone.

Head back 1 block west to Zelenářská ulice and follow it away from the square to Malá Mikulášká ulice, which leads to the Gothic **St. Nicholas Church** and behind it the bilevel **St. Wenceslas Chapel.** The church is supposed to be open only for services and the occasional concert, but check the door just in case.

Farther on you'll come to the 11th-century **Rotunda sv. Kateřiny,** one of the oldest and best examples of Romanesque architecture still standing in the Czech Republic. Inside are painstakingly restored frescoes of the Přemyslid rulers dating back to the mid–12th century.

At the edge of the embankment lies the **Znojmo Castle,** which now houses the **Jihomoravské Muzeum (South Moravian Museum)** (☎ **0624/224 961**). The museum focuses on the role of Znojmo through the ages, especially as a lookout against the Austro–Hungarian Empire. Admission is 20Kč (59¢); if you take the tour, note that both sights are included in the tour price. It's open Tuesday to Sunday from 9am to 4pm.

WHERE TO STAY

There's not much in the way of quality accommodations in Znojmo, which is probably one reason why so few people spend the night. If you choose to stay, your best

Seven Dwarfs, as well as the Šatov coat of arms. Running off of the main tunnel are five smaller rooms, each depicting a separate theme and carved and painted to painstaking detail.

It's almost as though Appeltauer was expecting one day to escape to his residence inside the cellar, celebrating his departure from life above ground. Indeed, celebrating had already taken place inside the dark cellar, as the inscription VINO, ŽENY A ZPĚV, ZAHLADÍ VEŠKERÝ HNĚV ("Wine, women, and song will remove all anger") indicates. Kučera will tell you that the cellar was at one time a popular place, where the masses gathered after mass, girlfriends and all. Wives searching for their husbands would often enter, sending girlfriends scurrying into the subcellar. Local lore has it that Hitler visited the cellar when inspecting the military bunkers set up to defend his southern flank.

Appeltauer left the cellar for good in 1968 and died 4 years later, never realizing his next dream—to paint farther into the cellar. Some cans of paint and a few jars still sit idly by at the point where he stopped, untouched after 25 years of waiting for the party that never came.

To get to Šatov by car or bike, take Highway 59 out of Znojmo to the south and turn right at the sign for Šatov. Buses and trains also run to the village from Znojmo on a regular basis.

Kučera will kindly give tours of the cellar for 15Kč (44¢) per person, but he speaks only Czech, so you'll need to take along someone who can translate or at least communicate in rudimentary Czech. His wife says that she will give tours in German if need be. Call ☎ **0624/7178** at least a couple of days in advance, so the Kučeras can arrange their schedule.

option may prove to be the information center, which can arrange a private room. Expect to pay around 500Kč ($15) per person.

Hotel Družba (Friendship Hotel). Pražská 100, 669 02 Znojmo. ☎ **0624/756 21.** 60 units. 750Kč ($23) double. No credit cards.

Just off the road leading to Prague, the Družba is exactly what a Communist-era hotel was meant to be—adequate but nothing more. The small rooms are sparsely furnished with 1970s beds. The ensuite bathrooms are a redeeming feature.

Hotel Dukla. Antonína Zápoteckého 5, Znojmo. ☎ **0624/763 20.** 110 units. 900Kč ($26.47) double. AE, DC, MC, V.

In the south part of Znojmo, the Dukla gets its name from the army but is nicer than the barracks. The rooms are functional and there is always a vacancy.

Morava. Horní nám. 17. No phone. Soups 12–25Kč (35¢–74¢); main courses 64–219Kč ($1.88–$6.44). No credit cards. Daily 10am–11pm. CZECH/INTERNATIONAL.

This small restaurant has a relatively big selection of meals, and, not surprisingly, a good choice of Moravian wines. A recent renovation has added a homey atmosphere that is relaxing and far nicer than the Communist-era surroundings of the hotel restaurants. Many items on the menu may look similar to those in other Czech restaurants, but the cooking has a south Moravian accent, so it's a pleasant surprise when meals like goulash come to the table with a little more spice. The Morava also has several pork dishes that are well prepared with a nice blend of piquant spices.

Appendix A: Prague in Depth

by John Mastrini & Hana Mastrini

1 The City Today

Prague in 2000 is enmeshed in its new capitalism, if not still trying to define it. The castles and cathedrals that draw most visitors are now surrounded by entrepreneurs trying to make back the bucks (or *koruny*) denied them under Communism. And they're trying to make money as quickly as possible. For example, a bottle of water that costs just 15Kč (44¢) in most shops can cost 50Kč ($1.47) or more when purchased from a cart in the main tourist areas. Supply and demand has caught on.

Developers are making the most of new opportunities as well. The pounding of jackhammers and the hollow thump of scaffolding being raised and lowered incessantly are now the sounds most familiarly mixed with the bells and whir of ubiquitous streetcars. There's hardly a corner you'll turn where cobblestones haven't been dug up or sidewalks torn out.

Prague is a city rebuilding its face and its spirit, trying to keep up with the massive new flood of cars and visitors and getting used to the pros and cons of its renewed affluence.

AT THE CROSSROADS OF EUROPE

Prague lies at the epicenter of Bohemia, which borders Germany to the north and west and Austria to the south. Slovakia to the east (which joined with the Czechs at the end of the Austro–Hungarian Empire in 1918 to form the Republic of Czechoslovakia) split with its Slavic neighbors in 1993 to form independent Czech and Slovak republics in the "Velvet Divorce."

About 10.3 million people inhabit the Czech lands of Bohemia and Moravia, with about 1.2 million living in the dozen districts comprising the Prague metropolitan area. A small percentage of Praguers live in the classical areas most frequented by visitors, and that number is dropping as many buildings are bought and remodeled to satisfy the high-paying demand for quality office space.

Most Praguers actually live in the satellite Communist-built housing estates (*paneláky*) ringing the city. In the high summer season, visitors outnumber locals two to one in most main areas in the city, taking away much of Prague's indigenous character.

THE CZECH LANGUAGE

Bohemia, through good times and bad, has been under a strong Germanic influence, and throughout a great deal of its history, German was the practiced language of the power elite. The Czech language, however, stems from the Slavic family, which includes Polish, Russian, Slovak, and others, though many Czech words have been altered from German. Czech uses a Latin alphabet with some letters topped by a small hat called a háček to denote Slavic phonic combinations like "sh" *š*, "ch" *č*, and everyone's favorite "rzh" *ř*. Slovak differs slightly from Czech, but Czechs and Slovaks understand each other's language.

English, however, has become the postrevolutionary foreign tongue of choice for Prague movers and shakers, though German is more abundant in border areas. Outside Prague, it's rare to find someone who speaks English fluently, so be patient, expect to be misunderstood, and cultivate a sense of humor. Many newer words in the Czech vocabulary derive from capitalist English (*marketink* and *e-byznys*) or pop culture (*rokenrol*).

2 History 101

IN THE BEGINNING
THE CELTS & THE NEW BOHEMIANS
A Celtic tribe, the Boii, first settled 300 years before Christ in the land around the Vltava River, which forms the heart of the present-day Czech territory. The Latin term *Bohemia* (Land of the Boii) became etched in history.

The Marcomanni, a Germanic tribe, banished the Boii around 100 B.C., only to be chucked out by the Huns by A.D. 450. The Huns, in turn, were expelled by a Turkic tribe, the Avars, about a century later.

Near the turn of the 6th century, Slavs crossed the Carpathian Mountains into Europe, and the westernmost of the Slavic tribes tried to set up a kingdom in Bohemia. The farming Slavs often fell prey to the nomadic Avars, but in 624 a Franconian merchant named Samo united the Slavs and began expelling the Avars from central Europe.

MORAVIAN EMPIRE Throughout the 9th century, the Slavs around the River Morava consolidated their power. Mojmír I declared his Great Moravian Empire—a kingdom that eventually encompassed Bohemia, Slovakia, and parts of modern Poland and Hungary—in a Christian order still outside the boundaries of the Holy Roman Empire.

In 863, the Greek brothers Cyril and Methodius arrived in Moravia to preach the Eastern Christian rite to a people who didn't understand them. They created a new language

Dateline
- **300 B.C.** Celtic people, the Boii, settle in the area of today's Czech Republic, giving it the name Bohemia.
- **A.D. 450** Huns and other Eastern peoples arrive in Bohemia.
- **870** Bohemia becomes part of Holy Roman Empire. Castle constructed in Hradčany.
- **973** Bishopric founded in Prague.
- **1158** First stone bridge spans the Vltava.
- **1234** Staré Město (Old Town) founded, the first of Prague's historic five towns.
- **1257** Malá Strana (Lesser Town) established by German colonists.
- **1306** Premyslid dynasty ends following the death of teenage Václav III, who leaves no heir.
- **1344** Prague bishopric raised to an archbishopric.
- **1346** Charles IV becomes king and later Holy Roman emperor, as Prague's Golden Age begins.
- **1403** Jan Hus becomes rector of the University of

continues

Prague and launches a crusade for religious reform.

- **1415** Hus burned at the stake by German Catholics, and decades of religious warfare begin.
- **1419** Roman Catholic councilors thrown from the windows of New Town Hall in the First Defenestration.
- **1434** Radical Hussites, called Taborites, defeated in the Battle of Lipany, ending religious warfare.
- **1526** Roman Catholic Habsburgs gain control of Bohemia.
- **1584** Prague made seat of the imperial court of Rudolf II.
- **1618** Second Defenestration helps ignite Thirty Years' War, entrenching Habsburg rule.
- **1648** Praguers defend the city against invading Swedes—stopping them on Charles Bridge in the last military action of the Thirty Years' War.
- **1784** Prague's four towns united.
- **1818** National Museum founded.
- **1848** Industrial Revolution begins in Prague, drawing villagers to the city and fueling Czech national revival.
- **1875** Horse-drawn trams operate on Prague's streets.
- **1881** National Theater completed during wave of Czech push for statehood against Austro-Hungarian rule.
- **1883** Franz Kafka born in Staré Město.
- **1918** Czechoslovakia founded at the end of World War I after the fall of the Austro-Hungarian Empire. Independence leader Tomáš G. Masaryk becomes first president.

continues

mixing Slavic with a separate script, which came to be known as Cyrillic. When Methodius died in 885, the Moravian rulers reestablished the Latin liturgy, though followers of Cyril and Methodius continued to preach their faith in missions to the east. Ultimately the Slavonic rite took hold in Kiev and Russia where the Cyrillic alphabet is still used, while western Slavs kept the Latin script and followed Rome.

The Great Moravian Empire lasted about a century—until the Magyar invasion of 896—and not until the 20th century would the Czechs and Slovaks unite under a single government. After the invasion, the Slavs living east of the Morava swore allegiance to the Magyars, while the Czechs, who lived west of the river, fell under the authority of the Holy Roman Empire.

BOHEMIA LOOKS TO THE WEST

Bořivoj, the first king of the now separate Bohemia and Moravia, built Prague's first royal palace at the end of the 9th century on the site of the present Prague Castle on Hradčany Hill. In 973, a bishopric was established in Prague, answering to the archbishopric of Mainz. Thus, before the end of the first millennium, the German influence in Bohemia was firmly established.

The kings who followed Bořivoj in the Premyslid dynasty ruled over Bohemia for more than 300 years, during which time Prague became a major commercial area along central Europe's trade routes. In the 12th century, two fortified castles were built at Vyšehrad and Hradčany and a wooden plank bridge stood near where the stone Charles Bridge spans the Vltava today. Václavské náměstí (Wenceslas Square) was a horse market, and the city's 3,500 residents rarely lived to 45. In 1234, Staré Město (Old Town), the first of Prague's historic five towns, was founded.

Encouraged by Bohemia's rulers, who guaranteed German civic rights to western settlers, Germans founded entire towns around Prague, including Malá Strana (Lesser Town) in 1257. The Premyslid dynasty of the Czechs ended with the death of teenage Václav III in 1306, who had no heirs. After much debate, the throne was offered to John of Luxembourg, husband of Václav III's younger sister, a foreigner who knew little of Bohemia. It was

John's first-born son who left the most lasting marks on Prague.

PRAGUE'S FIRST GOLDEN AGE

Charles IV (Karel IV), christened first as Václav, took the throne when his father died while fighting in France in 1346. Educated among French royalty and fluent in four languages (but not Czech), Charles almost single-handedly ushered in Prague's first golden age (the second came in the late 16th century).

Even before his reign, Charles wanted to make Prague a glorious city (he eventually learned to speak Czech). In 1344, he won an archbishopric for Prague independent of Mainz. When he became king of Bohemia, Charles also became, by election, Holy Roman emperor.

During the next 30 years of his reign, Charles transformed Prague into the bustling capital of the Holy Roman Empire and one of Europe's most important cities, with some of the most glorious architecture of its day. He commissioned St. Vitus Cathedral's construction at Prague Castle as well as the bridge that would eventually bear his name. He was most proud of founding Prague University in 1348, the first higher education institution in central Europe, now known as Charles University. In 1378, Charles died of natural causes at age 62.

PROTESTANT REFORMATION

Charles IV was the most heralded of the Bohemian kings, but the short reign of his son Václav IV was marked by social upheaval, a devastating plague, and the advent of turbulent religious dissent.

Reformist priest Jan Hus drew large crowds to Bethlehem Chapel, where he preached against what he considered the corrupt tendencies of Prague's bishopric. Hus became widely popular among Czech nationals who rallied behind his crusade against the German-dominated establishment. Excommunicated in 1412 and charged with heresy 2 years later, Hus was burned at the stake on July 6, 1415, in Konstanz (Constance), Germany, an event that sparked widespread riots and, ultimately, civil war. Czechs still commemorate the day as a national holiday.

THE HUSSITE WARS

The hostilities began simply enough. Rioting Hussites threw several Roman Catholic councilors to their deaths

- **1921** Prague's boundaries expand to encompass neighboring villages and settlements.
- **1938** Leaders of Germany, Great Britain, Italy, and France meet to cede Czech border territories (the Sudetenland) to Hitler in the Munich Agreement.
- **1939** Hitler absorbs the rest of the Czech lands as a German protectorate; puppet Slovak Republic established.
- **1940s** In World War II, more than 130,000 Czechs murdered, including more than 80,000 Jews.
- **1942** Nazi protectorate leader Reinhard Heydrich assassinated in Prague by soldiers trained in England. Hitler retaliates with the mass murder and destruction of the nearby village of Lidice.
- **1945** American army liberates western Bohemia and Soviet army liberates Prague; 2.5 million Germans expelled, their property expropriated under decrees of returning President Edvard Beneš.
- **1946** Communist leader Klement Gottwald appointed prime minister after his party wins 38% of vote.
- **1948** Communists seize power amid cabinet crisis.
- **1950s** Top Jewish Communists executed in purge as Stalinism reaches its peak. Giant statue of Stalin unveiled on Letná plain overlooking Prague (then destroyed after his death).
- **1968** Alexander Dubček becomes general secretary of the Communist Party and launches "Prague Spring" reforms; in August, Soviet-led Warsaw Pact troops invade and occupy Czechoslovakia.

continues

- **1977** Czech dissidents form Charter 77 to protest suppression of human rights during Communist "normal-ization."
- **1989** Student-led antigov-ernment protests erupt into revolution; Communist government resigns; Parlia-ment nominates playwright Václav Havel as president.
- **1990** Free elections held; Havel's loose movement Civic Forum captures 170 of 300 parliamentary seats.
- **1991** Country begins massive program of priva-tizing shares in thousands of companies by distributing coupons that could be exchanged for stock.
- **1992** Havel resigns, saying he doesn't want to preside over the division of Czecho-slovakia.
- **1993** Czechoslovakia splits into independent Czech and Slovak states—the "Velvet Divorce"—by mutual agreement of cabinets. Havel accepts new 5-year term as president of the independent Czech Republic. Country given first investment-grade rating of any post-Communist country by U.S. bond agencies.
- **1995** Czech Republic invited to join the OECD, the organization of the world's richest countries.
- **1996** Chain-smoking Havel nearly dies after surgery to remove a cancerous lung tumor; he later has two more.
- **1997** Prague-born Madeleine Albright, the daughter of a Czechoslovak diplomat, becomes the highest-ranking woman ever in the U.S. government as Secretary of State. July floods devastate much of the eastern part of the country.
- **1998** Havel wins another 5-year term, his final allowed

continues

from the windows of Prague's New Town Hall (Novoměstská radnice) in 1419, a deed known as the First Defenestration. It didn't take long for the pope to declare a crusade against the Czech heretics. The conflict widened into class struggle, and by 1420 sev-eral major battles were fought between the peasant Hussites and the Catholic crusaders, who were supported by the nobility. A schism split the Hussites when a more moderate fac-tion, known as the Utraquists, signed a 1433 peace agreement with Rome at the Council of Basel. Still the more radical Taborites con-tinued to fight, until they were decisively defeated at the Battle of Lipany.

HABSBURG RULE Following this, the nobility of Bohemia concentrated its power, forming fiefdoms called the Estates. In 1526, the nobles elected Archduke Ferdinand king of Bohemia, marking the beginning of Roman Catholic rule by the Austrian Habs-burgs, which continued until World War I. Rudolf II ascended to the throne in 1576 and presided over what was to become known as Prague's second golden age. He reestablished Prague as the seat of the Habsburg empire; he invited the great astronomers Johannes Kepler and Tycho de Brahe to Prague and endowed the city's museums with some of Europe's finest art. The Rudolfinum, which was recently restored and houses the Czech Phil-harmonic, pays tribute to Rudolf's opulence.

Conflicts between the Catholic Habsburgs and Bohemia's growing Protestant nobility came to a head on May 23, 1618, when two Catholic governors were thrown out of the windows of Prague Castle, in the Second Defenestration. This event marked the start of a series of complex politico-religious conflicts known as the Thirty Years' War. After a Swedish army was defeated on Charles Bridge by a local force that included Prague's Jews and students, the war came to an end with the Peace of Westphalia. The Catholics won a decisive victory, and the empire's focus shifted back to Vienna. Fresh waves of immigrants turned Prague and other towns into Germanic cities. By the end of the 18th century, the Czech language was on the verge of dying out.

INTO THE 20TH CENTURY

THE CZECH REVIVAL In the 19th cen-tury, the Industrial Revolution drew Czechs from the countryside into Prague, where a Czech national revival began.

As the industrial economy grew, Prague's Czech population increased in number and power, overtaking the Germans. In 1868, the Czech people threw open the doors to the gilded symbol of their revival, the neo-Renaissance National Theater (Národní divadlo), with the bold proclamation *"Národ sobě"* ("The Nation for Itself") inscribed over the proscenium. Then came the massive National Museum Building (Národní muzeum), completed in 1890 at the top of Wenceslas Square, packed with exhibits proclaiming the rich history and culture of the Czech people.

As the new century emerged, Prague was on the cusp of the art nouveau wave sweeping Europe. Moravian Alfons Mucha's sensuous painting of Sarah Bernhardt wowed Paris.

THE FOUNDING OF THE REPUBLIC OF CZECHOSLOVAKIA

As Czech political parties continued to call for more autonomy from Vienna, Archduke Ferdinand and his wife, Sophie, were assassinated in Sarajevo, setting off World War I. Meanwhile, a 65-year-old philosophy professor named Tomáš Masaryk seized the opportunity to tour Europe and America, speaking in favor of creating a combined democratic Czech and Slovak state. He was supported by a Slovak scientist, Milan Štefánik.

As the German and Austrian armies wore down in 1918, the concept of "Czechoslovakia" gained international support. U.S. President Woodrow Wilson backed Masaryk on October 18, 1918, in Washington, D.C., as the professor proclaimed the independence of the Czechoslovak Republic in the Washington Declaration. On October 28, 1918, the sovereign Republic of Czechoslovakia was founded in Prague. Masaryk returned home in December after being elected (in absentia) Czechoslovakia's first president.

THE FIRST REPUBLIC

The 1920s ushered in an exceptional but brief period of freedom and prosperity in Prague. Czechoslovakia, its industrial strength intact after the war, was one of the 10 strongest economies in the world. Prague's capitalists lived the Jazz Age on a par with New York's industrial barons. Palatial art nouveau villas graced the fashionable Bubeneč and Hanspaulka districts, where smart parties were held nonstop.

The Great Depression gradually spread to Prague, drawing sharper lines between the classes and nationalities. As ethnic Germans in Czech border regions found a champion in new German Chancellor Adolf Hitler in 1933, their calls to unify under the Third Reich grew louder.

In 1938, Britain's Neville Chamberlain and France's Edouard Daladier, seeking to avoid conflict with the increasingly belligerent Germans, met Hitler and Italy's Benito Mussolini in Munich. Their agreement to cede the Bohemian areas, which Germans called the Sudetenland, to Hitler on September 30 marked one of the darkest days in Czech history.

Chamberlain returned to London to tell a cheering crowd that he'd achieved "peace in our time." But within a year, Hitler absorbed the rest of the Czech

under the constitution. Special elections in June result in a center-left government being sworn in by Havel after the center-right cabinet, in power for 6 years, resigns due to a party financing scandal.

- **1999** The Czech Republic, along with Hungary and Poland, become the first ex–Soviet Bloc states to join NATO, while talks on joining the European Union drag on.
- **2000** Prague joins eight other cities named by the European Union as *European Cities of Culture 2000,* with celebrations and events to be held throughout the year (see "Schedule of Events— European City of Culture 2000" in chapter 2 for a schedule of selected events).

lands and installed a puppet government in Slovakia. Soon Europe was again at war.

WORLD WAR II   During the next 6 years, more than 130,000 Czechs were systematically murdered, including more than 80,000 Jews. Though Hitler ordered devastation for other cities, he sought to preserve Prague and its Jewish ghetto as part of his planned museum of the extinct race.

The Nazi concentration camp at Terezín, about 30 miles northwest of Prague, became a waystation for many Czech Jews bound for death camps at Auschwitz and Buchenwald. Thousands died of starvation and disease at Terezín even though the Nazis used it as a "show" camp for Red Cross investigators.

Meanwhile, the Czechoslovak government in exile, led by Masaryk's successor, Edvard Beneš, tried to organize resistance from friendly territory in London. One initiative was launched in May 1942 when two Czechoslovak paratroopers, in a mission called Anthropoid, attempted to assassinate Hitler's lead man in Prague, Reich Protector Reinhard Heydrich. Setting a charge at an intersection north of Prague, the soldiers stopped Heydrich's limousine and opened fire, fatally wounding him.

Hitler retaliated by ordering the total liquidation of a nearby Czech village, Lidice, where 192 men were shot dead and more than 300 women and children were sent to concentration camps. Every building in the town was bulldozed to the ground.

The soldiers, Jozef Gabčík and Jan Kubiš, were hunted down by Nazi police and trapped in the Cyril and Methodius church on Resslova street near the Vltava. They reportedly shot themselves to avoid the indignity of capture. The debate still rages whether Anthropoid brought anything but more terror to occupied Bohemia.

THE ADVENT OF COMMUNISM   The final act of World War II in Europe played out where the Nazis started it, in Bohemia. As U.S. troops liberated the western part of the country, General George Patton was told to hold his troops at Plzeň and wait for the Soviet army to sweep through Prague because of the Allied Powers agreement made at Yalta months before. Soviet soldiers and Czech civilians liberated Prague in a bloody street battle on May 9, 1945, a day after the Germans had signed their capitulation. Throughout Prague you can see small wall memorials on the spots where Czechs fell that day battling the Germans.

On his return from exile in England, Edvard Beneš ordered the expulsion of 2.5 million Germans from Czechoslovakia and the confiscation of all their property. (An agreement between Prague and Bonn in early 1997 tried to put an end to compensation demands from the families of expropriated Germans and the Czech victims of war crimes by setting up a joint fund, but the demands continue.) Meanwhile, the government, exhausted and bewildered by fascism, nationalized 60% of the country's industries, and many looked to Soviet-style Communism as a new model. Elections were held in 1946, and Communist leader Klement Gottwald became prime minister after his party won about one-third of the vote.

Through a series of cabinet maneuvers, Communists seized full control of the government in 1948, and Beneš was ousted. Little dissent was tolerated, and a series of show trials began, purging hundreds of perceived threats to Stalinist Communist authority. Another wave of political refugees fled the country. The sterile, centrally planned Communist architecture began seeping into classical Prague.

THE PRAGUE SPRING In January 1968, Alexander Dubček, a career Slovak Communist, became first secretary of the Czechoslovak Communist Party. Long before Mikhail Gorbachev, Dubček tinkered with Communist reforms that he called "socialism with a human face." His program of political, economic, and social reform (while still seeking to maintain one-party rule) blossomed into a brief intellectual and artistic renaissance known as the "Prague Spring."

Increasingly nervous about what seemed to them as a loss of party control, Communist hard-liners in Prague and other Eastern European capitals conspired with the Soviet Union to remove Dubček and the government. On August 21, 1968, Prague awoke to the rumble of tanks and 200,000 invading Warsaw Pact soldiers claiming "fraternal assistance." Believing that they'd be welcomed as liberators, these soldiers from the Soviet Union, Poland, East Germany, Bulgaria, and Hungary were bewildered when angry Czechs confronted them with rocks and flaming torches. The Communist grip tightened, however, and Prague fell deeper into the Soviet sphere of influence. Another wave of refugees fled. The following January, a university student named Jan Palach, in a lonely protest to Soviet occupation, doused himself with gasoline and set himself afire in Wenceslas Square. He died days later, becoming a martyr for the dissident movement. But the Soviet soldiers stayed for more than two decades during the gray period the Communists called "normalization."

CHARTER 77 In 1976, during the worst of "normalization," the Communists arrested a popular underground rock band called the Plastic People of the Universe on charges of disturbing the peace. This motivated some of Prague's most prominent artists, writers, and intellectuals, led by playwright Václav Havel, to establish Charter 77, a human-rights advocacy group formed to pressure the government—then Europe's most repressive—into observing the human rights principles of the 1975 Helsinki Accords. In the years that followed, Havel, the group's perceived leader, was constantly monitored by the secret police, the StB. He was put under house arrest and jailed several times for "threatening public order."

THE VELVET REVOLUTION & BEYOND

THE VELVET REVOLUTION Just after the Berlin Wall fell and with major change imminent in Eastern Europe, thousands of students set out on a chilly candlelit march on November 17, 1989. As part of their nonviolent campaign, they held signs simply asking for a dialogue with the government. Against police warnings, they marched from the southern citadel at Vyšehrad and turned up National Boulevard (Národní třída), where they soon met columns of helmeted riot police. Holding fingers in peace signs and chanting "our hands are free," the bravest 500 sat down at the feet of the police. After an excruciating standoff, the police moved in, squeezing the students against buildings and wildly beating them with clubs.

Although nobody was killed and the official Communist-run media played the story as the quiet, justified end to the whims of student radicals, clandestine videotapes and accounts of the incident blanketed the country. By the next day, Praguers began organizing their outrage. Havel and his artistic allies seized the moment and called a meeting of intellectuals at the Laterna Magika on Národní, where they planned more nonviolent protests. Students and theaters went on strike, and hundreds of thousands of Praguers began pouring into Wenceslas Square, chanting for the end of Communist rule. Within days,

From Prisoner to President: Václav Havel

In an atmosphere of decency, creativity, tolerance, and quiet resolution, we shall bear far more easily the trials we have yet to experience, and resolve all the large problems we must face.

> —Václav Havel addressing the nation (January 1, 1992)

Václav Havel's often frustrating personal crusade for morality and honesty in politics made him a most unlikely world leader.

Born in 1936 to a wealthy building developer, he was on the wrong side of Communism's bourgeois divide and wasn't allowed a top education. His interest in theater grew from his stint as a set boy and led to the staging of his first plays at Prague's Theater on the Balustrade (Divadlo Na Zábradlí). His play *The Garden Party* was widely acclaimed, and he became the playwright from the place he'd later call Absurdistan. After Havel publicly criticized the Soviet invasion and Communist policies, his plays and essays were banned.

In 1977, he helped draft Charter 77, a manifesto urging the government to respect human rights and decency; it was condemned by the politburo as a subversive act. Under almost constant surveillance by the StB, Havel was placed under house arrest and imprisoned several times. His philosophical writings about life under repression during the period—especially his essay "The Power of the Powerless"—became world-renowned for their insight into the dark gray world behind the Iron Curtain.

He was the natural leader when the well-read students and artists decided that the time was ripe for revolution.

Soon after Havel led the citizen's movement Civic Forum that ousted the Communist government in 1989, he told a joint session of the U.S. Congress why he accepted the offer to be president: "Intellectuals cannot go on forever avoiding their share of responsibility for the world and hiding their distaste for politics under an alleged need to be independent." Virtually overnight, he moved from the prison dungeon to the presidential throne, though he chose to live in his modest apartment on the river even when he could have lived in Prague Castle. (Havel now lives in a stylish villa in the smart part of town.)

After the peaceful split of Czechoslovakia into two countries in 1993, he was elected the first president of the now-independent Czech Republic.

factory workers and citizens in towns throughout the country joined in a general strike. In Wenceslas Square, the protesters jingled their keys, a signal to the politburo that it was time to go. On November 24, General Secretary Miloš Jakeš resigned, and by the end of year, the Communist government fell. By New Year's Eve, Havel, joined by Dubček, gave his first speech as president of a free Czechoslovakia. Because hardly any blood was spilled, the coup d'état was dubbed the "Velvet Revolution."

ECONOMIC & POLITICAL CHANGES   In June 1990, the first free elections in 44 years gave power to the Civic Forum, the movement led by Havel. But it was Václav Klaus who launched the country on its course of economic reform. First as federal finance minister and then as Czech prime minister, Klaus, an economist, helped form a right-wing offshoot of the Civic Forum called the Civic Democratic Party; it won the 1992 elections on a program of

In late 1996, the chain-smoking 60-year-old Havel was diagnosed with a small malignant tumor on his lung. The surgery to remove half of one lobe almost cost him his life less than a year after his wife, Olga, died of cancer. He has since survived no fewer than three life-threatening illnesses. In the midst of the first painful and frightening recuperation, Havel shocked the country by marrying again, this time to a popular (and much younger) stage and screen actress, Dagmar Veškrnová.

In an interview in mid-1997, the normally reserved Havel railed at the media's negative reaction to his surprise marriage. "I would not hold a referendum on this. I am the one who has to live with my wife, not anyone else," he told (John) in an uncommonly terse and gruff way. Havel also bristles at anyone who suggests that he should become an antismoking advocate after his ordeal, saying that people should have "the right to decide how to kill themselves."

After returning to full duties, the still-popular philosopher won his last 5-year term allowed under the constitution in early 1998. Havel, however, hasn't dirtied his hands much in the rough and tumble of postrevolutionary politics, instead using his mostly ceremonial post to act as a moral balancing wheel, warning against possible excesses of the new freedoms.

"From the West we have learned to live in a soulless world of stupid advertisements and even more stupid sitcoms and we are allowing them to drain our lives and our spirits," he told the nation in a speech marking the fifth anniversary of the Velvet Revolution.

Havel has an office full of honors from abroad, including the Roosevelt Four-Freedoms Medal, the Philadelphia Freedom Medal, France's Grande Croix de la Légion d'Honneur, and India's Indira Gandhi Prize. He has been shortlisted for the Nobel Peace Prize numerous times, but has never won. An unabashed fan of rock music, Havel kept close company with Frank Zappa until his death, and he has had friendly meetings with Bruce Springsteen, Lou Reed, Pink Floyd, Bob Dylan, and Joan Baez. He once held up traffic at an Australian airport to have a conversation on the tarmac with Mick Jagger.

massive privatization. First, thousands of small businesses were auctioned off for a song. By the end of 1994, shares in some 1,800 large companies were privatized by giving citizens government coupons they could exchange for stock or fund shares. In less than 5 years, private companies churned out 80% of the Czech economy.

THE VELVET DIVORCE In 1992, leaders of the Czech and Slovak republics peacefully agreed to split into separate states. The Slovaks wanted to get out of the shadow of Prague (Slovak nationalists had been calling for that since 1918), and the Czech government was happy to get rid of the expected financial burdens of Slovakia's slower reconstruction. The "Velvet Divorce" was final on January 1, 1993, with common property split on a 2-to-1 ratio, without lawyers taking anything—yet. They're still arguing over gold assets and bank accounts, just like a divorced couple would.

Privatization, however, did little to bring in new capital or energize management at larger companies. Meanwhile, Czechs bought up Western goods and equipment and ignored domestic suppliers. Speculators pounced on the imbalance to force the central bank to float the Czech crown, causing it to dive in the spring of 1997.

As voices of discontent have grown louder as socioeconomic divisions have widened, Czech reforms hit a wall in 1997, damaged by a series of financial scandals and poor competitiveness. Klaus and his center-right government barely clung to power in 1996 elections. In November 1997, a fund-raising scandal blew up around Klaus and his party, forcing the government to resign. New elections were held in mid-1998, bringing the first left-wing government to power since the revolution, the center-left Social Democrats, not the Communists.

Still, Czech politicians pushed to prove that the country belongs in the big leagues. The Czechs became one of the first former Soviet-bloc states to join NATO in 1999, along with Poland and Hungary (though about half of the country, according to polls, isn't sure it's a good idea). The government is also deep into talks on joining the European Union early in the new century, although the process looks like it will drag on for a while.

CRIME & RACISM Throughout Eastern Europe, overt racism appears to be an unwelcome by-product of revolution. Romanies (Gypsies) and Jews have been the targets of many attacks. The government has stepped up efforts to weed out and crack down on racist groups (most called Skinheads) after several violent incidents. In 1997, hundreds of Romanies sold their meager possessions to pay for plane tickets to Canada because of a local TV report that said they would find asylum there. They didn't, and most were sent back, penniless and hopeless. Since then, many more have tried to win asylum in Britain, Sweden, and Finland, creating friction in talks on EU membership.

With police carrying a smaller stick, crime has risen sharply, as pickpockets and car thieves take advantage of Prague's new prosperity. Violent crime, while rising, is still well under American levels, and Prague's streets and parks are safer than those in most large Western cities.

3 The Spoils of Revolution: Capitalism & Culture

Prague has once again become a well-heeled business center in the heart of central Europe. Nostalgic and successful Czechs say it's capitalism, not Communism, that comes most naturally here.

THE FIRST REPUBLIC LIVES ON

If you talk to a Praguer long enough, the conversation will often turn into a lecture about how the country had one of the world's richest economies, per capita, between the world wars. Communism, a Praguer will say, was just a detour. The between-wars period, lovingly called the First Republic, recalls a time when democracy and capitalism thrived and Prague's bistros and dance halls were filled with dandies and flappers swinging the night away, until the Nazi invasion in 1939 spoiled the party.

The First Republic motif has been revived in many clubs and restaurants, and you can see shades of this style in Czech editions of top Western fashion magazines.

Since the Velvet Revolution, Praguers have been obsessed with style. Many people—especially the *novobohatí* (nouveau riche)—rushed out to buy the flashiest Mercedes or BMW they could find with the quick money gained from the restitution of Communist-seized property.

While the average annual income per person is still less than $7,000, the trappings of conspicuous consumption are evident throughout Prague, from the designer boutiques in the city center to the newly developed luxury suburbs with split-level ranch homes and tailored lawns. Women's fashion has had the most stunning revolution: The blur of loud polyester minidresses that used to dominate the streets has been replaced by the latest looks from Europe's catwalks.

Prague's avant-garde community used to thrive in secret while mocking Communism but now has to face the realities of capitalism, such as rising rents and stiff competition. Many have had to find more mainstream work to survive. But if you look hard enough, you still might find an exhibition, a dance recital, or an experimental performance that's surprising, shocking, and satisfying. The *Prague Post,* the English-language weekly, usually serves as a good source for finding these events.

In the evening, you can find a typical Bohemian playing cards with friends at the neighborhood hospoda or *pivnice* (beer hall) or debating at a *kavárna* (cafe). Most likely, though, the characteristic Czech will be parked in front of the TV, as the country maintains one of the highest per capita nightly viewing audiences in Europe. TV Nova—launched by New York cosmetics scion Ronald Lauder's company—attracts around 60% of the population with a nightly mix of dubbed American action films, sitcoms (*M*A*S*H* has been wildly popular), and tabloid news shows. In 1999, in the most public example of foreign investment gone awry, Lauder's company was thrown out of TV Nova by his Czech partners, and hundreds of millions of dollars in lawsuits are pending.

Pop literature has also overwhelmed the classics since the Velvet Revolution, with scandal sheets surging in newspaper sales and pulp fiction romances ruling the bookshops.

CZECH POLITICAL & RELIGIOUS BELIEFS

While Praguers tend to look Westward and insist that they never belonged in the Soviet Bloc, the average Czech has been ambivalent about the government's push to join the European Union and the NATO security alliance. According to opinion polls, a majority of Czechs have doubts about NATO membership and slightly more than half favor entering the EU. That's understandable after a long history of living under various foreign spheres of influence.

In contrast to neighboring Poland, Hungary, and former partner Slovakia, the Czech Republic isn't deeply religious. Although Prague was once the seat of the Holy Roman Empire and churches lace the city, less than 20% of Czechs today say that they believe in God and around 10% say that they're religious. One opinion poll showed that more Czechs believe in UFOs than believe in God.

Czechs may not be religious, but they're often superstitious. One piece of folk wisdom is similar to Groundhog Day in the United States. If it rains on the day of Medard (June 8), Czechs plan to carry an umbrella another 40 consecutive days. They also believe that having a baby carriage in the house before a child is born is extremely bad luck for your expected child's future.

Each day on the calendar corresponds to one or more of the Czech first names, and it's customary to present a gift to close friends and colleagues on their *svátek* (name day)—it's like having two birthdays a year.

The American Invasion

After the Velvet Revolution, Czechs sought the antithesis of Communism—anything that could be called Western. And Westerners became quite curious about life on the other side of the raised Iron Curtain and excited to find a new market.

So postrevolutionary Prague quickly came to know a once-rare species: the American. An estimated 30,000 lived here either legally or illegally. Many were twentysomethings who heard that the inevitable job hunt could be postponed in a place where free love, cheap beer, and bad poetry were the order of the day. Some claimed that it was a chance to get a taste of the 1960s their parents had always talked about.

But Prague didn't replicate the rebelliousness of the Left Bank of Paris in the 1920s or San Francisco's Haight-Ashbury in the 1960s, its environment instead charged with the first feel of freedom after years of repression. Yet today's increasingly Western consumer habits make being Bohemian in Bohemia somewhat ironic. "There's no bathtub" or "I can't find any iceberg lettuce," complain sandaled masses, yearning to drink cheap beer and write haiku.

With the American invasion came the inevitable array of shops and services for those who really didn't want to wander so far from home. At the spot on Národní třída (National Boulevard) where the Velvet Revolution began, the U.S. discount retailer Kmart bought out an old Communist state department store known as the Máj. The store, Kmart's first in Europe, featured its famous half-off "Blue Light Special" sales (the flashing *modré světlo* in Czech). The store has since been sold to the British chain Tesco, which has actually added to shelf on shelf of peanut butter, microwave popcorn, nacho cheese tortilla chips, and fudge brownie mix.

Rising rents and beer prices and a lack of jobs with Western-level pay have pushed many back home. While many Czechs welcomed the Američany soon after the Velvet Revolution, they're now using the pejorative moniker Amíci more frequently. Perhaps familiarity does breed contempt. At this writing, one general weekly newspaper, the *Prague Post*, dominates the English-language audience, after a flurry of other postrevolutionary attempts failed. Several business magazines and weeklies have popped up, the best of which is the *Prague Business Journal*. Sports bars, taco bars, and Chicago-style pizzerias thrive.

TODAY'S CHALLENGES

The city now faces a host of problems that didn't occur under Communism. Taxi drivers, who were strictly licensed under the old regime and formed a small exclusive club, have become one of the mayor's biggest headaches. Reports that these new entrepreneurs have been gouging tourists have grown exponentially with the number of drivers and visitors. And prostitutes, who were kept behind closed doors in the old days, now display their wares on convent steps.

Leaders have tried to keep a lid on anything obscuring the best sights, including a tornado of billboards and the blight of graffiti. They're also searching for a way to curb the traffic rambling through the ancient streets.

Though eyesores keep popping up, the traffic keeps getting worse, and finicky phones wear you down . . . Prague is still a magical romp of a city.

4 Famous Czechs

Princess Libuše (pre–9th century)   Fabled mother of Bohemia. Legend holds that the clairvoyant Libuše, the daughter of Bohemian philosopher Krok, stood on a cliff on Vyšehrad Hill looking over the Vltava and conjured that on this land a great city would stand. She and Prince Přemysl Oráč declared the first Bohemian state, launching the Premyslid dynasty, which lasted from the 10th to the 12th centuries.

St. Wenceslas (Svatý Václav) (ca. 907–935)   Patron saint of Bohemia. Prince Wenceslas was executed at the site of the present-day city of Stará Boleslav—on the orders of his younger brother, Boleslav, who took over the Bohemian throne. A popular cult arose proclaiming the affable and learned prince Wenceslas as the perpetual spiritual ruler of all Czechs. The horse market, Prague's traditional meeting place, was the scene of a brief thrust of Czech nationalism against the Austrian Empire in 1848, when people named the place Wenceslas Square (Václavské náměstí). A statue at the top of the square, depicting the horse-mounted warrior, was erected in 1912.

Charles IV (Karel IV) (1316–78)   Bohemian king, Holy Roman emperor, and chief patron of Prague. Born to John of Luxembourg and Eliška, the sister of the last Premyslid king, Charles, originally christened as Václav, was reared as John's successor; John had taken over the Bohemian crown in 1310. Charles was educated in the royal court in Paris and spent much of his adolescence observing rulers in Luxembourg and Tuscany. Charles ascended the throne in 1346, and during his reign he made Prague the seat of the Holy Roman Empire and one of Europe's most advanced cities. He also inspired several key sites through the country, including Prague's university (Universita Karlova), stone bridge (Karlův most), largest New Town park (Karlovo náměstí), and the spa town of Karlovy Vary.

Master Jan Hus (1369 or 1370–1415)   Religious reformer, university lecturer, and Czech nationalist symbol. Upset with what he thought was the misuse of power by Rome and the German clergy in Prague, Hus questioned the authority of the pope and called for the formation of a Bohemian National Church. From his stronghold at Bethlehem Chapel in Old Town, he advocated that the powerful clergy cede their property and influence to more of the people. In 1414, he was summoned to explain his views before the Ecclesiastic Council at Konstanz in Germany but was arrested on arrival. He was burned at the stake as a heretic on July 6, 1415, a day considered the precursor to the Hussite Wars and now commemorated as a Czech national holiday. His church lives on today in the faith called the Czech Brethren.

K. I. Dienzenhofer (1689–1751)   High baroque architect and builder. He and his son, Kryštof, were responsible for some of the most striking Czech church designs, including the Church of St. Nicholas in Lesser Town, the Church of St. Nicholas in Old Town, and the Church of St. John of Nepomuk on Hradčany.

Bedřich Smetana (1824–84)   Nationalist composer. After studying piano and musical theory in Prague, Smetana became one of Bohemia's most revered composers, famous for his fierce nationalism. His *Vltava* movement in the symphony *Má Vlast* (My Country) is performed the opening night of the

Prague Spring music festival; it's also used as a score in Western movies and TV commercials. His opera *The Bartered Bride* takes a jaunty look at Czech farm life.

Antonín Dvořák (1841–1904)   Neoromantic composer and head of Prague Conservatory. Dvořák is best known for his symphony *From the New World*, which was inspired by a tour of the United States. His opera about a girl trapped in a water world, *Rusalka*, remains an international favorite; it became a popular film in Europe, starring Slovak actress Magda Vašáryová.

Franz Kafka (1883–1924)   Writer. Author of the depressing but universally read novel *The Trial*, Kafka was a German-Jewish Praguer who, for much of his adult life, worked in relative obscurity as a sad Prague insurance clerk. In works like *Metamorphosis, The Castle,* and *Amerika,* Kafka described surreal and suffocating worlds of confusion. Now many use the adjective *kafkaesque* to mean "living in absurdity." Anyone who tries to apply for anything at a state office here will know that Kafka's world lives on.

Tomáš G. Masaryk (1850–1937)   Philosopher, professor, Czechoslovakia's first president. Educated in Vienna and Leipzig, Masaryk spent decades advocating Czech statehood. In 1915, he made a landmark speech in Geneva calling for the end of the Habsburg monarchy. He traveled to Washington and received the backing of President Woodrow Wilson at the end of World War I for a sovereign republic of Czechs and Slovaks, which was founded in October 1918. During his nearly 17 years as president, Masaryk played the stoic grandfather of the new republic. He resigned for health reasons in 1935 and died less than 2 years later.

Klement Gottwald (1896–1953)   Communist leader. He was named prime minister after his Communist Party won the highest vote count in the first postwar election in 1946. By February 1948, he had organized the complete Communist takeover of the government and eventually forced out President Edvard Beneš. When he became president in June 1948, the name of his hometown Zlín was changed to Gottwaldov (it changed backed to Zlín after the 1989 revolution). He was abhorred for his role in the 1950s show trials that purged hundreds.

Alexander Dubček (1921–92)   Government leader. Though he's not a Czech, Dubček is a key figure in the history of Prague and the country. A Slovak Communist, he became the first secretary of the Communist Party in January 1968, presiding over the Prague Spring reforms. After he was ousted in the August 1968 Soviet-led invasion, Dubček faded from view, only later to stand with Havel to declare the end of hard-line Communist rule in 1989. He returned to become speaker of Parliament after the Velvet Revolution but was killed in a dubious car accident in 1992. The cause of the crash is still under investigation.

Václav Havel (b. 1936)   Author, dissident, president. Absurdist playwright in the 1960s, Havel became a leading figure in the pro-democracy movement Charter 77 and the first president after leading the Velvet Revolution. See the box "From Prisoner to President: Václav Havel," above.

Among other famous Czech ex-pats are Oscar-winning film director **Miloš Forman** (*Amadeus, The People vs. Larry Flynt*) and **Milan Kundera,** the author of *The Unbearable Lightness of Being* and other controversial works about 20th-century Czech life. Kundera is now a French citizen and bitterly refuses to make a public return to his homeland, after leaving during the dark days of Communist "normalization."

Former tennis superstars **Ivan Lendl** and **Martina Navrátilová,** now of Greenwich, Connecticut, and Aspen, hail from Ostrava and Řevnice. Two of the greatest stars in NHL ice hockey, **Jaromír Jágr** and **Dominik "The Dominator" Hašek,** have made millions playing for Pittsburgh and Buffalo respectively, but both say they miss home and will move back. Hašek is to retire after the 1999–2000 season to raise his family in his hometown of Pardubice.

Supermodel and Wonderbra icon **Eva Herzigová** hails from the blue-collar northern Bohemian industrial berg of Litvínov—whose smokestacks are about as far removed as you can get from the catwalks where she works.

A mention should also go to **Ivana Trump** (pronounced Ee-*vah*-nah), born in Gottwaldov (now known again as Zlín), east of Prague. The woman who first brought meaning to the term "Velvet Divorce" starred as a skier on the Czechoslovak National Team and as a model before going down the slippery slope with billionaire husband "The Donald" and then with her rebound mate Riccardo Mazzucchelli. Her first novel, *For Love Alone,* blatantly autobiographical, took place partly in Bohemia.

5 Prague's Architectural Mix

Look up. That's maybe the best advice we can give you. Prague's majestic mix of medieval, Renaissance, and art nouveau architecture shares one fairly universal element—the most elegant and well-appointed facades and fixtures aren't at eye level or even street level, but are on top floors and roofs. Hundreds of buildings are decorated with intricately carved cornices or ornamental balconies and friezes depicting mythical, religious, or heroic figures.

The grime of Prague pollution has been gradually stripped away, and each restored building reveals some previously hidden detail. What's interesting, though, is how visitors react to the grime. When people visit Paris or Venice and see dirty, crumbling buildings, they consider them quaint. When they see the same old, dirty, crumbling buildings in Prague, however, they point to the failure of Communism—not entirely fair. If you look at photos of Prague taken in 1900, you'll also see dirty, crumbling buildings.

The city's earliest extant forms are Romanesque, dating from 1100 to 1250. The long Gothic period followed from 1250 to 1530. You'll find many Gothic buildings in Staré Město. Plus Prague Castle's most visible superstructure, St. Vitus Cathedral, is a Gothic masterpiece—that is, its older east-facing half (the cathedral's western sections exemplify Renaissance and neo-Gothic styles). From 1500 to the early 1600s, the Italian Renaissance style prevailed.

Many of the best-known structures are baroque and rococo, sharply tailored in the high Austrian style inspired by the Habsburgs of the 17th and 18th centuries.

Some of the most flamboyant buildings are art nouveau, popular from 1900 to 1918. The movement that swept across Europe developed with the Industrial Revolution. Innovative building materials—primarily steel and glass—opened endless possibilities for artistic embellishments. Architects abandoned traditional stone structures, built in a pseudo-historic style. Art nouveau is characterized by rich, curvaceous ornamentation that seems sadly to have vanished in the push for functionalism later in the century.

Several intriguing cubist designs from that era have also been hailed for their ingenuity. As an architectural style, cubism thrived in Bohemia, and you can find many examples in the neighborhood below Vyšehrad Park.

The late 20th century has played havoc with Prague's architecture. Communists were partial to functionalism with virtually no character. Their buildings shed all decorative details. You shouldn't leave Prague before taking the metro out to Prosek to see the thousands of Communist-era flats, called "rabbit huts" even by their occupants. Created partly out of socialist dogma and partly out of economic necessity, these prefabricated apartment buildings (*paneláky*) were named after the concrete slabs used to build them. Cheap and unimaginatively designed, the apartment buildings are surrounded by a featureless world. Exteriors were made of plain, unadorned cement and halls were lined with linoleum. The same room, balcony, and window design was stamped out over and over.

But panelák living wasn't always viewed as a scourge. Unlike the larger, older apartments, paneláks had modern plumbing and heating and were once considered the politically correct way to live. They're also amazingly cheap: Some rents still only amount to about 1,000Kč ($29) per month, though price deregulation is just beginning.

Two major post-Communist projects have already triggered a new debate among the progressives and the traditionalists. The Myslbek shopping/office complex on Na Příkopě near Wenceslas Square is the business district's first attempt at blending the new with the old in a functional yet elegant way. And the so-called Dancing Building on the embankment at the Rašínovo nábřeží has conservative tongues wagging. Its design strays from the 19th-century Empire classical houses lining the river, but in a most peculiar way. Controversial U.S. architect Frank Gehry, who designed the American Center in Paris, and new wave designer Vlado Milunič have created a building that ironically pays tribute to the most classical of film dancing pairs: Fred Astaire and Ginger Rogers. Built as the Prague office of a Dutch insurance company, the building depicts the two intertwined in a spin above the Vltava. See the box "The Art of Prague's Architecture" in chapter 6 for more.

6 Recommended Films & Books

FILMS

Czech filmmaking has a long tradition, as the Prague studios in the Barrandov hills churned out glossy pre-Communist romantic comedies and period pieces rivaling the output of Paris, Berlin, and even Hollywood at the time.

While Czech literature and music have carved their places in classical culture, the country's films and their directors have collected the widest praise in the mid– to late 20th century. Cunning, melancholy views of Bohemian life (before the Soviets moved in for a few decades) were captured by some of the finest filmmakers in the era known as the "Czech New Wave" of the 1960s.

Directors Jiří Menzel and Miloš Forman were in the vanguard. An easy-to-find example of this period's work (with English subtitles) is Menzel's Oscar-winning *Closely Watched Trains*, a snapshot of the odd routine at a rural Czech rail station.

Forman made his splash with a quirky look at a night in the life of a town trying to have fun despite itself. *The Fireman's Ball* shows Forman's true mastery as he captures the essence of being stone bored in a gray world, yet still makes it strangely intriguing. Of course, this was made before Forman emigrated to the big budgets of Hollywood and first shocked Americans with *Hair.* He then directed the Oscar-winning *One Flew Over the Cuckoo's Nest.* For *Amadeus,* Forman sought authenticity, so he received special permission from the Communists to return to Prague; while filming, he brought back to life the original Estates' Theater (Stavovské divadlo), where Mozart first performed. Forman also consulted a friend, President Václav Havel, before choosing Courtney Love as the pornographer's wife in the Oscar-nominated *The People vs. Larry Flynt.* Havel loved the choice but refused to attend a private 1996 screening in Prague along with Flynt himself.

Czech-based directors after the New Wave mostly disappeared from view, but one stunningly brave film was made in 1970, as the repressive postinvasion period known as "normalization" began its long, cold freeze of talent. In *The Ear (Ucho),* director Karel Kachyňa presents the anguished story of a man trapped in an apartment wired for sound, subject to the Communist leaders' obsession and paranoia with Moscow. That *The Ear* was made in the political environment of the time was astounding. That it was quickly banned wasn't. Fortunately, local TV has dusted off copies from the archives, and it has begun playing to art-house audiences again.

But maybe a new Czech wave has begun. The father-and-son team of Zdeněk and Jan Svěrák won the Best Foreign Film Oscar in 1997 for *Kolja,* the bittersweet tale of an abandoned Russian boy grudgingly adopted by an aging Czech bachelor on the cusp of the 1989 revolution. After a previous Oscar nomination for the 1992 *Elementary School (Obecná škola),* the thirty-something director Jan and his actor father are making an industry out of golden reflections about Czech life. Both films can now be found subtitled in the United States and their first original English-language project is expected in 1998.

Prague has become a popular location for major motion pictures, in spite of itself. Producer/actor Tom Cruise and director Brian De Palma chose it for the stunning night shots around Charles Bridge in the early scenes of *Mission: Impossible.* During shooting, a verbal brawl broke out with Czech officials, who jacked up the rent for use of the riverside palace that acts as the American Embassy in the film (the palace is actually claimed by the von Liechtenstein family). *Immortal Beloved,* a story of Beethoven, made use of Prague's timeless streets (shooting around the graffiti).

Finally, *The Beautician and the Beast,* starring "Bond" hunk Timothy Dalton and nasal-siren Fran Drescher, uses Prague as a mythical East European capital invaded by a Brooklyn hairdresser (who makes pretty good use of her Frommer's guide while traveling through faux-Prague).

Still, the film about Prague probably most familiar is *The Unbearable Lightness of Being,* based on the book by émigré author Milan Kundera. Set in the days surrounding the Soviet invasion, the story draws on the psychology of three Czechs who can't escape their personal obsessions while the political world outside collapses around them. Many Czechs find the film disturbing, some because it hits home, others because they say it portrays a Western stereotype.

BOOKS

Any discussion of Czech literature with visiting foreigners usually begins with Milan Kundera. Reviled among many Czechs who didn't emigrate, Kundera creates a visceral, personal sense of the world he chose to leave in the 1970s for the freedom of Paris. In *The Unbearable Lightness of Being,* the anguish over escaping the Soviet-occupied Prague he loves tears the libidinous protagonist Dr. Tomáš in the same way the love for his wife and the lust for his lover does. More Czech postnormalization angst can be found in *The Book of Laughter and Forgetting* and *Laughable Loves.* Kundera's biting satire of Stalinist purges in the 1950s, *The Joke,* however, is regarded by Czech critics as his best work.

Arnošt Lustig, a survivor of the Nazi-era Terezín concentration camp and author of many works, including *Street of Lost Brothers,* shared the 1991

Publishers Weekly Award for best literary work with John Updike and Norman Mailer. In 1995, he became the editor of the Czech edition of *Playboy.*

The best work of renowned Ivan Klíma, also a survivor of Terezín, is translated as *Judge on Trial,* a study of justice and the death penalty.

Jaroslav Hašek wrote the Czech harbinger to *Forrest Gump* in *The Good Soldier Švejk,* a post–World War I satire about a simpleton soldier who wreaks havoc in the Austro–Hungarian army during the war.

Bohumil Hrabal, author of the Czech everyman and maybe the country's all-time favorite, died in early 1997 when he fell (so they said officially) out of a fifth-story window while trying to feed pigeons. His death was eerily similar to the fate of a character in one of his stories. He had two internationally acclaimed hits: *Closely Watched Trains* (also translated as *Closely Observed Trains,* on which the Menzel film was based), and *I Served the King of England.* When President Bill Clinton visited Prague in 1994, he asked to have a beer with Hrabal in the author's favorite Old Town haunt, the pub U Zlatého tygra (At the Golden Tiger). Clinton may have gotten more than he bargained for, as the gruff but lovable Hrabal, who turned 80 that year, lectured the president on his views of the world.

No reading list would be complete without reference to Franz Kafka, Prague's most famous novelist, who wrote his originals in his native German. *The Collected Novels of Franz Kafka,* which includes *The Castle* and *The Trial,* binds his most claustrophobic works into a single volume.

If it's contemporary philosophy you want, there is, of course, the philosopher president. Václav Havel's heralded dissident essay "The Power of the Powerless" explained how the lethargic masses were allowing their complacency with Communism to sap their souls. His "Letters to Olga," written to his wife while in prison in the 1980s, takes you into his cell and his view of a moral world. Available are two solid English-translated compilations of his dissident writings: *Living in Truth* and *Open Letters. Disturbing the Peace* is an autobiographical meditation on childhood, the events of 1968, and Havel's involvement with Charter 77. His first recollections about entering politics are in "Summer Meditations," a long essay written during a vacation.

While he hasn't had much time to write since becoming president, Havel says that his speeches given around the world each continue a dialogue about morality in politics. If you read the anthology of his presidential speeches, *Toward a Civil Society,* you'll find it clear that Havel hasn't stopped being the dissident. Only now his target is incompetence and corruption in politics and society, including in democracies.

Madeleine Albright's father, diplomat Dr. Josef Koerbel, wrote a definitive contemporary history of his homeland in his final book before dying in 1977, *Twentieth Century Czechoslovakia.* More than an academic study, it reads as a personal memoir of Prague's chaotic events, many of which he witnessed.

Finally, for an epic intellectual tour of the long, colorful, and often tragic history of the city, try the 1997 release of *Prague in Black and Gold* by native son and Yale literature professor Peter Demetz.

Appendix B:
Useful Terms & Phrases

Although Czech is a very difficult language to master, you should at least make an attempt to learn a few phrases. Czechs will appreciate the effort and will be more willing to help you out.

1 Basic Phrases & Vocabulary

CZECH ALPHABET

There are 32 vowels and consonants in the Czech alphabet, and most of the consonants are pronounced about as they are in English. Accent marks over vowels lengthen the sound of the vowel, as does the *kroužek*, or little circle ("°"), which appears only over "o" and "u."

A, a f*a*ther

B, b *b*oy

C, c get*s*

Č, č *ch*oice

D, d *d*ay

Ď, ď *Di*or

E, e n*e*ver

F, f *f*ood

G, g *g*oal

H, h un*h*and

Ch, ch Lo*ch* Lomond

I, i n*ee*d

J, j *y*es

K, k *k*ey

L, l *l*ord

M, m *m*ama

N, n *n*o

N', n' Ta*n*ya

O, o *aw*ful

P, p *p*en

R, r slightly trilled *r*

Ř, ř slightly trilled *r* + *zh* as in P*er*sian

S, s *s*eat

Š, š cru*sh*

T, t *t*oo

Ť, ť no*t y*et

U, u r*oo*m

V, v *v*ery

W, w *v*ague

Y, y funn*y*

Z, z *z*ebra

Ž, ž a*z*ure, plea*s*ure

CZECH VOCABULARY

Everyday Expressions

English	Czech	Pronunciation
Hello	**Dobrý den**	*doh*-bree den
Good morning	**Dobré jitro**	*doh*-breh *yee*-troh
Good evening	**Dobrý večer**	*doh*-bree *veh*-chair
How are you?	**Jak se máte?**	*yahk* seh *mah*-teh
Very well	**Velmi dobře**	*vel*-mee *doh*-brsheh
Thank you	**Děkuji vám**	*dyek*-ooee vahm
You're welcome	**Prosím**	*proh*-seem
Please	**Prosím**	*proh*-seem
Yes	**Ano**	*ah*-no
No	**Ne**	neh

Excuse me	**Promiňte**	*proh*-min-teh
How much does it cost?	**Kolik to stojí?**	*koh*-leek taw *stoh*-ee
I don't understand.	**Nerozumím.**	*neh*-roh-zoo-meem
Just a moment.	**Moment, prosím.**	*moh*-ment, *proh*-seem
Good-bye	**Na shledanou**	*nah* skleh-dah-noh-oo

Traveling

Where is the . . . ?	**Kde je . . . ?**	*gde* yeh . . .
bus station	**autobusové nádraží**	*au*-toh-boos-oh-veh *nah*-drah-zhee
train station	**nádraží**	*nah*-drah-zhee
airport	**letiště**	*leh*-tyish-tyeh
baggage check	**úschovna zavazadel**	*oo*-skohv-nah *zah*-vahz-ah-del
Where can I find a taxi?	**Kde najdu taxi?**	*gde nai*-doo *tahks*-eh
Where can I find a gas station?	**Kde najdu benzínovou pumpu?**	*gde nai*-doo *ben*-zeen-oh-voh *poomp*-oo
How much is gas?	**Kolik stojí benzín?**	*koh*-leek *stoh*-yee *ben*-zeen
Please fill the tank.	**Naplňte mi nádrž, prosím.**	*nah*-puln-teh mee *nah*-durzh, *proh*-seem
How much is the fare?	**Kolik je jízdné?**	*koh*-leek yeh yeesd-neh
I am going to . . .	**Pojedu do . . .**	*poh*-yeh-doo doh . . .
One-way ticket	**Jízdenka**	*yeez*-den-kah
Round-trip ticket	**Zpáteční jízdenka**	*zpah*-tech-nee *jeez*-den-kah
Car-rental office	**Půjčovna aut**	*poo*-eech-awv-nah ah-oot

Accommodations

I'm looking for . . .	**Hledám . . .**	*hleh*-dahm . . .
a hotel	**hotel**	*hoh*-tel
a youth hostel	**studentskou ubytovnu**	*stoo*-dent-skoh *oo*-beet-ohv-noo
I am staying . . .	**Zůstanu . . .**	*zoo*-stah-noo . . .
a few days	**několik dnů**	*nyeh*-koh-leek dnoo
two weeks	**dva týdny**	dvah tid-*neh*
a month	**jeden měsíc**	*yeh*-den *myeh*-seets
I have a reservation.	**Mám zamluvený nocleh.**	mahm *zah*-mloo-veh-ni *nohts*-leh
My name is . . .	**Jmenuji se . . .**	*meh*-noo-yee seh . . .
Do you have a room . . . ?	**Máte pokoj . . . ?**	*mah*-teh *poh*-koy . . .
for tonight	**na dnešek**	*nah* dneh-sheck
for three nights	**na tři dny**	*nah* trshee dnee
for a week	**na týden**	*nah* tee-den
I would like . . .	**Chci . . .**	khtsee . . .
a single	**jednolůžkový pokoj**	*jed*-noh-loosh-koh-vee *poh*-koy
a double	**dvojlůžkový pokoj**	*dvoy*-loosh-koh-vee *poh*-koy
I want a room . . .	**Chci pokoj . . .**	khtsee *poh*-koy . . .
with a bathroom	**s koupelnou**	*skoh*-pehl-noh
without a bathroom	**bez koupelny**	*behz* koh-pehl-nee

with a shower	**se sprchou**	*seh* spur-choh
without a shower	**bez sprchy**	*bez* sprech-eh
with a view	**s pohledem**	*spoh*-hlehd-ehm
How much is the room?	**Kolik stojí pokoj?**	*koh*-leek *stoh*-yee *paw*-koy
with breakfast?	**se snídaní?**	*seh* snee-dan-nyee
May I see the room?	**Mohu vidět ten pokoj?**	*moh*-hoo *vee*-dyet ten *paw*-koy
The key	**Klíč**	kleech
The bill, please.	**Dejte mi účet, prosím.**	*day*-teh mee *oo*-cheht, *praw*-seem

GETTING AROUND

I'm looking for . . .	**Hledám . . .**	*hleh*-dahm . . .
a bank	**banku**	*bahnk*-oo
the church	**kostel**	*kohs*-tell
the city center	**centrum**	*tsent*-room
the museum	**muzeum**	*moo*-zeh-oom
a pharmacy	**lékárnu**	*lek*-ahr-noo
the park	**park**	pahrk
the theater	**divadlo**	*dee*-vahd-loh
the tourist office	**cestovní kancelář**	*tses*-tohv-nee *kahn*-tseh-larsh
the embassy	**velvyslanectví**	*vehl*-vee-slahn-ets-tvee
Where is the nearest telephone?	**Kde je nejbližší telefon?**	gde yeh *nay*-bleesh-ee *tel*-oh-fohn
I would like to buy . . .	**Chci koupit . . .**	khtsee *koh*-peet . . .
a stamp	**známku**	*znahm*-koo
a postcard	**pohlednici**	*poh*-hlehd-nit-seh
a map	**mapu**	*mahp*-oo

Useful Terms & Phrases

SIGNS

No Trespassing	**Cizím vstup zakázán**	No Smoking	**Kouření zakázáno**
No Parking	**Neparkovat**	Arrivals	**Příjezd/Přílet**
Entrance	**Vchod**	Departures	**Odjezd/Odlet**
Exit	**Východ**	Toilets	**Toalety**
Information	**Informace**	Danger	**Pozor, nebezpečí**

NUMBERS

1	**jeden** (*yeh*-den)	16	**šestnáct** (*shest*-nahtst)
2	**dva** (dvah)	17	**sedmnáct** (*seh*-doom-nahtst)
3	**tři** (trzhee)	18	**osmnáct** (*aw*-soom-nahtst)
4	**čtyři** (*chtee*-rshee)	19	**devatenáct** (*deh*-vah-teh-nahtst)
5	**pět** (pyet)	20	**dvacet** (*dvah*-tset)
6	**šest** (shest)	30	**třicet** (*trshee*-tset)
7	**sedm** (*seh*-duhm)	40	**čtyřicet** (*chti*-rshee-tset)
8	**osm** (*aw*-suhm)	50	**padesát** (*pah*-deh-saht)
9	**devět** (*deh*-vyet)	60	**šedesát** (*she*-deh-saht)
10	**deset** (*deh*-set)	70	**sedmdesát** (*seh*-duhm-deh-saht)
11	**jedenáct** (*yeh*-deh-nahtst)	80	**osmdesát** (*aw*-suhm-deh-saht)
12	**dvanáct** (*dvah*-nahtst)	90	**devadesát** (*deh*-vah-deh-saht)
13	**třináct** (*trshee*-nahtst)	100	**sto** (staw)
14	**čtrnáct** (*chtur*-nahtst)	500	**pét set** (*pyet* set)
15	**patnáct** (*paht*-nahtst)	1,000	**tisíc** (*tyee*-seets)

DINING

Restaurant	**Restaurace**	*rehs*-tow-rah-tseh
Breakfast	**Snídaně**	*snee*-dah-nyeh
Lunch	**Oběd**	*oh*-byed
Dinner	**Večeře**	*veh*-chair-sheh
A table for two, please. (Lit.: There are two of us.)	**Jsme dva.**	*ees*-meh dvah
Waiter	**Číšník**	*cheess*-neek
Waitress	**Servírka**	ser-*veer*-ka
I would like . . .	**Chci . . .**	khtsee . . .
a menu	**jídelní lístek**	*yee*-del-nee *lees*-teck
a fork	**vidličku**	*veed*-leech-koo
a knife	**nůž**	noosh
a spoon	**lžičku**	lu-*shich*-koo
a napkin	**ubrousek**	*oo*-broh-seck
a glass (of water)	**skleničku (vody)**	*sklehn*-ich-koo (vod-*dee*)
the check, please	**účet, prosím**	*oo*-cheht, *proh*-seem
Is the tip included?	**Je v tom zahrnuto spropitné?**	yeh *ftohm*-zah *hur*-noo-toh *sproh*-peet-neh

2 Menu Terms

GENERAL

Soup	**Polévka**	*poh*-lehv-kah
Eggs	**Vejce**	*vayts*-eh
Meat	**Maso**	*mahs*-oh
Fish	**Ryba**	*ree*-bah
Vegetables	**Zelenina**	*zehl*-eh-nee-nah
Fruit	**Ovoce**	*oh*-voh-tseh
Desserts	**Moučníky**	*mohch*-nee-kee
Beverages	**Nápoje**	*nah*-poy-yeh
Salt	**Sůl**	sool
Pepper	**Pepř**	*peh*-psh
Mayonnaise	**Majonéza**	*mai*-o-neza
Mustard	**Hořčice**	*hohrsh*-chee-tseh
Vinegar	**Ocet**	*oh*-tseht
Oil	**Olej**	*oh*-lay
Sugar	**Cukr**	*tsoo*-ker
Tea	**Čaj**	chye
Coffee	**Káva**	*kah*-vah
Bread	**Chléb**	khlehb
Butter	**Máslo**	*mahs*-loh
Wine	**Víno**	*vee*-noh
Fried	**Smažený**	*smah*-sheh-nee
Roasted	**Pečený**	*pech*-eh-nee
Boiled	**Vařený**	*vah*-rsheh-nee
Grilled	**Grilovaný**	*gree*-loh-vah-nee

Useful Terms & Phrases

SOUP

Bramborová potato
Čočková lentil
Gulášová goulash

Rajská tomato
Slepičí chicken
Zeleninová vegetable

MEAT

Biftek steak
Guláš goulash
Hovězí beef
Játra liver
Jehněčí lamb
Kachna duck

Klobása sausage
Králík rabbit
Skopové mutton
Telecí veal
Telecí kotleta veal cutlet
Vepřové pork

FISH

Karp carp
Kaviár caviar
Rybí filé fish fillet
Sleď herring

Štika pike
Treska cod
Úhoř eel
Ústřice oysters

EGGS

Míchaná vejce scrambled eggs
Smažená vejce fried eggs
Varená vejce boiled eggs

Vejce naměkko soft-boiled eggs
Vejce se slaninou bacon and eggs
Vejce se šunkou ham and eggs

SALAD

Fazolový salát bean salad
Hlávkový salát mixed green salad

Okurkový salát cucumber salad
Salát z červené řepy beet salad

VEGETABLES

Brambory potatoes
Celer celery
Chřest asparagus
Cibule onions
Houby mushrooms

Květák cauliflower
Mrkev carrots
Paprika peppers
Rajská jablíčka tomatoes
Zelí cabbage

DESSERT

Koláč cake
Cukroví cookies
Čokoládová zmrzlina
  chocolate ice cream

Jablkový závin apple strudel
Palačinky pancakes
Vanilková zmrzlina
  vanilla ice cream

FRUIT

Citrón lemon
Hruška pears

Jablko apple
Švestky plums

BEVERAGE

Čaj tea
Káva coffee
Mléko milk
Víno wine

Červené red
Bílé white
Voda water

Index

See also Accommodations and Restaurant indexes, below.

General Index

General Index

Accommodations Index

Restaurant Index

FROMMER'S® COMPLETE TRAVEL GUIDES

Alaska
Amsterdam
Arizona
Atlanta
Australia
Austria
Bahamas
Barcelona, Madrid & Seville
Beijing
Belgium, Holland & Luxembourg
Bermuda
Boston
Budapest & the Best of Hungary
California
Canada
Cancún, Cozumel &
  the Yucatán
Cape Cod, Nantucket & Martha's Vineyard
Caribbean
Caribbean Cruises & Ports of Call
Caribbean Ports of Call
Carolinas & Georgia
Chicago
China
Colorado
Costa Rica
Denmark
Denver, Boulder & Colorado Springs
England
Europe
Florida
France
Germany
Greece
Greek Islands
Hawaii
Hong Kong
Honolulu, Waikiki & Oahu
Ireland
Israel
Italy
Jamaica & Barbados
Japan
Las Vegas
London
Los Angeles
Maryland & Delaware
Maui
Mexico
Miami & the Keys

Montana & Wyoming
Montréal & Québec City
Munich & the Bavarian Alps
Nashville & Memphis
Nepal
New England
New Mexico
New Orleans
New York City
Nova Scotia, New Brunswick &
  Prince Edward Island
Oregon
Paris
Philadelphia & the
  Amish Country
Portugal
Prague & the Best of the Czech Republic
Provence & the Riviera
Puerto Rico
Rome
San Antonio & Austin
San Diego
San Francisco
Santa Fe, Taos &
  Albuquerque
Scandinavia
Scotland
Seattle & Portland
Singapore & Malaysia
South Africa
Southeast Asia
South Pacific
Spain
Sweden
Switzerland
Thailand
Tokyo
Toronto
Tuscany & Umbria
USA
Utah
Vancouver & Victoria
Vermont, New Hampshire
  & Maine
Vienna & the Danube Valley
Virgin Islands
Virginia
Walt Disney World & Orlando
Washington, D.C.
Washington State

FROMMER'S® DOLLAR-A-DAY GUIDES

Australia from $50 a Day
California from $60 a Day
Caribbean from $70 a Day
England from $70 a Day
Europe from $60 a Day
Florida from $60 a Day

Hawaii from $70 a Day
Ireland from $50 a Day
Israel from $45 a Day
Italy from $70 a Day
London from $85 a Day
New York from $80 a Day

New Zealand from $50 a Day
Paris from $85 a Day
San Francisco from $60 a Day
Washington, D.C.,
   from $60 a Day

FROMMER'S® PORTABLE GUIDES

Acapulco, Ixtapa &
   Zihuatanejo
Alaska Cruises & Ports of Call
Bahamas
Baja & Los Cabos
Berlin
California Wine Country
Charleston & Savannah
Chicago

Dublin
Hawaii: The Big Island
Las Vegas
London
Maine Coast
Maui
New Orleans
New York City
Paris

Puerto Vallarta, Manzanillo
   & Guadalajara
San Diego
San Francisco
Sydney
Tampa & St. Petersburg
Venice
Washington, D.C.

FROMMER'S® NATIONAL PARK GUIDES

Family Vacations in the
   National Parks
Grand Canyon

National Parks of the
   American West
Rocky Mountain

Yellowstone & Grand Teton
Yosemite & Sequoia/
   Kings Canyon
Zion & Bryce Canyon

FROMMER'S® GREAT OUTDOOR GUIDES

New England
Northern California

Southern California & Baja
Washington & Oregon

FROMMER'S® MEMORABLE WALKS

Chicago
London

New York
Paris

San Francisco
Washington D.C.

FROMMER'S® IRREVERENT GUIDES

Amsterdam
Boston
Chicago
Las Vegas

London
Los Angeles
Manhattan

New Orleans
Paris
San Francisco

Seattle & Portland
Vancouver
Walt Disney World
Washington, D.C.

FROMMER'S® BEST-LOVED DRIVING TOURS

America
Britain
California

Florida
France
Germany

Ireland
Italy
New England

Scotland
Spain
Western Europe

THE UNOFFICIAL GUIDES®

SPECIAL-INTEREST TITLES